A Secret Location

A Sourcebook of Information

by

Steven Clay and Rodney Phillips

A Secret
Location

on the

Lower East
Side

Adventures in Writing,
1960–1980

The New York Public Library and Granary Books

Lines on page 54 from "Asphodel, That Greeny Flower," from
volume 2 of William Carlos Williams, *Collected Poems 1939–
1962,* copyright © 1962 by William Carlos Williams. Reprinted
by permission of New Directions Publishing Corporation.

Additional permissions for the use of copyrighted material
appear on page 342, which constitutes an extension of this page.

Library of Congress Cataloging-in-Publication Data

Clay, Steven, 1951–
   A secret location on the Lower East Side: adventures in
writing, 1960–1980: a sourcebook of information /
by Steven Clay and Rodney Phillips.
       p.   cm.
   Accompanies an exhibition held at The New York
Public Library.
   Includes bibliographical references (p.   ) and index.
   ISBN 1–887123–19–9 (cloth: alk. paper). —
ISBN 1–887123–20–2 (pbk.: alk. paper)
   1. American poetry — 20th century — Bibliography —
Exhibitions. 2. Postmodernism (Literature) — United
States — Exhibitions. 3. Bibliographical exhibitions — New
York (State) — New York. 4. Literature publishing — United
States — Exhibitions. 5. Small presses — United States —
Exhibitions. I. Phillips, Rodney, 1946– . II. New York Public
Library. III. Title.
Z1231.P7C58   1998
[PS325]
016.811'5408 — DC21   98-24027
                                             CIP

Designed by Marc Blaustein

First published 1998

Printed on acid-free paper
Printed and bound in the United States of America

Distributed to the trade by D.A.P./Distributed Art Publishers
155 Avenue of the Americas, Second Floor
New York, NY 10013-1507
Orders: (800) 338-BOOK • Tel.: (212) 627-1999
Fax: (212) 627-9484

www.nypl.org • www.granarybooks.com

Allen Ginsberg's inscription on his 1984 photograph reads:

"Out my kitchen window, Ed Sanders' *Fuck You/A Magazine of the Arts* was 'mimeo'd in a secret location in the Lower East Side' circa 1964 in a backyard house down below. 1984 I focused on the clothesline raindrops after looking out this window at breakfast 8 years."

Contents

Pre-Face

Since everyone loves a paradox, let me start off with this now-familiar one: the mainstream of American poetry, the part by which it has been & will be known, has long been in the margins, nurtured in the margins, carried forward, vibrant, in the margins. As mainstream & margin both, it represents our underground economy as poets, the gray market for our spiritual/corporeal exchanges. It is the creation as such of those poets who have seized or often have invented their own means of production and of distribution. The autonomy of the poets is of singular importance here – not something we've been stuck with *faute de mieux* but something we've demanded as a value that must (repeat: *must*) remain first & foremost under each poet's own control. And this is because poetry as we know & want it is the language of those precisely at the margins – born there, or more often still, self-situated: a strategic position from which to struggle with the center of the culture & with a language that we no longer choose to bear. Poetry is another language, as it is another orientation, from that of the other, more familiar mainstream, which has, in Paul Blackburn's words, "wracked all passion from the sound of speech." For many of us, so positioned, it is the one true counter-language we possess – even, to paraphrase Alfred Jarry (& to be almost serious about it), our language (& our science) of exceptions.

by
Jerome Rothenberg

The model figure here – a hundred years before the Lower East Side works presented in these pages – was surely Walt Whitman, whose 1855 *Leaves of Grass*, self-published, was the work of his own hands as well as mind, from manuscript to printed book to first reviews ghost-written by the man himself. And contemporaneous with that, our second founding work was that of Emily Dickinson, who never would be published in her lifetime but, more secretly & privately than any, hand-wrote & stitched together a series of single-copy booklets (fascicles) as testimony to her own experiments with voice & line. Along with William Blake before them, she & Whitman are the poets of our language who first brought inspiration & production back together as related, undivided acts.

The work of the (still) present century is the continuation & expansion of those acts. In Europe the years immediately before & after the first world war – what Marjorie Perloff calls & chronicles as "the futurist moment" – saw a proliferation of poet-&-artist driven publications, from the collaborative "prose of the transsiberian" of Blaise Cendrars and Sonia Delaunay (a powerful multicolored foldout extravaganza) to the rough-hewn books of the Russian constructivists and the movement-centered magazines & books (Expressionist, Futurist, Dada, Surrealist) under the command, nearly always, of their poet/founders. The American equivalent was the first (golden)

OPPOSITE: Bernadette Mayer, *Studying Hunger* (New York and Bolinas, Calif.: Adventures in Poetry & Big Sky, 1975). Cover photograph of the author by Ed Bowes.

age of "little" magazines & presses – central publications for what was emerging as a bona-fide American avant-garde. Writers who sought new ways & languages took charge of their own publication – Gertrude Stein a case in point, whose works for years were published by herself & Alice Toklas – while others (Pound, Loy, Williams, among many) drew from a network (noncommercial, often poet-run) that ranged from Robert McAlmon's Contact Editions to Harry Crosby's Black Sun offerings to the important publications by George and Mary Oppen's To Publishers, linking Imagist(e)s to "Objectivists" & both to the new poetries that would emerge post–World War Two. James Laughlin's New Directions – alive & vital to the present day – came from the same fertile source, which also included magazines & reviews like Margaret Anderson and Jane Heap's *Little Review* and Eugene Jolas's *Transition* as first publishers respectively of works like Joyce's *Ulysses* and *Finnegans Wake* (the latter then known as "Work in Progress").

The disruption of all that came with the new mid-century war & holocaust, prelimi-nary to the cold war that defined the next four decades. The great European movements were long since gone or – notably in the case of Surrealism – had splintered into warring factions. A number of once marginal poets had received more general recognition (Eliot, Moore, Stevens, among the Americans) and with it access to the commercial literary net-works. Others, like the American "Objectiv-ists" (Zukofsky, Oppen, Reznikoff, Rakosi), had fallen between the cracks & into a life of near nonpublication. And the climate, in the decade following the war, seemed unremit-tingly reactionary, both on its "new critical" literary side & in its McCarthyite political retrenchments.

The story by now is well known, but it is also true – that it was against this background that the second great awakening of twentieth-century poetry was starting up, not only in the U.S. but in Europe, in Latin America, & in much of what was becoming, increasingly, the post-colonial world. Its two American centers – as everybody also knows – were New York and San Francisco, with links to other places large & small. If San Francisco was the great "refuge city" overall (I think that's Robert Duncan's term), New York was where a counterpoetics flourished in what Richard Schechner spoke of – for theater & related arts – as "a resistance and alternative to the conglomerate . . . [that] exist[s] only in the creases of contemporary society, and off leavings, like cockroaches . . . not marginal [he adds, but] . . . run[ning] through the actual and conceptual center of society, like faults in the earth's crust." But the actual topography of the new poetry (circa 1960) was at a necessary distance from the commercial hub of American publishing (the concentration of media power in mid-Manhattan). Its terrain included not only the old bohemia of Greenwich Village but moved increasingly, significantly, into surrounding regions – eastward & southward into the tene-ment & loft areas of the Lower East Side, or into what came to be called the East Village, Soho, Tribeca, & so on. Rents then were cheap, & the cheapness, the economic advantage of life in the creases, was one of the attractions for the writers & artists who entered that territory. It was also – at least at the start – a time that was favorable for producing works on the cheap, either printing abroad (the dollar was still at its postwar high) or utilizing new & inexpensive means for the setting & manufacture of maga-zines & books: increasingly available photo-off-set technologies, but also more rough & ready means such as mimeo, ditto, & (somewhat later) Xerox & other photocopying processes.

The result is what this book is all about: the emergence on the Lower East Side & environs (stretching all the way to Highlands, North Carolina, & Kyoto, Japan) of that kind of intellectual & spiritual energy that Pound, in the context of an earlier independent magazine & movement, had called a vortex: a place of cultural intersections & fusions, into which "all experience rushes," to make past & the present into something new. The publishers & publications included here represent the vortex, the vital center, of their own time & place. At its beginnings it was also part of that wave of liberations and resistances, still largely self-generated & unfinanced, that marked the 1960s and 70s in fact as well as in the popular imagination. The activity, with its spin-offs into readings & performances, was intense & (in its size & scope) unprecedented. The movements or groupings then active included the kingpins of the New American Poetry from the time of its 1960 emergence: Black Mountain poets, Beats, New York School, along with Fluxus, concrete poetry, Black Arts, deep image, ethnopoetics, L=A=N=G=U=A=G=E. Under such headings – or in some fertile space between – the poets directly involved in the work of publication included the likes of Robert Creeley, Jonathan Williams, Cid Corman, Amiri Baraka, Lawrence Ferlinghetti, James Laughlin, Jack Spicer, Ed Sanders, Diane di Prima, Vito Acconci, Bernadette Mayer, Ted Berrigan, Ron Padgett, Lewis Warsh, Larry Fagin, Anne Waldman, John Ashbery, Clark Coolidge, Aram Saroyan, Ron Silliman, Charles Bernstein, Bruce Andrews, Bob Perelman, James Sherry, Lyn Hejinian, Margaret Randall, James Koller, Dick Higgins, Emmett Williams, Jackson Mac Low, David Henderson, Ishmael Reed, Lorenzo Thomas, Dennis Tedlock, David Antin, Robert Kelly, Nathaniel Mackey, even (at several points) the present writer. Yet even so large a list – limited as it is to poets who doubled as publishers – fails to catch the full breadth & force of what was happening there & throughout the world.

By 1980 – the terminal date for this presentation – the situation was no longer as clear as it had been earlier. The Vietnam War had shattered the image of American hegemony & the cold war had begun to simmer down. And while the Reagan years might have brought about a new resistance (& sometimes did), they also brought a new defensiveness in what became increasingly a culture war directed *against* the avant-garde rather than *by* it. The secret locations of this book's title were no longer secret but had come into a new & far less focused visibility & a fusion/confusion, often, with the commercial & cultural conglomerates of the American center. Increasingly too there had developed a dependence on support from institutional & governmental sources – the National Endowment for the Arts, say, as the major case in point. The result was to impose both a gloss of professionalism on the alternative publications & to make obsolete the rough & ready book works of the previous two decades. But the greatest danger of patronage was that the denial of that patronage, once threatened, became an issue that would override all others.

At the present time, then, the lesson of the works presented here is the reminder of what is possible where the makers of the works seek out the means to maintain & fortify their independence. It seems possible that with the new technologies now opening – computer-generated publication & the still wide-open possibilities of Internet & Web – that the great tradition of an independent American poetry is still alive & well. Toward that end, the contents of the present work may prove to be a guideline & an inspiration.

January 1998

A Little History of the
Mimeograph Revolution

A Little History of the
Mimeograph Revolution

A Little History of the
Mimeograph Revolution

A Little History of the
Mimeograph Revolution

A Little History of the
Mimeograph Revolution

A Little History of the
Mimeograph Revolution

A Little History of the
Mimeograph Revolution

Pound and William Carlos Williams, it has built on their achievements and gone on to evolve new conceptions of the poem. These poets have already created their own tradition, their own press, and their public. They are our avant-garde, the true continuers of the modern movement in American poetry."[1]

Allen's anthology was prophetic in another way. It assigned poets to large overall groupings that have persisted for nearly forty years and have entered the critical nomenclature: Black Mountain, San Francisco Renaissance, Beat Generation, and New York Poets – as well as identifying a group of younger poets "who have been associated with and in some cases influenced by the leading writers of the preceding groups" (p. xiii). Allen was circumspect to a fault concerning his classifications: "Occasionally arbitrary and for the most part more historical than actual, these groups can be justified finally only as a means to give the reader some sense of milieu . . ." (p. xiii).

There was no more significant poetry anthology in the second half of the twentieth century than **The New American Poetry, 1945–1960,** edited by Donald M. Allen and published by Grove Press in 1960. Poised almost at mid-century, it provides a summing up of a very particular situation in poetry as it looks back to the achievements of the 1950s and ahead to the possibilities of the 60s.

Allen's anthology was a self-conscious counter to *New Poets of England and America*, edited by Donald Hall, Robert Pack, and Louis Simpson and published by Meridian in 1957. It was to prove prophetic (the two anthologies have not one poet in common) and to serve as both a calling for and a permission to younger writers. The goal, according to Allen, was to present poetry that "has shown one common characteristic: a total rejection of all those qualities typical of academic verse. Following the practice and precepts of Ezra

When the Allen anthology came out, several of the featured poets had barely been published. Of necessity, they existed on the margins, outside mainstream publication and distribution channels. Of necessity, they invented their own communities and audiences (typically indistinguishable), with a

---

1. Donald Allen, *The New American Poetry* (New York: Grove Press, 1960), p. xi.

small press or little magazine often serving as the nucleus of both.

Direct access to mimeograph machines, letterpress, and inexpensive offset made these publishing ventures possible, putting the means of production in the hands of the poet. In a very real sense, almost anyone could become a publisher. For the price of a few reams of paper and a handful of stencils, a poet could produce, by mimeograph, a magazine or booklet in a small edition over the course of several days. Collating, stapling, and mailing parties helped speed up production, but, more significantly, they helped galvanize a literary group. The existence of independent bookstores meant that it was actually possible to find these publications in all their raw homemade beauty. In several instances (for example, Wallace Berman's *Semina* and LeRoi Jones and Diane di Prima's *The Floating Bear*), the magazines were available only to a mailing list; they were produced for a community of kindred spirits as a literary newsletter – a quick way to get new work out. And they were the cutting edge of new explorations in and through language. As Ron Loewinsohn noted, "[M]ore important than the quality of their contents was the fact of these magazines' abundance and speed. Having them, we could see what we were doing, as it came, hot off the griddle. We could get instant response to what we'd written last week, & we could respond instantly to what the guy across town or across the country had written last week." [2]

At the other pole were magazines like *Evergreen Review*, which published equally subversive material – but with the financial backing and distribution of a large publishing house.

Donald Allen, San Francisco, 1969. Photograph by Ann Charters.

2. Ron Loewinsohn, "Reviews: After the (Mimeograph) Revolution," *TriQuarterly* 18 (Spring 1970): 222.

Comparatively slick and "professional," it helped to bring new writing and new thinking to a much larger and geographically diverse audience.

These extremes of production quality and availability are comfortably subsumed under the concept of the "mimeo revolution," the unprecedented outpouring of poetry books and magazines that took place roughly between 1960 and 1980; the writing and publishing with which this survey is concerned are those which emerged precisely at the point at which the New American Poetry met the mimeo revolution. The "mimeo revolution," as a term, is a bit of a misnomer in the sense that well over half the materials produced under its banner were not strictly produced on the mimeograph machine; however, the formal means of production are not as important in identifying the works of this movement as is the nature of their content. Looking back at them now, the books and magazines of the mimeo revolution appear imbued with a vivid purity of intention which it is nearly impossible to conceive of creating in today's publications.

Loomings: Waldport and Berkeley

1940 *The Experimental Review*, edited by Robert Duncan and Sanders Russell

1940 Kenneth Rexroth's *In What Hour* published by Macmillan

1943 *The Untide* published at the Conscientious Objectors' Camp, Waldport, Oregon

1943 William Everson's *X War Elegies* published by the Untide Press

1946 Philip Lamantia's *Erotic Poems* published by Bern Porter (the poet is nineteen years old)

1947 *The Ark*, edited by Sanders Russell, Philip Lamantia, and Robert Stock

1947 Robert Duncan's *Heavenly City, Earthly City* published by Bern Porter

1948 *The Berkeley Miscellany*, edited by Robert Duncan

Although the earliest mimeographed literary item we have been able to identify is Yvor Winters's *Gyroscope* (published for his classes at Stanford in 1929 and early 1930), we'll start our story in 1943 in the conscientious objectors' camp at Waldport, Oregon. There, William Everson published poems in an unofficial newsletter, *The Untide*, and helped run the mimeograph machine to produce his own *X War Elegies*, among other small volumes. The last book produced at the Untide Press in Waldport was Kenneth Patchen's *An Astonished Eye Looks Out Of the Air*, which Everson printed via letterpress in 1945 as the war was ending. Everson was soon to move down to Berkeley and purchase a Washington hand press to continue his printing. His poems from this period, including those originally written in Waldport, were collected by James Laughlin and published by New Directions in 1948, as *The Residual Years*.

In 1947, the first issue of *The Ark*, strongly committed to literary and political writings influenced by anarchist and pacifist principles, appeared in San Francisco. Contributors included Kenneth Rexroth, Richard Eberhardt, Paul Goodman, and William Everson. Another contributor was Robert Duncan, whose essay "The Homosexual in Society," published in Dwight MacDonald's *Politics* in August 1944, had occasioned John Crowe Ransom to renege on publishing Duncan's previously accepted "African Elegy" in *The Kenyon Review*. Despite his feeling that the article was courageous, Ransom felt the poem was a "homosexual advertisement." On a sojourn to the East Coast, Duncan had co-edited with Sanders Russell *The Experimental Review* – a formal beginning to his long experience with small presses and little magazines. In California, he produced two issues of *The Berkeley Miscellany* (in 1948 and 1949),

as well as his own *Poems 1948–1949* under the imprint of Berkeley Miscellany Editions. In the two issues of the magazine, Duncan published his own work as well as that of Mary Fabilli, Jack Spicer, and Gerald Ackerman.

Spicer, like Duncan and Robin Blaser, was then a student at the University of California at Berkeley. These three were the center of the "Berkeley Renaissance," a group heavily influenced by the study of medieval and Renaissance culture. The Duncan-Spicer-Blaser circle created "a spiritual and artistic brotherhood out of shared homosexual experience, occultism, and the reading of modern literature."[3] The Berkeley group held regular meetings for discussions and readings influenced in part by Kenneth Rexroth's evenings in San Francisco. Spicer went on to produce his own magazine, *J*, in 1959, and was influential on Stan Persky's beginning *Open Space* in 1964. Both of these magazines were produced via mimeograph in San Francisco. In 1957, Spicer conducted the Poetry as Magic Workshop attended by, among others, John Wieners, then in the middle of producing his own little magazine, *Measure*. The Berkeley group consolidated important shared tendencies and were to exert a considerable force as they moved to San Francisco in the early 1950s.

3. Michael Davidson, *The San Francisco Renaissance: Poetics and Community at Mid-century* (New York: Cambridge University Press, 1989), p. 40.

A Little History of the Mimeograph Revolution

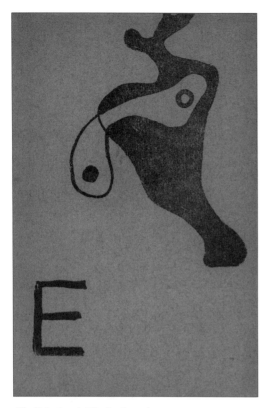

The Experimental Review (1940).
Cover by Robert Duncan and
Sanders Russell.

The San Francisco Renaissance and California

1951 The Jargon Society founded by
Jonathan Williams in San Francisco

1953 City Lights Bookstore opens in
North Beach

1955 Six Gallery reading, the first public
reading of Allen Ginsberg's *Howl*

1955 *Semina*, edited by Wallace Berman

1956 Allen Ginsberg's *Howl* published
by City Lights

1957 *Howl* confiscated by customs;
Lawrence Ferlinghetti and Shigeyoshi
Murao arrested

1957 Jack Spicer's Poetry as Magic Workshop, San Francisco Public Library

1957 Charles Olson reads and lectures
in San Francisco

1957 First book from White Rabbit Press,
Steve Jonas's *Love, the Poem, the Sea &
Other Pieces Examined*

1958 First book from Auerhahn Press,
John Wieners's *The Hotel Wentley Poems*

1958 Richard Brautigan's *The Galilee Hitch-
hiker* published by White Rabbit Press

1958 George Stanley's *The Love Root* published by White Rabbit Press

1959 Philip Lamantia's *Ekstasis* published
by Auerhahn Press

A Little History of the Mimeograph Revolution

```
6 POETS AT 6 GALLERY

Philip Lamantia reading mss. of late John
Hoffman-- Mike McClure, Allen Ginsberg,
Gary Snyder & Phil Whalen--all sharp new
straightforward writing-- remarkable coll-
ection of angels on one stage reading
their poetry. No charge, small collection
for wine and postcards. Charming event.

              Kenneth Rexroth, M.C.

   8 PM Friday Night October 7,1955

        6 Gallery 3119 Fillmore St.
                San Fran
```

Allen Ginsberg's postcard announcing the Six Gallery reading, 1955.

1959	Bob Kaufman's *The Abomunist Manifesto* published by City Lights	**1966**	Lenore Kandel's *The Love Book* published by Stolen Paper Editions
1959	*J*, edited by Jack Spicer	**1966**	Philip Lamantia's *Touch of the Marvelous* published by Oyez Press
1959	Cid Corman's Origin Press publishes Gary Snyder's first book, *Riprap*	**1966**	John Martin's Black Sparrow Press begins in Los Angeles
1960	Gary Snyder's *Myths and Texts* published by Corinth Books	**1967**	*The Pacific Nation*, edited by Robin Blaser in Vancouver
1960	Lew Welch's *Wobbly Rock* published by Auerhahn Press	**1968**	Janine Pommy-Vega's *Poems to Fernando* published by City Lights
1960	William S. Burroughs and Brion Gysin's *The Exterminator* published by Auerhahn Press	**1969**	Gary Snyder's book of essays *Earth House Hold* published by New Directions
1963	Vancouver Poetry Conference	**1975**	Jack Spicer's *Collected Books* published by Black Sparrow
1964	Open Space publishes Robin Blaser's first book, *The Moth Poem*		
1965	Berkeley Poetry Conference		
1965	Joanne Kyger's *The Tapestry and the Web* published by the Four Seasons Foundation		
1965	Lew Welch's *Hermit Poems* published by the Four Seasons Foundation		
1965	Jack Spicer's *Language* published by White Rabbit Press		
1965	Jack Spicer dies		

Meanwhile, across the bay in San Francisco, the commingling of several activities helped to prepare the ground for the remarkable literary explosion that was soon to take place. The Libertarian Circle held regular literary events; poet members included Kenneth Rexroth, Muriel Rukeyser, William Everson, Robert Duncan, Jack Spicer, and Thomas

Parkinson. Rexroth also ran a literary program on KPFA, the country's first listener-sponsored radio station. Madeline Gleason (assisted by Rexroth and Duncan) founded the San Francisco Poetry Center, housed at San Francisco State College and managed by Ruth Witt-Diamant. The magazines *Circle*, *Ark*, *City Lights*, *Goad*, *Inferno*, and *Golden Goose* helped to consolidate the growing literary underground.

The famous reading at Six Gallery on Fillmore Street was publicized by Allen Ginsberg (via a hundred mailed postcards and a few flyers) thus: "6 POETS AT 6 GALLERY Philip Lamantia reading mss. of late John Hoffman – Mike McClure, Allen Ginsberg, Gary Snyder & Phil Whalen – all sharp new straightforward writing – remarkable collection of angels on one stage reading their poetry. No charge, small collection for wine and postcards. Charming event. Kenneth Rexroth, M.C. 8 PM Friday Night October 7, 1955 6 Gallery 3119 Fillmore St. San Fran." On October 7, 1955, in a room measuring 20 × 25 feet with a dirt floor, Ginsberg "read *Howl* and started an epoch."[4] Gary Snyder, Philip Lamantia, Michael McClure, and Philip Whalen shared the bill and, by all reports, also read brilliantly. Aside from Rexroth and Whalen, all the readers were in their twenties. Again, in the words of Kenneth Rexroth, "What started in SF and spread from there across the world was public poetry, the return of a tribal, preliterate relationship between poet and audience."[5]

These events, along with the flourishing of Lawrence Ferlinghetti's City Lights Bookshop and publishing house, helped to inaugurate and consolidate what has become known as

Fran Herndon's drawing for the cover of Jack Spicer's *Heads of the Town up to the Aether* (San Francisco: Auerhahn, 1962).

4. Kenneth Rexroth, *American Poetry in the Twentieth Century* (New York: Herder and Herder, 1971), p. 141.
5. Ibid.

A Little History of the Mimeograph Revolution

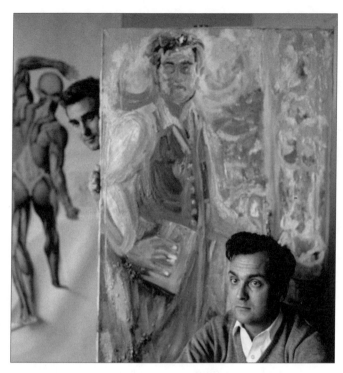

Jess Collins and Robert Duncan, San Francisco, 1958. Photograph by Harry Redl.

the San Francisco Renaissance. City Lights published *Howl* in 1956 (Ferlinghetti asked Ginsberg for the manuscript the same night it was read at the Six Gallery) as Number Four in the Pocket Poets Series. (It had been preceded by an extremely rare mimeographed edition, typed by Martha Rexroth and mimeographed by none other than Robert Creeley. Ginsberg's *Siesta in Xbalba* had been mimeographed by the man himself on a freighter in the Alaskan Ocean.) Among the audience members that night was one who added his own chant, the young novelist Jack Kerouac, whose *On the Road*, published in 1957, was to make this reading and its readers legendary.

It was also in 1957 that Charles Olson, rector of the experimental Black Mountain College, visited San Francisco and gave a series of lectures on Alfred North Whitehead at the Portrero Hill home of Robert Duncan and his companion, the painter Jess Collins. Among the attendees at the lectures were, of course, Duncan himself, but also Michael McClure, Gary Snyder's Reed College friend Philip Whalen, Jack Spicer, and Richard Duerden. The same year saw the "San Francisco Scene" issue of *Evergreen Review*. Poet Helen Adam's flamboyant 1961 ballad opera, entitled *San Francisco's Burning*, epitomized the time, outrageous both aesthetically and socially. Other writers associated with the San Francisco Renaissance included James Broughton, Lew Welch, Ron Loewinsohn, Madeline Gleason, David Meltzer, Kirby Doyle, and Lenore Kandel.

Experimentation with forms of literature and lifestyle had long been an attractive characteristic of life in San Francisco. But the tolerance felt in Northern California was not as evident in Los Angeles. In 1957, an exhibit of work by assemblage artist Wallace Berman at the Ferus Gallery was closed by the Los Angeles Police Department, and Berman was jailed on charges of exhibiting "lewd and lascivious pornographic art." Found guilty (by the same judge who ruled against Henry Miller), Berman and family left L.A. for San Francisco that year. Berman edited and published a fascinating assemblage magazine called *Semina.* After the raid of his exhibit at Ferus, he announced in *Semina 2* that "I will continue to print Semina from locations other than this city of degenerate angels." Berman's friend, artist George Herms, designed his own books and provided the artwork for others, including Diane di Prima. Herms had likewise found the political climate in L.A. intolerable and had preceded the Bermans to Northern California.

In the mid-1960s, John Martin's Black Sparrow Press began publishing broadsides and booklets and has, over the years, published a wide variety of experimental and alternative poetry and prose, including work by Duncan, Olson, Spicer, and Creeley among very many others. Black Sparrow continues to publish in 1998 from Santa Rosa, California.

Because of the previous associations of house printer/designer Graham Mackintosh, Black Sparrow is linked to earlier literary small presses of Northern California, particularly White Rabbit Press (at the urging of Jack Spicer, Mackintosh resurrected the press in 1962, printing Spicer's own *Lament for the Makers*); Robert Hawley's Oyez Press (Mackintosh had printed its first book in 1963); and Dave Haselwood's Auerhahn Press, which flourished during the 1960s and early 70s in San Francisco. Auerhahn

Poster for Wallace Berman's July 1977 retrospective exhibition at the Timothea Stewart Gallery, Los Angeles.

A Little History of the Mimeograph Revolution

Left to right: Jack Spicer, Robin Blaser, Carolyn Dunn, Joe Dunn, Robert Duncan, Dick Bratset, probably in Newburyport (on the way from Boston to Cape Ann), probably Spring 1956. Photograph by Kent Bowker.

published a wide variety of well-designed books, including *The Exterminator,* an early example of William S. Burroughs and Brion Gysin's cut-up technique, in 1960. Auerhahn also published John Wieners's first book, *The Hotel Wentley Poems.* Oyez published many memorable volumes including Philip Lamantia's *Touch of the Marvelous.* Joe Dunn's White Rabbit Press, which had begun publishing in 1957 with Steve Jonas's rough work *Love, the Poem, the Sea & Other Pieces Examined,* produced books somewhat less elegant than Auerhahn's or Oyez's but with a beauty all their own.

The editorial genius behind White Rabbit was the irrepressible Jack Spicer, who published his own remarkable mimeographed magazine, *J.* Spicer emphasized the inclusion of writers who were not well published elsewhere, and accepted contributions for consideration in a box that was kept in one of three bars in the North Beach area of San Francisco. *J* is representative of the best of the mimeograph revolution: an uncompromising editorial stance combined with a playful, even colorful, formal character thanks to Fran Herndon, who edited the

artwork for the magazine. Spicer's model for *J* was *Beatitude,* which had begun publication in San Francisco slightly before *J.* And a recalcitrant model it was, since Spicer was not a fan of the Beats and carried on a running war against Ferlinghetti in particular. He imagined Ferlinghetti had become commercial and financially successful, thereby, in Spicer's mind, "selling out" to the establishment. Magnificently consistent with his principles, Spicer never copyrighted his own work, anticipating the "no copyright, no nuthin" statements of Tom Clark's London-based Once series. The performative aspects of Spicer's poetics as well as his personality also prefigured the rise of poetry readings in the 1950s, particularly those sponsored by the Poetry Center at San Francisco State, which featured mimeographed programs and booklets printing selections from the poets who were reading, among them, Charles Olson, Denise Levertov, and Louis Zukofsky.

Although Spicer's *J* didn't publish the works of "established" poets, Spicer did include the work of Robert Duncan in four issues of his magazine. Duncan and

Jess Collins (whose work adorned the cover of many magazines and books of the period, including *Open Space, Caterpillar*, and *The Floating Bear*) were important influences on the literary and artistic scene in San Francisco in the 60s. Duncan's early work was published in Berkeley or North Carolina (his *Song of the Borderguard* was published by the Black Mountain College Press with a cover by Cy Twombly in 1952). Other earlier works were multilithed (*Fragments of a Disordered Devotion* in San Francisco in 1952) or mimeographed (the first hundred copies of *Faust Foutu* were mimeographed by Duncan himself, and the next 150 or so of one act of the play were multilithed by Joe Dunn of White Rabbit Press at his place of employment, the Greyhound Bus offices in San Francisco). The multilithed third edition of *Faust Foutu*, although also produced by Dunn, was published under Duncan's own imprint, Enkidu Surrogate, of Stinson Beach. Duncan's work was published by an amazing variety and number of publishers, including Oyez, Auerhahn, White Rabbit, Black Sparrow, Divers Press, Jargon, Perishable Press, City Lights, Grove Press, New Directions, and Scribners.

Slightly outside the Spicer circle (although some of his own poems were published in *J*) was Donald Allen, who, after the publication of *The New American Poetry, 1945–1960* and before his removal to New York, established the Four Seasons Foundation in San Francisco, which published the work of a number of the writers from the anthology, including Charles Olson, Ed Dorn, Ron Loewinsohn, Philip Lamantia, Michael McClure, Joanne Kyger, Robin Blaser, and Robert Creeley. Among the early Four

Beatitude 17 (1960–1961). Cover photograph by Fortunato Clementi.

City Lights Journal 3 (1966). Front cover: Poets at City Lights Bookstore, December 5, 1965 (photo by Larry Keenan, Jr.). *Back row, left to right:* Stella Levy, Lawrence Ferlinghetti (with umbrella). *Next row, left to right:* David Meltzer (with scarf over shoulder), Michael McClure, Allen Ginsberg, Daniel Langton, Steven Bornstein, Richard Brautigan, Gary Goodrow in jester hat. *Front row, sitting down, left to right:* Robert LaVigne, Shigeyoshi Murao, Larry Fagin, Lelan Meyezove (in Larry Fagin's lap), Lew Welch, Peter Orlovsky.

CITY LIGHTS
JOURNAL

$2.50   NUMBER THREE

A Little History of the Mimeograph Revolution

Seasons publications were two important works by poet Gary Snyder (the Reed College roommate of Lew Welch and Philip Whalen and the "Japhy Ryder" of Kerouac's *The Dharma Bums*): *Six Sections from Rivers and Mountains Without End* and *Riprap and Cold Mountain Poems*, both published in 1965. *Riprap*, it should be noted, was originally published in 1959 as a booklet by Cid Corman's Origin Press. Snyder's *Myths and Texts* was published in 1960 by Corinth Books. Snyder was out of the country on an extended stay in Japan, and the text used for the Corinth publication was probably from a manuscript that LeRoi Jones had hand-copied from one that Robert Creeley had received from Snyder in 1955 or 1956. Snyder's poetry was extremely popular in the 60s and was often used as text for broadsides by small presses, particularly those whose owners were ecologically minded. For instance, Snyder's poem "Four Changes" was published in 1969 by Earth Read Out, a Berkeley environmental protection group, as four mimeographed pages, as well as in a folded, printed version in 200,000 copies by environmentalist Alan Shapiro for free distribution to schools and citizens' groups.

Literary scenes with strong affiliations to the New American Poetry were in evidence elsewhere in California – most notably Bolinas in the 1970s, when that somewhat remote hippie village north of San Francisco became home to many poets. In particular, the transplanted easterner and Poetry Project veteran Bill Berkson and his press Big Sky flourished there in the decade, publishing both a magazine and a series of books. Bolinas residents of the period also included Robert Creeley, Bobbie Louise Hawkins, David Meltzer, Lewis Warsh, Tom Clark, Lewis MacAdams, Philip Whalen, Aram Saroyan, Joanne Kyger, Jim Carroll, and Duncan McNaughton, among others. Ted Berrigan, Alice Notley, and Joe Brainard were among many occasional visitors, with Joe Brainard's *Bolinas Journal* providing an interesting record of one such extended stay.

Tom Clark *(left)* and Lewis Warsh on the beach at Bolinas, California, 1968. Photograph by Anne Waldman from *Bustin's Island '68* by Lewis Warsh (New York: Granary Books, 1996).

A Little History of the Mimeograph Revolution

The Poetry Conferences at Vancouver and Berkeley

Charles Olson.
Photograph by Jim
Hatch from *Charles
Olson Reading at
Berkeley* (N.p.: Coyote
Books, 1966).

Poetry conferences at Vancouver (1963) and Berkeley (1965) were significant events that brought together and introduced a range of poets from diverse locations and temperaments. Warren Tallman was the man behind the conference in Vancouver, an event Robert Creeley described as "landmark" in that it brought "together for the first time, a decisive company of then disregarded poets such as Denise Levertov, Charles Olson, Allen Ginsberg, Robert Duncan, Margaret Avison, Philip Whalen and myself, together with as yet unrecognized younger poets of that time, Michael Palmer, Clark Coolidge and many more." The conference at Berkeley in July of 1965 further galvanized the gains made by the Allen anthology and the Vancouver event. Mostly organized and emceed by Thomas Parkinson and Robert Duncan, it featured readings and lectures by, among many others, Charles Olson, Jack Spicer, Allen Ginsberg, Gary Snyder, Ed Dorn, Robert Creeley, John Wieners, Ed Sanders, Ted Berrigan, Joanne

Robert Creeley in
the audience at the
Berkeley Poetry
Conference, 1965.

Kyger, Lew Welch, Ron Loewinsohn, John
Sinclair, and Victor Coleman. For the senior
poets, the Berkeley conference was at once a
triumphant victory and the beginning of the
end. In the years immediately following the
conference, a general emigration of spirits
took place. Jack Spicer's lecture on poetry
and politics was to be his last public appearance; he died a month later. Within the next
couple of years, a great many of the participants in the San Francisco Renaissance had
moved from the area or passed away. Yet for
many of the younger poets in attendance, the
Berkeley Poetry Conference was the flash
point of the mimeo revolution, the place
from which much of the writing and publishing just ahead was to locate its identity and
its momentum.

The Beats

1955 City Lights Pocket Poets series begins
with Lawrence Ferlinghetti's *Pictures
of the Gone World*

1957 "San Francisco Scene" issue of
Evergreen Review

1957 Jack Kerouac's *On the Road* published
by Viking

1958 Jack Kerouac's *The Dharma Bums*
published by Viking

1958 Beat article in *Esquire*: Jack Kerouac
on the term "Beat"

1958 *Yugen*, edited by LeRoi Jones and
Hettie Cohen

1958 *The Beat Generation and the Angry
Young Men*, edited by Gene Feldman
and Max Gartenberg, published by
Citadel

1959 Jack Kerouac's *Mexico City Blues* published by Grove Press

1959 Gary Snyder's *Riprap* published by
Origin Press

1959 William S. Burroughs's *Naked Lunch*
published by Grove Press

1960 Selections from Jack Kerouac's *Visions
of Cody* published by New Directions

1960 Gary Snyder's *Myths and Texts* published by Corinth Books

1960 William S. Burroughs, Brion Gysin,
Gregory Corso, and Sinclair Beiles's
Minutes to Go published in Paris by
Two Cities

A Little History of the Mimeograph Revolution

1960	Fred McDarrah's *The Beat Scene*, edited by Eli Wilentz, published by Corinth Books
1961	January, first issue of *The Floating Bear*, edited by Diane di Prima and LeRoi Jones
1961	October, LeRoi Jones arrested for *The Floating Bear* 9
1965	Gary Snyder's *Six Sections from Rivers and Mountains Without End* published by the Four Seasons Foundation
1967	The Gathering of the Tribes for a Human Be-In, Golden Gate Park, San Francisco
1967	*San Francisco Earthquake,* edited by Jacob Herman, Claude Peliau, and Norman Mustill
1968	Diane di Prima's *Revolutionary Letters* published by Communications Co.
1969	Jack Kerouac dies
1971	Jack Kerouac's *Scattered Poems* published by City Lights
1973	Jack Kerouac's *Visions of Cody* published by McGraw-Hill

Allen Ginsberg,
New York City, 1960.
Photograph by
Fred McDarrah.

Among those writers at the 1955 reading at the Six Gallery in San Francisco were, of course, both Allen Ginsberg and Jack Kerouac. Both were to become literary idols of a generation, and both were heavily connected to life in the West. Ginsberg's poem *Howl* had been written on Montgomery Street in San Francisco, where he was to meet his lover and companion Peter Orlovsky. Kerouac's most famous books all deal in one way or another with the myth of the West and its place in the American imagination. However, Kerouac and Ginsberg, who, with William S. Burroughs and Gregory Corso, were to form the nucleus of the Beat writers, had met in the 1940s in New York City, where they had begun their writing as well. New York was to become a Beat capital in the 1950s, with its plethora of coffeehouses and jazz bars, where poetry was occasionally performed, with or without musical accompaniment. One enterprising young man, Dan Saxon, collected the manuscripts that poets read in the East Seventh Street coffeehouses and published an early mimeographed magazine, *Poems Collected at Les Deux Mégots*, and its continuation, *Poets at Le Metro*, directly reproducing the original handwritten manuscript or typescript. In 1960, Corinth Books published the defining anthology, *The Beat Scene*, edited by Eli Wilentz, with spectacular and intimate photographs by Fred McDarrah. That same year, Corinth also published (sometimes in association with Totem Press) Jack Kerouac's *The Scripture of the Golden Eternity*, Philip Whalen's *Like I Say*, and Gary Snyder's *Myths and Texts*. In 1961, Corinth published Diane di Prima's *Dinners and Nightmares*, Ginsberg's early poems in *Empty Mirror*, and LeRoi Jones's breakthrough *Preface to a Twenty Volume Suicide Note.*

LeRoi Jones started the little magazine *Yugen* in 1958 with Hettie Cohen, and its pages were full of writings by core Beat writers, including Kerouac, Burroughs, Orlovsky, Snyder, and

San Francisco Earthquake, vol. 1, no. 3 (Spring 1968).

Whalen, as well as Jones himself. In 1961, Jones and Diane di Prima started the mimeo magazine *The Floating Bear*, early issues of which were typed up by di Prima and produced on the mimeograph machine at Robert Wilson's Phoenix Bookstore in New York in exchange for finished copies of the magazine. Jones and di Prima intended their "newsletter" to be an engine for quick and informal communication, particularly for younger and unpublished experimental poets who practiced "the open and implied rebellion – of form and content." *The Floating Bear* 9 (October 1961) was apparently a little *too* rebellious for the authorities, as it contained an excerpt from Jones's *The System of Dante's Hell* and Burroughs's *Routine*. Jones was arrested and charged with sending obscene material through the U.S. mails. But he was not indicted by the grand jury, who listened patiently to his reading great literature of all types, once deemed obscene. *The Floating Bear* had a bold and colorful editorial style, and a simple design. It emphasized the publication of new work from a variety of sources, be they Black Mountain, Beat, San Francisco Renaissance, or New York School.

Black Mountain, Intermedia, Deep Image, Ethnopoetics

1947 Charles Olson's *Call Me Ishmael* published by Reynal & Hitchcock

1948 Charles Olson's *Y & X* published by Black Sun Press

1951 *Origin*, edited by Cid Corman, begins life near Boston; the first issue features Olson, the second, Robert Creeley

1951 Charles Olson arrives at Black Mountain College as Rector

1951 *The Dada Painters and Poets*, edited by Robert Motherwell, published by Wittenborn, Schultz

1953 Charles Olson's *Mayan Letters* published by the Divers Press

1954 *The Black Mountain Review*, edited by Robert Creeley

1956 Black Mountain College closes

1957 John Cage begins teaching classes on experimental music composition at the New School; classes continue to 1960

1958 *The Fifties*, edited by Robert Bly

1959 *Poems from the Floating World*, edited by Jerome Rothenberg

1959 Charles Olson's *Projective Verse* published by Totem Press

1959 Allan Kaprow's *18 Happenings in 6 Parts* performed at the Ruben Gallery

1960 Performance events held at Yoko Ono's loft on Chambers Street, 1960–1961	**1975** George Oppen's *Collected Poems* published by New Directions
1960 Ed Dorn's *What I See in The Maximus Poems* published by Migrant Books	**1975** Paul Blackburn's *Journals* published by Black Sparrow Press
1960 *Trobar*, edited by George Economou, Joan Kelly, and Robert Kelly	**1977** *New Wilderness Letter*, edited by Jerome Rothenberg
1961 John Cage's *Silence* published by Wesleyan University Press	**1978** Louis Zukofsky's *"A"* (complete version) published by the University of California Press
1962 *El Corno Emplumado*, edited by Margaret Randall	**1980** Volume 1 of Charles Olson's and Robert Creeley's correspondence published by Black Sparrow Press
1962 Robert Creeley's *For Love* published by Scribners	**1981** *Sulfur*, edited by Clayton Eshleman

1960 Performance events held at Yoko
Ono's loft on Chambers Street,
1960–1961
1960 Ed Dorn's *What I See in The Maximus
Poems* published by Migrant Books
1960 *Trobar*, edited by George Economou,
Joan Kelly, and Robert Kelly
1961 John Cage's *Silence* published by
Wesleyan University Press
1962 *El Corno Emplumado*, edited by
Margaret Randall
1962 Robert Creeley's *For Love* published
by Scribners
1962 George Oppen's *The Materials* published by New Directions
1963 *Wild Dog*, edited by John Hoopes and
Ed Dorn
1963 *An Anthology of Chance Operations*,
edited by La Monte Young, published
by Young and Jackson Mac Low
1963 *Matter* and Matter Books, edited and
published by Robert Kelly
1966 *Maps*, edited by John Taggart
1967 *Caterpillar*, edited by Clayton Eshleman
1968 Jerome Rothenberg's *Technicians of the
Sacred: A Range of Poetries from Africa,
America, Asia, & Oceania* published by
Doubleday Anchor
1969 Celia and Louis Zukofsky's Catullus
translations published by Cape
Goliard/Grossman
1970 *Alcheringa*, edited by Jerome
Rothenberg and Dennis Tedlock
1972 *Shaking the Pumpkin: Traditional Poetry
of the Indian North Americas*, edited by
Jerome Rothenberg, published by
Doubleday Anchor
1973 *America: A Prophecy. A New Reading of
American Poetry from Pre-Columbian
Times to the Present*, edited by Jerome
Rothenberg and George Quasha, published by Random House

1975 George Oppen's *Collected Poems* published by New Directions
1975 Paul Blackburn's *Journals* published by
Black Sparrow Press
1977 *New Wilderness Letter*, edited by Jerome
Rothenberg
1978 Louis Zukofsky's *"A"* (complete version) published by the University of
California Press
1980 Volume 1 of Charles Olson's and
Robert Creeley's correspondence published by Black Sparrow Press
1981 *Sulfur*, edited by Clayton Eshleman

Black Mountain

Among the several streams which made up
the New American Poetry was a group known
as the Black Mountain poets, so named for
the experimental college in North Carolina
where many of them taught or attended
classes in the 1950s. The most prominent
of these poets were of course Charles Olson,
rector of the college in its last five years, and
Robert Creeley, who edited *The Black Mountain Review*. The work of both has exerted
an extraordinary influence on the course
of American poetry in the latter half of this
century. Closely allied with many of the
Black Mountain writers, but especially influential on Creeley, were the poets occasionally known as the Objectivists, such as Louis
Zukofsky, George Oppen, and Charles
Reznikoff, who were in fact too individualistic to be part of any school. Still, the spare
lyricism, historical knowledge, and social
conscience found in all three poets were
highly regarded in the camps of the New
American Poetry.

Those who taught or listened at Black
Mountain constitute a veritable roll-call
of the American avant-garde; among those

A Little History of the Mimeograph Revolution

most relevant to our literary purposes are John Cage, Merce Cunningham, Fielding Dawson, Ed Dorn, Robert Duncan, Buckminster Fuller, Basil King, Joel Oppenheimer, M. C. Richards, Michael Rumaker, John Wieners, and Jonathan Williams. *The Black Mountain Review* was founded to supplement allied magazines such as *Origin* (Olson succinctly described the importance of *Origin* when he told editor Cid Corman, "The thing is, because *Origin* exists, I write better, I write more …")[6] and attempted to extend this work by creating a critical grounding for the new writing through the publication of theoretical writings. The magazine also acted as a bridge to writers outside the Black Mountain milieu, publishing work by Lorine Niedecker, James Purdy, Allen Ginsberg, Hubert Selby, Jr., and Jack Kerouac, among others. Jonathan Williams returned from San Francisco to his home-state to study photography with Aaron Siskind and Harry Callahan at Black Mountain College. Williams's nascent Jargon Society flourished in part as a result of his stay at the college – books published during and just after this period include Olson's *The Maximus Poems*, Creeley's *A Form of Women*, Louis Zukofsky's *Some Time*, Larry Eigner's *On My Eyes*, Duncan's *Letters*, Denise Levertov's *Overland to the Islands*, Paul Metcalf's *Genoa*,

and Williams's own *Empire Finals at Verona* (illustrated by Fielding Dawson), to name just a few. *The Black Mountain Review* had a distinctive squat format and was very well produced. Published in part as an attempt to draw attention to the college in a last-ditch effort to increase enrollment, the edition size never exceeded 750 copies.

The bringing together of unusual talents from diverse arts in the cloistered setting at Black Mountain played a crucial role in the development of postmodernism later in the 1960s. Having the likes of Buckminster Fuller, John Cage, Merce Cunningham, Robert Rauschenberg, Willem de Kooning, David Tudor, Stephen Volpe, Paul Goodman, and Cy Twombly (along with the poets mentioned above) under one roof pinpoints the location of one of several influential force fields in America that surely extended the boundaries of the various arts into new kinds of expression and new ways of making art.

Robert Creeley and Dan Rice at Black Mountain College, 1955. Photograph by Jonathan Williams.

6. Sherman Paul, *Olson's Push: Origin, Black Mountain and Recent American Poetry* (Baton Rouge: Louisiana State University Press, 1978), p. 32.

A Little History of the Mimeograph Revolution

Intermedia

New York in the late 1950s saw the emergence of radical changes in dance, painting, film, sculpture, and theater as well as in writing. Indeed, writing or "text" was foregrounded in much of the new art. Language was newly seen as a material form, and could thus be worked with as one would work with paint or movement or sound. Concrete and sound poetry flourished. Conceptual and minimal artists began publishing their works in the form of books (later to be called "artists' books") – Edward Ruscha's early published booklets (for example, *Twenty-six Gasoline Stations*) were important extenders of the book as an art form. Other artists, such as Dan Graham, Adrian Piper, Sol LeWitt, Vito Acconci, Lawrence Weiner, and Carl Andre, were publishing both artists' books (i.e., books as works of art) as well as poetry and other writings, sometimes in the same places as those writers most easily identified as poets. Painter Carolee Schneemann was (and continues to be) crucial in highlighting the value of the ecstatic body as a source of knowledge. Her early performances and films are the source books for much of the performance art that followed in the 70s. *Parts of a Body House Book*, published by Beau Geste Press in 1972, connects text and image to ritual, performance, and dream and links her work to that of the writers working in ethnopoetics.

John Cage's influence, in part disseminated through his class in "Composition of Experimental Music" at the New School for Social Research, was crucial in the development of both Happenings and Fluxus. In the summer of 1958, class members included Dick Higgins, Jackson Mac Low, Jim Dine, Allan Kaprow, and George Brecht. Cage's collection of lectures and writings, entitled *Silence*,

was published in 1961 by Wesleyan University Press. George Maciunas met La Monte Young in Richard Maxfield's New School class in electronic music. In early 1961, Young and Maciunas hosted a series called "Literary Evenings and Musica Antiqua et Nova" at the latter's AG Gallery. Participants included Trisha Brown, Yvonne Rainer, Jackson Mac Low, Dick Higgins, and Ray Johnson. In 1960, Young was invited to guest edit an issue of *Beatitude East* focusing on performance and poetry. The project for *Beatitude East* was canceled but was resurrected as *An Anthology of Chance Operations*, edited by Young, designed and produced by Maciunas, and published by Young and Mac Low in 1963. The anthology, a collection of music and performance scores, essays, stories, and poems, included work by Emmett Williams, George Brecht, Henry Flynt, Robert Morris, Terry Riley, Yoko Ono, Simone Forti, Jackson Mac Low, and others. Mac Low's own work as a writer dates to 1937; he stands, in the words of Jerome Rothenberg, alongside John Cage as "one of the two major artists bringing systematic chance operations into our poetic & musical practice since the Second World War."[7] His first book, *The Twin Plays*, was mimeographed in 1963, and was soon followed by *The Pronouns* in 1964, which was mimeographed at the Judson Memorial Church.

The year 1964 saw the founding of one of the most interesting presses of the period: Dick Higgins's Something Else Press. As an editor, Higgins seemed to be interested in everything having to do with the new arts – his interest in and knowledge of the

---

7. Jerome Rothenberg, Pre-Face to Jackson Mac Low, *Representative Works: 1938–1985* (New York: Roof, 1986), p. v.

Jackson Mac Low, The Bronx, New York, 1975. Photograph by Gerard Malanga.

history of bookmaking, printing, design, and typography helped him to accomplish something very few of the previously mentioned publishers ever managed to achieve: distribution. One of the most radical achievements of the Something Else Press was to slip avant-garde content into what looked like "regular books" and then to get those books into bookstores and libraries around the world. The list of titles published by Something Else in its regular series as well as the series of Great Bear Pamphlets is astonishing for its range and depth. A few examples are Daniel Spoerri's *An Anecdoted Topography of Chance*, *Notations* by John Cage with Alison Knowles, *An Anthology of Concrete Poetry*, edited by Emmett Williams, *Breakthrough Fictioneers*, edited by Richard Kostelanetz, *Store Days* by Claes Oldenburg, and *Stanzas for Iris Lezak* by Jackson Mac Low. It is interesting to note that Higgins's own first book, *What Are Legends*, was published by Bern Porter in 1961. Porter, himself an important writer and visual artist, also published the first books of Philip Lamantia and Robert Duncan.

The Deep Image and Ethnopoetics

In the late 50s and early 60s, another group important to the New American Poetry was emerging, primarily in New York. They were a sort of "in-between" generation – younger than most of the poets in the Allen anthology but older than the second-generation New York School or the Language poets. This group began publishing in magazines such as *Some/thing*, *Poems from the Floating World*, *Trobar*, *Matter*, and *Caterpillar*. Poets most closely allied with this group include Jerome Rothenberg, Robert Kelly, Clayton Eshleman, Diane Wakoski, David Antin, Paul Blackburn, Frank Samperi, Armand Schwerner, and George Economou. The basic sense of deep image poetry, as distinct from Imagism, was, according to Robert Kelly, to "generate a kind of poetry not necessarily dominated by the images, but in which it is the rhythm of images which forms the dominant movement of the poem."[8] Jerome Rothenberg would later describe the "deep image" as "a power, among several, by which the poem is sighted & brought close." Investigations

---

8. *The Little Magazine in America: A Modern Documentary History*, edited by Elliott Anderson and Mary Kinzie (Yonkers, N.Y.: Pushcart Press, 1978), p. 400.

A Little History of the Mimeograph Revolution

into deep image existed alongside and resonated with work in translation, performance, and an awareness of earlier avant-gardes and poetry from "those anonymous tribal & subterranean predecessors." Consequently, these poets were keenly aware of the need to build on the insights and discoveries of Dada and Surrealism. Ethnopoetics developed, in part, out of a growing awareness "that we weren't just doing something new (which we were) but were getting back in our own terms to fundamental ways of seeing & languaging from which we (the larger 'we' of the Western enterprise) had long been cut off."[9] Thus, Ethnopoetics is a recognition of the "primitive" as a way to ease ourselves into the future. *Alcheringa: Ethnopoetics*, "a first journal of the world's tribal poetries," edited by Jerome Rothenberg and Dennis Tedlock, published five numbers in its first series (1970–1973) and continued forward with a second series in 1975. Several of the issues contained phonograph records, including readings by Jaime de Angelo, Jackson Mac Low, and Anne Waldman. *New Wilderness Letter* (edited primarily by Jerome Rothenberg but with the help of co- and guest editors) extended the ethnopoetics project into an exploration of the relation between old and new forms of art-making across the full spectrum of arts. One of the most interesting issues was *New Wilderness Letter* 11 (1982), entitled *The Book, Spiritual Instrument*, which Rothenberg co-edited with anthropologist/poet David Guss. A significant contribution to the ethnopoetic project is to be found in the collection of anthologies edited by Rothenberg, including *Technicians of the Sacred, Shaking the Pumpkin, America: A Prophecy* (with George Quasha), and *A Big Jewish Book*.

Technicians of the Sacred: A Range of Poetries from Africa, Asia, & Oceania, edited with commentaries by Jerome Rothenberg (Garden City, N.Y.: Doubleday Anchor, 1969). Cover design by Richard Mantel.

9. Jerome Rothenberg, *Pre-Faces and Other Writing* (New York: New Directions, 1981), pp. 52, 139.

The New York School: The First Generation

1949 John Ashbery, as editor of the *Harvard Advocate*, publishes stories and poems by Frank O'Hara

1953 *Folder*, edited by Daisy Alden

1953 John Bernard Myers of Tibor de Nagy Gallery publishes Frank O'Hara's *Oranges* as well as other books

1953 Frank O'Hara teaches at the New School

1957 Frank O'Hara's *Meditations in an Emergency* published by Grove Press

1958 James Schuyler's *Alfred and Guinevere* published by Harcourt, Brace

1959 Kenneth Koch's *Ko: or, A Season on Earth* published by Grove Press

1960 Barbara Guest's *The Location of Things* published by Tibor de Nagy

1962 John Ashbery's *The Tennis Court Oath* published by Wesleyan University Press

1962 Kenneth Koch's *Thank You and Other Poems* published by Grove Press

1965 Frank O'Hara's *Lunch Poems* published by City Lights

1966 Frank O'Hara dies

1966 John Ashbery's *Rivers and Mountains* published by Holt, Rinehart and Winston

1966 James Schuyler's *May 24th or So* published by Tibor de Nagy

1968 Barbara Guest's *The Blue Stairs* published by Corinth Books

1969 Kenneth Koch's *When the Sun Tries to Go On* published by Black Sparrow Press

1970 Kenneth Koch's *Wishes, Lies and Dreams: Teaching Children to Write Poetry* published by Chelsea House Publishers

1971 Frank O'Hara's *Collected Poems*, edited by Donald Allen, published

1972 *49 South*, an anthology/one-shot magazine edited by James Schuyler

1973 Barbara Guest's *Moscow Mansions* published by Viking

1974 *ZZZ* publishes *Play*, a play by Frank O'Hara, Kenneth Koch, and John Ashbery, the first act originally written at Koch's apartment in 1953

1978 *Big Sky* 11/12 presents an homage to Frank O'Hara (later published by Creative Arts Press in Berkeley in an expanded edition)

The New York School really began, strangely enough, in Cambridge, Massachusetts, at Harvard University where several of its most famous members were students along with other postwar poets Robert Bly, Robert Creeley, Donald Hall, Adrienne Rich, and Richard Wilbur. It was at Harvard that Kenneth Koch met John Ashbery and that John Ashbery published Frank O'Hara, later meeting him in the flesh at an opening of a show of Edward Gorey's watercolors (Gorey was Ashbery's roommate). All three eventually ended up in New York City, where they became involved with each other and with a number of painters, including Jane Freilicher, Nell Blaine, Larry Rivers, and Fairfield Porter.

Everyone, it seems, wrote for *Art News* or worked at the Museum of Modern Art, except for Koch who taught and pioneered the teaching of poetry to children. The poetry and art worlds were deeply intertwined, and collaboration between visual artists and writers continues to be a salient characteristic of the New York School. In 1953, for instance, John Bernard Myers of the Tibor de Nagy Gallery published O'Hara's *Oranges* in an edition of about twenty mimeographed copies. Issued in gray "three-clasp binders," some of the copies contained oil paint sketches by Grace Hartigan (the publication was in fact to accompany the exhibition of her work at the gallery). In 1952, Myers had produced, somewhat more "professionally," O'Hara's *A City Winter*, with some copies containing drawings by Larry Rivers. This was followed in 1953 by Koch's *Poems*, with prints by Nell Blaine, and Ashbery's *Turandot*, with plates by Jane Freilicher. These volumes were all printed letterpress with decorative covers. In 1969, Myers published an anthology, *The Poets of the New York School*, which included O'Hara, Koch, and Ashbery as well as James Schuyler, Barbara Guest, Joe Ceravolo, Kenward Elmslie, Frank Lima, and Tony Towle. James Schuyler, whose *May 24th or So* was published (unaccompanied by art) by Tibor de Nagy in 1966, had arrived on the scene (he was to become one of the most famous of the residents of New York City's Chelsea Hotel) and, in 1972, had published the mimeographed anthology *49 South*. His *Freely Espousing* was published by Paris Review Press in 1969 with a jacket by Alex Katz, and *Hymn to Life, The Crystal Lithium*, and *The Morning of the Poem* were all published by Random House with covers by Fairfield Porter.

All the major figures of the New York School were to find commercial publishers,

Left to right: Arthur Gold, Julia Gruen, Harold Clurman, Bobby Fizdale, John Ashbery, Jane Freilicher, Joe Hazan, and Jane Wilson, Water Mill, New York, 1962. Photograph by John Gruen.

but continued to provide work to the small presses and mimeograph magazines (Barbara Guest, for instance, appeared in several issues of *"C"* magazine, and Ashbery's *The New Spirit* was published by Larry Fagin's Adventures in Poetry). In 1970, *An Anthology of New York Poets*, edited by Ron Padgett and David Shapiro (with a cover by Joe Brainard), was published by Vintage. It featured work by Schuyler, Koch, Ashbery, and O'Hara scattered throughout the book, which also included Clark Coolidge, Kenward Elmslie, Ted Berrigan, Harry Matthews, Tony Towle, Tom Clark, Tom Veitch, Lewis MacAdams, Frank Lima, John Giorno, Joe Ceravolo, Jim Brodey, John Perrault, Bill Berkson, Michael Brownstein, Ed Sanders, Peter Schjeldahl, Aram Saroyan, Ron Padgett, Dick Gallup, Bernadette Mayer, Edwin Denby, and David Shapiro.

The New York School:
Second and Third Generations

1959 *White Dove Review* published in Tulsa
1960 Ron Padgett arrives in New York
1960 Dick Gallup arrives in New York
1960 Joe Brainard arrives in New York
1960 Ted Berrigan arrives in New York
in December (or possibly in
January 1961)
1961 Bill Berkson's *Saturday Night Poems*
published by Tibor de Nagy
1962 *Fuck You, a magazine of the arts*, edited
by Ed Sanders
1963 Vancouver Poetry Conference
1963 *"C," a Journal of Poetry*, edited by Ted
Berrigan
1964 Ted Berrigan's *The Sonnets* published
by "C" Press; it was reissued by Grove
in 1967 and again by United Artists
in 1982
1964 Carol Bergé's *The Vancouver Report*
published by Fuck You
1964 *Joglars*, edited by Clark Coolidge and
George [Michael] Palmer
1964 Ron Padgett's *In Advance of the Broken
Arm* published by "C" Press
1964 Tom Clark becomes poetry editor of
The Paris Review, his editorship continues through 1974
1964 *Mother*, edited by David Moberg,
Jeff Giles, Peter Schjeldahl,
Lewis MacAdams, and others

1965 Berkeley Poetry Conference
1965 Joe Ceravolo's *Fits of Dawn* published
by "C" Press
1966 The Poetry Project at St. Mark's
Church begins
1966 *Angel Hair*, edited by Anne Waldman
and Lewis Warsh
1966 *Lines*, edited by Aram Saroyan
1967 *The World*, edited by Joel Sloman,
Anne Waldman, and others
1967 Tom Veitch's *Toad Poems* published in
London by Tom Clark's Once Books

Lewis Warsh, *Dreaming as
One: Poems* (New York:
Corinth Books, 1971).
Cover by Joe Brainard.

Best and Company picnic. Photograph by L. Fagin taken at the Staten Island Ballfield, Easter Sunday, 1968. *Back row, left to right:* Peter Schjeldahl (with hand on head), Jim Carroll, Linda Schjeldahl, George Kimball. *Next row, left to right:* Susan Kimball (with dark glasses), Lewis Warsh, Anne Waldman, Ted Berrigan, Bill Berkson, George Schneeman, Ron Padgett, Dick Gallup (with cigarette), Carol Gallup. *Next row, left to right:* Tessie Mitchell (holding Emma Rivers), Katie Schneeman (holding Gwen Rivers), Sandy Berrigan (with hat and polka dot dress), Emilio Schneeman (kneeling between two baseballs), David Berrigan (holding baseball bat), Pat Padgett (wearing sunglasses, holding Wayne Padgett), Joan Fagin (wearing wristwatch), Elio Schneeman (in striped shirt).

1967 Ted Berrigan and Ron Padgett's *Bean Spasms*, with drawings by Joe Brainard, published by Kulchur

1967 Ron Padgett's *Tone Arm* published by Once Press

1967 *0 to 9*, edited by Bernadette Mayer and Vito Acconci

1968 Bernadette Mayer's *Story* published by 0 to 9

1968 *Adventures in Poetry*, edited by Larry Fagin

1968 Larry Fagin's *Parade of the Caterpillars* published by Angel Hair

1968 Clark Coolidge's *Ing*, with a cover by Philip Guston, published by Angel Hair

1969 *Telephone*, edited by Maureen Owen

1969 Tom Clark's *Stones* published by Harper & Row

1969 Ron Padgett's *Great Balls of Fire* published by Holt, Rinehart and Winston

A Little History of the Mimeograph Revolution

1970	Anne Waldman's *Giant Night* published by Corinth Books
1970	*An Anthology of New York Poets*, edited by Ron Padgett and David Shapiro, published by Vintage
1970	Clark Coolidge's *Space* published by Harper & Row
1971	Lewis Warsh's *Dreaming as One* published by Corinth Books
1972	*The Poetry Project Newsletter*, edited by Ron Padgett and others
1973	*Z*, edited by Kenward Elmslie
1975	Bernadette Mayer's *Studying Hunger* published by Adventures in Poetry/ Big Sky and her *Memory* published by North Atlantic
1976	Alice Notley's *Alice Ordered Me to Be Made* published in Chicago by Yellow Press
1977	*United Artists*, edited by Lewis Warsh and Bernadette Mayer
1977	*Mag City*, edited by Greg Masters, Gary Lenhart, and Michael Scholnick
1977	*Un Poco Loco*, edited by Larry Fagin
1977	*Dodgems*, edited by Eileen Myles
1979	*Rocky Ledge*, edited by Anne Waldman and Reed Bye
1980	Ted Berrigan's *So Going Around Cities* published by Blue Wind

Some of the great New York–based magazines were *"C"*, *Fuck You, a magazine of the arts*, *Mother*, *Angel Hair*, *The World*, *o to 9*, *Lines*, and *Adventures in Poetry*, all born in the turbulent literary and social atmosphere of the East Village in the 1960s.

Ed Sanders came from Kansas to study classics at NYU. Poet, editor, publisher, bookstore owner (Peace Eye), singer/songwriter (founding member of the Fugs), political activist, and relentless archivist, Sanders founded *Fuck You, a magazine of the arts* in 1962. Unabashed and unashamed on every front, *Fuck You* reveled in an attitude best described by William Blake 150 years before: "Energy is eternal delight."

Fuck You published the likes of Charles Olson, Lenore Kandel, Carol Bergé, Ted Berrigan, Tuli Kupferberg, W. H. Auden, and Ezra Pound. The energy and ethos of the magazine is vividly expressed in the following statement: "Fuck You: A Magazine of the Arts is edited, published, zapped, designed, freaked, groped, stomped, & ejaculated by Ed Sanders at a secret location in the lower east side, New York City, U.S.A." Almost forty years later, it is still completely original and a total delight.

Mother was edited by several different poets including David Moberg, Jeff Giles, Peter Schjeldahl, Lewis MacAdams, and Duncan McNaughton from such diverse locations as Northfield, Minnesota; Galesburg, Illinois; New York City; and Buffalo, New York. Yet it was always associated with the New York School and published work by such poets as John Ashbery, Bernadette Mayer, Ed Sanders, John Wieners, Tony Towle, Kenneth Koch, and Joe Ceravolo, and artwork by many including Les

Left to right: Ken Irby, Robert Duncan, and Anne Waldman, Cambridge, Massachusetts, April 1972. Photograph by Elsa Dorfman. Photograph © 1998 by Elsa Dorfman. http://elsa.photo.net

A Little History of the Mimeograph Revolution

An Anthology of New
York Poets, edited by
Ron Padgett and
David Shapiro (New
York: Vintage Books,
1970). Cover by Joe
Brainard.

Levine, Andy Warhol, and Joe Brainard. Issue 7 included the infamous interview with John Cage conducted by Ted Berrigan. Actually, Berrigan was responsible for both questions *and* answers, most of which were appropriated from other sources, a circumstance that caused some embarrassment when the interview was honored with a cash award from *The National Literary Anthology.*

Ted Berrigan, in many ways the focal point of the East Village literary outburst, arrived in New York from Tulsa in late 1960 (or early 1961), having completed his Master's thesis on G. B. Shaw. While in the army, he had learned to operate the mimeograph machine, a skill that would serve him well. The first issue of *"C"* was published by Lorenz Gude in May 1963 – the contributors were editor Berrigan and his three best friends, all from Tulsa: Ron Padgett, Dick Gallup, and Joe Brainard. *"C"* was preceded

by the one and only issue of a mimeographed magazine entitled *The Censored Review,* which published poems by Berrigan ("I Was Born Standing Up"), Jonathan Cott, Dick Gallup ("Ember Grease"), Nancy Ward, and David Omer Bearden, and the very long and anonymous "Eli's Story" about a group of characters who were "All orbits in Brian Benedict's universe." In 1963, *"C"* published the Edwin Denby issue with its cover by Andy Warhol. Berrigan's breakthrough book, *The Sonnets,* was mimeographed and published by "C" Press in 1964. Ron Padgett edited the work and typed the stencils.

Among the other early mimeograph publications of the East Village were several collaborations: *Some Things* (a collaboration late in 1963 between Berrigan, Padgett, and Brainard) and *Seventeen* (plays by Ted Berrigan and Ron Padgett, and by the two in collaboration, 1964).

In the early years, Berrigan and Padgett were the best of friends, and their combined talents were crucial ingredients in the emerging scene. Padgett's high school experience in Tulsa editing the *White Dove Review* proved invaluable. His wisdom and learning mixed with Berrigan's enthusiasm and energy to provide an atmosphere of friendly competition and collaboration that inspired and encouraged other poets and writers throughout the 60s.

Lines was edited by Aram Saroyan and, like *0 to 9* (edited by Bernadette Mayer and Vito Acconci), published works somewhat more visually and conceptually based than many of the other literary magazines of the period. *The World*, the magazine of The Poetry Project, was first published in 1967. Mimeographed at St. Mark's Church-in-the-Bowery, it has long been a cohesive, unifying element in the downtown New York literary scene and has always been identified with a broad range of new and interesting writing. Remarkably, *The World* is still publishing in 1998. Angel Hair was born at Robert Duncan's reading at the Berkeley Poetry Conference, where Anne Waldman and Lewis Warsh first met. They edited six issues of the magazine and a series of books. Larry Fagin moved to New York from San Francisco where he was associated with the Spicer circle. His eclectic Adventures in Poetry published both the magazine and a series of books.

It is interesting to note that, at least for a short while, trade publishers in New York and elsewhere did take considerable interest in the new writing. A great many anthologies of new and experimental poetry were published, including *The World*, *Another World*, *An Anthology of New York Poets*, and *Naked Poetry*, to name a few. Also, a significant number of books by individual writers –

including Anne Waldman, Tom Clark, Carol Bergé, Joel Oppenheimer, Clark Coolidge, Lewis MacAdams, Michael Brownstein, Ron Padgett, and Dick Gallup – were published in the late 60s and early 70s by the likes of Bobbs-Merrill and Harper & Row.

The third generation of New York School writers emerged at roughly the same time that the poets associated with language writing began to be identified as a group. The magazine *United Artists* served to a great extent as a bridge between the generations, publishing many of the newcomers to the scene alongside the more established members of the St. Mark's school. *United Artists* was also in many ways the apotheosis of the mimeograph magazine, spectacular in its simple design (the first twelve covers were simply tables of content) and adventuresome in its combination of the personal and the experimental, pioneering in the publication of journal and diary entries. The third generation was largely based at The Poetry Project, and much influenced by teachers there such as Ted Berrigan, Alice Notley, Lewis Warsh, and Bernadette Mayer. In the mid- to late 70s and early 80s, East Village magazines and presses such as *Mag City*, Frontward Books, *4, 3, 2 Review*, *KOFF*, *Tangerine*, *Ghandhabba*, *Ladies Museum*, and *Dodgems* published writings by Greg Masters, Ed Friedman, Eileen Myles, Susie Timmons, Tom Weigel, Michael Scholnick, Maggie Dubris, Jeff Wright, Simon Schuchat, Elinor Nauen, and Gary Lenhart, among others who identified with and extended the heritage of the New York Schools. A similar scene developed in the Los Angeles area with the Beyond Baroque reading series in Venice, and many of its trends can be seen in the magazine *Little Caesar*, which further blurred the lines between literature, music, and the visual arts.

A Little History of the Mimeograph Revolution

Language Writing

1970 *Tottel's*, edited by Ron Silliman

1971 *This*, edited by Barrett Watten and Robert Grenier

1972 *Vort*, edited by Barry Alpert

1972 *L*, edited by Curtis Faville

1973 The "Wiater/Andrews issue" of *Toothpick, Lisbon & the Orcas Islands*

1973 *Hills*, edited by Bob Perelman

1973 *Poetics of the New American Poetry*, edited by Donald Allen and Warren Tallman, published by Grove Press

1973 *Shirt*, edited by Ray DiPalma

1974 Susan Howe's *Hinge Picture* published by Telephone Books

1975 David Melnick's *PCOET* published in part by *Tottel's* and also as a chapbook by G.A.W.K.

1975 "The Dwelling Place: 9 Poets," edited by Ron Silliman, published in *Alcheringa*

1975 Geoffrey Young and Laura Chester's The Figures begins

1976 Lyn Hejinian's Tuumba begins

1976 *A Hundred Posters*, edited by Alan Davies

1976 *Roof*, edited by James Sherry and Tom Savage

1977 "Politics of the Referent," edited by Steve McCaffery, a symposium in *Open Letter*

1977 Bob Perelman's Talk Series begins in San Francisco

1978 *L=A=N=G=U=A=G=E*, edited by Charles Bernstein and Bruce Andrews

1978 Ear Inn Reading Series founded by Ted Greenwald and Charles Bernstein

1978 Hannah Weiner's *Clairvoyant Journal* published by Angel Hair

1978 "A Symposium on Clark Coolidge," edited by Ron Silliman; published as *Stations* 5

1978 Ron Silliman's *Ketjak* published by This Press

1978 Charles Bernstein's *Shade* is published, the first Sun & Moon Press book

1978 *E pod*, edited by Kirby Malone and Marshall Reese

1979 "Talks" issue (no. 6/7) of *Hills*, edited by Bob Perelman

1979 *QU*, edited by Carla Harryman

1980 Lyn Hejinian's *My Life* published by Burning Deck

1980 Charles Bernstein, Steve McCaffery, Bruce Andrews, and Ray DiPalma's *Legend* published by L=A=N=G=U=A=G=E/Segue

1980 *The Difficulties*, edited by Tom Beckett

1982 *Poetics Journal*, edited by Lyn Hejinian and Barrett Watten

1983 *HOW(ever)*, edited by Kathleen Fraser, Rachel Blau DuPlessis, Frances Jaffer, and others

Clairvoyant Journal

Hannah Weiner

Hannah Weiner,
Clairvoyant Journal 1974
(New York: Angel Hair,
1978). Cover photo-
graph of the author by
Tom Ahern.

In 1982, two literary journals as disparate as *Ironwood* and *The Paris Review* both featured collections of language writing. Ron Silliman, in his introduction to the collection in *Ironwood*, traces a kind of "anti-history" back to the early 70s with the publication of two important journals, *Tottel's* and *This*. Silliman makes the important point that the phenomenon is based on a created audience and that language writing is most significantly identified as community based, with almost all its practitioners sharing "the responsibility of creating the institutions through which the work can be made public." He goes on to say that "the project of this writing is the discovery of a community."[10] In his introduction to the selection of language writing published in *The Paris Review*, Charles Bernstein offers the useful hint that this is a "writing that takes as its medium, or domain of intention, every articulable aspect of language."

Although language writing surely flourished in the 1980s, a fact amply demonstrated by several anthologies (such as *In the American Tree: Language Realism Poetry*, edited by Ron Silliman, and *"Language" Poetries: An Anthology*, edited by Douglas Messerli) and critical works (*Code of Signals*, a special issue of *Io* edited by Michael Palmer; Barrett Watten's *Total Syntax*; Charles Bernstein's *Content's Dream*; Bernstein and Bruce Andrews's *The L=A=N=G=U=A=G=E Book*; and Ron Silliman's *The New Sentence*), it was, from its beginnings in the early 70s, an influential and always controversial presence in the poetry community at large. At first, the lines between the soon-to-be-identified language poets and various other vaguely defined schools or groups were not so clearly drawn.

10. Ron Silliman, ed., "Language Writing," *Ironwood* 20 [vol. 10, no. 2] (Fall 1982): 64.

For instance, Barrett Watten's first book, *Opera-Works*, was published by Bill Berkson's New York School–identified Big Sky, and *Roof* magazine, an important New York–based outlet for language writing, was born at Naropa Institute in 1976. Its early issues included both Beat and New York School poets. The second small anthology of language writing appeared in the ethnopoetics journal *Alcheringa* in 1975 – but by the end of the 70s, those associated with language writing had thoroughly established their presence and made visible their various unique and shared tendencies through an incredible network of magazines, presses, and reading and talk series located primarily in San Francisco and New York, with a smaller group active in Washington, D.C. Magazines and presses such as *L=A=N=G=U=A=G=E*, *This*, *A Hundred Posters*, *E pod*, *Hills*, *Vanishing Cab*, *Miam*, *Roof*, *Sun & Moon*, The Figures, *Asylum's*, Tuumba, *The Difficulties*, *Poetics Journal*, and others served as venues for writing (poetry as well as critical prose) by Ron Silliman, Charles Bernstein, Lyn Hejinian, Bruce Andrews, Barrett Watten, Robert Grenier, Steve Benson, Rae Armantrout, Bob Perelman, Nick Piombino, Diane Ward, Carla Harryman, Alan Davies, and Johanna Drucker, among many others.

BELOW AND OPPOSITE:
Big Table 1 (Spring 1959),
front and back covers.

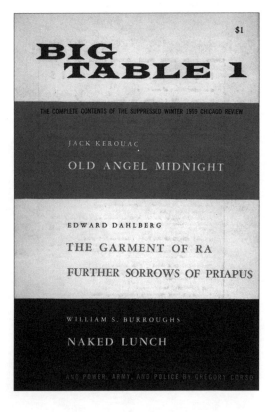

$1

BIG
TABLE 1

THE COMPLETE CONTENTS OF THE SUPPRESSED WINTER 1959 CHICAGO REVIEW

JACK KEROUAC

OLD ANGEL MIDNIGHT

EDWARD DAHLBERG

THE GARMENT OF RA

FURTHER SORROWS OF PRIAPUS

WILLIAM S. BURROUGHS

NAKED LUNCH

AND POWER, ARMY, AND POLICE BY GREGORY CORSO

Other Places (Chicago, Michigan, Ohio, Rhode Island, Iowa, and Beyond)

Chicago

The literary climate in the Midwest began to heat up in 1958 when *The Chicago Review*, as its Spring number, presented an issue devoted to the San Francisco Renaissance. This included a chapter from the then-unpublished *Naked Lunch* by the notorious William S. Burroughs, as well as work by Duncan, Ginsberg, Ferlinghetti, McClure, and others. Editors Irving Rosenthal and Paul Carroll gathered and published more such "Beat" material in the Autumn 1958 issue. As they prepared the Winter issue, the *Chicago Daily News* published an article entitled "Filthy Writing on the Midway"; as a consequence, that issue was suppressed by a cowardly administration, galvanizing and energizing the literary underground.

Carroll and Rosenthal, along with a half dozen other editors, resigned from *The Chicago Review*. With the suppressed material they founded *Big Table* (so named by Jack Kerouac in a telegram: "CALL IT BIG TABLE"). The first issue, which featured Kerouac, Dahlberg, and Burroughs, was impounded by the U.S. Post Office. The ACLU challenged the Post Office in a hearing presided over by Judge Julius S. Hoffman, who later presided over the Chicago Seven conspiracy trial. Judge Hoffman followed Judge Woolsey's decision regarding Joyce's *Ulysses*, and *Big Table* continued publishing through five issues. The aura, even the glamour, of censorship helped to increase its distribution, and its audience consequently grew significantly. Like *Evergreen Review*, *Big Table* was crucial in bringing the underground to those of us waiting in the wings in small-town America.

(Three editors of the geographically distant *Northwest Review* at the University of Oregon, in Eugene, were to face this same issue later, when their publication was suspended by the university after the publication of eight poems by Philip Whalen and work by Antonin Artaud in its Fall 1963 issue. Also included were an interview with Fidel Castro and a portfolio of photographs of contemporary Cuba. Like their fellows in Chicago, the group, led by editor Edward Van Aelstyne, started their own periodical, entitled *Coyote's Journal*, which in its first three issues used material gathered for the *Northwest Review*.) Other important

Chicago periodicals and presses of the 1960s and 70s included Alice Notley's *Chicago*, Art Lange's *Brilliant Corners* (which, in addition to poetry, printed writings on improvisational jazz), the Surrealist/anarchist/leftist-oriented Black Swan (still in operation), Yellow Press, and *Milk Quarterly*, principally edited by Darlene Pearlstein with Bob Rosenthal, Peter Kostakis, and Richard Friedman. Interestingly, some of the poets in Chicago were taught how to use the mimeograph machine in the 1960s and 70s by Ted Berrigan on one of his visits to Chicago or during teaching stints at Northwestern.

Brilliant Corners 4 (Fall 1976). Cover photograph of Thelonious Monk by Jim Marshall.

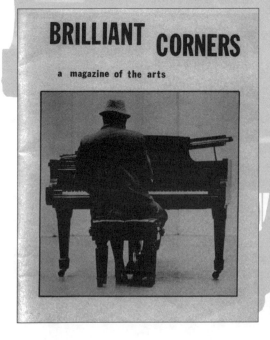

Michigan, Ohio, and Rhode Island

Other activities in the Midwest included the Artists' Workshop Press in Detroit, which published (often in broadside format) work by such poets as George Tysh, John Sinclair, and John Wieners. The use of colored "construction" papers (of the sort favored by grade school teachers) was a particularly distinctive characteristic of this press, which also cultivated a sort of hard-core working-class aesthetic. Dudley Randall's Broadside Press of Detroit was very important for the Black Arts Movement during the late 60s and 70s and published a great many writers including Gwendolyn Brooks, Sonia Sanchez, and Sterling Brown. Ken and Anne Mikolowski's The Alternative Press, also of Michigan, has published an avalanche of interesting work over the past thirty years, most of which has taken the form of broadsides, postcards, bookmarks, bumper-stickers, and other ephemera. In 1971, they began to issue annual packets of printed matter by subscription, the announcement for which carried the slogan "Art Poetry Melodrama." Artists and writers published include Faye Kicknosway, John Sinclair, Ted Berrigan, Allen Ginsberg, Robert Creeley, Jerome Rothenberg, Lewis Warsh, Tom Clark, George Tysh, William Wantling, Joel Oppenheimer, Robert Bly, Philip Guston, and others. Burning Deck Press (as in "the boy stood on the") began as a literary magazine in Ann Arbor in 1961. Three issues were published in Michigan before editors Keith and Rosmarie Waldrop moved to Durham, Connecticut, where the fourth issue came out. Material for a fifth issue was gathered but never published. In 1968, the editors moved to Providence,

Lyn Hejinian, *My Life*
(Providence, R.I.:
Burning Deck, 1980).
Cover collage by Keith
Waldrop.

Rhode Island, the city where Clark Coolidge had earlier co-published his influential magazine *Joglars*. Burning Deck has published over 200 books and broadsides, primarily by younger writers, and is generally recognized as one of the most important and interesting literary presses publishing in English. Its books are often designed and printed by the editors by letterpress. It is interesting to note that letterpress, previously the mark of more upscale publishing with a distinctly mainstream flavor, was then in the process of undergoing its own revolution. As photo-offset became the standard in commercial printing, the letterpress machines became available for next to nothing. Poets like the Waldrops picked them up cheaply and produced works very much in the spirit of those working with mimeo, thus transforming letterpress aesthetics into the service of the revolution. The Waldrops are both accomplished writers and translators with wide-ranging tastes. Over the years they have published works from John Heath-Stubbs, Bruce Andrews, X. J. Kennedy, Rochelle Owens, Mark Strand, Ron Silliman, Edwin Honig, Lisa Jarnot, Marcia Southwick, William Bronk, Lyn Hejinian, and Barbara Guest, among others.

465: An Anthology of Cleveland Poetry published the work of T. L. Kryss, Russell Atkins, Grace Butchert, d.a.levy, and others. d.a.levy was an important catalyst in Cleveland on several fronts. His aptly named Renegade Press (later 7 Flowers Press) produced some fifty volumes of levy's work, much of which takes the form of amazingly beautiful and prescient concrete poetry (see, for example, *Fortuitons Motherfucer*, *Zen Concrete*, and *The Tibetan Stroboscope*). levy also edited several anthologies, serials, and magazines including *The Buddhist 3rd Class Junkmail Oracle* and the *Marrahwannah Newsletter*. As Ed Sanders later said of Ted Berrigan and Paul Blackburn,

d.a.levy,
The Tibetan Stroboscope
(Cleveland: Ayizan
Press, 1968).

levy "lived it 24 hours a day" and he paid a heavy price. levy was arrested and jailed along with Jim Lowell (proprietor of the great Asphodel Bookshop, a welcoming home for new poetry for over thirty years) on charges of distributing obscene material. One of the truly unique and authentic spirits of the mimeo revolution, levy became famous as the poetry world gathered in his support, but in 1968, at the age of twenty-six, he committed suicide.

Ray DiPalma began publishing, among others, writers associated with scenes in Iowa City and around The Poetry Project in New York in his magazine *Doones* in 1969 out of Bowling Green, Ohio. A considerable range of poets such as Ted Berrigan, Merrill Gilfillan, Ted Greenwald, Darrell Gray, Anselm Hollo, Robert Kelly, James Tate, Bill Knott, Ron Silliman, and Larry Fagin published in *Doones* as well as in DiPalma's series of booklets and one-shot "supplements" such as *Painted Horses* and *Shelter*. DiPalma moved to New York in the mid-70s. He has been associated with language writing since the beginning and has published many impressive volumes of his own work under such imprints as Sun & Moon, Segue, and Burning Deck.

Iowa

Whether because or in spite of the University of Iowa Writers' Workshop, a vibrant literary scene developed in Iowa City during the late 60s and early 70s. Ted Berrigan and Anselm Hollo were both in residence as teachers at the famous workshop for a spell, but probably wielded greater influence in the bars and cafes off campus. More than thirty small presses and magazines sprouted up during the period. Among the most interesting were

A Little History of the Mimeograph Revolution

Poetry Comics 1 (1979), edited and drawn by Dave Morice.

This, *Toothpaste* (later *Dental Floss*), *Gum, Hills, Matchbook, Search for Tomorrow,* Blue Wind, *Poetry Comics,* and *The Spirit That Moves Us.* A genuine "movement" evolved, and Darrell Gray's articulate and rousing manifesto of "Actualism" appeared in *Gum* 9 (January 1973). It begins, "Actuality is never frustrated because it is complete." And ends, "Why belabor the impossible?" *The Actualist Anthology* appeared in 1977. *Toothpaste* was edited by poet and printer Allan Kornblum, who is now the director of its direct descendant, The Coffee House Press. Dave Morice (a.k.a. Dr. Alphabet, a.k.a. Joyce Holland) has been an important poet and teacher in Iowa City since the mid-6os. His magazines and books continue to stretch the limits of language (and publishing) in subtle ways. *Matchbook,* for instance, was a magazine of one-word poetry, and each copy was stapled to the inside of a found matchbook. "Joyce Holland" edited *The Alphabet Anthology* in

1973. Contributors to this anthology of one-letter poetry include Bruce Andrews ("O"), Larry Eigner ("e"), and Bernadette Mayer ("n"). Dave Morice began publishing his *Poetry Comics* in 1979, and Simon & Schuster later published (and then remaindered) a collection of this excellent work.

Beyond

Interesting magazines and presses flourished throughout the country as a network of literary publications kept far-flung poets and writers in contact with one another. Fine work could be found in *Margins* (which published reviews and writings on poetics), *Grist* (established in Kansas in 1964 by John Fowler, *Grist* is now publishing online at http://www.thing.net/~grist/), *Quixote, The Wormwood Review, Io, Truck, Suck-Egg Mule, Duende, Wild Dog, The Fifties, The Sixties,* and *The Outsider. The Outsider* represents an extreme act of publishing and deserves special mention. Edited and published in New Orleans by Jon Edgar and Louise "Gypsy Lou" Webb, *The Outsider* was lavishly (one imagines even maniacally) produced by letterpress with a wide range of interesting and unusual materials. Yet in spite of its formal sophistication, it still manifests the indomitable spirit of the mimeo revolution by virtue of its devotion to such writers as Charles Bukowski and Kenneth Patchen, both of whom were recipients of the "Outsider of the Year" award. Other contributors to this "book periodical" were Robert Creeley, Douglas Woolf, Gary Snyder, Larry Eigner, William S. Burroughs, Michael McClure, and Barbara Moraff.

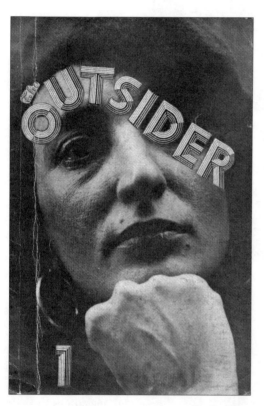

The Outsider 1 (1960).

A Little History of the Mimeograph Revolution

bill bissett, *th fifth sun*
(Vancouver: blewoint-
mentpress, 1975). Cover
design by the author.

bill bissett, *th fifth sun*
(Vancouver: blewoint-
mentpress, 1975). Cover
design by the author.

Canada, England, Scotland, Europe, and Australia

Of course, kindred acts of experimental writing and publishing were committed around
the world. For a time, in the 60s and 70s,
Toronto might well have boasted the largest
number of avant-garde poets per capita of any
city on the face of the earth. The great Coach
House Press has been a vortex for innovative
writing and publishing since its inception in
1966. Among the many Coach House titles
are Michael Ondaatje's *The Dainty Monsters,
Journeying and the Return* by bp Nichol, *Excellent Articles of Japan* by David Rosenberg, *The
Great Canadian Sonnet* by David McFadden
and Greg Curnoe, *Neil Young* by Tom Clark,
Ow's Waif by Steve McCaffery, *Bill Jubobe* by
Bob Cobbing, and Nicole Brossard's *A Book*,
to mention only a few of the works published
during its first decade. Throughout Canada,
writers, editors, performers, publishers –
instigators-at-large – worked through such
presses and magazines as *Contact, blewointment*,
Coach House Press, the *Ant's Forefoot, Tish*,
Periwinkle Press, Intermedia, Talonbooks,
Very Stone House, Ganglia Press, Oberon,
grOnk, Open Letter, and *Weed*. A great deal of
memorable work, particularly in the realms
of concrete and sound poetry, emanated
from Canada (especially Toronto and Vancouver) during the period. bp Nichol's

presence and example were an inspiration for
many, and his untimely death in 1988 was a
great tragedy.

A quick sketch of presses and magazines
operating in other parts of the world would
have to include, in England, *My Own Mag*,
Aloes, *Stereo Headphones*, Fulcrum Press,
Coracle Press, *Aggie Weston's*, Writers' For-
um, Beau Geste Press, Gaberbocchus, and
Cape Goliard/Grossman; in Scotland, *Poor.
Old. Tired. Horse.* (and the work of its editor,
Ian Hamilton Finlay, in general); in the
Netherlands, *Kontexts*; in Germany, Edition
Hansjörg Mayer; in France, *Merlin* and *OU*;
and in Australia, *The Ear in a Wheatfield*.

Women's and Feminist Writing

Great strides were made in the development of women's and feminist writing during the late 60s and through the 70s. Ron Silliman observed in 1982 that "the single most significant change in American poetry over the past two decades is to be seen in the central role of writing within feminist culture, which in 1982 is (for good reason) the largest of all possible verse audiences."[11] Important developments among women and feminist poets run parallel to the New American Poetry but rarely intersect during the 1960–1980 period, except perhaps as they relate to the creation of independent poet-operated women's presses. The establishment, for example, of Judy Grahn's The Women's Press Collective in Oakland in 1969 and Alta's Shameless Hussy Press in Berkeley were crucial in providing a venue for women's literary voices to speak out. These writers (with significant exceptions) felt self-consciously apart from the more experimental side of poetry and determined that their concerns might perhaps be more directly served through populist modes of expression. The example of work by such writers as Adrienne Rich, Judy Grahn, Pat Parker, Ntozake

Shange, and Susan Griffin, among many others, was important in defining and foregrounding issues particular to women and feminists that would be further explored over the next two decades. It is no coincidence that the magazine *HOW(ever)*, edited by Kathleen Fraser and first published in May 1983, opens with the questioning "And what about the women who were writing experimentally? Oh, were there women poets writing experimentally? Yes there were, they were." Fraser, working with contributing editors Frances Jaffer, Beverly Dahlen, Rachel Blau DuPlessis, and Carolyn Burke (and later with Susan Gevirtz, Chris Tysh, Myung Mi Kim, Meredith Stricker, Diane Glancy, and Adalaide Morris), published sixteen issues (in six volumes) between 1983 and 1992. Unlike many other feminist magazines, *HOW(ever)* was framed in a literary context and traced its history to include Emily Dickinson, Gertrude Stein, Virginia Woolf, and Dorothy Richardson. Thus, *HOW(ever)* set out to be, as Jaffer expressed it in the first issue, "A vehicle for experimentalist poetry – post-modern if you will, to be thought of seriously as an appropriate poetry for women and feminists." Contributors and topics include Norma Cole, Karen Riley, Kathy Acker on humility, Lyn Hejinian, Caroline Burke on Mina Loy, Johanna Drucker on canon formation, a group of writings on Barbara Guest, Laura Moriarty, Joan Retallack, Gail Scott, and the various editors, among many others.

---

11. Ron Silliman, ed., "Language Writing," *Ironwood* 20 [vol. 10, no. 2] (Fall 1982): 68.

HOW(ever), vol. 2, no. 3 (1985).

African American Writing

African American literary magazines of the years 1960–1980 were rarely devoted exclusively to literary concerns – more often they presented a mix of cultural expression and political commentary in an ongoing effort to battle the racism, oppression, and violence that characterized the era. The history of the African American little magazine runs rich and deep, and a beginning look would include such publications as *Freelance, Confrontation, Callaloo, Soulbook, Umbra,* the *Journal of Black Poetry,* and *Hambone,* among many others. As with feminist writing, third-world writing, and writing by people of color in general, the trajectory of African American poetry charts a somewhat different course than that of the New American Poetry and nearly always speaks to its own audience of its own issues and on its own terms. One fascinating and eclectic example is *Yardbird Reader.* Edited by Ishmael Reed, Al Young, Shawn Wong, Frank Chin, and William Lawson, it ran for five volumes, from 1972 to 1976. A vast range of writing from many cultures was presented, including African Americans, Asian Americans, Colombians, Puerto Ricans, Filipino-Americans, Franco-Americans, Anglo-Americans, North Africans, Kenyans, and Caribbeans. *Y'Bird,* edited by Ishmael Reed, continued the work after the demise of *Yardbird Reader.* In 1978, Grove Press

Yardbird Reader, volume 1, edited by Al Young and Ishmael Reed (Berkeley: Yardbird Publishing, 1972).

published a collection of work from *Yardbird Reader* entitled *Yardbird Lives!* Dudley Randall's Broadside Press in Detroit was a prominent venue for the Black Arts Movement, and during the late 60s and throughout the 70s published such writers as June Jordan, Lucille Clifton, Raymond Patterson, Etheridge Knight, Audre Lorde, Dudley Randall, Alice Walker, and Sonia Sanchez, among many others. LeRoi Jones and Larry Neal edited the provocative *Black Fire: Anthology of Afro-American Writing,* published in 1968.

Conclusion

In 1982, Grove Press published *The Postmoderns: The New American Poetry Revised*. Edited by Donald Allen and George Butterick, this anthology confirms the prophecy of its predecessor. In the opening sentence of its introduction, it boldly proclaims its intention "not to deal comprehensively with the full range of recent American poetry but with that poetry written in America since the Second World War which, by its vitality alone, became the dominant force in the American poetic tradition." It is this vitality which is the unifying element in all the various intertwined and tangled schools and movements described above. In the heyday of the mimeo revolution it was called "the indomitable spirit," and it is our hope that this collection will serve as a vivid reminder for those who were there, and as a source of inspiration for poets and publishers now and of the future. As William Carlos Williams reminds us,

```
                It is difficult
    to get the news from poems
            yet men die miserably every day
                    for lack
    of what is found there.
```

...erground, 1950–1980

1971

Another World
This
A Caterpillar Anthology
Death of Paul Blackburn (age 44)
Stanzas for Iris Lezak
Big Sky
On the Mesa
Unmuzzled Ox
Memorial Day
The Harris Review
Moving
Apparent death of Lew Welch (age 44)
Mulch

1973

Hills
America: A Prophecy
The Ear in a Wheatfield
Mohawk
Open Poetry
Z
Life Notes
Living Hand
Ring of Bone
Poetics of the New American Poetry
The "Wiater/Andrews" issue of *Toothpick, Lisbon & the Orcas Islands*

1975

THE FIGURES
Oculist Witnesses
The Collected Books of Jack Spicer
Montemora
Essaying Essays
Adult Life of Toulouse Lautrec
Wch Way
Fast Speaking Woman
Dental Floss
All This Everyday
Brilliant Corners
Slinger

1977

Mag City
Talk series
Un Poco Loco
New Wilderness Letter
United Artists
Abracadabra
The Olson Festival
The Ladies Museum
Co-Accident (performance group)
The Actualist Anthology
Miam

1979

Rocky Ledge
Poetry Comics

1981

Sulfur

1972

Sixpack
Parts of a Body House Book
Unnatural Acts
A Little Anthology of Surrealist Poems
Contact (Philadelphia)
Shaking the Pumpkin
The Poetry Project Newsletter
Seventh Heaven
Chicago
The Crystal Lythium
Vort
The Martyrology Books I & II
Clown War
Part of My History

1974

Rhymes of a Jerk
Blues of the Sky (first and only mimeo book ever reviewed in the *New York Times*)
Revolution of the Word
Spanner
Hinge Picture
Poets of the Cities
Jack Kerouac School of Disembodied Poetics
I Dreamt I Became a Nymphomaniac: Imagining

1976

4,3,2 Review
None of the Above
Sun & Moon
Là-Bas
Death of Wallace Berman (age 50)
Bombay Gin
TUUMBA
bill joubobe
Little Caesar
Roof
The Countess from Minneapolis
Doc(k)s
A Hundred Posters

1978

Ketjak
L=A=N=G=U=A=G=E
Shade (Sun & Moon's first book)
"A"
White Walls
Gesualdo
Talking Poetics from Naropa Institute
"A Symposium on Clark Coolidge" issued as *Stations 5*
A Big Jewish Book
The Basketball Diaries
Death of Louis Zukofsky (age 74)
The Day Our Turtle Was Kidnaped
Train Ride
Ear Inn series
Loba I–VII

1980

Legend
The Liberties
The Difficulties
My Life
Dr. Williams' Heiresses
So Going Around Cities
Olson/Creeley Correspondence Vol. 1

1982

The Postmoderns: The New American Poetry Revised

The checklists that follow are only occasionally "complete" – they are intended as an indication of some of the relevant titles issued by the various publishers and should therefore be seen as guidelines for further research. In the bibliographic entries, complete information (when available) is given for periodicals; citations for books and broadsides give year of publication only. The presence of an item in a division of The New York Public Library's research collections (as of March 1998) is indicated by one or more of the following abbreviations:

AT THE CENTER FOR THE HUMANITIES:

APP	Miriam and Ira D. Wallach Division of Art, Prints and Photographs
BRG	Henry W. and Albert A. Berg Collection of English and American Literature
GRD	General Research Division
JWS	Jewish Division
MSS	Manuscripts and Archives Division
RBK	Rare Books Division

AT THE NEW YORK PUBLIC LIBRARY FOR THE PERFORMING ARTS:

DAN	Dance Collection

SC	Schomburg Center for Research in Black Culture

The Presses

In organizing the material in this section, we have attempted to proceed along a line that moves somewhat chronologically, somewhat geographically, and somewhat intuitively, grouping the presses and magazines in clusters or communities and moving from one to the next in a progression that, although not precisely linear, contains within it some sense of inevitability. The basic categories of "San Francisco Renaissance," "Beat," "Black Mountain," etc., provide a useful but by no means tidy model. From the outset, we wanted to focus attention on the publishers

and Publications

and the publications, but in attempting to do so discovered that they exist in a snarled labyrinth of associations and allegiances most vividly revealed in hindsight. Hence the "secret location on the Lower East Side" of the title (with thanks to Ed Sanders) is presented as both a real and imagined place – the everywhere present (and necessary) margin or "underground" of writing and publishing. We have consciously weighted the book (and the exhibition it documents) toward the New York School, in particular the second generation, in part as a reflection of our residence in that great city but more importantly to pay special respect to The Poetry Project at St. Mark's Church-in-the-Bowery.

In addition to Steven Clay and Rodney Phillips, the following poets, artists, editors, and publishers generously contributed their memories and reflections to this section of the book – in order of appearance: Eloyde Tovey (p. 71), Aaron Fischer (p. 95), Gerrit Lansing (p. 135), Jackson Mac Low (pp. 140–142), Ed Sanders (p. 167), Anne Waldman (pp. 177, 180, 187–188), Lewis Warsh (pp. 179, 199), Bill Berkson (p. 183), Ed Friedman (pp. 184–185, 189), Larry Fagin (pp. 195–196, 201), Carol Bergé (p. 205), Aram Saroyan (p. 211), Bob Rosenthal (p. 219), Johnny Stanton (p. 221), Eileen Myles (p. 223), Annabel Lee (p. 225), Maureen Owen (p. 227), Steve Levine (p. 230), Greg Masters (p. 233), Charles Bernstein (p. 235), Bruce Andrews (p. 235), Clark Coolidge (p. 237), James Sherry (p. 251), and Lyn Hejinian (p. 257).

J

Jack Spicer; art editor Fran Herndon

San Francisco
1959–1961

Jack Spicer listening to a
baseball game on the radio
at the beach at Plum Island,
Newbury, Massachusetts,
ca. 1958. Photograph by
Kent Bowker.

"His parents were professional bridge players from Southern California."

— Josephine Miles on Jack Spicer, from an unpublished
manuscript in the collections of the Bancroft Library,
University of California, Berkeley

In many ways the most beautiful of all the
mimeo magazines, *J* had an eight-issue
run. The first five issues were edited from
North Beach bars by Jack Spicer with Fran
Herndon as art editor. Spicer, who embodied
the spirit of poetry in the Bay area, collected
pieces for his magazine from a box marked "J"
in The Place, a bar at 1546 Grant Avenue in
San Francisco. A refugee from Los Angeles
with two degrees from Berkeley, he had been
a student of Josephine Miles there in the mid-
1940s. They became close friends, and Spicer
participated in the Friday afternoon poetry
readings in Wheeler Hall during the late 1940s
as well as the readings organized with Rocke-
feller money by Ruth Witt-Diamant at the new
Poetry Center at San Francisco State. Into the
cauldron of poetic politics surrounding Miles,
Kenneth Rexroth, Robert Duncan, Lawrence
Ferlinghetti, and others, Spicer introduced his
freest of spirits, sometimes more Caliban than
Ariel. Spicer lived for words (even making his
living as a research assistant on a lexicographi-
cal project at Berkeley). He could be found
most evenings in one of the North Beach bars
or coffeehouses leading the discussion on
poetry, poetics, myth, linguistics, and other
mysteries. Like Blake and Yeats (with the help
of Mrs. Yeats), Spicer attempted to clear his
mind and open himself to "dictation" from
other sources, which he devotedly pursued.
Spicer also believed wholeheartedly in the
necessity of human beings' helping each other
through communication, which he confronted
in the editorship of *J*, a little newsletter of the
poetic spirit. Donald Allen acted as *J*'s distributor in New York ("New York Contributions
are not forbidden. But quotaed"), selling
copies for Spicer to the Wilentz brothers of
the Eighth Street Book Shop. In an early letter
to Spicer, Allen eagerly wondered "what your
editorial policy may be. Seduction by print."

*J*5 (1959). Cover by Fran Herndon.

J. Nos. 1–8 (1959–1961).
Nos. 6 and 7 (*An Apparition
of the Late J*) edited (and
with cover art) by George
Stanley from San Francisco
and New York City respec-
tively. No. 8 (1961) edited
by Harold Dull from Rome.
Covers by Russell FitzGerald
(3), Fran Herndon (1, 2,
4, 5), George Stanley (6, 7).

BRG has: nos. 1–3, 5, 6.

Open Space

Stan Persky

*San Francisco
1964*

THIS IS NOT THE COVER OF OPEN SPACE #1
IT'S A MASK YOU CAN WEAR IN CASE
YOU'RE SUDDENLY CALLED TO A MASKED BALL.

Open Space 1 (January
1964). Cover drawing
of George Stanley by
Bill Brodecky.

Open Space was published during 1964 for fifteen issues (number 0 or the "Prospectus" was published in the same month as the first issue, and two separate number 2's and 4's were published). The unofficial organ of the group of poets centered around Jack Spicer at Gino and Carlo's Bar on Green Street and The Place on Grant Avenue, both in San Francisco's bohemian North Beach, it was the production of Stan Persky, recently relocated from Los Angeles, who printed only fifty copies of each issue on a "multilith machine." It was really intended for those whose poems appeared in its pages, such as Helen Adam, Robin Blaser, Ebbe Borregaard, Richard Duerden, Harold Dull, Larry Fagin (who later produced his own *Adventures in Poetry* in New York), Jess Collins, Jack Spicer, and George Stanley, all locals from North Beach or Berkeley. The covers of *Open Space* featured imaginative and unusual artwork by Jess Collins, Graham Mackintosh, Fran Herndon, and others. The magazine was quite spicy and a little gossipy, for instance, labeling the famed 1955 reading at the Six Gallery as "creamed cottage cheese." Persky, somewhat standoffish from the others in the scene, lampooned any number of them, including Donald Allen and Madeline Gleason (she of the pre-punk red hair and attachment to the Virgin Mary who had in the 1940s begun poetry readings everywhere in San Francisco, while composing poetry as she messengered securities throughout the financial district). Gleason, along with Helen Adam and James Broughton, formed one of the poetic coteries of San Francisco in the 1950s and 60s, often at odds with the others, such as those centered around Spicer in North Beach or Robert Duncan

in Berkeley, and all of whom were fairly irritated by Kenneth Rexroth and his "Beat Renaissance." One editorial salvo irrupting from Persky began: "*Open Space* isn't Group-Soup, bar set or queer coterie." Nevertheless, *Open Space* was still a curious mixture of humor and high literary seriousness, publishing correspondence between Spicer and Lawrence Ferlinghetti on publishing ethics or Charles Olson's "Against Wisdom as Such," alongside a hoax or an appropriation or a baseball issue.

Open Space. Nos. 0–12 (January 1964–December 1964); no. 1, January 1964, preceded by an undated issue called no. 0; no. 2, February 1964, preceded by an issue called *Open Space Valentine*; no. 4, April 1964, followed by an issue called *Open Space Taurus* issue 4.

BRG has: complete file.

Open Space books include:

Alexander, James. *Eturnature.* 1965. (BRG)

Alexander, James. *The Jack Rabbit Poem.* Drawings by Paul Alexander. 1966. Published with White Rabbit Press. (BRG)

Blaser, Robin. *The Moth Poem.* 1964. (BRG)

Duerden, Richard. *The Fork.* 1965. (GRD)

Duncan, Robert. *The Sweetness and Greatness of Dante's Divine Comedy.* Cover drawing by the author. 1965. (BRG)

Miles, Josephine. *Saving the Bay.* 1967. (BRG)

Nerval, Gérard de. *Les Chimères.* Translated by Robin Blaser. 1965. (BRG)

White Rabbit Press

Joe Dunn and Graham Mackintosh

San Francisco and Oakland, California
1957–1972

Robert Duncan, *The Cat and the Blackbird* (1967).
Cover by Jess (Collins).

White Rabbit Press books include:

Adam, Helen. *The Queen o' Crow Castle*. Drawings by Jess (Collins). 1958. (GRD)

Alexander, James. *The Jack Rabbit Poem*. Drawings by Paul Alexander. 1966. Published with Open Space. (BRG)

Borregaard, Ebbe. *The Wapitis*. Cover drawing by Robert Duncan. 1958. (GRD)

Brautigan, Richard. *The Galilee Hitch-hiker*. Illustrated by Kenn Davis. 1958. (BRG)

Brautigan, Richard. *Please Plant This Book*. 1968. Printed by Graham Mackintosh. (BRG)

Dorbin, Sanford. *The Ruby Woods*. Illustrated by Chuck Miller. 1971. (RBK)

Dull, Harold. *Bird Poems*. Illustrated by Nugent. 1958. (GRD)

Duncan, Robert. *As Testimony: The Poem and the Scene*. 1964. (BRG)

Duncan, Robert. *The Cat and the Blackbird*. Cover by Jess (Collins). 1967. (BRG)

The Presses and Publications

The first book of the White Rabbit Press was Boston poet Steve Jonas's *Love, the Poem, the Sea & Other Pieces Examined*, published in 1957 with a cover by San Francisco artist Jess Collins. It was followed closely by poet Jack Spicer's breakthrough book *After Lorca* in the same year ("Things fit together. We knew that – it is the principle of magic."). The press was owned by Joe Dunn, who started it to print the work of the group who surrounded Spicer at The Place in North Beach, a bar owned by Leo Krikorian, an alumnus of Black Mountain College. Dunn, who worked for Greyhound Bus Lines in San Francisco, took a secretarial course at Spicer's insistence and learned to operate a multilith machine. He produced the first ten or eleven titles of the press at work, squeezing out time here and there. Among the books he produced were Denise Levertov's *5 Poems*, with a cover by Jess Collins, Richard Brautigan's *The Galilee Hitch-hiker*, Helen Adam's *The Queen o' Crow Castle*, George Stanley's *The Love Root*, Charles Olson's *O'Ryan 2, 4, 6, 8, 10*, and Ebbe Borregaard's *The Wapitis*, with a cover drawn by Robert Duncan. These pieces were all uniformly lithographed from typescripts or even manuscripts provided by the authors, and each book was sized 8 1/2 by 6 1/2 inches. In many ways they are perfect examples of the printing of poetry. After Joe Dunn's relationship with methamphetamines ended in tragedy, the presswork at White Rabbit was taken over in 1962 by a close friend of Spicer's, Graham Mackintosh, dubbed "the ruffian printer" by the elegant San Francisco pressman Robert Grabhorn. As a graduate student at Berkeley in 1961, Mackintosh had worked closely with Spicer on *The Linguistic Atlas of the Pacific Coast*. His first experience in printing was Spicer's *Lament for the Makers,* for which he also provided the collage cover. Mackintosh, who was Robert Duncan's favorite printer, went on to print books for Oyez and to design and print, along with Saul Marks of the Plantin Press, the first few books of the Black Sparrow Press.

Logo of White Rabbit Press, drawn by Robert Duncan.

Duncan, Robert. *Faust Foutu.* Decorations by the author. 1958. (BRG)

Dunn, Joe. *The Better Dream House.* Cover and illustrations by Jess (Collins). 1968. (GRD)

Garcia, Luis. *The Mechanic.* Cover drawing by Walter Dusenberry. 1970. (BRG)

Liddy, James. *A Munster Song of Love & War.* 1971. (BRG)

Olson, Charles. *O'Ryan 1, 2, 3, 4, 5, 6, 7, 8, 9, 10.* Cover by Jess (Collins). 1965. (GRD)

Olson, Charles. *O'Ryan 2, 4, 6, 8, 10.* Cover by Jess (Collins). 1958. (GRD)

Persky, Stan. *Lives of the French Symbolist Poets.* 1966. (BRG)

Spicer, Jack. *After Lorca.* Introduction by "Federico García Lorca." Cover by Jess (Collins). 1957. (BRG)

Spicer, Jack. *Book of Magazine Verse.* 1966.

Spicer, Jack. *A Book of Music.* Cover illustration by Graham Mackintosh. 1969.

Spicer, Jack. *Collected Poems, 1945–1946.* 1981. Published with Oyez. (BRG)

Spicer, Jack. *The Holy Grail.* 1964.

Spicer, Jack. *Lament for the Makers.* Cover collage by Graham Mackintosh. 1962. (BRG)

Spicer, Jack. *Language.* 1965. (GRD)

Spicer, Jack. *A Redwood Forest Is Not Invisible at Night.* Broadside. 1965.

Wieners, John. *Reading in Bed.* Broadside. 1970. (BRG, RBK)

For further information on White Rabbit Press, the reader is referred to: Alastair M. Johnston, *A Bibliography of the White Rabbit Press* (Berkeley: Poltroon Press, 1985).

From the Introduction by "Federico García Lorca," outside Granada, October 1957:

"It must be made clear at the start that these poems are not translations. In even the most literal of them Mr. Spicer seems to derive pleasure in inserting or substituting one or two words which completely change the mood and often the meaning of the poem as I had written it. More often he takes one of my poems and adjoins to half of it another half of his own, giving rather the effect of an unwilling centaur. (Modesty forbids me to speculate which end of the animal is mine.) Finally there are an almost equal number of poems that I did not write at all (one supposes that they must be his) executed in a somewhat fanciful imitation of my early style. The reader is given no indication which of the poems belong to which category, and I have further complicated the problem (with malice aforethought I must admit) by sending Mr. Spicer several poems written after my death which he has also translated and included here. Even the most faithful student of my work will be hard put to decide what is and what is not Garcia Lorca as, indeed, he would if he were to look into my present resting place. The analogy is impolite, but I fear the impoliteness is deserved."

Jack Spicer, *After Lorca* (1957). Cover by Jess (Collins).

The Pacific
Nation 1
(June 1967).

The Pacific Nation

Robin Blaser

Vancouver, British Columbia, Canada
1967–1969

The Pacific Nation.
Nos. 1–2 (June 1967, 1969).

BRG has: complete file.

The youngest poet of the immediate Spicer circle, Robin Blaser gained his own experience of mimeography as an assistant in 1955 for the *Pound Newsletter* produced by the English Department at the University of California at Berkeley. Blaser was devoted to his friend and mentor Jack Spicer and edited his collected books, appending a long, well-argued essay on Spicer's work. Blaser shares Spicer's concern for the structure of language: "syntax is arrangement, it's all the word means, the way the sentence is arranged. Generally speaking it is subject, verb & object (the way the sentence moves), a sentence is a way of feeling/thinking both (not just thinking which is in your head) but the materialisation of it. Language is the instrument and you are the musician. We all are. It's wonderful to listen to language in the street." After his first two books were published by Open Space, Blaser left Berkeley to teach at Simon Fraser University in Vancouver (or more correctly Burnaby), British Columbia, where he started *The Pacific Nation*. The first issue included poems and an essay (semi-autobiographical and theoretical) by Blaser, one poem by Jack Spicer, a Blaser translation of a letter of Artaud's on Nerval, Michael McClure's "The Moon Is the Number 18," an early John Button drawing, and the first printing of the first five chapters of Richard Brautigan's *Trout Fishing in America*.

The Four Seasons Foundation

Donald Allen

San Francisco and Bolinas, California
1964–1985

Richard Brautigan,
*Trout Fishing in
America* (1967).
Cover photograph
by Erik Weber.

The Four Seasons Foundation was the publishing project of poet and anthologist Donald Allen, who began the concern in 1964 to publish the authors who had been included in his epoch-defining anthology *The New American Poetry* (1960). At first, Allen intended to publish a little magazine to be entitled variously *The Four Seasons Quarterly* or *The New Review*, but the material he had collected for the magazine was instead published in the second and third of the Four Seasons publications, *Prose 1* (there was never another number) and *12 Poets and 1 Painter*, which were published in 1964 as "Writing 2" and "Writing 3." *Prose 1* contained work by Edward Dorn, Michael Rumaker, and Warren Talman as well as various reviews of fiction and belles lettres, including LeRoi Jones's *Blues People*. The poets in *12 Poets and 1 Painter* were Jones, Joanne Kyger, Robert Duncan, Robert Creeley, Denise Levertov, Lawrence Ferlinghetti, Gary Snyder, Lew Welch, Allen Ginsberg, Charles Olson, Max Finstein, and Bruce Boyd. The painter is Jess Collins. "Writing 1," published at the same time, consists appropriately of Charles Olson's *A Bibliography on America for Ed Dorn*. Six other Olson titles were also published by Four Seasons, along with three Creeley titles, four titles by Gary Snyder, two by Philip Whalen, three by Richard Brautigan (*The Pill Versus the Springhill Mine Disaster*, 1968; *In Watermelon Sugar*, 1968; and *Trout Fishing in America*, 1967), two by Michael McClure (*Love Lion Book*, 1966; and *The Sermons of Jean Harlow and the Curses of Billy the Kid*, 1968), and two by Philip Lamantia (*The Blood of the Air*, 1970; and *Touch of the Marvelous*, 1974).

Four Seasons Foundation books include:

Blaser, Robin. *Cups*. 1968. (Writing 17.) (BRG)

Brautigan, Richard. *Trout Fishing in America*. 1967. (Writing 14.) (BRG, GRD)

Creeley, Robert. *A Quick Graph: Collected Notes & Essays*. Edited by Donald Allen. 1970. (Writing 22.) (BRG, GRD)

Dorn, Edward. *Interviews*. Edited by Donald Allen. 1980. (Writing 38.) (GRD)

Hadley, Drummond. *The Webbing*. 1967. (Writing 15.) (GRD)

Kyger, Joanne. *The Tapestry and the Web*. 1965. (Writing 5.) (GRD)

Lamantia, Philip. *The Blood of the Air*. Cover photograph of the author by Stanley Reade. 1970. (Writing 25.) (GRD)

Loewinsohn, Ron. *Against the Silences to Come*. 1965. (Writing 4.) (BRG)

McClure, Michael. *Love Lion Book*. 1966. (Writing 11.) (BRG, GRD)

Olson, Charles. *A Bibliography on America for Ed Dorn*. 1964. (Writing 1.) (BRG, GRD)

Olson, Charles. *In Cold Hell, in Thicket*. 1967. (Writing 12.) (BRG, GRD)

Olson, Charles. *Stocking Cap: A Story*. 1966. (Writing 13.) (BRG, GRD)

Prose 1. With contributions by Edward Dorn, Michael Rumaker, Warren Tallman. 1964. (Writing 2.) (BRG)

Snyder, Gary. *Riprap and Cold Mountain Poems*. 1965. (Writing 7.) (BRG, GRD)

Snyder, Gary. *Six Sections from Mountains and Rivers Without End*. 1965. (Writing 9.) (BRG, GRD)

12 Poets and 1 Painter. 1964. (Writing 3.) (BRG, GRD)

Upton, Charles. *Time Raid*. 1969. (Writing 19.) (BRG)

Whalen, Philip. *Heavy Breathing: Poems, 1967–1980*. 1983. (Writing 42.) (BRG, GRD)

Whalen, Philip. *The Kindness of Strangers: Poems 1969–1974*. 1976. (Writing 33.) (GRD)

Whalen, Philip. *Off the Wall: Interviews with Philip Whalen*. Edited by Donald Allen. 1978. (BRG, GRD)

Whalen, Philip. *Severance Pay: Poems, 1967–1969*. Cover drawing by the author. 1970. (Writing 24.) (GRD)

Oyez Press

Robert Hawley

Berkeley, California
1963–1968

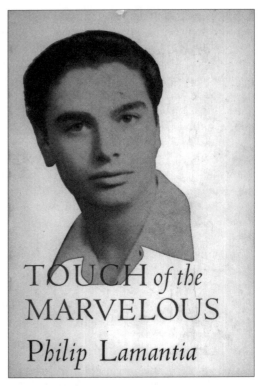

Philip Lamantia, *Touch of the Marvelous* (1966).

Oyez Press books include:

Charters, Ann. *Olson/ Melville: A Study in Affinity.* 1968. (BRG)

Duncan, Robert. *Medea at Kolchis.* Cover drawing by the author. 1965. (BRG)

Duncan, Robert. *Passages 22–27 of the War.* 1966. (BRG)

Duncan, Robert. *The Years as Catches: First Poems, 1939–1946.* 1966. (BRG)

Eigner, Larry. *Selected Poems.* Edited by Samuel Charters and Andrea Wyatt. 1972. (BRG)

[Everson, William] Brother Antoninus. *The City Does Not Die.* 1969. (BRG)

Everson, William. *Earth Poetry: Selected Essays and Interviews, 1950–1977.* Edited by Lee Bartlett. 1980. (BRG, GRD)

Everson, William. *In the Fictive Wish.* 1967. (BRG, GRD)

Everson, William. *Single Source: The Early Poems of William Everson.* Introduction by Robert Duncan. 1966. (BRG. GRD)

Fabilli, Mary. *The Animal Kingdom: Poems, 1964–1974.* 1975.

Robert Hawley, founder of Oyez Press, was in the last days of Black Mountain College a student of John Wieners, and of Robert Duncan and Charles Olson. Along with many of his fellow students, Hawley, originally from Wisconsin, landed in San Francisco, where he worked as a book scout and later with the Holmes Book Company for nearly twenty years. The Oyez Press was conceived in a series of conversations with Stevens Van Strum of Cody's Books at the Jabberwock Coffee House on Berkeley's Telegraph Avenue. The first Oyez publications were ten broadside poems, one each by Robert Duncan, Robert Creeley, Michael McClure, Denise Levertov, David Meltzer, Josephine Miles, Charles Olson, Brother Antoninus (William Everson), Gary Snyder, and William Bronk, designed and printed across the bay by David Haselwood at the Auerhahn Press. The first Oyez book was poet David Meltzer's *The Process*, printed by Graham Mackintosh, who also printed many of the early Black Sparrow books. Both Meltzer and Mackintosh were great influences on the growth of Oyez, which published multiple works by Charles Olson, Duncan, Sister Mary Norbert Körte, Mary Fabilli, and William Everson, as well as books by Thomas Parkinson and Josephine Miles, professors at the nearby University of California (Parkinson was an early defender of the Beats). Among the last books published by the Press was a facsimile reprint of a unique copy of Jack Spicer's ironically titled *Collected Poems* (1968) from the library of Josephine Miles. The Press also published many items anonymously, including a free *Checklist of the Separate Publications of Poets of the First Berkeley Poetry Conference of 1965*. This conference, a two-week-long extravaganza of readings, seminars, and workshops, was planned to increase the visibility of the New American Poetry and to introduce new poets to each other. It was in some ways a continuation of a similar conference in Vancouver two years earlier, described in Carol Bergé's *The Vancouver Report*, published by Ed Sanders in 1964.

Fabilli, Mary. *Aurora Bligh & Early Poems*. 1968. (BRG)

Fabilli, Mary. *The Old Ones: Poems*. Linoleum blocks by the author. 1966. (BRG)

Garcia, Luis. *Beans*. 1976.

Ginsberg, Allen. *Kral Majales*. Illustrated by Robert LaVigne. Broadside. 1965. (RBK)

Gitin, David. *Legwork*. 1977.

Korn, Richard. *The Judgment of the Condor*. 1978.

Körte, Mary Norbert. *Beginning of Lines: Response to Albion Moonlight*. Cover photograph by Betty Berenson. 1968. (BRG)

Körte, Mary Norbert. *Lines Bending*. 1978. (RBK)

Körte, Mary Norbert. *Mammals of Delight*. 1978. (GRD)

Lamantia, Philip. *Touch of the Marvelous*. 1966. Printed at the Auerhahn Press. (BRG, GRD)

Levertov, Denise. *Summer Poems, 1969*. 1970. (BRG)

Meltzer, David. *Blue Rags*. 1974. (BRG)

Meltzer, David. *The Dark Continent*. Cover by Peter LeBlanc. 1967. (BRG)

Meltzer, David. *Two Way Mirror: A Poetry Notebook*. 1977. (BRG)

Miles, Josephine. *Fields of Learning*. 1968.

Olson, Charles. *The Special View of History*. Edited with an introduction by Ann Charters. 1970. (BRG)

Parkinson, Thomas. *Thanatos: Earth Poems*. Illustrated by Ariel Parkinson. 1965. (GRD)

Spicer, Jack. *Collected Poems, 1945–1946*. 1981. Published in association with White Rabbit Press. (BRG)

Torregian, Sotère. *The Wounded Mattress*. Introduction by Philip Lamantia. 1970. (SC)

Vinograd, Julia. *Berkeley Street Cannibals: New and Selected Work, 1969–1976*. 1976. (GRD)

Welch, Lew. *On Out*. Frontispiece photograph of the author by Jim Hatch. 1965.

Wyatt, Andrea. *A Bibliography of Works by Larry Eigner, 1937–1969*. 1970. (BRG)

Wyatt, Andrea. *Three Rooms*. 1970. (RBK)

Auerhahn Press

David Haselwood

San Francisco
1958–1963

Philip Lamantia,
Narcotica (1959). Cover
photographs by Wallace
Berman.

Logo of Auerhahn
Press, designed by
Dion Wright.

In the unpublished "A Guide to Sources for a History of the New American Poetry," Eloyde Tovey writes:

While he was stationed with the Army in Germany during the 1950s, David Haselwood conceived the idea of becoming a publisher. At the time he was corresponding with Michael McClure in San Francisco – who needed a publisher for his *Hymns to St. Geryon.* When Haselwood, a native of Wichita, Kansas, was released from the Army ca. 1958, he came to live in San Francisco's North Beach and joined the Beats. He became familiar with all the poets and the new poetry being created at that time – some of it live, some in manuscript form, and saw that a small press would be a kind of surrogate wish fulfillment. He too had dreamed of becoming a poet. The first book under the Auerhahn Press imprint was John Wieners's *The Hotel Wentley Poems* in 1958. An unfortunate experience with a commercial printing firm led Haselwood to decide to study the rudiments of printing and book design. Then, he figured, he could personally print all future titles bearing his imprint. The printers had expurgated Wieners's text by removing certain "dirty" words and leaving the spaces blank. Haselwood's first real printing job was Philip Lamantia's *Ekstasis* (1959). He discovered what a difficult task printing really is, or what it means to "express" the poet's intent. But he wanted it known that his was the first press on the West Coast seeking to print the works of younger poets – and in cooperation with them. Nothing was ever that simple. . . . David Haselwood first published the Beat writers: William S. Burroughs, Lew Welch, Philip Whalen, Philip Lamantia, and Michael McClure. He also published books by William Everson, Charles Olson, Jack Spicer, Ronald Johnson, and Andrew Hoyem. Some of Haselwood's later titles were considered outrageously overpriced when they were first offered for sale at $10 each.

John Wieners, *The Hotel Wentley Poems* (1958). Portrait of the author by Jerry Burchard.

Auerhahn Press books include:

Lamantia, Philip. *Destroyed Works.* Cover reproduction of a no-longer-extant collage by Bruce Conner. 1962. (BRG)

Lamantia, Philip. *Ekstasis.* Cover design by Robert LaVigne. 1959. (BRG)

Lamantia, Philip. *Narcotica.* Cover photographs by Wallace Berman. 1959. (BRG)

McClure, Michael. *Hymns to St. Geryon.* Cover emblem by the author. 1959. (BRG)

Spicer, Jack. *The Heads of the Town up to the Aether.* Lithographs by Fran Herndon. 1962. (GRD)

Van Buskirk, Alden. *Lami.* Collected from his writings by David Rattray, with an introductory note by Allen Ginsberg. 1965. (BRG, GRD)

Whalen, Philip. *Memoirs of an Interglacial Age.* Cover by Robert LaVigne. 1960. (BRG)

Whalen, Philip. *Self-portrait from Another Direction.* Broadside. 1959.

Wieners, John. *The Hotel Wentley Poems.* Cover photograph by Jerry Burchard. Drawing by Robert LaVigne. 1958. (BRG)

For further information on Auerhahn Press, including a complete bibliography of its publications, the reader is referred to: Alastair M. Johnston, *A Bibliography of the Auerhahn Press & Its Successor Dave Haselwood Books.* Compiled by a printer (Berkeley: Poltroon Press, 1976).

Yugen 5 (1959).
Cover by
Basil King.

Yugen

LeRoi Jones [Imamu Amiri Baraka] and Hettie Cohen (assistant editor for nos. 6–8)

*New York City
1958–1962*

Yugen. Nos. 1–8 (1958–1962). Covers by Norman Bluhm (7), Fielding Dawson (4), Basil King (1, 5, 6, 8), Peter Schwarzburg (3), Tomi Ungerer (back cover, 2).

BRG has: complete file.

In the 1950s and 60s, LeRoi Jones was as deeply involved as an editor and publisher as he was as a poet and playwright. His publishing ventures included *Zazen, The Floating Bear, Kulchur, Yugen,* and *Totem.* Subtitled "a new consciousness in arts and letters," *Yugen* ran for eight issues from 1958 to 1962 and published an ever-widening group of writers, starting in issue 1 with such Beat writers as Allen Ginsberg, William S. Burroughs, Jack Kerouac, and Gregory Corso. By issue 3, *Yugen* was publishing writers associated with Black Mountain College and the New York School, including Charles Olson, Robert Creeley, Joel Oppenheimer, Fielding Dawson, Barbara Guest, and Frank O'Hara. Jones also paid considerable attention to a range of Eastern, Native American, and other minority cultures. The final issues included correspondence and essays exploring the theoretical side of alternative and experimental literatures; as contributor Gilbert Sorrentino noted, "the new writers had been appearing in magazines for about a decade, and it was time for the establishment of a critical position." *Yugen*'s willingness to engage in debates over theory prefigures a growing concern within the avant-garde to define a poetic principle and thus establishes *Yugen* as one of the most important precursors of the New American Poetry. *Yugen* always *looked* interesting, too, with covers illustrated by such artists as Basil King and Norman Bluhm.

The Floating Bear

Diane di Prima and LeRoi Jones [Imamu Amiri Baraka]; later Diane di Prima

New York City; later San Francisco
1961–1971

THE FLOATING BEAR
a newsletter

semi-monthly — issue # 1 — — —

Editors: Diane Di Prima   Floating Bear is distributed solely by
          LeRoi Jones   mailing list. Send mss. & inquiries to:

The Floating Bear / 309 East Houston Street / New York City 2, New York

THE SMILE SHALL NOT BE MORE MUTABLE THAN THE FINAL EXTINCTION OF MEAT. THE
/SMILE
          WITH TEETH SUNK IN LOWER LIP.
     The Smile with upturned corners
     that squints the eyes to sight beyond
     sight. I watch the dance and I smile, the figures
     are silhouettes, rounded and black sensual figures. OH
     see how they gesticulate to me. I confuse them by smiling.
     They call to me! THEY KNOW I NO LONGER AM OF THEM!!

     I am happy - OH see my huge teeth in the smile of my happiness!
          They call to me and realize I will not join
     the dancers. I WILL NOT DANCE IN THE ACTS OF YOUR LIFE!
          BUT I SMILE!
     Oh see my smile. Anarchic and black past destruction!
     The Open Smile sla hed over my face. My eyes half-
     closed with it. The smile is a sign of the eyes.
          I SHALL ALWAYS SMILE NOW! I want you
     to know what I'm thinking when I smile -- I DO NOT THINK!
     My mind is blank as a rose, convoluted
     white blank red cold, empeopled by the beasts of my love, hot
     and eternal. I am happy. I AM HAPPY. AND I SMILE
     I am served by Cherubim that float on
     plump bodies about me. CAN YOU SEE THEM? I am served
     by tall benign profiles of Godhead and spirit
          that spin in the air about me,
     by trails of black kisses and ghosts of Heroin.
     THE SMILE THE SMILE is the kiss of my own beauty
          upon myself. The solid memories of love
                    support me
     more real than statuary twined by vines
          and twisted by cracks along all ancient flaws

The Floating Bear,
a newsletter 1
(1961).

74

Named for Winnie-the-Pooh's boat made of a honey pot ("Sometimes it's a Boat, and sometimes it's more of an Accident"), *The Floating Bear*, started in February 1961, was a mimeographed "newsletter" distributed by mailing list whose mission was the speedy dissemination of new literary work. Under the editorship of Diane di Prima and LeRoi Jones (guest editors included Billy Linich [a.k.a. Billy Name], Alan Marlowe, Kirby Doyle, John Wieners, and Bill Berkson), twenty-five issues came out in the magazine's first two years. Contributing writers included Charles Olson, Robin Blaser, Robert Creeley, Philip Whalen, Paul Blackburn, and Ed Dorn, while Ray Johnson and Wallace Berman were among the many visual artists whose work was presented. This tremendous output was due at least in part to Jones's experience as editor at *Yugen* and Totem Press and to his voracious working habits. Di Prima recalls, "LeRoi could work at an incredible rate. He could read two manuscripts at a time, one with each eye. He would spread things out on the table while he was eating supper, and reject them all – listening to the news and a jazz record he was going to review, all at the same time." Occasionally a group would convene to put out the *Bear*. "In the winter of 1961–1962, we held gatherings at my East Fourth Street pad every other Sunday. There was a regular marathon ball thing going on there for a few issues. Whole bunches of people would come over to help: painters, musicians, a whole lot of outside help. The typing on those particular issues was done by James Waring, who's a choreographer and painter. Cecil Taylor ran the mimeograph machine, and Fred Herko and I collated, and we all addressed envelopes." One of the recipients of *Bear* 9 was Harold Carrington, a poet who was in prison in New Jersey. The censor read his mail and objected to the contents

of the issue, which included Jones's *The System of Dante's Hell* and William S. Burroughs's *Routine*. Jones and di Prima were subsequently arrested on obscenity charges on October 18, 1961. Di Prima remembers, "I heard a knock on my door early in the morning which I didn't answer because I never open my door early in the morning in New York City. In the morning in New York City is only trouble. It's the landlords, it's Con Edison, it's the police, it's your neighbors wanting to know why you made so much noise last night, it's something awful, and before noon I never open my door." There was a grand jury hearing, but after Jones's two-day testimony, they failed to return an indictment. Jones resigned from *The Floating Bear* in 1963 after issue 25. Di Prima moved briefly to California in 1962 and the magazine came out irregularly over the next several years, culminating in a very large issue in 1971 guest edited by Allen De Loach in Buffalo. It was called *The Intrepid-Bear Issue: Intrepid 20/Floating Bear 38.*

The Floating Bear.
Nos. 1–37 (1961–1969), and no. 38, *The Intrepid-Bear Issue* (1971).

BRG has: complete file.

Measure 1
(Summer 1957).

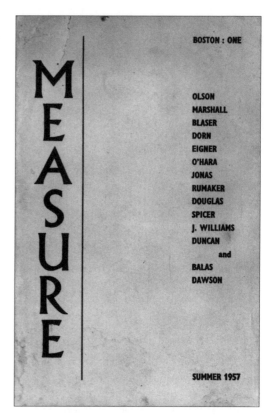

Measure

John Wieners

Boston and
San Francisco
1957–1962

Measure. Nos. 1–3
(1957–1962).

BRG has: complete file.

The three simple, almost starkly working-class issues of *Measure* followed glorious and overlooked "underground" poet John Wieners from Black Mountain College home to Boston, across country to San Francisco (issue 2), and back to Boston again. In his years in San Francisco, from 1958 to 1960, Wieners attended (sometimes serving as host at his Scott Street apartment) the legendary Sunday afternoon poetry workshops of the charismatic poets Robert Duncan and Jack Spicer (editor of *J*). Also present at the workshops were poet George Stanley (editor of *Open Space*), Harold Dull, Robin Blaser (*The Pacific Nation*), and many others (including visitors such as Stephen Spender, teaching at Berkeley in 1959). These workshops were an outgrowth of the 1957 series sponsored by the Poetry Center at San Francisco State and held in a public room at the San Francisco Public Library. *Measure* 3, published in Boston, included West Coast poets Helen Adam, Madeline Gleason, Robert Duncan, Philip Lamantia, and Jack Spicer, as well as Charles Olson, Larry Eigner, and James Schuyler from the East Coast. Except for Adam and Gleason, all had also appeared in the first Boston issue.

Newspaper 11
(1963).

Newspaper

Jack Green

New York City
1957–1965

Newspaper. Nos. 1–15
(1957–1965).

BRG has: no. 11.

Newspaper was part conceptual art, part political tract, and part 'zine. Between 1957 and 1965, fifteen issues were written, edited, and distributed by "Jack Green," reportedly the son of novelist Helen Grace Carlisle. A Princeton dropout, student of gambling systems and the theories of Wilhelm Reich, actuary of the Metropolitan Life Insurance Company, and then a free-lance proofreader, "Green" used his underground tabloid for cultural commentary and deliciously satirical (yet superbly well-documented) assaults against institutionalized publishing and book reviewing in America. Jack Green was quite vocal (some might even say fanatical) in his appreciation of William Gaddis's *The Recognitions*, taking out a full-page ad in the *Village Voice* in 1962 to extol the virtues of a book he considered to be "as much the novel of our generation as *Ulysses* was of its." His master critique was "Fire the Bastards!," which originally appeared in *Newspaper* 12–14, wherein he dissected the overwhelmingly negative criticism dished out to *The Recognitions. Fire the Bastards!* was reprinted by Dalkey Archive Press in 1992.

Semina

Wallace Berman

Los Angeles and San Francisco
(principally)
1955–1964

Semina 1 (1955).
Cover by Wallace
Berman.

Semina 4 (1959). Cover
by Wallace Berman.

Visual artist Wallace Berman published
and distributed nine issues of the assemblage magazine *Semina* between 1955 and
1964. Its circulation never exceeded a few
hundred copies. You could not buy *Semina*;
it was sent to you. Consequently, some claim
it as the precursor to "mail art." The poet
Robert Duncan has said, "*Semina* was a cult
magazine. It meant to reveal the possibility
of the emergence of a new way of feeling.
Cult means the cultivation of something. . . .
Wallace Berman gathered writers and artists
he knew that gave him a sense of his own
personal identity, and of taking hold of the
beginnings of his art." In the words of writer
Rebecca Solnit, "the magazine depicts the
emerging subculture's aesthetics, and its
values." *Semina* printed the work of two of
Berman's heroes, Hermann Hesse and Jean
Cocteau, as well as W. B. Yeats, Paul Éluard,
Charles Baudelaire, and Paul Valéry, alongside William S. Burroughs, Michael McClure,
Charles Bukowski, Allen Ginsberg, Philip
Lamantia, David Meltzer, e. i. alexander,
Bob Kaufman, and Berman himself, writing
under the pseudonym Pantale Xantos. Berman's first art exhibit, at the Ferus Gallery
in Los Angeles in 1957, resulted in his arrest
for exhibiting "lewd and lascivious pornographic art." He was found guilty and fined
by the same judge who found Henry Miller
guilty on similar charges. The motto of *Semina*
2, later the same year, was "ART IS LOVE IS
GOD." Wallace Berman was killed in an auto-
mobile accident near his home in Topanga
Canyon in 1976 on his fiftieth birthday.

Semina. Nos. 1–9
(1955–1962).

BRG has: complete file.

Beatitude

John Kelly, Bob
Kaufman, William J.
Margolis, John
Richardson, Bernie
Uronowitz, and others

San Francisco
1959–1987
(publication suspended
1961–1969)

Beatitude. Nos. 1–34
(May 1959–March 1987).

GRD has: nos. 1–33.

Beatitude, perhaps the quintessential "Beat" publication, was originally published in mimeograph at the Bread and Wine Mission on Grant Avenue in San Francisco's very hip North Beach. The Bread and Wine Mission was the creation of a Congregationalist minister, incongruously called "Father," Pierre Delattre, on a mission of social action among the Italian Catholics of North Beach. *Beatitude* was originally planned as a weekly newsletter, "designed to extol beauty and promote the beatific life among the various mendicants, neo-existentialists, christs, poets, painters, musicians and other inhabitants and observers of North Beach," as Bob Kaufman (quoted by Lawrence Ferlinghetti) put it in the *Beatitude Anthology* (1960). The first issue, the brainchild of Ginsberg, Bob Kaufman, and John Kelly, was published in May of 1959; thereafter, *Beatitude* was never anything like weekly,

but it *was* vital. The magazine was a very local North Beach Beat phenomenon; although it did have a longer reach in its later years, it still retained the look and spirit of the San Francisco coffeehouse literary scene. The magazine included work by its legendary founders, and by Jack Kerouac and Michael McClure as well, but its flare and power are perhaps better represented by the haunting work of the jazz poet ruth weiss, a frequent contributor, or by the spectacularly outrageous Lenore Kandel, whose "First They Slaughtered the Angels" nearly jumps off the pages of *Beatitude Anthology*.

Bill Margolis, Eileen Kaufman, and Bob Kaufman printing the first issue of *Beatitude* at the Bread and Wine Mission, San Francisco, April 1959. Photograph by Fortunato Clementi (from *Beatitude 17*).

Poems Collected at Les Deux Mégots/Poets at Le Metro

Dan Saxon

New York City
1962–1965

Poems Collected at Les Deux Mégots 1 (December 1962).

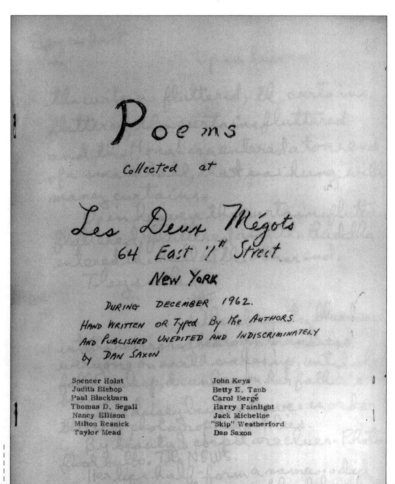

During the 1950s, East Tenth Street between Third and Fourth Avenues housed a number of art galleries exhibiting the most advanced art in America on a street that until then had been occupied by pawnshops, pool rooms, and sheet metal shops. During that decade, the area became a primary stomping ground for the young Abstract Expressionist painters and their attendant theorists/promoters, Harold Rosenberg and Clement Greenberg. Here, also, poet Frank O'Hara served as an important link between artists and poets in the East Village. Art openings became mandatory for "networking," and several of the galleries along Tenth Street also offered poetry readings and jazz. The Tenth Street Coffee House, owned by Micky Ruskin, was the scene from 1960 until 1962 of the first poetry readings in the area (organized by Chester Anderson, Howard Ant, and Ree Dragonette and including Carol Bergé, Jackson Mac Low, and Diane Wakoski among the readers). Ruskin then moved his cafe and the readings to a larger basement storefront at 64 East Seventh Street, christened Les Deux Mégots Coffee House. The Monday and Wednesday night readings organized there by poet Paul Blackburn were transferred a year later, in February 1963, to the Cafe Le Metro, owned by Moe and Cindy Margulies (Ruskin went on to open Max's Kansas City, a famous night spot frequented by Andy Warhol and other stars of the downtown art and music scene in the 1960s). At both Les Deux Mégots and the Cafe Le Metro, poet Dan Saxon collected hand- and typewritten manuscripts from the readers and produced a mimeographed magazine that he circulated for free. Among those who spoke or sang in the coffeehouses were Julian Beck of the Living Theatre, Ted Berrigan, Paul Blackburn, Allen Ginsberg, William S. Burroughs, Diane di Prima, Bob Dylan, Frank O'Hara, Gerard Malanga, LeRoi Jones, Denise Levertov, Charles Reznikoff, Lawrence Ferlinghetti, John Wieners, and Gregory Corso, most of whom also appeared in the pioneering mimeos produced by Saxon. In February 1964, the Cafe Le Metro became the battleground for one of the most important First Amendment fights in New York City's literary history. A city license inspector appeared at a reading by Jackson Mac Low and issued a summons, citing the New York Coffee House Law of 1962, which outlawed unlicensed "entertainment." Enforcement of this law in such cases would have put the small neighborhood coffee houses that did not serve liquor out of business, because cabaret licenses were expensive, and were accompanied by more stringent fire department codes and other regulations. The poetry community, led by Allen Ginsberg, Paul Blackburn, and Ted Berrigan, fought for and won the right to read poetry without a cabaret permit.

[Information adapted from Bill Morgan's *The Beat Generation in New York: A Walking Tour of Jack Kerouac's City* (San Francisco: City Lights, 1997).]

Poems Collected at Les Deux Mégots/ Poets at Le Metro.
Nos. 1–20 (December 1962–January 1965).

BRG has: complete file.

Kulchur

Marc Schleifer, Lita Hornick, and others

New York City
1960–1966

Ted Berrigan and Ron Padgett, *Bean Spasms* (1967).
Cover by Joe Brainard.

Kulchur. Nos. 1–20 (Spring 1960–Winter 1965).

BRG has: nos. 3, 4, 5, 7–10, 17. GRD has: complete file.

Kulchur Press books include:

Adam, Helen. *Stone Cold Gothic*. Paintings by Auste. 1984. (GRD)

Adam, Helen. *Turn to Me, and Other Poems*. 1977. (GRD)

Antin, David. *Talking*. Cover by the author. 1972. (GRD)

Berrigan, Ted, and Ron Padgett. *Bean Spasms*. Cover and drawings by Joe Brainard. 1967. (GRD)

Throughout its twenty issues, *Kulchur* maintained the character of a magazine of high seriousness and wide-ranging interest and investigation, in this resembling the compendious *Guide to Kulchur* by Ezra Pound. *Kulchur* included commentary or criticism (rather than poetry or fiction) by most of the writers of the avant-garde, and in a variety of areas including literature, film, theater, books, politics, and music. Gilbert Sorrentino, who edited *Kulchur* 4 and was associated with the magazine as a contributing editor for two years, remarks on its impact: "*Kulchur* evolved a review style that, for better or worse, has persisted in little-magazine writing to this day. It was personal, colloquial, wry, mocking, and precisely vulgar when vulgarity seemed called for . . . nothing was ever explained, the writing was elliptical, casual, and obsessively conversational. We had wanted a flashing, brilliant magazine that had nothing to do with the academic world and we had got one." Among the high points of the twenty issues were Charles Olson on "Proprioception," and Julian Beck of the Living Theatre on "The Life of the Theatre," in issue 1.

Subsequent issues featured Jerome Rothenberg and Robert Creeley on deep image poetry, Paul Blackburn's article on *The Black Mountain Review*, Ed Dorn on Olson's *Maximus* poems (reprinted from his Migrant pamphlet), Edwin Denby on Balanchine, Clayton Eshleman's translations of Peruvian poet César Vallejo, and a good number of Ted Berrigan's *Sonnets*. Covers were contributed by a variety of artists including Franz Kline, Robert Indiana, and Joe Brainard. The artistic community of the early 1960s was reflected in the instability of its contentious editorial history: there were at least four single editors, including Marc Schleifer for three issues and Sorrentino and Jerome Rothenberg for one each; an editorial board consisting of Sorrentino, LeRoi Jones, Frank O'Hara, Bill Berkson, and Joseph LeSueur for several issues; followed by the single editorship of Lita Hornick, who was also the publisher and the financier for most of the magazine's feisty life.

Brainard, Joe. *Selected Writings.* Cover and endpapers by Ron Padgett. 1971. (GRD)

Ceravolo, Joe. *Millenium Dust.* Cover by Monica Da Vinci. 1982. (GRD)

Clark, Tom. *At Malibu.* Cover by the author. Cover photograph of the author by Angelica Clark. 1975. (GRD)

Elmslie, Kenward. *Album.* Cover and drawings by Joe Brainard. 1969.

Elmslie, Kenward, and Joe Brainard. *Sung Sex.* 1989.

Fagin, Larry. *Rhymes of a Jerk.* Cover by Ed Ruscha. 1974. (GRD)

Ferrari, Mary. *The Isle of the Little God.* Covers by Jennifer Bartlett. 1981. (GRD)

Giorno, John. *Balling Buddha.* Cover by Les Levine. 1970. (GRD)

Giorno, John, and Richard Bosman. *Grasping at Emptiness.* Cover and drawings by Richard Bosman. 1985. (GRD)

Greenwald, Ted. *The Licorice Chronicles.* Cover by James Starrett. 1979. (GRD)

Hartman, Yuki. *Ping.* Cover and drawings by Susan Greene. 1984. (GRD)

Hornick, Lita. *Night Flight.* Cover painting by Susan Hall. Back cover by Jennifer Bartlett. 1982. (GRD)

Hornick, Lita. *Nine Martinis.* 1987. (GRD)

Howe, Susan. *The Defenestration of Prague.* Cover from a drawing by Inigo Jones. Design by Susan B. Laufer. 1983. (GRD)

Jones, Hettie, ed. *Poems Now.* 1966. (BRG)

Katz, Alex, and Kenneth Koch. *Interlocking Lives.* Cover by Alex Katz. 1970. (BRG)

Kostelanetz, Richard. *I Articulations.* 1974.

Lavin, Stuart. *Let Myself Shine.* Cover by Bruce Chandler. 1979. (GRD)

MacAdams, Lewis. *Live at the Church.* Cover photograph of the author by Gerard Malanga. 1977. (GRD)

Continued on page 86

One of the most vibrant issues of *Kulchur*, no. 4, was guest edited by Gilbert Sorrentino at Lita Hornick's request. As Sorrentino recounted in "Neon, Kulchur, etc.," *TriQuarterly* (Fall 1978):

"I asked Zukofsky (whom I badly wanted to begin to use the magazine for an outlet), Duncan, Ron Loewinsohn, and [Hubert] Selby for contributions, and they all responded. Zukofsky gave me 'Modern Times,' a beautiful essay on Charlie Chaplin, written in 1936 and never before published; Duncan sent his matchless 'Ideas of the Meaning of Form'; Loewinsohn sent 'A Credo Sandwich,' a piece on poetics that complemented Duncan's; and Selby, writing as 'Harry Black,' submitted 'Happiness House,' a bitter assault on New York State mental institutions. [LeRoi] Jones, as an editor, gave me a chapter from his as yet unpublished book, *Blues People*, and I asked Edward Dorn if I might reprint his 'What I See in the *Maximus* Poems,' originally published in Gael Turnbull's *Migrant*. Paul Goodman sent a comment on the material that had appeared in number 3. An oddly curious Freudian study of L. Frank Baum, and in particular the Oz books, came in unsolicited from Osmond Beckwith, of whom I have never again heard, and seemed to me exactly right for the issue. The reviews were by [Fielding] Dawson, Jones, Cid Corman (on Zukofsky), [Joel] Oppenheimer (on Dorn), and Walter Lowenfels, who sent a review of *Tropic of Cancer*, written in Paris on the appearance of Miller's novel in 1934 and previously unpublished. Marian Zazeela, Marc Schleifer's wife, gave me a snapshot of Kerouac and Burroughs taken in Paris about 1955, and that became the cover; the title page identifies it as a photograph of Inspector Maigret and Sam Spade."

Malanga, Gerard. *Screen Tests: A Diary.* Cover and illustrations by Andy Warhol. 1967. (GRD)

Mayer, Bernadette. *Poetry.* Cover by Rosemary Mayer. 1976. (GRD)

North, Charles. *Leap Year: Poems 1968–1978.* Cover and drawings by Paula North. 1978. (GRD)

Notley, Alice. *Waltzing Matilda.* Covers by George Schneeman. 1981. (GRD)

Owen, Maureen. *Hearts in Space.* Cover and drawings by Joe Giordano. 1980. (GRD)

Owens, Rochelle. *How Much Paint Does the Painting Need.* 1988. (GRD)

Owens, Rochelle. *I Am the Babe of Joseph Stalin's Daughter.* Cover and drawings by the author. 1972. (GRD)

Perreault, John. *Luck.* 1969. (GRD)

Plymell, Charles. *The Trashing of America.* Covers by Les Levine. 1975. (GRD)

Pommy-Vega, Janine. *The Bard Owl.* Cover and drawings by Martin Carey. 1980. (GRD)

Ratcliff, Carter. *Fever Coast.* 1973. (GRD)

Torregian, Sotère. *The Age of Gold.* Cover and pictures by the author. 1976. (GRD)

Towle, Tony. *New and Selected Poems.* Cover painting by Jean Holabird. 1983. (GRD)

Violi, Paul. *Baltic Circles.* Cover painting of the author by Paula North. 1973.

Waldman, Anne. *No Hassles.* Cover by Brigid Polk and art by Joe Brainard, Donna Dennis, and George Schneeman. 1971.

Waldman, Anne, and Susan Hall. *Invention.* Drawings by Susan Hall. 1985.

Warsh, Lewis. *Blue Heaven.* Cover by George Schneeman. 1978. (BRG)

$1.00 KULCHUR 4

Kulchur 4 (1961). Photograph of William S. Burroughs and Jack Kerouac in Paris, ca. 1955.

Poets Press

Diane di Prima

New York City
1963–1969

"Growing up in the fifties, you had to figure it out for yourself – which she did, and stayed open – as a woman, uninterested in any possibility of static investment or solution. Her search for a human center is among the most moving I have witnessed – and she took her friends with her, though often it would have been simpler indeed to have gone alone. God bless her toughness and the deep gentleness of her hand!"

— Robert Creeley, "Foreword for Diane" in
  Diane di Prima's *Pieces of a Song: Selected Poems*
  (San Francisco: City Lights, 1990)

One of the most influential people in Diane di Prima's life was her grandfather, Domenico Mallozi, a writer for the anarchist newspaper *Il Martello* (*The Hammer*) on New York City's Lower East Side. His granddaughter followed in his footsteps, both as a writer and as an activist and internationalist, during the 1960s co-founding the New York Poets Theatre (which from 1961 to 1965 produced one-act plays by poets, with sets and decorations by a variety of artists), co-editing *The Floating Bear* with LeRoi Jones [Imamu Amiri Baraka], and serving as a contributing editor to both *Yugen* and *Kulchur*. From her apartment at 54 East Fourth Street in New York, and later from Kerhonkson in upstate New York, she ran the Poets Press. About its beginnings, she is characteristically to the point: "I bought a Davidson 241 and put it in a store-front . . . I went to 'printing school' for a week and learned how to run the machine (I was the only woman in the class), and I got on with it." Poets Press published nearly thirty books, including many of di Prima's own, as well as the first books of Audre Lorde, Jay Wright, and David Henderson, and works by Herbert Huncke and Michael McClure. Di Prima lived in Timothy Leary's psychedelic community in Millbrook, New York, for six months in 1966–1967 and published Leary's *Psychedelic Prayers* in 1966. John Ashbery's *Three Madrigals* was published in holograph reproduction in 1968. Di Prima moved in 1968 to the West Coast, where she continues her active involvement in poetry, publishing, and antiwar and ecological projects. She has taught in the Poetics Program at the New College of San Francisco and founded the San Francisco Institute of Magical and Healing Arts.

Poets Press books include:

Ashbery, John. *Three Madrigals*. 1968. (BRG)

Creeley, Robert. *Mazatlan: Sea*. 1969. Printed at the Cranium Press.

Creeley, Robert. *5 Numbers*. Cover design, rubberstamp print by William Katz. 1968.

Di Prima, Diane. *Earthsong: Poems, 1957–1959*. Cover drawings by George Herms. 1968. (BRG)

Di Prima, Diane. *Hotel Albert Poems*. 1968. (BRG)

Di Prima, Diane. *L.A. Odyssey*. Cover by George Herms. 1969. (BRG)

Di Prima, Diane. *The New Handbook of Heaven*. 1964 (reprint of Auerhahn Press edition of 1963). (BRG)

Di Prima, Diane. *New Mexico Poem*. 1968.

Di Prima, Diane, trans. *Seven Love Poems from the Middle Latin*. 1965. (BRG)

Di Prima, Diane, ed. *War Poems*. Cover by John Braden. 1968. (BRG)

Doyle, Kirby. *Sapphobones*. 1966.

Duncan, Robert. *Play Time Pseudo Stein*. Cover by the author. 1969. (BRG)

Henderson, David. *Felix of the Silent Forest*. Introduction by LeRoi Jones. Cover by Brett Rohmer. 1967. (BRG, SC)

Huncke, Herbert. *Huncke's Journal*. Drawings by Erin Matson. 1965.

Leary, Timothy. *Psychedelic Prayers After the Tao Te Ching*. 1966. (GRD)

Lorde, Audre. *The First Cities*. Introduction by Diane di Prima. 1968.

Marlowe, Alan. *A Handbook of Survival into the New Age*. Broadside. 1964.

Marlowe, Alan. *John's Book*. Introduction by Robert Creeley. 1969. (BRG)

Marlowe, Alan. *To a Growing Community (To Allen Ginsberg)*. Broadside. 1968.

Matson, Clive. *Mainline to the Heart*. Introduction by John Wieners. Drawings by Erin Matson. 1966.

McClure, Michael. *Little Odes, Jan.–March 1961*. 1968. (BRG)

Spellman, A. B. *The Beautiful Days*. Introduction by Frank O'Hara. Drawings by William White. Cover by Ross Perez. 1965. (SC)

Totem Press

LeRoi Jones [Imamu Amiri Baraka]

New York City
1958–1962

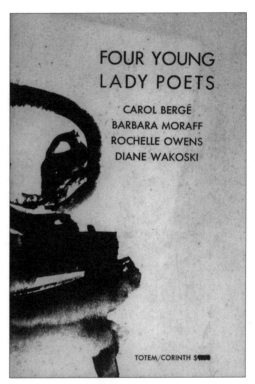

Four Young Lady Poets: Carol Bergé, Barbara Moraff, Rochelle Owens and Diane Wakoski (1962). Cover drawing by Jesse Sorrentino. Published in association with Corinth Books.

Totem Press books include:

Blackburn, Paul. *Brooklyn-Manhattan Transit.* 1960. (Blueplate No. 3.) (BRG)

Di Prima, Diane. *This Kind of Bird Flies Backward.* Introduction by Lawrence Ferlinghetti. 1958. (BRG, GRD)

Finstein, Max. *Savonarola's Tune.* Foreword by Gilbert Sorrentino. 1959. Published by Laurence Hellenberg and distributed by Totem Press. (GRD)

Jones, LeRoi, ed. *Jan 1st 1959: Fidel Castro.* Includes poems by Joel Oppenheimer, Max Finstein, LeRoi Jones, Gilbert Sorrentino, Ron Loewinsohn, and Jack Kerouac. 1959. (Blueplate No. 1.) (BRG)

Loewinsohn, Ron. *Watermelons.* Introduction by William Carlos Williams. 1959. (BRG)

McClure, Michael. *For Artaud.* 1959. (Blueplate No. 2.) (BRG)

Olson, Charles. *Projective Verse.* Cover by Matsumi Kanemitsu. 1959. (BRG)

Totem Press books in association with Corinth Books include:

Dorn, Edward. *Hands Up!* Cover by William White. 1964. (GRD)

Four Young Lady Poets. Includes poems by Carol Bergé, Barbara Moraff, Rochelle Owens, Diane Wakoski. 1962. (BRG)

Ginsberg, Allen. *Empty Mirror.* Introduction by William Carlos Williams. Cover by Jesse Sorrentino. 1961. (BRG)

Jones, LeRoi. *Preface to a Twenty Volume Suicide Note.* Cover drawing by Basil King. 1961. (BRG)

Kerouac, Jack. *The Scripture of the Golden Eternity.* Cover drawing of Kerouac by Robert LaVigne. 1960. (BRG)

O'Hara, Frank. *Second Avenue.* Cover by Larry Rivers. 1960. (BRG)

Oppenheimer, Joel. *The Love Bit and Other Poems.* Cover by Dan Rice. 1962. (GRD)

Snyder, Gary. *Myths and Texts.* Cover and drawings by Will Peterson. 1960. (BRG)

Sorrentino, Gilbert. *Black and White.* 1964. (GRD)

Whalen, Philip. *Like I Say.* 1960. (BRG)

On the same small offset press, and as an arm of his magazine *Yugen*, LeRoi Jones's Totem Press imprint published thirteen pamphlets, beginning with Diane di Prima's *This Kind of Bird Flies Backward* in 1958. The press also published work by Ron Loewinsohn *(Watermelons,* 1959), Michael McClure (*For Artaud,* 1959), and Jack Kerouac (*The Scripture of the Golden Eternity,* 1961), as well as Charles Olson's influential and much-admired *Projective Verse* in 1959 and Paul Blackburn's *Brooklyn-Manhattan Transit* in 1960. However, the most important (at least to Jones himself) of the Totem Books was the little six-page pamphlet he edited in 1959 as the second book of the press. Entitled *Jan 1st 1959: Fidel Castro,* it included poems by Joel Oppenheimer, Max Finstein, Gilbert Sorrentino, Ron Loewinsohn, and Jack Kerouac in addition to Jones's own "A Poem Some People Will Have to Understand." Jones's arguments with his friends (then mostly white) over the relationship of poetry to politics caused him to reevaluate his own position on non-violence and political action, which eventually led him to break with most of his white colleagues and friends. In late 1960, Jones entered into a relationship with Eli Wilentz of Corinth Books to co-publish and distribute Totem Press titles.

Charles Olson, *Projective Verse* (1959). Cover by Matsumi Kanemitsu.

Corinth Books

*Eli and Ted Wilentz; later
Ted and Joan Wilentz*

New York City
1959–1973

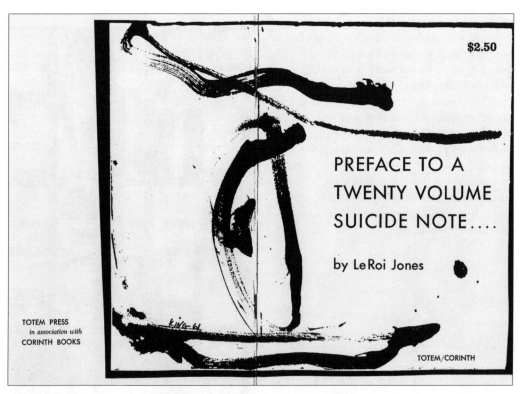

LeRoi Jones, *Preface to a Twenty Volume Suicide Note* (1961). Cover drawing by Basil King. Published in association with Totem Press.

One of New York's literary landmarks was the Eighth Street Book Shop, which began in 1947 when brothers Ted and Eli Wilentz bought an old Womraths "bookstore" (really a lending library and card shop) and transformed it into a thriving center of literary activity. In addition to selling books, the Wilentzes began a small publishing concern in 1959. As Ted remembers: "Both of us were interested in publishing, so we jumped in. For a while we thought we might make Corinth into a full-fledged business, but that fantasy dwindled as time went on. . . . These new writers, then, began appearing sometime in the early fifties. They would come in the shop, often to leave their books. . . . There were many now-important writers whom I had the pleasure of working with and getting to know. LeRoi Jones, for instance, who today prefers to be known as Imamu Amiri Baraka. I met Roi when Hettie Jones, his first wife, worked as my secretary for a time. . . . I still recall the time when Ginsberg came to me and asked if I would lend him some money to bring Philip Whalen and Mike McClure to New York City for a reading. . . . Jonathan Williams, at some point, used to pack books for us at the shop. We did four books with Jonathan, and published them under the Jargon/Corinth imprint." A remarkable number of important writers of the period were published by Corinth, including, in cooperation with Jargon, Robert Creeley, Charles Olson, and Louis Zukofsky. Corinth also co-published books with LeRoi Jones's Totem Press, including Frank O'Hara's *Second Avenue* (1960), Gary Snyder's *Myths and Texts* (1960), Ginsberg's *Empty Mirror* (1961), and Kerouac's *The Scripture of the Golden Eternity* (1961). For a number of years the press was active in publishing the work of promising young African American poets, including Tom Weatherly, Al Young, Clarence Major, and Jay Wright. Some of the second-generation New York Schoolers were also published by the Wilentzes, including Anne Waldman and Ted Berrigan.

Corinth books include:

Berrigan, Ted. *Many Happy Returns.* Cover by Joe Brainard. 1969. (BRG)

Di Prima, Diane. *Dinners and Nightmares.* 1961. (BRG)

Ginsberg, Allen. *Empty Mirror.* Introduction by William Carlos Williams. Cover collage from photographs by Ann Charters and Elsa Dorfman. Revised edition. 1970. (BRG)

Guest, Barbara. *The Blue Stairs.* Cover by Helen Frankenthaler. 1968.

Joans, Ted. *The Hipsters.* 1961. (BRG)

Jones, LeRoi, ed. *The Moderns: An Anthology of New Writing in America.* Introduction by LeRoi Jones. 1963. (BRG)

Major, Clarence. *Symptoms & Madness.* Cover by Joan Wilentz. 1971. (BRG, SC)

Schjeldahl, Peter. *White Country.* 1968. (BRG)

Waldman, Anne. *Giant Night.* Cover by Joe Brainard. 1970. (BRG)

Warsh, Lewis. *Dreaming as One: Poems.* Cover by Joe Brainard. 1971. (BRG)

Weatherly, Tom. *Maumau American Cantos.* 1970. (SC)

Wilentz, Eli, ed. *The Beat Scene.* Photographs by Fred McDarrah. 1960. (BRG)

Wright, Jay. *The Homecoming Singer.* 1971. (GRD, SC)

For a more complete list of Corinth and Totem/Corinth books, the reader is referred to the list by Ted Wilentz and Bill Zavatsky, appended to their article "Behind the Writer, Ahead of the Reader: A Short History of Corinth Books," which appeared in *Tri-Quarterly* 43 (1978) and is reprinted in Elliott Anderson and Mary Kinzie's *The Little Magazine in America: A Modern Documentary History* (Yonkers, N.Y.: Pushcart Press, 1978).

New Directions

James Laughlin
New York City
1936–

Kenneth Patchen, *Selected Poems*
(1957). Cover photograph of the
author by Harry Redl. Cover design by
David Ford.

"No, Jaz, it's hopeless. You're never going to make a writer." "Jaz" was James Laughlin IV, a bored college freshman who had taken 1934–1935 off to study with Ezra Pound at the poet's "Ezuversity." Pound counseled Laughlin, "Go back to Haavud to finish up your studies. If you're a good boy your parents will give you some money and you can bring out books. I'll write to my friends and get them to provide you with manuscripts." Pound was right about the money, although Laughlin didn't wait for the manuscripts to roll in. In 1936, with help from his father and his aunt, he founded New Directions. His first title, *New Directions in Prose and Poetry 1936*, featured a poem, short story, and essay by William Carlos Williams, whom Laughlin had first published as an editor of the *Harvard Advocate*. Williams's *White Mule* followed in 1937. Pound's *Guide to Kulchur* was published in 1938. It would be easy to dismiss Laughlin as a gentleman publisher (Pound invariably did, when frustrated by delays or mistakes), but consider this: New Directions has kept Williams and Pound in print for sixty years. And they are just two poets on a list that includes David Antin, Apollinaire, Baudelaire, Edwin Brock, Ernesto Cardenal, Hayden Carruth, Cid Corman, Gregory Corso, Robert Creeley, Robert Duncan, Richard Eberhart, Russell Edson, William Everson, Lawrence Ferlinghetti, García Lorca, Goethe, H.D., Robinson Jeffers, Bob Kaufman, Irving Layton, Denise Levertov, Michael McClure, Eugenio Montale, Pablo Neruda, Charles Olson, George Oppen, Wilfred Owen, Nicanor Parra, Boris Pasternak, Kenneth Patchen, Octavio Paz, Raymond Queneau, John Crowe Ransom, Raja Rao, Pierre Reverdy, Kenneth Rexroth, Rilke, Rimbaud, Selden Rodman, Jerome Rothenberg, Delmore Schwartz, Stevie Smith, Gary Snyder, Nathaniel Thomas, and Yvor Winters – not to mention Buddha.

— *Aaron Fischer*
Fort Lee, New Jersey, October 1997

New Directions books include:

Antin, David. *Talking at the Boundaries.* 1976. (BRG)

Corman, Cid. *Livingdying.* Cover by Shiryu Morita. 1970. (BRG)

Corman, Cid. *Sun Rock Man.* 1970. (BRG)

Corso, Gregory. *Elegiac Feelings American.* Cover photograph of the author by Ettore Sottass, Jr. 1970. (BRG)

Corso, Gregory. *The Happy Birthday of Death.* 1960. (BRG)

Corso, Gregory. *Long Live Man.* 1962. (BRG)

Duncan, Robert. *Bending the Bow.* Book and dust jacket designed by Graham Mackintosh. Cover photograph of the author by Nata Piaskowski. 1968. (BRG)

Duncan, Robert. *The Opening of the Field.* 1973. (BRG)

Ferlinghetti, Lawrence. *A Coney Island of the Mind.* 1958. (BRG)

Ferlinghetti, Lawrence. *Her.* 1960. (BRG)

Ferlinghetti, Lawrence. *The Secret Meaning of Things.* 1968. (BRG)

Kaufman, Bob. *Solitudes Crowded with Loneliness.* 1965. (GRD, SC)

Kerouac, Jack. *Excerpt from Visions of Cody.* 1959. (BRG)

Levertov, Denise. *The Cold Spring & Other Poems.* 1968. (BRG)

Levertov, Denise. *The Collected Earlier Poems.* 1979. (BRG)

Levertov, Denise. *Footprints.* Cover photograph by Liebe Coolidge. 1972. (BRG)

Levertov, Denise. *The Freeing of the Dust.* Cover photograph of work by Antonio Tàpies. 1975. (BRG)

Levertov, Denise. *Life in the Forest.* Cover photograph by Harry Callahan. 1978. (BRG)

Levertov, Denise. *O Taste and See.* Cover photograph by Roloff Beny. 1964. (BRG)

Levertov, Denise. *The Poet in the World.* Cover photograph of the author's desk by Suzy Gordon. 1973. (BRG)

Levertov, Denise. *The Sorrow Dance.* Cover photograph by Roloff Beny. 1966. (BRG)

Continued on page 96

Denise Levertov, *The Sorrow Dance* (1966).
Cover photograph by Roloff Beny.

Levertov, Denise. *With Eyes at the Back of Our Heads.* 1959. (BRG)

McClure, Michael. *September Blackberries.* 1974. (BRG)

Olson, Charles. *Selected Writings.* Edited, with an introduction, by Robert Creeley. 1966. (BRG)

Oppen, George. *The Collected Poems of George Oppen.* 1975. (GRD)

Oppen, George. *The Materials.* 1962.

Oppen, George. *Of Being Numerous.* 1968. (BRG)

Oppen, George. *This in Which.* 1965. (BRG)

Patchen, Kenneth. *Because It Is: Poems and Drawings.* 1960. (GRD)

Patchen, Kenneth. *But Even So.* 1968. (GRD)

Patchen, Kenneth. *Hallelujah Anyway.* 1966. (GRD)

Patchen, Kenneth. *In Quest of Candlelighters.* 1972. (GRD)

Patchen, Kenneth. *Memoirs of a Shy Pornographer.* Cover photograph of the author by Ray Johnson. 1958. (GRD)

Patchen, Kenneth. *Red Wine & Yellow Hair.* 1949. (GRD, BRG with cover painted by the author)

Patchen, Kenneth. *Selected Poems.* Cover photograph of the author by Harry Redl. Cover design by David Ford. 1957. (GRD)

Patchen, Kenneth. *Sleepers Awake.* 1969. Published originally by Padell Books, 1946. (GRD)

Randall, Margaret. *Part of the Solution: Portrait of a Revolutionary.* 1973. (GRD)

Rexroth, Kenneth. *The Collected Longer Poems.* 1968.

Rexroth, Kenneth. *The Collected Shorter Poems.* 1966.

Rexroth, Kenneth. *Natural Numbers: New and Selected Poems.* 1963.

Rexroth, Kenneth, trans. *One Hundred Poems from the Chinese.* 1965.

Reznikoff, Charles. *By the Waters of Manhattan: Selected Verse.* Introduction by C. P. Snow. 1962. (BRG, GRD)

Rothenberg, Jerome. *Poland/1931.* 1974.

Rothenberg, Jerome. *Pre-Faces and Other Writings.* 1981. (BRG)

*Journal for the
Protection of All
Beings: A Visionary
and Revolutionary
Review* 1 (1961).

Journal for the Protection of All Beings: A Visionary and Revolutionary Review

*Michael McClure, Lawrence Ferlinghetti,
and David Meltzer*

*San Francisco
1961–1978*

**Journal for the
Protection of All Beings.**
Nos. 1–4 (1961–1978).

BRG has: no. 1.

Similar in spirit and philosophy to *Ark II/Moby 1*, the *Journal for the Protection of All Beings* was one of the first radical ecology journals. The brainchild of Michael McClure and David Meltzer, it melded the anarchist thought of the 1950s (*The Ark*) with the pacifism evidenced in the very early mimeo journal *The Illiterati*, published in the late 1940s by Kermit Sheets and Kemper Nomland at the camp for conscientious objectors in Waldport, Oregon. The newest element in the mix was work from the San Francisco Renaissance poets. The first issue led off with Thomas Merton's "Chant to be used in procession around a site with furnaces" and included work by all three editors as well as an interview with Ginsberg by Gregory Corso, an interview with Ginsberg and Corso by William S. Burroughs, as well as Gary Snyder's "Buddhist Anarchism." This issue also reprinted two famous documents, Percy Bysshe Shelley's "Declaration of Rights" and the famous statement by Chief Joseph of the Nez Perce Indians.

City Lights

Lawrence Ferlinghetti

San Francisco

1955–

Michael McClure, *Ghost Tantras* (1964). Cover by Wallace Berman.

City Lights Journal.
Nos. 1–4 (1963–1978).

BRG has: complete file.

City Lights books include:

Beatitude Anthology. 1960.

Corso, Gregory. *Gasoline.* Introduction by Allen Ginsberg. 1958. (Pocket Poets Series, No. 8.) (BRG)

Di Prima, Diane. *Revolutionary Letters.* Cover design by Lawrence Ferlinghetti. 1971. (Pocket Poets Series, No. 27.) (BRG)

Duncan, Robert. *Selected Poems.* 1959. (Pocket Poets Series, No. 10.) (BRG)

Ferlinghetti, Lawrence. *Pictures of the Gone World.* 1955. (Pocket Poets Series, No. 1.) (BRG)

Ginsberg, Allen. *Howl and Other Poems.* 1956. (Pocket Poets Series, No. 4.) (BRG)

Ginsberg, Allen. *Kaddish and Other Poems 1958–1960.* 1961. (Pocket Poets Series, No. 14.) (BRG)

Kerouac, Jack. *Book of Dreams.* Cover photograph of the author by Robert Frank. 1961.

Kerouac, Jack. *Scattered Poems.* Cover photograph of the author by William S. Burroughs. 1971. (Pocket Poets Series, No. 28.) (BRG)

Lamantia, Philip. *Selected Poems, 1943–1966.* 1967. (Pocket Poets Series, No. 20.)

The very image of the counterculture, the City Lights Bookstore opened its doors on Columbus Avenue in San Francisco's North Beach neighborhood in 1953. At first, under the name of the Pocket Bookshop, Lawrence Ferlinghetti and Peter Martin sold only paperbacks and magazines; the name was changed in 1955 when the famous Pocket Poets Series began with Ferlinghetti's own *Pictures of the Gone World*. The series and the bookshop flourish to this day. In 1956, a few months after the famous Six Gallery reading, Ferlinghetti published Allen Ginsberg's *Howl and Other Poems*, causing a firestorm of controversy when he was arrested and tried for the sale of obscene material in 1957. Ferlinghetti was acquitted, and the powerful little book of poems has since sold over a million copies. The poem itself was a watershed work for the New American Poetry, and is still contemporary in its angry protest. Ferlinghetti started the *City Lights Journal* in 1963, basing it on such older and distinguished European literary journals as *Botteghe Oscure* and *Transition* and on the yearly American anthologies from New Directions. The entire Beat pantheon, including Ginsberg, Burroughs, Kerouac,

Ed Sanders, Gary Snyder, and Neal Cassady, contributed to the first issue. The *Journal* did not stay on schedule, however; it numbered only four issues, the last of which was not published until fifteen years after the first. But the *Journal* was notable for the catholicity of its taste, combining writing from around the world. Under the City Lights imprint, Ferlinghetti has published a truly international selection of avant-garde literature, including works in translation by García Lorca, Rimbaud, Picasso, Prévert, Neruda, and others, as well as original work by almost all the Beat, Black Mountain, and San Francisco Renaissance writers. Ferlinghetti today is an incarnation of his own hero, Charlie Chaplin, a symbol of integrity, of a life lived for art. Chaplin's famous film provided Ferlinghetti with the name for his equally famous and truly exemplary bookstore.

Levertov, Denise. *Here and Now.* 1957. (Pocket Poets Series, No. 6.) (BRG)

Mailer, Norman. *The White Negro.* Cover, negative of photograph by Harry Redl. 1957. (BRG)

McClure, Michael. *Ghost Tantras.* Cover by Wallace Berman. 1964. (BRG)

McClure, Michael. *Meat Science Essays.* 1963. (BRG)

O'Hara, Frank. *Lunch Poems.* 1964. (Pocket Poets Series, No. 19.) (BRG)

Pickard, Tom. *Guttersnipe.* Cover photograph of the author by Elsa Dorfman. 1971. (GRD)

Rothenberg, Jerome, ed. and trans. *Nine Young German Poets.* 1959. (Pocket Poets Series, No. 11.) (GRD)

Waldman, Anne. *Fast Speaking Woman.* Cover photograph of the author by Sheyla Baykal. 1975. (BRG)

Watts, Allen. *Beat Zen, Square Zen, and Zen.* 1959. (BRG)

Weishaus, Joel, ed. *On the Mesa: An Anthology of Bolinas Writing.* Cover photograph by Steven Lazar. 1971.

Williams, William Carlos. *Kora in Hell.* 1957. (Pocket Poets Series, No. 7.)

For further information on City Lights, the reader is referred to: Ralph T. Cook, *City Lights Books: A Descriptive Bibliography* (Metuchen, N.J.: Scarecrow Press, 1992).

Grove Press

Barney Rosset

New York City
1948–

THE
NEW
AMERICAN
POETRY
1945-1960
EDITED BY
DONALD M. ALLEN

Donald Allen, ed.,
The New American
Poetry, 1945–1960
(1960).

Grove Press, named for Grove Street in Greenwich Village, started as a small reprint house in 1948. By 1951, when Barney Rosset became a partner (and then owner), the firm had published only three paperbacks: a book of poetry by seventeenth-century mystical writer Richard Crashaw, Melville's *The Confidence Man,* and *The Selected Writings of the Ingenious Mrs. Aphra Behn;* the first book brought to Grove by Rosset was Henry James's *The Golden Bowl.* Very much influenced by New Directions, Faber & Faber, and Chatto and Windus, Rosset soon introduced the writings of Beckett, Genet, Robbe-Grillet, Gide, and Ionesco to an American audience. Barney Rosset believed in "combat publishing," and his ongoing challenge to mainstream American sensibilities has landed him in court many, many times. He fought and won battles for D. H. Lawrence's *Lady Chatterley's Lover* and Henry Miller's *Tropic of Cancer* (for which he went to court in sixty separate state and local prosecutions, six state supreme court rulings, and a U.S. Supreme Court hearing). For many, Grove Press really defined the character of the international literary underground. Donald Allen, the first editor at Grove (other than Rosset), edited the anthology *The New American Poetry, 1945–1960,* the importance and influence of which cannot be overestimated – San Francisco Renaissance, Black Mountain, Beat, the New York School, are all here brought together and center stage. This book might well be considered the "flash point" for the renaissance in literary writing and small press publishing that would flourish within a few short years of its publication. Along with its stable of European writers, Grove also published such Americans as Ted Berrigan (*The Sonnets* went through two printings totaling 6,000 copies), Paul Blackburn, William S. Burroughs, Hubert Selby, Jr., Richard Brautigan, Robert Duncan, and Charles Olson, among many others.

Grove Press books include:

Allen, Donald, ed. *The New American Poetry, 1945–1960.* 1960. (BRG)

Berrigan, Ted. *The Sonnets.* 1967.

Blackburn, Paul. *The Cities.* 1967.

Brautigan, Richard. *A Confederate General from Big Sur.* Cover from a painting by Larry Rivers. 1964. (BRG)

Burroughs, William S. *Naked Lunch.* 1959. (BRG)

Burroughs, William S. *Nova Express.* 1964. (BRG)

Burroughs, William S. *The Soft Machine.* Cover reproduction of a drawing by the author. 1966. (BRG)

Burroughs, William S. *The Wild Boys: A Book of the Dead.* 1971. (BRG)

Duncan, Robert. *The Opening of the Field.* Title page designed by Jess (Collins). 1960. (BRG)

The Evergreen Review Reader, 1957–1967. Edited by Barney Rosset. 1968.

Fanon, Frantz. *The Wretched of the Earth.* 1966. (GRD)

Ginsberg, Allen. *Journals: Early Fifties, Early Sixties.* Edited by Gordon Ball. 1977. (BRG)

H.D. (Hilda Doolittle). *Helen in Egypt.* 1961. (GRD)

Jones, LeRoi. *The Dead Lecturer.* Cover photograph of the author by Leroy McLucas. 1964. (BRG)

Jones, LeRoi. *The System of Dante's Hell.* 1965. (BRG)

Continued on page 102

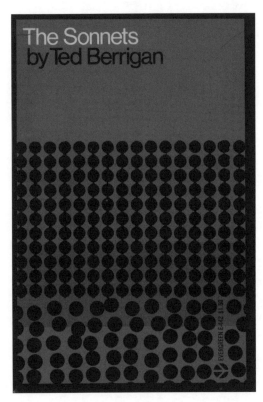

Ted Berrigan, *The Sonnets* (1967).

Kandel, Lenore. *Word Alchemy.* 1967.

Kerouac, Jack. *Mexico City Blues.* Cover by Roy Kuhlman. 1959. (BRG)

Kerouac, Jack. *Satori in Paris.* 1966. (BRG)

Koch, Kenneth. *The Pleasures of Peace, and Other Poems.* 1969. (BRG)

Kupferberg, Tuli. *1001 Ways to Beat the Draft.* 1967. (GRD)

Kupferberg, Tuli. *1001 Ways to Live Without Working.* 1967.

Kupferberg, Tuli. *1001 Ways to Make Love.* 1969.

Machiz, Herbert, ed. *Artists' Theatre: Four Plays.* 1960.

McClure, Michael. *The New Book/A Book of Torture.* 1961. (BRG)

Miller, Henry. *Tropic of Cancer.* 1961.

Miller, Henry. *Tropic of Capricorn.* 1961.

Odier, Daniel. *The Job: Interviews with William Burroughs.* Revised and enlarged edition. 1974. (BRG)

O'Hara, Frank. *Meditations in an Emergency.* 1957. (BRG)

Olson, Charles. *The Distances: Poems.* 1960. (GRD)

Olson, Charles. *Human Universe and Other Essays.* 1967. (GRD)

Rechy, John. *City of Night.* Cover photograph by Richard Seaver. 1963. (BRG)

Reynolds, Frank. *Freewheelin Frank, Secretary of the Angels,* as told to Michael McClure. 1967. (BRG)

Sanders, Ed. *Shards of God.* 1970. (BRG)

Selby, Hubert, Jr. *Last Exit to Brooklyn.* 1964. (GRD)

Tyler, Parker. *Underground Film: A Critical History.* 1969.

Woolf, Douglas. *Fade Out.* 1959.

*Evergreen Review 2
(1957): "San
Francisco Scene"
issue. Cover
photograph by
Fred Lyon.*

Evergreen Review

*Barney Rosset,
with Donald Allen for nos. 1–6*

*New York City
1957–1973*

Evergreen Review.

Nos. 1–97 (1957–1973).

BRG has: complete file.

In 1957, with the backing of Grove Press, Barney Rosset and Donald Allen began editing *Evergreen Review*, whose early issues reveal "preoccupations with European philosophical and political debates, an enthusiasm for relatively accessible forms of American and European mainstream literary experimentalism and a compulsion to challenge censorship by publishing old and new 'great outlaw masterpieces.'" The first issue included work by Jean-Paul Sartre, Samuel Beckett, and Henri Michaux as well as an article on *Lady Chatterley's Lover*. The second issue, the famous "San Francisco Scene" issue, featured Allen Ginsberg, Michael McClure, Jack Kerouac, Kenneth Rexroth, Robert Duncan, Lawrence Ferlinghetti, Gregory Corso, and others. *Evergreen Review* was typically published in print runs exceeding 100,000 copies and thus was able to deliver the "underground" to a large audience. To many, particularly those waiting in the wings in small-town (and even not-so-small-town) America, *Evergreen Review* broadcast the first stirrings of the counterculture that would flourish within a few short years. Donald Allen left *Evergreen* after the sixth issue, and one can chart the magazine's gradual decline from that point. Although the magazine continued into the 1970s, the editorial movement was toward soft-focus nude photo-essays and pornographic stories, albeit printed alongside the staples, among them, Beckett.

Black Sparrow Press

John Martin

Los Angeles, Santa Barbara, and Santa Rosa
1966–

David Meltzer, *Round the Poem Box, Rustic & Domestic Home Movies for Stan & Jane Brakhage* (1969). Cover by David Meltzer.

Sparrow. Santa Barbara. Nos. 1–72 (October 1972–September 1978) (each issue devoted to the work of a single author).

RBK has: complete file.

Black Sparrow books include:

Antin, David. *Code of Flag Behavior.* 1968. (BRG)

Dawson, Fielding. *Krazy Kat, The Unveiling and Other Stories.* Cover collage by the author. 1969. (GRD)

Dorn, Edward. *Gunslinger. Book I.* 1968. (GRD)

Dorn, Edward. *Gunslinger. Book II.* 1969. (GRD)

Duncan, Robert. *Epilogos.* 1967. (BRG)

Duncan, Robert. *Tribunals, Passages 31–35.* 1970. (BRG)

Enslin, Theodore. *The Median Flow: Poems 1943–1973.* 1975. (RBK)

Eshleman, Clayton. *Indiana.* Cover by Robert Indiana. 1969. (GRD)

Grossinger, Richard. *Solar Journal (Oecological Sections).* 1970. (GRD)

Kelly, Robert. *Finding the Measure.* Linoleum cut by the printer, Graham Mackintosh. 1968. (BRG)

Koch, Kenneth. *When the Sun Tries to Go On.* Cover by Larry Rivers. 1969. (BRG)

Kyger, Joanne. *Places to Go.* Illustrations by Jack Boyce. 1970. (BRG)

Loewinsohn, Ron. *L'Autre.* 1967. (BRG)

Loewinsohn, Ron. *Lying Together, Turning the Head & Shifting the Weight, The Produce District & Other Places, Moving: A Spring Poem.* 1967. (BRG)

Mac Low, Jackson. *22 Light Poems.* 1968. (GRD)

Malanga, Gerard. *The Last Benedetta Poems.* Cover photograph by the author. 1969. (GRD)

McClure, Michael. *Little Odes & The Raptors.* 1969. (BRG)

Meltzer, David. *Luna.* Cover by Wallace Berman. 1970. (BRG)

Meltzer, David. *Round the Poem Box: Rustic & Domestic Home Movies for Stan & Jane Brakhage.* Cover by David Meltzer. 1969. (BRG)

Perhaps the most familiar of all the literary small presses, Black Sparrow began life with the money John Martin got from selling (for $50,000) his collection of modern literature, which he had purchased over a period of fifteen years (primarily through trading the collection of more classical books he had inherited from his father). The first six publications of the press were broadsides (five of them by Charles Bukowski, who is published to this day by the press). The first book was Ron Loewinsohn's *L'Autre*. In an essay included in Brad Morrow and Seamus Cooney's *Bibliography of the Publications of the Black Sparrow Press* (1981), poet Robert Kelly assesses the press that printed so much of his own work: "How much of these past two decades is represented in the Black Sparrow checklist? How much of it is still in print? What are the high points? Antin's *Meditations*, Palmer's first book, Dorn's first *Gunslinger*, The Collected Spicer, Blackburn's *Journals*, Grossinger's *Solar Journal*, these stand out for me. The dynamic plurality of our poetry, so aptly and widely reflected by Black Sparrow (publisher of those uncousins Bukowski and Ashbery, Wakoski and Creeley), may go under any day – control freaks are afoot in the land. . . . What has been truest of our time is the variety of means, the variety of textures, the variety of texts leading all the Sacred Ways. These may retract. The liberty of the spirit, always polemic but never doctrinaire, lives a life ever in jeopardy – as it must. The press takes risks, surely; but the biggest risk is the sheer accumulation of alternatives it has struggled to keep before the audience. There are Black Sparrow poets – but they are not a stable, not a uniform cadre of uniform product, often they share no other contact but that press."

David and Tina Meltzer, San Francisco, 1969. Photograph by Ann Charters.

Logo of Black Sparrow Press, designed by Barbara Martin.

Meltzer, David. *Six. Drawings by the author.* 1976. (BRG)

Morgenstern, Christian. *Gallowsongs.* Translated by Jess Collins. 1970. (APP)

Palmer, Michael. *Blake's Newton.* 1972. (GRD)

Palmer, Michael. *The Circular Gates.* 1974. (RBK)

Reznikoff, Charles. *By the Well of the Living & Seeing: New & Selected Poems, 1918–1973.* Edited, and with an introduction, by Seamus Cooney. 1974. (BRG, RBK)

Wakoski, Diane. *The Magellanic Clouds.* 1970.

Yau, John. *Radiant Silhouette: New and Selected Work, 1974–1988.* 1989.

For further information on Black Sparrow, including a bibliography of its publications, the reader is referred to: Bradford Morrow and Seamus Cooney, *A Bibliography of the Black Sparrow Press, 1966–1978* (Santa Barbara: Black Sparrow, 1981).

The Black Mountain Review

Robert Creeley

Palma de Mallorca, Spain, and Black
Mountain, North Carolina
1954–1957

*The Black
Mountain Review,*
vol. 1, no. 1
(Spring 1954).
Cover by Katsué
Kitasono.

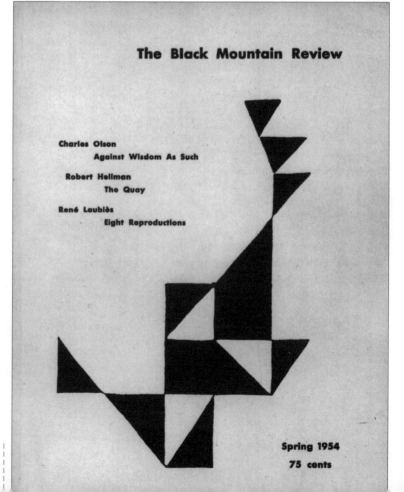

The Black Mountain Review

Charles Olson
    Against Wisdom As Such

Robert Hellman
    The Quay

René Laubiès
    Eight Reproductions

Spring 1954
75 cents

From 1933 to 1956, Black Mountain College flourished as a unique experimental college and community in a remote North Carolina valley. A local resident remembered the college people as "Godless eccentrics who lived in open dormitories and ran around in shorts and blue jeans," but poet Robert Creeley recalls the openness and self-determination of those at the school, where there was often a one-to-one ratio of students to teachers. Charles Olson, Josef Albers, Eric Bentley, Buckminster Fuller, John Cage, Merce Cunningham, Franz Kline, Willem de Kooning, Robert Rauschenberg, Robert Duncan, Fielding Dawson, and Francine du Plessix Gray were only some of those. *The Black Mountain Review*, printed in Palma de Mallorca where Creeley was producing his Divers Press books, developed from the friendship in daily correspondence between Creeley and Black Mountain Rector Charles Olson, who thought a quality literary journal might help increase enrollment. Editorially, Creeley followed advice given him earlier by Ezra Pound: "He suggested I get at least four others, on whom I could depend unequivocally for material, and to make their work the mainstay of the magazine's form. But then, he said, let the rest of it, roughly half, be as various and hogwild as possible. . . ." Olson's poem "On First Looking Out of La Cosa's Eyes" led off the first issue, which also included Olson's long essay on Robert Duncan, entitled "Against Wisdom as Such," and poems by Paul Blackburn, who, along with Louis Zukofsky, Denise Levertov, and Robert Duncan, became the core of the magazine. Distribution was difficult, and effected mainly by Jonathan Williams, who hauled the *Review* around with his Jargon publications, or by Blackburn, who pushed it on vendors in New York. A dramatic feature of all seven issues of *The Black Mountain Review* was the inclusion of reproductions of visual work. Each issue included at least one portfolio (8 pages out of 64 for each of the first four issues, for instance). The second issue included "Mayan Heads" by Charles Olson, which introduced photographs of exquisite Mayan pottery ("because they refresh us"). Other issues reproduced work from Franz Kline and Jess Collins, as well as photographs by Aaron Siskind and Harry Callahan. The standard cover for the first four issues was designed by Katsué Kitasono, with Black Mountaineers John Altoon, Dan Rice, and Edward Corbett being responsible for the final three issues (these latter in a smaller and thicker format of over 200 pages each). The seventh and prophetic last issue included work by Allen Ginsberg ("America"), Jack Kerouac, Michael McClure, Philip Whalen, and Gary Snyder and a chapter from "William Lee's" *Naked Lunch*.

Charles Olson, San
Francisco, ca. 1957.
Photograph by
Harry Redl.

"It is difficult… to appreciate the excitement (in certain very limited circles, of
course) produced by the appearance of the *Review*. Today 'The Black
Mountain Poets' have far less trouble getting their work published:
and their counterparts in unfashion among more recent generations
of poets have such a variety of mimeographed (sometimes even
glossy) outlets, that it's hard to recall the lack of reputation and lack
of publishing opportunities characteristic of the literary scene during those damp, encased, mid-fifties McCarthyite years. Yes, there
had been *Origin* – and after *The Black Mountain Review* folded in 1957,
there was again to be an outlet for innovation: Gil Sorrentino's *Neon*,
LeRoi Jones's *Yugen*, Ron Padgett's *White Dove Review*. But not until
the early sixties – coincidentally with the breaking open of so many
areas of American life – was there to be a variety, happily almost a
tumult, of corresponding energies and outlets."

— Martin Duberman, *Black Mountain: An Exploration in Community*
  (New York: Dutton, 1972)

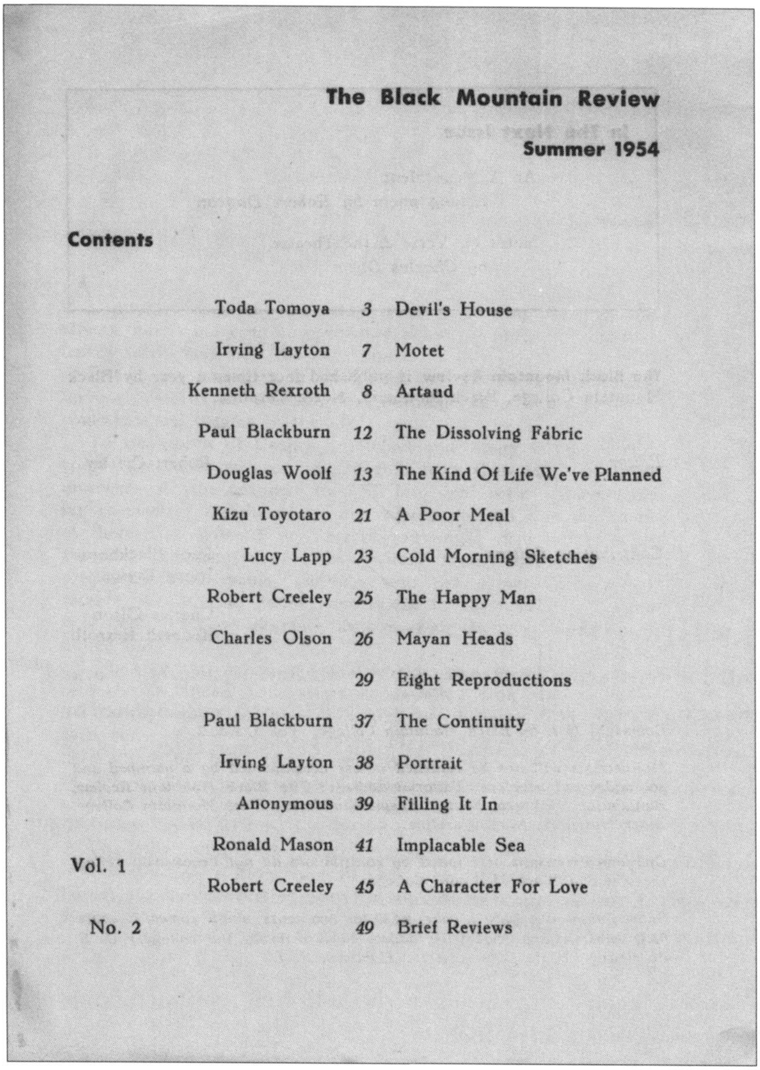

The Black Mountain Review, vol. 1, no. 2 (Summer 1954). Title page.

The Black Mountain Review

Summer 1954

Contents

Vol. 1

No. 2

The Black Mountain Review. Nos. 1–7 (Spring 1954– Autumn 1957).

BRG has: complete file.

Divers Press

Robert Creeley

Banalbufar, Mallorca

1953–1955

Charles Olson, *Mayan Letters* (1953 [i.e., 1954]).

"What I felt was the purpose of the press has much to do with my initial sense of [*The Black Mountain Review*] also. For me, and the other writers who came to be involved, it was a place defined by our own activity and accomplished altogether by ourselves – a place wherein we might make evident what we, as writers, had found to be significant, both for ourselves and for that world – no doubt often vague to us indeed – we hoped our writing might enter ... there had to be both a press and a magazine absolutely specific to one's own commitments and possibilities. Nothing short of that was good enough."

— Robert Creeley, Introduction to the AMS Press reprint (1969) of *The Black Mountain Review*

Raising pigeons and chickens on a farm in Littleton, New Hampshire, Robert Creeley heard, through "a fluke of airwaves," poet Cid Corman's weekly radio program from Boston, "This Is Poetry." Inspired, Creeley read on the program during a weekend in 1950 when he was showing chickens at the Boston poultry show. And so began a network of literary friendships that inspired a generation of poets ("A knows B, B knows C, and there begins to be increasing focus. And I think that we were curiously lucky that that focus was not literally a question of whether we were all living together or not."). Galvanized, Creeley tried unsuccessfully to start his own little magazine, but ended up giving Cid Corman at *Origin* much of the material he had collected, including work by Denise Levertov, Paul Blackburn, and Charles Olson, to whom the first issue of *Origin* was devoted. Against this background it is not surprising that Creeley, called "The Figure of Outward" by Olson, whom he met through Corman, would himself venture forth as a publisher in 1953 with Martin Seymour-Smith's *All Devils Fading*. In addition to two volumes by Paul Blackburn and one each by Larry Eigner and Robert Duncan, in 1954 Creeley issued a volume of poems by Canadian poet Irving Layton and Japanese poet Katué Kitasono's self-translated poems, *Black Rain*. The last volume he published, in 1955, was American novelist Douglas Woolf's "painful rite of passage," *The Hypocritic Days*. Creeley published his own *The Kind of Act of* in 1953 and *A Snarling Garden of Xmas Verses* and *The Gold Diggers*, both in 1954. In 1982, Creeley wistfully remembered the serious, edgy nature of the press: "I don't recall that the Divers Press paid anybody anything – it was my first wife's modest income that kept any of it going – and so our choices had to be limited to writers as existentially defined as ourselves."

Divers Press books include:

Blackburn, Paul. *The Dissolving Fabric.* 1955. (BRG)

Creeley, Robert. *The Gold Diggers.* 1954. (RBK)

Creeley, Robert. *The Kind of Act of.* 1953.

Creeley, Robert. *Printing Is Cheap in Mallorca.* 1953.

Creeley, Robert. *A Snarling Garland of Xmas Verses.* 1954.

Duncan, Robert. *Caesar's Gate.* Cover collage by Jess (Collins). 1955. (BRG)

Eigner, Larry. *From the Sustaining Air.* 1953. (BRG)

Kitasono, Katsué. *Black Rain: Poems & Drawings.* 1954.

Layton, Irving. *The Blue Propeller.* 1955.

Layton, Irving. *In the Midst of My Fever.* 1954.

Olson, Charles. *Mayan Letters.* 1953 [i.e., 1954]. (RBK)

Proensa: from the Provençal of Guillem de Peitau, Arnaut de Marueill, Raimbautz de Vaqueiras, Sordello, Bernart de Ventadorn, Peire Vidal, Bertran de Born. Selected and edited by Paul Blackburn. 1953. (BRG)

Seymour-Smith, Martin. *All Devils Fading.* 1953.

Woolf, Douglas. *The Hypocritic Days.* 1955.

Origin

Cid Corman

*Dorchester, Boston, and Ashland,
Massachusetts; Orono, Maine;
and Kyoto, Japan
1951–1984*

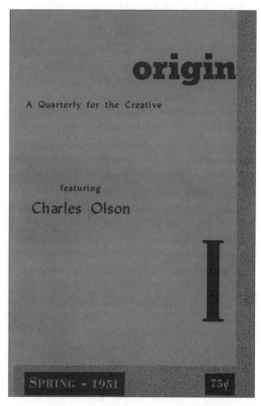

Origin 1 (Spring 1951): Charles Olson issue.

Origin. Nos. 1–20 (Spring 1951–Winter 1957); second series, nos. 1–14 (April 1961–July 1964); third series, nos. 1–20 (April 1966–1971); fourth series, nos. 1–20 (October 1977–July 1982); fifth series, nos. 1–4 (Fall 1983–Fall 1984). First series published from Dorchester, Mass.; second and third series from Kyoto, Japan; fourth series from Boston; fifth series from Orono, Maine.

BRG has: first and second series. GRD has: complete file.

Origin Press books include:

Bronk, William. *Light and Dark.* Illustrations by Ryohei Tanaka. 1956. (BRG)

Corman, Cid. *Cool Gong.* 1959. (BRG)

Corman, Cid. *The Descent from Daimonji.* 1959. (BRG)

Corman, Cid. *For Good.* 1964.

Corman, Cid. *For Instance.* 1962. (BRG)

Corman, Cid. *Hearth.* 1968. (BRG)

Around 1950, while living in New Hampshire, Robert Creeley abandoned plans for his yet-to-be-launched little magazine. Among the material he had already gathered was work from poet Cid Corman, who was then hosting a weekly radio show in Boston entitled "This Is Poetry." Corman expressed his disappointment over the loss of the magazine to a listener, one Evelyn Shoolman, who responded by offering to back Corman in a magazine of his own if he wished. Thus began *Origin: a quarterly for the creative*. Material gathered by Creeley along with work brought in by Corman helped to establish, in Creeley's words, "a Place defined by our own activity." The first issue featured a major section of work by Charles Olson, then barely published, and established the presence of an important magazine for new writing. As Olson wrote to Corman, *Origin* gave him "the fullest satisfaction i have ever had from print, lad, the fullest. And i am so damned moved by yr push, pertinence, accuracy, taste, that it is wholly inadequate to say thanks." The second issue featured Robert Creeley. *Origin* published a wide range of writers working in poetry and prose – contributions to the first series of issues included work by Paul Blackburn, Robert Duncan, Ed Dorn, Margaret Avison, Denise Levertov, Theodore Enslin, Larry Eigner, Irving Layton, William Bronk, William Carlos Williams, Wallace Stevens, and Gael Turnbull, and translations of Antonin Artaud, Gottfried Benn, Federico García Lorca, Henri Michaux, and Giuseppe Ungaretti among many others. The possibilities for writing explored and enacted in the pages of *Origin* exerted considerable influence in the postwar literary scene – indeed, as Paul Blackburn wrote in the early 1960s, "*Origin* and *The Black Mountain Review*: What other solid ground was there in the last decade?"

Corman, Cid. *In Good Time.* 1964. (BRG)

Corman, Cid. *In No Time.* Illustrations by Will Peterson. 1963. (BRG)

Corman, Cid. *The Marches & Other Poems.* Cover by Edwina Curtis. 1957. (BRG)

Corman, Cid. *The Responses.* Cover by Stasha Halpern. 1956. (BRG)

Corman, Cid. *Stances and Distances.* Cover by Edwina Curtis. 1957. (BRG)

Corman, Cid. *Sun Rock Man.* 1962. (BRG)

Corman, Cid. *A Table in Provence.* Drawings by Barnet Rubinstein. 1959. (GRD)

Corman, Cid. *Unless.* 1975. (BRG)

Enslin, Theodore. *The Work Proposed.* 1958.

Snyder, Gary. *Riprap.* 1959. (BRG, RBK)

Turnbull, Gael. *Bjarni Spike-Helgi's Son and Other Poems.* 1956. (GRD)

Zukofsky, Louis. *"A,"* *1–12.* Essay on the poetry by the author and a final note by William Carlos Williams. 1959. (BRG)

Zukofsky, Louis. *It Was.* 1961. (BRG)

For further information on *Origin*, the reader is referred to: Cid Corman, ed., *The Gist of Origin, 1951–1971: An Anthology* (New York: Grossman Publishers, 1975).

The Jargon Society

Jonathan Williams

Highlands, North Carolina
(principally)
1951–

Robert Creeley, *A Form of Women* (1959). Cover photograph by Robert Schiller. Published in association with Corinth Books.

Jargon Society books include:

Broughton, James. *A Long Undressing: Collected Poems, 1949–1969.* Cover photograph by Imogen Cunningham. 1971. (Jargon 55.) (GRD)

Creeley, Robert. *All That Is Lovely in Men.* Drawings by Dan Rice. 1955. (Jargon 10.) (GRD)

Creeley, Robert. *The Immoral Proposition.* Drawings by Rene Laubies. 1953. (Jargon 8.) (GRD)

Davenport, Guy. *Do You Have a Poem Book on E. E. Cummings.* 1969. (Jargon 67.)

Davenport, Guy. *Flowers and Leaves.* Cover photograph by Ralph Eugene Meatyard. 1966. (Jargon 46.) (BRG)

Duncan, Robert. *Letters, Poems mcmliii–mcmlvi.* Drawings by the author. 1958. (Jargon 14.) (BRG)

Eigner, Larry. *On My Eyes.* Note by Denise Levertov. Photographs by Harry Callahan. 1960. (Jargon 36.) (BRG)

Johnson, Ronald. *A Line of Poetry, a Row of Trees.* Drawings by Thomas George. 1964. (Jargon 42.)

Johnson, Ronald. *The Spirit Walks, the Rocks Will Talk: Eccentric Translations from Two Eccentrics.* Vignettes by Guy Davenport. 1969. (Jargon 72.)

Levertov, Denise. *Overland to the Islands.* 1958. (Jargon 19.) (BRG)

Loy, Mina. *Lunar Baedeker & Time-Tables: Selected Poems.* Introductions by William Carlos Williams, Kenneth Rexroth, Denise Levertov. Drawings by Emerson Woelffer. 1958. (Jargon 23.) (BRG)

McClure, Michael. *Passage.* Cover by Jonathan Williams. 1956. (Jargon 20.) (BRG)

Niedecker, Lorine. *T & G: The Collected Poems.* Plant prints by A. Doyle Moore. 1968. (Jargon 48.) (BRG)

Jonathan Williams describes himself as "a poet, essayist, publisher of the Jargon Society, photographer, occasional hiker of long distances, and aging scold." Jargon's first booklet, which contained a poem by Williams with an engraving by David Ruff, was published in San Francisco in 1951. The press blossomed at Black Mountain College where its peripatetic director moved to study photography with Harry Callahan and Aaron Siskind. Jargon's second publication was a poem by Joel Oppenheimer ("The Dancer") with a drawing by Robert Rauschenberg. Over the next several years the press would publish Kenneth Patchen, Robert Creeley, *The Maximus Poems* by Charles Olson, more work by Williams, Louis Zukofsky, Denise Levertov, Michael McClure, Mina Loy, Robert Duncan, Fielding Dawson, Irving Layton, Guy Davenport, Paul Metcalf – the list goes on and on. The Jargon Society married excellence in the art of book making with important writing, to become what critic Hugh Kenner aptly called "the custodian of snowflakes." When asked why he has published what he has, Jonathan Williams replied, "For *pleasure* surely. I am a stubborn, mountaineer Celt with an orphic, priapic, sybaritic streak that must have come to me, along with H. P. Lovecraft, from Outer Cosmic Infinity. Or maybe Flash Gordon brought it from Mongo? Jargon has allowed me to fill my shelves with books I cared for as passionately as I cared for the beloved books of childhood – which I still have: *Oz, The Hobbit, The Wind in the Willows, Dr. Doolittle*, Ransome, Kipling, et al."

Olson, Charles. *Maximus 1–10*. Calligraphy by Jonathan Williams. 1953. (Jargon 7.) (RBK)

Olson, Charles. *Maximus 11–22*. Calligraphy by Jonathan Williams. 1956. (Jargon 9.) (RBK)

Oppenheimer, Joel. *The Dancer*. Drawing by Robert Rauschenberg. 1951. (Jargon 2.)

Oppenheimer, Joel. *The Dutiful Son*. 1956. (Jargon 16.) (GRD)

Patchen, Kenneth. *Fables and Other Little Tales*. 1953. (Jargon 6.)

Sorrentino, Gilbert. *The Darkness Surrounds Us*. Cover by Fielding Dawson. 1960. (Not in series.) (BRG)

Williams, Jonathan. *Garbage Litters the Iron Face of the Sun's Child*. 1951. (Jargon 1.)

Williams, Jonathan. *Red/Gray*. Drawings and declaration by Paul Ellsworth. 1952. (Jargon 3.)

Zukofsky, Louis. *Some Time: Short Poems*. 1956. (Jargon 15.) (BRG)

Jargon also published the following in association with Corinth Books:

Brown, Bob. *1450–1950*. 1959. (Jargon 29.) (GRD)

Creeley, Robert. *A Form of Women*. Photograph by Robert Schiller. 1959. (Jargon 33.) (BRG)

Olson, Charles. *The Maximus Poems*. 1960. (BRG)

Zukofsky, Louis. *A Test of Poetry*. 1964. Originally published in 1948 by the Objectivist Press. (BRG)

For a more complete listing of the early Jargon publications, the reader is referred to: Millicent Bell, "The Jargon Idea," *Books at Brown* 19 (May 1963), reprinted separately, 1963; and to J. M. Edelstein, *A Jargon Society Checklist 1951–1979*, published in conjunction with an exhibition of Jargon publications at Books & Co., New York City, March 15–April 14, 1979.

Hawk's Well Press/ Poems from the Floating World

Jerome Rothenberg

New York City
1958–1964

Jerome Rothenberg, *White Sun, Black Sun* (1960).
Cover drawing by Mildred Gendell.

Poems from the Floating World.
Nos. 1–5 (1959–1963).

BRG has: complete file.

Hawk's Well Press books include:

Buber, Martin. *Tales of Angels, Spirits and Demons.* Translated by Jerome Rothenberg and David Antin. 1958.

Faust, Seymour. *The Lovely Quarry.* 1958. (GRD)

Gunn, Thom. *Fighting Terms.* 1958. (BRG)

Jess [Collins]. *O!* 1960. (BRG)

Kelly, Robert. *Armed Descent.* Cover design by Jerome Rothenberg from an Aztec drawing in the Codex Mendoza. 1961. (BRG)

Owens, Rochelle. *Futz.* 1961. (GRD)

Rothenberg, Jerome. *Black Sun, White Sun.* Cover drawing by Mildred Gendell. 1960. (BRG)

Rothenberg, Jerome. *Sightings* / Robert Kelly. *Lunes.* Drawings by Amy Mendelson. 1964. (GRD)

Wakoski, Diane. *Coins & Coffins.* Cover by Jor. 1962. (BRG)

Hawk's Well Press, under the irrepressible Jerome Rothenberg, published five issues of *Poems from the Floating World* and half a dozen small books of big poetry, most of them printed in Ireland, including, amazingly, the first books of Rothenberg, Robert Kelly, and Diane Wakoski. Clues to the territory mapped by *Poems from the Floating World* are contained in the poems published, as well as in the short, unattributed statements (presumably the words of the editor) that appeared in each of the first three issues. For example, inside the front cover of issue 3 one reads: "The poem is the record of a movement from perception to vision. Poetic form is the pattern of that movement thru space and time. The vehicle of movement is passion-speaking-thru-things. The condition of movement is freedom. The deep image is the content of vision emerging in the poem." The magazine's five issues included work by James Wright, Gunnar Ekelof, Robert Bly, André Breton, Rothenberg, Paul Celan, Denise Levertov, Pablo Neruda, Robert Creeley, Gary Snyder, David Antin, Robert Kelly, Philip Lamantia, Robert Duncan, Anselm Hollo, and Jackson Mac Low. Rothenberg went on to become a fine and prolific poet, translator, and anthologist. His first book, a collaboration with David Antin (who along with David Witt was a co-founder of Hawk's Well), was a translation of Martin Buber's *Tales of Angels, Spirits and Demons.* In this work, published by Hawk's Well in 1958, one can see Rothenberg turning the ground that will result in the remarkable group of anthologies that have made him a major force in contemporary poetry; they include *Revolution of the Word: A New Gathering of American Avant Garde Poetry, 1914–1945* (1974) and, most recently, *Poems for the Millennium: The University of California Book of Modern & Postmodern Poetry* (edited with Pierre Joris; 2 volumes, 1995–98). His

sensitivity to a wide variety of traditions and enthusiasm for the "forgotten" have been motivating sources since his young adulthood, as he notes in the "Pre-Face" to *Revolution of the Word*: "It was 1948 & by year's end I was seventeen. I had been coming into poetry for two years. My head was filled with Stein & Cummings, later with Williams, Pound, the French Surrealists, the Dada poets who made 'pure sound' three decades earlier. Blues. American Indian things from Densmore. Cathay. Bible, Shakespeare, Whitman. Jewish liturgies. Dali & Lorca were ferocious possibilities. Joyce was incredible to any of our first sightings of his work. The thing was to get off on it, to hear one's mind, learn one's own voice. But the message clear & simple was to move. To change. To create one's self & thus one's poetry. A process."

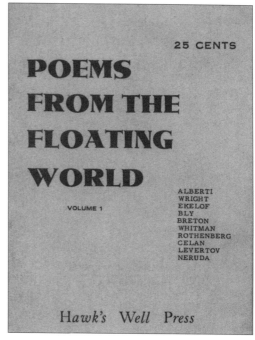

Poems from the Floating World 1 (1959).

Some/thing

Jerome Rothenberg and
David Antin

New York City
1965–1968

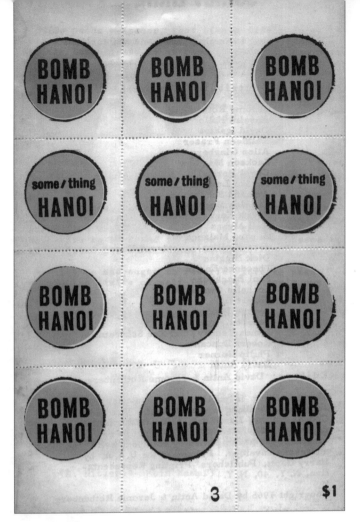

Some/thing 3 (1966).
Cover by Andy Warhol.

David Antin's first separate book was in preparation at Hawk's Well Press (*Definitions* was ultimately published by Caterpillar in 1967) when he joined with veteran poet and editor Jerome Rothenberg to create *Some/thing*. The first issue, published by Rothenberg's Hawk's Well Press in New York in the Spring of 1965, leads off with "Aztec Definitions: Found Poems from the Florentine Codex," translated from Bernardino de Sahagun's *General History of the Things of New Spain*. The issue also includes work by Paul Blackburn, Anselm Hollo, Diane Wakoski, and Rothenberg, deep image poets all, and, on red paper, "The Presidents of the United States," the first series, including Washington through Fillmore, of one of Jackson Mac Low's chance compositions. Carolee Schneemann's "Meat Joy," with pictures from the performance at the Judson Memorial Theater in October 1964, is the highlight of the second issue, which includes a cover picture of a sculpture by Robert Morris. Issue three, with a yellow perforated sticker cover by Andy Warhol, is devoted to "A Vietnam Assemblage." Published in 1966, early in the Vietnam War, it includes Allen Ginsberg's long poem "Who Be Kind To" ("Be kind to yourself, it is only one and perishable of many on the planet") and works by Mac Low and others, interspersed with quotations from newspapers, magazines, and photo captions from the Associated Press and elsewhere. The last, double issue of Summer 1968, with a cover by Fluxus artist George Maciunas, integrated the deep image poets with the performance poets; it includes Clayton Eshleman's "Travel Journal in Peru," from October of 1965, as well as five poems by Margaret Randall, editor of *El Corno Emplumado*, and one by Carol Bergé, editor of *Center*. It also contains Rothenberg's "'Doings' and 'Happenings': Notes on a Performance of the Seneca Eagle Dance." All the issues of *Some/thing* feature a log taken from a Southwestern Indian drawing described by the editors as an emblem for the magazine: "a Pima drawing: of the pathways: searchings: stopping places: where the god has stopped: a wave length: energy: cessation: strife: emergence into: something."

Some/thing. Nos. 1–4/5 (1965–1968).

GRD has: complete file.

Alcheringa

Jerome Rothenberg and Dennis Tedlock

New York City and Boston
1970–1980

Alcheringa. Nos. 1–5
(1970–1973); new series,
vol. 1, no. 1–vol. 4, no. 2
(1975–1980). 13 issues.
Some issues contain
phonodiscs.

BRG has: new series, vol. 1,
no. 2. GRD has: complete
file.

Also issued was: Jerome
Rothenberg. *Gift Event 2:
From Alcheringa. Midwinter
Poem 1973.* Illuminated by
Michael Manfredo after a
traditional Seneca Indian
beaver clan mask. Folded
sheet. 1973.

From the Arunta of Australia comes the word "Alcheringa," "The Eternal Dream Time, The Dreaming of a sacred heroic time long ago when man and nature came to be, a kind of narrative of things that once happened." The ethnopoetics magazine *Alcheringa*, "A First Magazine of the World's Tribal Poetries," was published from 1970 to 1980 and edited by Jerome Rothenberg and Dennis Tedlock (Rothenberg left the magazine in 1976 to found *New Wilderness Letter*). Their intention was to publish "transcriptions of oral poems from living traditions, ancient texts with oral roots, and modern experiments in oral poetry. There will be songs, chants, prayers, visions and dreams, sacred narratives, fictional narratives, histories, ritual scenarios, praises, namings, word games, riddles, proverbs, sermons. These will take the shape of performable scripts (meant to be read aloud rather than silently), experiments in typography, diagrams, and insert disc recordings." The editors encouraged against literal translation and toward innovation in transcribing what are often works located in an oral tradition. The first issue includes, in translation, work from the Seneca and the Quiche Maya; from New Guinea; and from the Serbo-Croatian. Over the years, contributors included Jackson Mac Low, Armand Schwerner, Jaime de Angulo, Anne Waldman, Gary Snyder, Charles Olson, Clayton Eshleman, W. S. Merwin, Nathaniel Tarn, Anselm Hollo, Simon Ortiz, and others, who presented their own work as well as transcriptions from a broad range of the world's tribal poetries including Eskimo, Hebrew Tribal poetry, Black Oral poetry, hunting and gathering songs, songs of ritual license, and much more. As Rothenberg noted, "The poets of ALCHERINGA start with the voice. The essayists will look, ultimately, to the very origins of poetry. ALCHERINGA will be radical – that is, going to the center – in approaching the Word."

Alcheringa, new series, vol. 1, no. 2 (1975).

"Ethnopoetics — my coinage, in a fairly obvious way, circa 1967 – refers to an attempt to investigate on a transcultural scale the range of possible poetries that had not only been imagined but put into practice by other human beings. It was premised on the perception that western definitions of poetry & art were no longer, indeed, had never been, sufficient & that our continued reliance on them was distorting our view both of the larger human experience & of our own possibilities within it. The focus was not so much inter*national* as inter*cultural with a stress* ... on those stateless & classless societies that an earlier ethnology had classified as 'primitive.' That the poetry & art of those cultures were complex in themselves & in their interconnections with each other was a first point that I found it necessary to assert.... *There are no primitive languages.*"

— Jerome Rothenberg, "Ethnopoetics & Politics/The Politics of Ethnopoetics" in Charles Bernstein, ed., *The Politics of Poetic Form: Poetry and Public Policy* (New York: Roof, 1990)

New Wilderness Letter

Jerome Rothenberg

New York City

1977–1982

*New Wilderness
Letter* 11 (1982).
Cover image by
Michael Gibbs.

A follow-up to *Alcheringa* and an offshoot of the New Wilderness Foundation (formed by Jerome Rothenberg and Charlie Morrow to "explore the relation between old & new forms of art-making"), *New Wilderness Letter,* edited by Rothenberg, offered the following opening statement: "The editor – a poet by inclination & practice – recognizes *poesis* in all arts & sciences, all human thoughts & acts directed toward such ends: the participation in what the surrealist master André Breton called a 'sacred action' or what Gary Snyder defined as the 'real work of modern man: to uncover the inner structure & actual boundaries of the mind.' The New Wilderness Letter will therefore not be specialized & limited by culture or profession but will be a report, largely through the creative work itself, of where that process takes us." That process led to some very interesting places indeed. Issues were devoted to such topics as the "role of poets/artists as 'technicians of the sacred,'" "writing and reading as co-existent with human origins," "poetics and performance," "dream-works," and, for issue 11, co-edited with David Guss, "The Book, Spiritual Instrument." Among the diverse contributors to the various issues are Carolee Schneemann, Barbara Einzig, Allen Ginsberg, Pauline Oliveros, Michael McClure, Allan Kaprow, Edmond Jabès, Dick Higgins, David Meltzer, George Herms, Howard Norman, Linda

Montano, and Jackson Mac Low. Eleven regular issues were published between January 1977 and December 1982, at which time *New Wilderness Letter* merged with *Wch Way.* Jerome Rothenberg characterized the role of *New Wilderness Letter* with these words: "There is a primal book as there is a primal voice, & it is the task of our poetry & art to recover it – in our minds & in the world at large."

New Wilderness Letter.
Nos. 1–13 (1977–1985)
(nos. 12 and 13 issued
with *Wch Way* nos. 5 and 6).

GRD has: nos. 1–11.

Also issued was: Jerome
Rothenberg. *A Poem in Yellow
After Tristan Tzara.* Metal felt-
tipped pen. ca. 1980.

Caterpillar

Clayton Eshleman

*New York City and Sherman Oaks,
California
1967–1973*

Caterpillar 12 (July 1970). Cover collage by
Robin Blaser.

Caterpillar. Nos. 1–20
(1967–1973). 20 issues
in 19.

BRG has: complete file.

Caterpillar books include:

Alexander, D. *Terms
of Articulation.* 1967.
(Caterpillar 7.) (GRD)

Antin, David. *Definitions.*
1967. (Caterpillar 6.)
(GRD)

Blackburn, Paul. *Sing-Song.*
1967. (Caterpillar 4.)
Published with the
Asphodel Bookshop,
Cleveland.

Césaire, Aimé. *State of
the Union.* Translated from
the French by Clayton
Eshleman and Dennis Kelly.
1966. (Caterpillar 1.) (SC)

Eshleman, Clayton.
*Lachrymae Mateo: 3 Poems
for Christmas 1966.* 1966.
(Caterpillar 3.) (BRG)

Eshleman, Clayton. *Walks.*
1967. (Caterpillar 10.)

Mac Low, Jackson.
August Light Poems.
Cover by Iris Lezak. 1967.
(Caterpillar 9.) (BRG)

Sampieri, Frank. *Crystals.*
1967. (Caterpillar 5.)
(GRD)

Vas Dias, Robert.
The Counted. 1967.
(Caterpillar 8.) (BRG)

Caterpillar was started by Clayton Eshleman as a series of chapbooks by such writers as Jackson Mac Low, David Antin, Paul Blackburn, and Louis Zukofsky. "The Caterpillar Glyph," an image of a small napalmed Vietnamese girl, was printed on the cover with the statement "until the end of the war this black caterpillar," revealing the outspoken and controversial stance taken by Eshleman as an editor. *Caterpillar,* "a magazine of the leaf, a gathering of the tribes," began publication in October 1967. Commercially produced and substantial in size, it provided considerable space, over the course of its twenty issues, for work by a wide range of younger writers and artists as well as many of those associated with its precursors, *The Black Mountain Review* and *Origin.* Says Eshleman: "I saw a poetry magazine as a granary of sorts, where writing could be stored until it was to be consumed or consummated in a book, a midpoint between its inception and its ultimate form." *Caterpillar*'s special attention to translation included a "test of translation" in which differing versions of a poem were set "side by side and with a minimum of comment, [to] encourage the reader to measure them as articulations of the original poem." Works of Vallejo, Montale, Cavafy, and Rilke, among others, were thus presented. The magazine was also attuned to important work in film, visual art, music, and performance; it was not unusual to find film stills by Carolee Schneemann or Stan Brakhage; or drawings and collages by Nancy Spero, Jess Collins, Leon Golub, Robert LaVigne, or Wallace Berman. Issue 12 devoted some 150 pages to work by Jack Spicer. Other regular contributors included Gary Snyder, Robert Duncan, Margaret Randall, Cid Corman, Diane Wakoski, Robert Kelly, and Jerome Rothenberg. On the name of the magazine, Eshleman recalled, "That special word was given me by Will Petersen on a Kyoto street corner in 1963, when he quoted Blake's couplet 'The Caterpillar on the Leaf / Repeats to thee thy Mother's grief.'"

Wch Way

*Jed Rasula; later Jed
Rasula and Don Byrd*

*Bloomington, Indiana;
Los Angeles; and
Albany, New York
1975–1985*

Wch Way 4 (Summer 1982).

The Presses and Publications

"BLOOMINGTON YOU ARE REAL DADA" reads the graffiti sign on the wall of an abandoned building in a photograph reproduced in *Wch Way* 1, and the magazine's epigraph is from a 1940 movie starring Errol Flynn and Alexis Smith: "Ride 'em thru town!" Symbolic of postmodern, midwestern intellectualism, *Wch Way* was centered in a group of individuals associated with the venerable landgranted Indiana University who advocated a sophisticated, literary back-to-the-land approach to things poetic. The title of a poem/essay by David Wevill in issue number 1 says it: "We have lost our natural images. All the images we make are twisted, hammered, brilliant." In its first four issues, the magazine presented a variety of long poems and prose works, including the romantic cavalier work of Tom Meyer (of Jargon) as well as selections from George Quasha's poetic sequence "Somapoetics." Transcriptions of discussions among the local members of the poetic community are included under titles such as "Multivocal Moontalk." The third issue (also known as number 2²) includes one of Jackson Mac Low's chance works from 1958, "Haiku, No Haiku," based on a Funk & Wagnall's dictionary and on a poetry anthology edited by Louis Untermeyer. By the fourth issue, Rasula had moved to Los Angeles and been joined by critic and language poet Don Byrd in his editorship; these two occurrences may explain the wild change in contributors for the issue, which includes Clark Coolidge, John Taggart, Barrett Watten, Charles Bernstein, and the Canadians Steve McCaffrey and Christopher Dewdney. The issue begins with Robert Duncan's poetic sequence "Santa Cruz Propositions," prefaced by a statement by the poet: "The authentic text [is] . . . in my case, not the manuscript, which is conceived of as a propositional sketch; and most certainly not the printed version, which represents the work and interpretational notion of someone else, but the present state of the typescript which comes from and is my own working hand and eye as concept ongoing."

Wch Way. Nos. 1–6 (1975–1985) (nos. 5 and 6 issued with *New Wilderness Letter* nos. 12 and 13).

GRD has: nos. 1, 2, 4.

Maps

John Taggart

*Chicago, New York City, and
Newberg, Pennsylvania
1966–1974*

Maps. Nos. 1–6
(1966–1974).

BRG has: nos. 4 (Charles
Olson), 5 (Louis Zukofsky).

"One draws a map to show where one is" reads the motto of *Maps*, edited by poet, translator, and critic John Taggart. Number 1 was issued from Chicago in 1966 and includes an editor's note that defines the purpose of the magazine: "In his *Critique of Pure Reason*, Kant writes of the need for making new maps of man's consciousness *now*, and of the past as seen from that now. The maps would be of those regions just discovered, somewhat known, but not to the extent of the older areas or of the most recent projections. MAPS, then, takes its title and purpose from Kant's observation. These poems are not on the furthermost borders of the avant-garde. They are of the now in the continuum sense of 'being' – eyes open, perhaps screaming, but not leaping out of the present – and occasionally, they are of the past as renovated by those open eyes." The work of Paul Blackburn, Ken Irby, and Clayton Eshleman was featured in the first small issue. Issue 2 (1967), from New York City, was an homage to the sculptor David Smith with contributions from Jerome Rothenberg, Joanne Kyger, Hannah Weiner, Douglas Blazek, Larry Eigner, and others. Issue 3 (1970), from Newberg, Pennsylvania, printed poems for John Coltrane. Issues 4–6 were devoted to Charles Olson, Louis Zukofsky, and Robert Duncan, respectively, with works by and about the poets. Contributors include Hugh Kenner, Ralph Eugene Meatyard, Guy Davenport, Theodore Enslin, Ronald Johnson, Ron Silliman, and many others. *Maps* ceased publication in 1974 with number 6.

Maps 2 (May 1967):
Homage to David Smith.

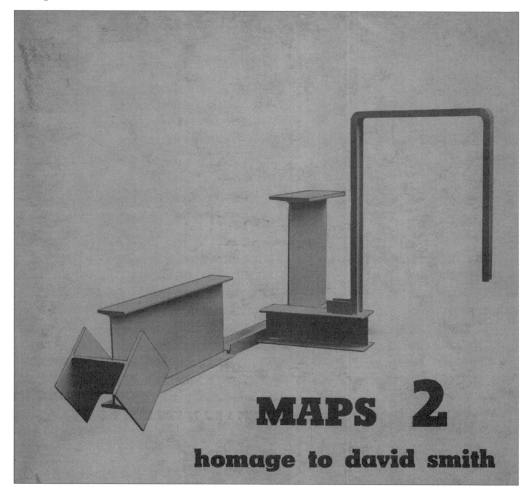

Trobar,
a magazine of the New
American Poetry

*George Economou, Joan Kelly,
and Robert Kelly*

*Brooklyn, New York
1960–1964*

T robar magazine was published in Brooklyn in
only five issues from 1960 to 1964, but it was
tremendously influential in spreading knowledge
about deep image poetry. Deep image poetry,
according to Robert Kelly, is "poetry not necessarily dominated by the image, but in which it is the
rhythm of the images which forms the dominant
movement of the poem." Of the three editors,
Kelly has been the most tireless and enthusiastic
poet, reader, and teacher, exerting a charismatic
influence. He has published nearly thirty-five volumes (his first, *Armed Descent*, was published by
Jerome Rothenberg's Hawk's Well Press) and was
a founding editor of *Chelsea Review* and *Matter* and
a contributing editor to *Caterpillar* and *Alcheringa*.
Kelly co-edited, with Paris Leary, the paperback *A
Controversy of Poets* (1965), which was an entrant in
the poetry anthology wars of the 1960s. Kelly's
essay "Notes on the Poetry of Deep Image," which
appears in *Trobar* 2, is a provocative statement
about an important thread in modern poetry
and is central to the concept of *Trobar* (the name
refers to the Troubadour tradition in Provençal
poetry). The press also issued a series of books,
which included works by Rochelle Owens, Jerome
Rothenberg, Paul Blackburn, and Louis Zukofsky.

Trobar. Nos. 1–5
(1960–1964).

BRG has: no. 3.

Trobar books include:

Blackburn, Paul. *The Nets.*
Cover by Michelle Stuart.
1961. (BRG)

Kelly, Robert. *Round Dances.*
Drawings by Josie Rosenfeld.
1964. (DAN)

Owens, Rochelle. *Not Be
Essence That Cannot Be.* 1961.

Rothenberg, Jerome.
*The Seven Hells of the Jigoku
Zoshi.* 1962.

Zukofsky, Louis.
I's (pronounced eyes).
1963. (BRG)

"...we have to try to see the world in all its natural and contemporary detail as if no differences existed between the seer and the things he sees. To see in this way – through the self (emotively) – results in certain necessary changes on the material emerging in the poem:

"a heightened sense of the emotional contours of objects (their dark qualities, or shadows);

"their free re-association in a manner that would be impossible to descriptive or logical thought, but is here almost unavoidable;

"the sense of these objects (and the poem itself) being informed with a heightened relevance, a quickened sense of life;

"the recognition of the poem as a natural structure arising at once from the act of emotive vision."

— Jerome Rothenberg, from "Why Deep Image?" in *Trobar* 3 (1962)

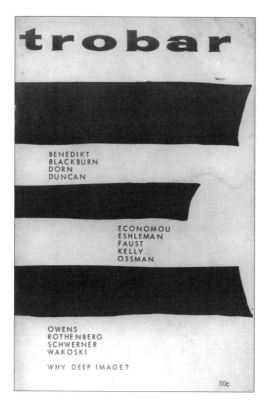

Trobar, a magazine of the New American Poetry 3 (1962).

Matter

Robert Kelly

*Annandale-on-Hudson,
New York*

1963–1966

Robert Kelly, *Twenty
Poems* (1967).

The Presses and Publications

"*Matter* is when it is for the sake of the work, & is the work therein contained, no more. . . . That is my axe now, & I hope the chips fall in a pile fed by other wielders; to get some kindling these cold days," says Robert Kelly in the editorial statement in the first issue. Overlapping only slightly with Kelly's Brooklyn-published little magazine *Trobar*, *Matter* was a newsletter from up the Hudson River, created to produce a sense of literary community and to overcome the isolation created by distance. *Matter* was simply but elegantly produced in four issues of 16–22 pages each, mimeographed on yellow, white, and blue paper, and carefully designed with a poem to a page and spacious margins. The first, third, and fourth issues were printed at Bard College, where Kelly has taught for many years, and the second came out of Buffalo's student bookstore (Kelly was a guest professor in the poetry program at the State University of New York at Buffalo). Like many mimeographed magazines, *Matter* was sold for a nominal amount ($1.00) at alternative bookstores such as the Eighth Street, Phoenix, and Peace Eye bookstores in New York, at City Lights Books in San Francisco, and at the legendary Asphodel Book Shop in Cleveland. The three New York bookstores no longer exist. *Matter* published a variety of material including the anthropoetically influenced work of Clayton Eshleman of *Caterpillar* magazine and the deep image/dream work of Kelly, Ted Enslin, Diane Wakoski, Rochelle Owens, and George Economou. Issue 2 includes Jackson Mac Low's poem "TO SAVE/WILDLIFE AND AID US, TOO," which consists of lines selected and arranged by schematic chance from a *New York Times*

article by Secretary of the Interior Stewart L. Udall. Issue 4 includes a three-page poem by the avant-garde filmmaker Stan Brakhage (who had at the age of nineteen been a poet living in the basement of Robert Duncan and Jess Collins's house). Matter Books, edited primarily by Joan Kelly, produced a dozen fine works, among them Gerrit Lansing's first book, *The Heavenly Tree Grows Downward*, and Charles Olson's long poem *Apollonius of Tyana*.

Matter. Nos. 1–4 (1963–1968).

GRD has: nos. 1–3.

Matter Books include:

Bialy, Harvey. *Love's Will: Poems, 1967.* 1968.

Enslin, Theodore. *The Diabelli Variations and Other Poems.* 1967. (GRD)

Irby, Kenneth. *The Flower of Having Passed Through Paradise in a Dream: Poems, 1967.* 1968.

Kelly, Robert. *Twenty Poems.* 1967. (BRG)

Lansing, Gerrit. *The Heavenly Tree Grows Downward.* Preface by John Wieners. 1966.

SET

Gerrit Lansing

*Gloucester,
Massachusetts
1961–1964*

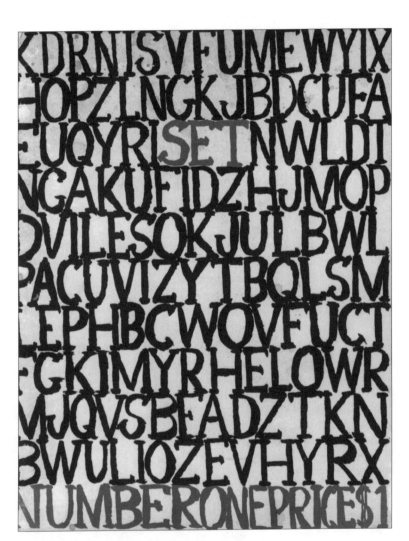

SET 1 (1961–1962). Cover by Harry Martin.

The Presses and Publications

In 1959, when I decided to produce a small magazine, I sent out a note (prodrome) about the magazine's content and format to a number of poets and poet-friends. I said that SET would be photo-offset, appear irregularly. As to intent and content I wrote: "SET will be about the poetic exploration of the swarming possibilities occult and/or unused in American life, urban and local, here & especially *now*, at this moment of the Aeon, i.e. the Vulgar Advent."

"The gates of memory and intuition, history and magic, open from a 'windowless' monad into Time," I wrote to Kenward Elmslie, amplifying a sentence in my prodromic statement, "Thus its (i.e. SET's) character will be dual *historical & magical*, the emphasized characters of Time." (The last phrase delighted Robert Duncan.)

"In this time-moment poetry and science meet. Hence the manifesto states that SET is interested in material 'relevant to the poetic-scientific study of American experience and nature . . .'" but "As I wrote to Frank O'Hara, 'I don't want SET to be polemick abt Amerika . . . will be more James Dean & Andrew Jackson Davis than Marcel Marceau or the Sar Peladan . . .'" I also wrote Frank, "Certainly I want neither the 'monumental' nor the 'study' . . . the 'study': the nature-morte ou vivante of the Misses Moore, Bishop, Wilbur, etc."

[the datedness of this now entertains me (1997)].

Around 1959 I wrote the poet Steve Jonas that the name of the proposed magazine come on like or in the places of its play, as:

(1) jazz (wch most readers will probably read primary)
(2) stance
(3) direction
(4) "theory of Sets" in *mathesis*
(5) (tennis, for those who like it)
(6) the God   — by the Chenoboskion gnostics identified w/ the Biblical Seth   — and and and
Shem   Melchizedek   Christ / Antichrist   Saturn
Typhon   Mercury   Dionysius (sacred ass)   Capricorn

"Enough ! or Too much " (Blake)

— *Gerrit Lansing*
  "*Statement: how SET was conceived*"
  Gloucester, Massachusetts, 1997,
  at the Equinox of Fall

SET. Nos. 1–2 (1961–1964).

BRG has: no. 1.

Something Else Press

Dick Higgins

New York City and Barton, Vermont (principally)
1964–1974

Logo of Some-
thing Else Press,
designed by
Dick Higgins.

"My job included copy editing, proofreading, managing the office and correspondence. I never knew what to expect, as Dick was always bursting with
ideas.... My most vivid editorial memory concerns ... Daniel Spoerri's
An Anecdoted Topography of Chance, translated from the French and anec-
dotally expanded by the author's friend, the expatriate American poet/
artist Emmett Williams. (Emmett, though still in Europe at the time, later
came to New York to follow me as editor at the Press.) Due to Emmett's
professionalism, the *Topography* made for tricky proofreading. Unaware
of Emmett and Dieter Roth's mnemonic 'the man with 5 A's in his name,'
I removed what appeared to be extra letters from the name Aagaard
Andersen. As the proofs traveled back and forth across the ocean in
those pre-fax days, Emmett kept putting the A's back in and I conscien-
tiously kept removing them. I got my comeuppance on that one when
about 12 or 15 years later, I was shackled with a typewriter that printed
double A's every time I hit the key."

— Barbara Moore, from *Some Things Else About Something Else*
   (New York: Granary Books, 1991)

The Presses and Publications

Designed, edited, and produced by Dick Higgins, the Something Else Press books contained offbeat and avant-garde writing in a neat and tidy, yet quirky and distinctive form. The press began in 1964 following Higgins's break with Fluxus founder George Maciunas and embodied many of the concerns of the then nascent art movement. Early titles included *Jefferson's Birthday/Postface*, Higgins's collection of performance scores; correspondence art pioneer Ray Johnson's *The Paper Snake*; Al Hansen's *A Primer of Happenings & Time/Space Art*; and Rumanian-born Nouveau Realiste artist Daniel Spoerri's *An Anecdoted Topography of Chance*. Higgins's *foew&ombwhnw* (a 1969 collection disguised as a prayer book) contains his important essay "Intermedia," in which he describes artworks which "fall between media," arguing that the social conditions of the time (early to mid-1960s) no longer allowed for a "compartmentalized approach" to either art or life. Indeed, the range of works published by Something Else exemplifies a very diverse approach: first American editions of several of Gertrude Stein's works, including *The Making of Americans*; a reprint of Henry Cowell's *New Musical Resources*; Merce Cunningham's *Changes: Notes on Choreography*; John Cage's anthology of unusual musical scores, *Notations*; Jackson Mac Low's *Stanzas for Iris Lezak*; R[ichard] Meltzer's *The Aesthetics of Rock*; *One Thousand American Fungi* by Charles McIlvaine and Robert K. Macadam; as well as Emmett Williams's important *Anthology of Concrete Poetry* among many others. Artists' books, critical theory, conceptual art, amusement, back-to-the-land hippie culture – through the use of conventional production and marketing strategies, Dick Higgins was able to place unconventional works into the hands of new and often unsuspecting readers. Something Else Press had published more than sixty books when it ended in 1974, in addition to pamphlets, newsletters, cards, posters, and other ephemera.

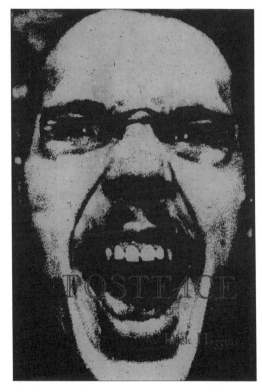

Dick Higgins, *Jefferson's Birthday/Postface* (1964). Cover photograph of the author by Wolf Vostell.

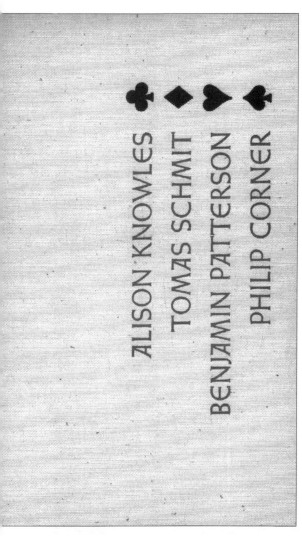

ALISON KNOWLES TOMAS SCHMIT BENJAMIN PATTERSON PHILIP CORNER

Alison Knowles, Tomas
Schmit, Benjamin
Patterson, and Philip
Corner, *The Four Suits*
(1965).

**Something Else Press
books include:**

Cage, John. *Diary: How to
Improve the World (You Will
Only Make Matters Worse)
Continued Part Three.* 1967.
(A Great Bear Pamphlet.)

Cage, John, with Alison
Knowles. *Notations.* 1969.
(BRG)

Cowell, Henry. *New Musical
Resources.* 1969. (MSS)

Cunningham, Merce.
Changes: Notes on Choreography. 1968. (DAN)

Filliou, Robert. *Ample Food
for Stupid Thought.* 1965.

Finlay, Ian Hamilton, and
Gordon Huntly. *A Sailor's
Calendar.* 1971. (BRG)

Gomringer, Eugen. *The Book
of Hours and Constellations.*
Translated and edited by
Jerome Rothenberg. 1968.
(GRD)

Gysin, Brion. *Brion Gysin Let
the Mice In.* Edited by Jan
Herman with contributions
by William S. Burroughs
and Ian Sommerville. 1973.

Hansen, Al. *A Primer of
Happenings & Time/Space
Art.* 1965. (GRD)

Higgins, Dick.
foew&ombwhnw. 1969.
(BRG, GRD)

Higgins, Dick. *Jefferson's
Birthday/Postface.* 1964.
(GRD)

Johnson, Ray. *The Paper
Snake.* 1965. (GRD)

Kaprow, Allan. *Some Recent
Happenings.* 1966. (A Great
Bear Pamphlet.) (BRG)

Knowles, Alison, Tomas
Schmit, Benjamin Patterson, and Philip Corner.
The Four Suits. 1965. (GRD)

McLuhan, Marshall.
Verbi-Voco-Visual Explorations.
1967.

Oldenburg, Claes.
Store Days. 1967. (APP)

Roth, Dieter. *246 Little
Clouds.* Introduction by
Emmett Williams. 1968.

Spoerri, Daniel. *An Anecdoted Topography of Chance.*
Translated from the French,
and further anecdoted
at random by Emmett
Williams. With one hundred reflective illustrations
by Topor. 1966. (GRD)

Stein, Gertrude. *The Making
of Americans.* 1966. (BRG)

Vostell, Wolf, and Dick
Higgins, eds. *Fantastic
Architecture.* 1971.

Williams, Emmett. *Anthology
of Concrete Poetry.* 1967.
(BRG)

Williams, Emmett.
Sweethearts. 1967.

**For a complete list of
Something Else publications,** the reader is referred
to: Peter Frank, *Something
Else Press: An Annotated Bibliography* (New Paltz, N.Y.:
Documentext/McPherson
& Company, 1983).

Performance Art and Intermedia

Much of the artwork produced during the 1960s and 70s can be described as "intermedial" in that it falls between media. For example, language and writing show up as the subject and material for many visual artists, while dance, cinema, theater, and sculpture stretch their boundaries in an attempt to create new forms to embody and enact newly emerging lifestyles and consciousness. The works of John Cage, Jackson Mac Low, Dick Higgins, the Fluxus group, Charlotte Moorman, Al Carmines and the Judson Memorial Church performances, Carolee Schneemann, and many others like them are closely allied to new developments in poetry during the intense period of cross-fertilization that this book documents. Illustrated on the following pages are several examples from this generative period.

An Anthology of Chance Operations

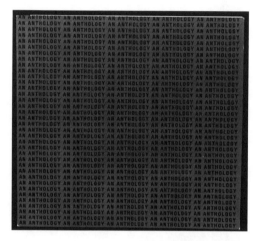

*An Anthology of Chance
Operations*, edited by
La Monte Young
(1963).

*In September 1997, Jackson Mac Low recounted
the history of* An Anthology:

AN ANTHOLOGY OF chance operations
concept art anti-art INDETERMINACY
IMPROVISATION meaningless work natural disasters plans of action STORIES Diagrams POETRY ESSAYS Music Dance con-
structions mathematics COMPOSITIONS . . .
(caps & lowercase as in the book) was gathered together by La Monte Young largely
in Autumn 1960 & Winter 1960–61 as a
response to Chester Anderson's request
that he guest-edit an issue of his new magazine *Beatitude East* (Chester had co-edited
the Bay Area magazine *Beatitude* just before
he came east). By late Spring Chester had
disappeared with all the materials La Monte
had gathered from composers, poets, concept artists, dancers, etc. here & in Europe.
He reappeared after a while & gave all the
mss. back to La Monte & me in front of the
23rd Street YMCA one cold night in late May.
La Monte had previously organized a series
at Yoko Ono's loft where a number of us
had our first one-person's-works concerts &
George Maciunas had attended the last few
of them. He had discovered our sector of
the ca. 1960 "New York Avant-Garde" when
he attended Richard Maxfield's electronic
music class, the successor of John Cage's
experimental music class at the New School,
& soon afterwards, the late Frank Kuenstler
had asked me to do something in a "variety

program" in June 1961 at the AG Gallery, run by George & a friend, located on Madison Avenue near the present site of the Whitney Museum. (A group of us including La Monte, Diane Wakoski, Iris Lezak & me performed my 1961 play *Verdurous Sanguinaria*, which we'd premiered [with Simone Forti] at Yoko's in April.) Soon George started several series at the gallery: music, verbal works, electronic works, etc. One Sunday, La Monte and I were having our pictures taken by George at the AG for flyers for these series, & we mentioned the collection of works La Monte had gathered. (I was concerned because 20 pages of my recent work were included.) George said: "*I'll* publish it! I've got *lots* of paper!" & sure enough, he had many shelves full of paper of all sorts, many colors, thicknesses, plainnesses, fancinesses, etc., on the shelves of the gallery's backroom. However, after a while the gallery went bust & our last concerts were done in candlelight because the electricity had been cut off. George had to escape his creditors by flying to Europe, where he got a job with the US Air Force at Wiesbaden, from which he sent us his first ukases announcing that we were all editors of something called "Fluxus." Just before he flew away, he sat down for 2 solid days in a friend's loft on Water Street and designed the 7 front title pages & the 23 title pages of the individual artists' sections while a number of us were typing a lot of the pieces on George's electric with its narrow gothic sans-serif typeface. He had sold his hi-fi to Dick Higgins & paid the money to his flyer printer (who'd probably never printed a book before) & told La Monte and me to get the pages and let the printer "wait" for the rest of the money. This printer was a bull & could've taken La Monte under one arm & me under the other and thrown us both thru a brick wall. So we had to raise the rest of the money ourselves. That's how we became the co-publishers of the 1st edition. I was doing most of the production work, proofreading, correcting negatives, etc., at the printshop, because La Monte couldn't stand the guy. This printer only did more work when we infused more money. We finally got the book out in May 1963 during Yam Day, a two-day concert at the Hardware Poets Theatre on 53rd Street, mainly organized by George Brecht & the late Bob Watts.

Jackson Mac Low, *The Pronouns*

In October 1997, Jackson Mac Low had this to say about The Pronouns:

The *Pronouns* is a collection of texts by Jackson Mac Low that are both poems and instructions for dancers and other performers. Each one may be realized by a dancer or performer in any way that interprets in action each line successively. They were written in February–March 1964, and this first edition was mimeographed by Mac Low (not long after March 22, 1964, when the last text was written) in the office of the Judson Memorial Church in Greenwich Village, at the request of members of the Judson Dance Workshop. The Workshop obtained permission from the Rev. Howard R. Moody, then the church's principal minister, for Mac Low to use the church's mimeograph machine, stencils, and paper. About 100 copies were mimeographed. The poems were derived by two sets of nonintentional operations from the Basic English List (850 words), designed (in England, 1926–1930, by C. K. Ogden and I. A. Richards) as a simple form of English to be used as an international language. Mac Low used it merely as a source of simple words. The first step (January 1961) drew words from the Basic list by random-digit chance operations to make up a "pack" of filing cards with 1–5 action phrases written on each. This "action pack," together with the Basic list itself, was first used to produce the "card pack" *Nuclei for Simone* [Forti]. Each card has on it 1–10 separated words and 1–5 phrases from the action pack. A performer (so far only Simone Forti and Trisha Brown) uses these words and phrases as "nuclei" around which she or he may build an improvisation. The second step (February–March 1964) used diastic deterministic text selection procedures (not chance operations) to draw a series of phrases from the action pack that "spelled out" the one of the phrases – arrived at by "cutting" the action pack – which became the poem's title. The phrases (other than the title of the poem) were converted into sentences. Each sentence in each *Pronouns* poem has, as its subject, one of forty pronouns (and pronoun-like nouns) as the subject of each sentence – the same pronoun throughout each poem. Mac Low chose the pronoun for each poem and inserted appropriate time expressions (e.g., "first," "then," and "finally"). Several groups of dancers and individual performers have realized the *Pronouns* poems, beginning with a group of eight (including Mac Low) organized by Meredith Monk in 1965 for performances during the 3rd Annual New York Festival of the Avant Garde (coordinated by Charlotte Moorman). A second, revised edition of *The Pronouns* – boxed folios with multicolored grid graphics by Ian Tyson – was published by Tetrad Press, London, in 1971. A third, newly revised edition, with new essays by Mac Low and photos of the first (1965) performances by Peter Moore, was published by Station Hill Press, Barrytown, New York, in 1979.

THE PRONOUNS -- A COLLECTION OF 40 DANCES -- FOR THE DANCERS -- 6 February-22 March 1964

by Jackson Mac Low

1ST DANCE -- MAKING THINGS NEW -- 6 February 1964

He makes himself comfortable,
& matches parcels.

Then he makes glass boil,
while having political material got in,
& coming by.

Soon after, he's giving gold cushions or seeming to do so,
taking opinions,
shocking,
pointing to a fact that seems to be an error & showing it to be other than it seems,
& presently raining by going or having waves.

Then he names things.

A little while later he gets out with things,
& finally either rewards someone for something or goes up under something.

2ND DANCE -- SEEING LINES -- 6 February 1964

She seems to come by wing,
&, keeping present being in front,
she reasons regularly.

Then -- making her stomach let itself down,
& giving a bit or doing something elastic,
& making herself comfortable,
she lets complex impulses make something.

She disgusts everyone.

She does a little penning,
& then she fingers a door.

Later she wheels awhile,
while either transporting a star or letting go of a street.

Performance Art and Intermedia

Carolee Schneemann, *Parts of a Body House Book*

Carolee Schneemann is a painter who has been a highly visible participant in several art and literary circles since 1960. She continues to be a pioneering, taboo-breaking performance artist, filmmaker, and writer on the subjects of feminism, sexuality, and the ecstatic body as a source of knowledge. She has created many influential solo improvisations and multimedia performances that incorporate movement, film, video, and text. She pioneered Body Art, choreographed for the Judson Dance Theater, established her own Kinetic Theater, and participated in Fluxus and the Women's Movement. Her *Parts of a Body House Book* grew out of a series of drawings made by Schneemann which explored the "body house" through investigations of its many "rooms," for example, the "liver room" and the "gut room." The book was designed by Felipe Ehrenberg, printed via mimeo, and published by his Beau Geste Press in 1972. The book, Schneemann says, is "an accumulation of letters, analyses of films and charts of sexual parameters which incorporate many of the issues that were of great concern in the early 1970s in London. The texts are centered on those aspects of the body that were then considered shameful or taboo or were simply ignored." These important texts found outlet in other publications of the period, including *Fantastic Architecture* (Something Else Press, 1971) and *Caterpillar* 3/4 (April–July 1968).

Carolee Schneemann,
*Parts of a Body House
Book* (1972). Front and
back covers.

El Corno Emplumado

Margaret Randall

Mexico City
1962–1969

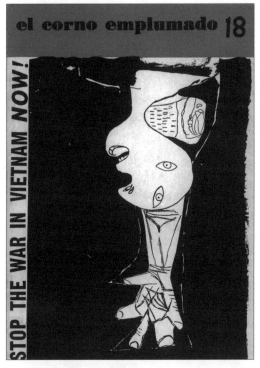

El Corno Emplumado 18 (April 1966).

"In the United States *Black Mountain Review* was already a classic, to be drawn upon. We saw ourselves connected in one way or another to *Evergreen Review* before it became slick, *City Lights Journal, Trobar,* George Hitchcock's hand-wrought *Kayak, Kulchur,* the outer edges of *Poetry,* Robert Bly's *The Sixties* for his concern with the great Latin voices, and many, many others. The radius included *Duende* in New Mexico, d. a. levy's *Renegade Press* in Cleveland, *Elizabeth* in New Rochelle, and Leavenworth's *New Era* (written and run by prisoners)."

— Margaret Randall, "El Corno Emplumado, 1961–1969: Some Notes in Retrospect, 1975," *TriQuarterly* 43 (Fall 1978)

In 1962, Margaret Randall, an expatriate American in Mexico City, founded *El Corno Emplumado/The Plumed Horn* ("the jazz horn of the U.S. and the plumes of Quetzal-coatl"), an international magazine that in its heart intended to help heal the break between the Americas, North and South. Randall wanted to provide "a showcase (outside politics) for the fact that WE ARE ALL BROTHERS." About this use of gender, she later commented: "We really thought we could all be brothers. (We didn't think, then, about being sisters. We were a few women, a minority among mostly men. Our intellectual pretensions took care of that ratio – women's consciousness was not part of us then.)" In its thirty-one issues, *El Corno Emplumado* introduced Latin American literature to the North, printing English translations of work by Vallejo, Neruda, and Gabriel García Marquez, among many others (a generation of new Cuban writers in issue 7, for instance). Conversely, the magazine, under the direction of co-editor Sergio Mondragon, printed translations into Spanish of work by Hart Crane, Walt Whitman, Ezra Pound, William Carlos Williams, and Paul Blackburn.

Increasingly political as the decade wore on, the magazine was vociferously opposed to U.S. intervention in Vietnam and just as vociferously positive about the Cuban revolution. Supported for its first seven years by various departments of the Mexican government as well as by private contributions from many Americans, the magazine was eventually harassed out of existence by the repressions of 1968–1969, which culminated in the massacre of nearly a thousand students in Mexico City. In an eloquent description of her own magazine, Randall could well have been describing any number of other American little magazines of the period: "*El Corno Emplumado* was never just a magazine; it was never just a collection of words and images on paper, put together by two people (it was always only two people: editing, raising money, supervising the printing, handling the secretarial work and distribution). *El Corno* was a network – letters going back and forth between poets, between people. It was a meeting of poets like spontaneous combustion. ..."

El Corno Emplumado.
Nos. 1–31 (1962–1969).

GRD has: complete file.

El Corno Emplumado books, some in English, some in Spanish, and some bilingual, include:

Bowering, George. *The Man in Yellow Boots/El Hombre de las Botas Amarillas.* Collages by Roy Kiyooka. 1965. (BRG)

Enslin, Theodore. *This Do and The Talents.* 1966. (GRD)

Greenberg, Alvin. *The Small Waves.* Drawings by Don McIntosh. 1965. (GRD)

Kelly, Robert. *Her Body Against Time.* 1963.

Kelly, Robert. *Weeks.* 1966.

Kiviat, Erik. *Museum of Memnon.* 1966. (BRG)

Lowenfels, Walter. *Land of Roseberries.* Drawings by David Siqueiros. 1965.

Mondragon, Sergio. *Yo Soy el Otro; I Am the Other.* Drawings by Arnold Belkin. 1965.

Moreno Colmenares, José. *Prontuario* [Compendium]. 1966. (GRD)

Ossman, David. *Set in a Landscape: Poems and Sequences, 1960–1964.* Drawings by Mowry Baden. 1966. (BRG)

Randall, Margaret. *October.* Photographs, sculpture by Shinkichi Tajiri. 1965. (GRD)

Rossi, Matti. *The Trees of Vietnam.* Translated from the Finnish by Anselm Hollo. 1966. (GRD)

Rothenberg, Jerome. *The Gorky Poems/Poemas a Gorky.* Translated into Spanish by Sergio Mondragon. 1966.

Silva, Ludovico. *Tenebra.* Drawings by Julius Tobias. 1964.

Swaan, Silvia de. *Dibujos de Vida y Muerte/Drawings of Life and Death.* 1966. (APP)

Truesdale, Calvin William. *In the Country of a Deer's Eye.* Drawings by Judith Gutierrez. 1966.

Migrant Books

Gael Turnbull

*Worcester, England, and
Ventura, California
1957–1966*

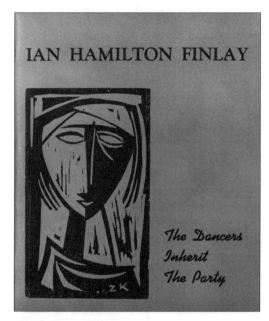

Ian Hamilton Finlay,
*The Dancers Inherit the
Party* (1960). Cover
woodcut by Zeljko
Kujundzic.

Migrant. Nos. 1–8 (July
1959–September 1960).
Superseded by: **Mica**.
Santa Barbara, California;
Helmut Bonheim and
Raymond Federman, eds.
Nos. 1–7 (December
1960–November 1962).

Migrant Books include:

Creeley, Robert. *The Whip.*
1957.

Creighton-Hill, Hugh.
Latterday Chrysalides. 1961.

Dorn, Ed. *What I See in the
Maximus Poems.* 1960.
(BRG)

Finlay, Ian Hamilton. *The
Dancers Inherit the Party:
Selected Poems.* Woodcuts
by Zeljko Kujundzic. 1962.
(BRG)

Hollo, Anselm. *& it is a
song: Poems.* Cover design

and section plates by John
Furnival. 1965. (GRD)

Mead, Matthew. *A Poem in
Nine Parts.* 1960.

Morgan, Edwin, trans.
*Sovpoems: Brecht, Neruda,
Pasternak, Tsvetayeva,
Mayakowsky, Martynov,
Yevtushenko.* 1961.

Shayer, Michael.
Persephone. 1961.

Turnbull, Gael. *The Small
Change.* 1980.

Turnbull, Gael.
To You, I Write. 1963.

English poet Gael Turnbull began Migrant Books by purchasing stock from several presses, including *Origin*, *Jargon*, and Divers Press, and his first solo publication was a single mimeographed sheet advertising these publications, which included Charles Olson's *Maximus Poems*. In a personal memoir of the press, Turnbull comments on his first real book publication: "In the summer of 1957, I published *The Whip*, a small volume of selected poems by Robert Creeley, who arranged and managed the printing for me on Mallorca (with Mosen Alcover who had printed the Divers Press books). There were 500 copies in paper wrappers and 100 hard cover . . . the bulk of the edition went out through Jargon (Jonathan Williams) in the United States. (I did have the intention of publishing Olson's *O'Ryan Poems* but it didn't get further than 'an intention' because I never got myself together enough to actually approach a printer in Worcester.)" Turnbull immigrated to the United States in 1958 and settled in Ventura, California, where he began to publish his books on a hand-operated Sears Roebuck duplicator. He used this machine to produce the little magazine entitled *Migrant*, which he sent to friends and colleagues, partly as a way to retain contact with his native England, to which he returned in 1964. Eight issues of *Migrant* appeared over the course of a year, and then Turnbull began publishing pamphlets, including Scottish artist and poet Ian Hamilton Finlay's *The Dancers Inherit the Party*, which was printed in two editions. Although it lasted only a few years, Migrant was an example to certain other presses in the United Kingdom, influencing (at least editorially) both Finlay's Wild Hawthorne Press and the more mainstream Fulcrum Press in London. An unassuming, simple affair, each Migrant book was focused on providing a readable text in more ways than one. The last publication of the press was *Few* by Pete Brown in 1966: "It was our biggest in sheer size, and somewhere, somehow, 1000 copies vanished into other bookshops and presumably into the hands of readers."

Duende 4 (April 1964): Kenneth Irby's *The Roadrunner Poem*. Cover drawing by Signe Nelson (Stuart).

Duende

Larry Goodell

Placitas, New Mexico
1964–1966

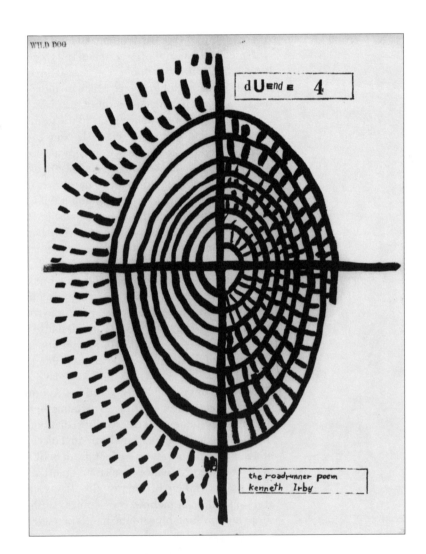

In the southwestern desert highlands of Placitas, New Mexico, flourished one of the most down-to-earth, and yet still lunar, of the mimeographed magazines of the 1960s, Larry Goodell's *Duende*. Each of its fourteen issues published the work of just one poet (a separate anthology, entitled *Oriental Blue Streak*, was published in the Spring of 1968 in Placitas without the *Duende* imprint). Among the individual titles were Ronald Bayes's *History of the Turtle (Book 1)* as number 1, Kenneth Irby's *The Roadrunner Poem* (number 4), Margaret Randall's *Some Small Sounds from the Bass Fiddle* (number 5), Larry Eigner's *Murder Talk* (number 6), Robert Kelly's *Lectiones* (number 7), and Kenneth Irby's *Movements/Sequences* (number 8). The final issue was devoted to Goodell's own *Cycles*. The press also published a series of half a dozen broadside poems. The press was named after the poetic view developed by Spanish poet Federico García Lorca, whose "Theory and Function of the *Duende*" was widely influential among American poets of the 6os and 7os: "All through Andalusia, from the rock of Jaén to the shell of Cádiz,

people constantly speak of the *duende*, and recognize it with unfailing instinct when it appears. The wonderful flamenco singer El Lebrijano, creator of the *Debla*, said: 'When I sing with *duende* nobody can equal me.' The old gipsy dancer La Malena exclaimed once on hearing Brailowsky play Bach: 'Olé! This has *duende*!,' yet she was bored by Gluck, Brahms, and Darius Milhaud. And Manuel Torres, a man with more culture in his veins than anybody I have known, when listening to Falla playing his own 'Nocturno del Generalife,' made this splendid pronouncement: 'All that has dark sounds has *duende*.' And there is no greater truth."

Duende. Nos. 1–14 (1964–1966).

BRG has: complete file.

Fervent Valley. Edited by Larry Goodell, Stephen Rodefer, Bill Perelman, and Charlie Vermont. Nos. 1–5 (Spring 1972–1975).

BRG has: nos. 1, 2, 4.

The fourteen issues of *Duende* **were:**

Bayes, Ronald. *History of the Turtle (Book 1)*. 1964. (Duende 1.) (BRG)

Bayes, Ronald. *History of the Turtle (Book 4)*. 1966. (Duende 10.) (BRG)

Dodd, William. *Se Marier.* 1965. (Duende 9.) (BRG)

Eigner, Larry. *Murder Talk; The Reception: (Suggestions for a Play); Five Poems; Bed Never Self Made.* 1965. (Duende 6.) (BRG)

Franklyn, A. Frederic. *Virgules and Déjà Vu.* 1964. (Duende 2.) (BRG)

Franks, David. *Touch.* 1966. (Duende 13.) (BRG)

Goodell, Larry. *Cycles.* 1966. (Duende 14.) (BRG)

Harris, William. *Poems 1965.* 1966. (Duende 12.) (BRG)

Irby, Kenneth. *Movements/Sequences.* 1965. (Duende 8.) (BRG)

Irby, Kenneth. *The Roadrunner Poem.* 1964. (Duende 4.) (BRG)

Kelly, Robert. *Lectiones.* 1965. (Duende 7.) (BRG)

Randall, Margaret. *Some Small Sounds from the Bass Fiddle.* 1964. (Duende 5.) (BRG)

Ward, Fred. *Poems.* 1966. (Duende 11.) (BRG)

Watson, Richard. *Cockcrossing.* 1964. (Duende 3.) (BRG)

Wild Dog

*John Hoopes, Ed Dorn,
Drew Wagnon, and
others*

*Pocatello, Idaho; Salt
Lake City, Utah; and
San Francisco
1963–1966*

Wild Dog 1 (April 1963).

The Presses and Publications

In many respects – name, form, and con-tent – *Wild Dog* boldly embodies much of what we identify as the "mimeo revolution." Preceded in Pocatello by *A Pamphlet, Wild Dog*, which joined the mimeograph revolution in April 1963, was the brain-child of Edward Dorn, who was familiar with the emergence of divergent American writing through his association with Black Mountain College, where he had studied under Charles Olson and Robert Creeley. The literary direction that Dorn brought to *Wild Dog* encompassed writing from diverse sources including, but not limited to, writers associated with *The Black Mountain Review*, the San Francisco Renaissance, the Beat generation, the New York School, and certain "hip" European and South American publications and poets. In its three-year history, *Wild Dog* moved from Pocatello, Idaho, to Salt Lake City, Utah, before ending its existence with number 21 of volume 3 in March of 1966, in San Francisco. In January 1966, *Wild Dog* published a book of poems, *The Disappearance of Mountains* by Max Finstein. *Wild Dog* had several editors in its brief history. While in Pocatello, John Hoopes edited the first issue with Ed Dorn and then edited number 2 with Geoffrey Dunbar and numbers 3 and 4 with Drew Wagnon. Drew Wagnon joined Hoopes for number 5 and stayed with the magazine through its final issue. He joined Gino Clays

(Sky) in Salt Lake City for number 10 and later went to San Francisco with Clays to edit numbers 11 through 18. A double issue, 19 and 20, and the last issue were edited by Wagnon and his wife, Terry. During the period of the magazine's existence, there were also several guest editors. Some of the writers and poets who submitted original manuscripts to *Wild Dog* were LeRoi Jones, Douglas Woolf, Robert Kelly, Larry Eigner, Fielding Dawson, Charles Olson, Denise Levertov, Louis Zukofsky, Robert Creeley, Diane Wakoski, Stan Brakhage, and Joanne Kyger.

Wild Dog. Nos. 1–21 (1963–1966).

BRG has: complete file.

Wild Dog books include:

Finstein, Max. *The Disappearance of Mountains: Poems 1960–63.* 1966. (GRD)

Umbra

Thomas C. Dent, Calvin
Hernton, and David Henderson

New York City
1963–1974

Umbra. Vol. 1, nos. 1–5
(Winter 1963–1974).
Cover photograph by
Henri de Chatillont (2).

BRG has: no. 3. SC has:
vol. 1, nos. 1, 2, 4.

The first literary magazines of the 1960s published exclusively by black writers and for black readers were *Soulbook, Black Dialogue,* and *The Journal of Black Poetry. Umbra* ("shadow-region"), which chronologically preceded them, presaged and shared the excitement they generated. Founded by the Society of Umbra, a workshop of musicians, poets, fiction writers, and visual artists, the journal was, unlike the others mentioned above, not a black nationalist literary organ. Aesthetically, however, it was born of the black struggle, as evidenced by this statement in its first issue: "*Umbra* is not another haphazard 'little literary' publication. *Umbra* has a defined orientation: (1) the experience of being Negro, especially in America; and (2) that quality of human awareness often termed 'social consciousness.'" The magazine was concerned primarily with issues facing African Americans as these were reflected in creative literature ("poetry, short stories, articles, essays") and prided itself on its high standards, choosing carefully among a large number of submitted manuscripts. Politically, for *Umbra* was political, the magazine tended toward the left, "as radical as society demands the truth to be." *Umbra* and its cousins *Umbra/Blackworks* and *Blackworks from the Black Galaxy* published many of the most important black writers of the 60s and 70s, including Dudley Randall, Ree Dragonette, Conrad Kent Rivers, Lorenzo Thomas, Ann Allen Shockley, Ishmael Reed, LeRoi Jones, Jayne Cortez, Nikki Giovanni, Bob Kaufman, Tom Weatherly, and Jay Wright. The periodical included writers from Africa, the Caribbean, Pasadena, Queens, New York, Illinois, West Africa, and elsewhere.

December, 1963   Number 2   75 cents

UMBRA

Umbra 2 (December 1963). Cover photograph by Henri de Chatillont.

Hambone

Nathaniel Mackey

Santa Cruz, California
1974, 1982–

The Presses and Publications

H*ambone*'s lineage includes the poetry of Black Mountain, the San Francisco Renaissance, language poetry, and the myths and traditions of West and North Africa, Haiti, and Papua/New Guinea as well as the history and rhythms of blues, jazz, and improvisatory music. Editor Nathaniel Mackey was born in Miami and grew up in Southern California, before attending both Princeton and Stanford universities. While at Stanford in 1974, he was one of the editors of the first issue of *Hambone*, which was not to appear again until 1982 when, as a better-established poet and scholar, Mackey revived the periodical (he has since gone on to publish a half dozen books of poetry, an anthology of jazz poetry, and, in 1993, a highly regarded critical work, *Discrepant Engagement: Dissonance, Cross-Culturality, and Experimental Writing*). The revived *Hambone* reflects the wide interests of its editor in "cross-cultural" and experimental writing as well as writing by people of color (two of Mackey's cultural heroes were Imamu Amiri Baraka and Guyanese novelist Wilson Harris). Mackey commented on his role as editor in an interview with Chris Funkhouser published in the print magazine *Callaloo* and at the Electronic Poetry Center from SUNY–Buffalo: "my idea was to simply put my sense of a community of writers and artists on a kind of map, in one place. So in *Hambone* 2, in which all of the material was solicited, that meant having a talk by Sun Ra and poems by Robert Duncan, poems by Beverly Dahlen, Jay Wright, fiction by Clarence Major, Wilson Harris, poems by Edward Kamau Brathwaite and so on. That issue was sort of saying, 'OK, here's my map, a significant part of it, and we're going to call it *Hambone*.' It seems to me that's what little magazines do, and do best. They put out a particular editor's sense of 'what's up' out there – and you find out who 'out there' is interested in that."

Hambone. To date: Nos. 1–14 (1974, 1982–1998). *Hambone* is still in operation.

BRG has: nos. 1–8.

White Dove Review

Ron Padgett

Tulsa, Oklahoma

1959–1960

Ron Padgett, Riverside Park, 1966. Snapshot photograph by Lorenz Gude.

Through his friendship with Ted Berrigan, whom he first met at Meyer's bookstore in Tulsa, Ron Padgett developed a network, most of whom soon moved together to New York: "There was a whole crew of young artists and wild people, sensitive, creative people. Ted seemed quite a bit older than me. He'd been in the army, for god's sake – he'd been to Korea. He'd grown up in Providence. He'd been to Japan. And he knew a lot of things I didn't know, so he was in many ways a mentor to me and to Dick [Gallup] and to other young people."

Editorially the predecessor to all the second-generation New York School little magazines, the *White Dove Review* was started by high school student Ron Padgett. The associate editor was Dick Gallup, and the art editors were Joe Brainard and Michael Marsh. The first issue contained poems by Paul Blackburn (described as a "well known poet living in New York") as well as Clarence Major and Ron Padgett, and an excerpt, here entitled "Thrashing Doves," from Kerouac's *Book of Blues*. The second issue included poems by Ted Berrigan, LeRoi Jones, Ron Loewinsohn, Fielding Dawson, Simon Perchick, and Clarence Major, among others. In a 1991 interview with Edward Foster, Padgett described his inspiration for the *Review*: "But my introduction to modern poetry came . . . when I was fifteen and working in a bookstore, the Louis Meyer Bookshop, run by a very nice and highly literate man, who was also a writer. It was there I found out about e. e. cummings and T. S. Eliot. Then I learned about *Evergreen Review* and suddenly started reading all these modernist poets such as LeRoi Jones and Frank O'Hara, and I subscribed to the magazines advertised in *Evergreen Review* like LeRoi Jones's *Yugen* and Wallace Berman's *Semina*. And when I looked at magazines like *Yugen*, I saw they were just little things stapled together, and so I went down to a local printer and asked, How do you do this? And he said, Oh, it's nothing – it's real easy. So I decided to start my own magazine. I invited Dick Gallup, who was [living] across the street and was writing poetry, to be co-editor and Joe Brainard, who was the best artist in school, to be the art editor." Padgett called his magazine the *White Dove Review* after an *Evergreen Review* cover showing a girl holding a white dove. That issue, *Evergreen Review*, vol. 2, no. 6 (Autumn 1958), includes "In Memory of My Feelings" by Frank O'Hara and "Cold Mountain Poems" by Gary Snyder. The photograph is by Susan Nevelson.

White Dove Review, vol. 2, no. 5 (1960). Cover by Joe Brainard.

White Dove Review.
Nos. 1–5 (1959–
May/August 1960).

BRG has: nos. 2–5.

"C" Press

Ted Berrigan

New York City
1963–1980

"C," vol. 2, no. 11 (Summer
1965). Cover by Joe Brainard.

egun in May 1963 by poet and editor
Ted Berrigan (with Lorenz Gude as
publisher), "C" Press and its mimeograph-
produced magazine and books provided
an important early outlet for the writings
of younger poets and their immediate predecessors. The first issue printed work by
the core group of Dick Gallup, Ron Padgett,
Joe Brainard (who was also a visual artist),
and Ted Berrigan. These four had recently
relocated to the East Village from Tulsa,
where they had produced and/or contributed to the *White Dove Review* (five issues,
1959–1960). However, the immediate precursor to *"C"* was *The Censored Review*, which
was published, also via the mimeo machine,
in 1963; its contents had been gathered
by Columbia student Ron Padgett for the
university literary magazine, but had been
suppressed by the dean. The title poem,
by "Noble Brainard," was a collaboration
between Berrigan and Padgett. Berrigan's
"C" magazine published poems, plays, essays,
translations, and comics by a growing number of writers and artists, but always bore
the distinctive imprint of its charismatic
editor. Issue 4 featured poet and dance writer Edwin Denby and included contributions by Frank O'Hara, John Wieners, and
Berrigan. The cover sported a silk-screen
by Andy Warhol of an image of Denby and
Gerard Malanga. *2 / 2 Stories for Andy Warhol*
by Ron Padgett, also with a cover by Warhol,
was published by "C" Press in 1965, as was
Joseph Ceravolo's *Fits of Dawn*. Berrigan's
own great book of the period was *The Sonnets*
(1964), which featured a cover by Brainard.
For many people, this work has come to sym-
bolize Berrigan, who was, in the words of Ken
Tucker, "fiercely unpretentious, intensely
self-absorbed, prodigious in his ambition
and energy, [and who] did more than create
a substantial body of poetry. He also embodied a spirit that gave meaning to many other
writers' lives."

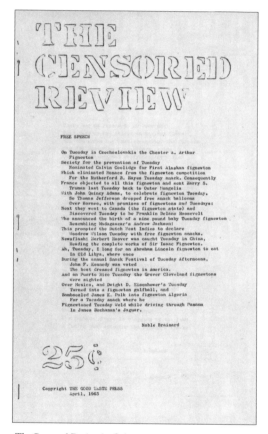

The Censored Review (1963).

"C" Press

Joseph Ceravolo,
Fits of Dawn (1965).
Cover by Rosemary
Ceravolo.

Elio Schneeman,
In February I Think
(1978). Cover by
George Schneeman.

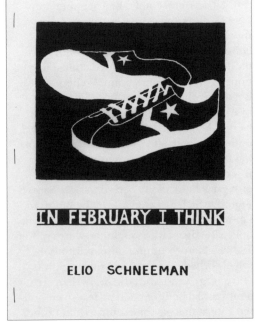

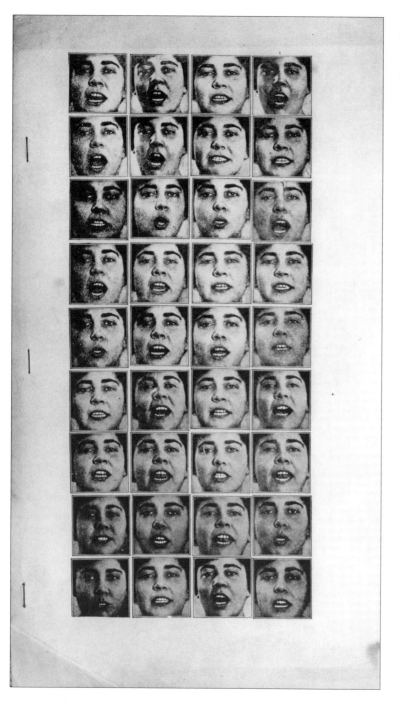

"C": a journal of poetry,
vol. 1, no. 6 (December
1963/January 1964).
Cover by Joe Brainard,
after Tristan Tzara.

Ted Berrigan, *The Sonnets* (1964). Cover by Joe Brainard.

"C," a Journal of Poetry.
Vol. 1, no. 1–vol. 2, no. 13 (May 1963–May 1966).

BRG has: vol. 1, nos. 1–3, 5, 7, 8; vol. 2, nos. 11, 13. RBK has: signed, annotated, editor's file, complete with the exception of vol. 2, no. 12.

"C" Comics. Edited by Joe Brainard. Nos. 1–2 (1964).

BRG has: no. 1.

"C" Press books include:

Berrigan, Ted. *The Sonnets.* Cover by Joe Brainard. 1964. (BRG)

Brownstein, Michael. *Behind the Wheel.* Cover by Alex Katz. 1967. (BRG)

Burroughs, William S. *Time.* Four drawings by Brion Gysin. 1965.

Ceravolo, Joe. *Fits of Dawn.* Covers by Rosemary Ceravolo. 1965. (GRD)

Elmslie, Kenward. *The Power Plant Poems.* Cover by Joe Brainard. 1967. (BRG)

Gallup, Dick. *Hinges.* Cover by Joe Brainard. 1965.

Notley, Alice. *165 Meeting House Lane (Twenty-four Sonnets).* Covers by Philip Whalen. 1971. (BRG)

Padgett, Ron. *Quelques Poèmes/Some Translations/ Some Bombs.* Translation by Padgett of poems by Pierre Reverdy. Cover by Joe Brainard. 1963. (GRD)

Padgett, Ron. *2 / 2 Stories for Andy Warhol.* Cover by Andy Warhol. 1965. (BRG)

Schneeman, Elio. *In February I Think.* Cover by George Schneeman. 1978. (BRG)

Veitch, Tom. *Literary Days.* Cover by Joe Brainard. 1964.

Ted Berrigan. Mixed-media portrait by George Schneeman, 1966–1967.

Painter George Schneeman and poet Ted Berrigan met in June 1966 just
after Schneeman moved to New York City. This is probably the first of the
many paintings of New York School poets executed by Schneeman at his
new studio on East Seventh Street.

Fuck You,
a magazine of the arts

Edward Sanders

New York City
1962–1965

Ed Sanders, New York
City, late 1960s.
Photograph by Elsa
Dorfman. Photograph
© 1998 by Elsa Dorfman.
http://elsa.photo.net

I n February of 1962 I was sitting in Stanley's Bar at 12th and B
with some friends from the *Catholic Worker*. We'd just seen Jonas
Mekas's movie *Guns of the Trees*, and I announced I was going to publish a poetry journal called *Fuck You, a magazine of the arts*. There was
a certain tone of skepticism among my rather inebriated friends, but
the next day I began typing stencils, and had an issue out within a
week. I bought a small mimeograph machine, and installed it in my
pad on East 11th, hand-cranking and collating 500 copies, which I
gave away free wherever I wandered. Fearful of getting arrested, I
nevertheless mailed it to my heroes around the world, from Charles
Olson to T. S. Eliot to Marianne Moore, from Castro to Samuel
Beckett, from Picasso to Lawrence Ferlinghetti and Allen Ginsberg.
Fuck You was part of what they called the Mimeograph Revolution,
and my vision was to reach out to the "Best Minds" of my generation
with a message of Gandhian pacifism, great sharing, social change,
the expansion of personal freedom (including the legalization of
marijuana), and the then-stirring messages of sexual liberation. I
published *Fuck You, a magazine of the arts* from 1962 through 1965,
for a total of thirteen issues. In addition, I formed a mimeograph
press which issued a flood of broadsides and manifestoes during
those years, including Burroughs's *Roosevelt After Inauguration*,
Carol Bergé's *Vancouver Report*, Auden's *Platonic Blow*, *The Marijuana
Review*, and a bootleg collection of the final Cantos of Ezra Pound.

— *Ed Sanders*
  Woodstock, New York, October 1997

**Fuck You, a magazine
of the arts.** Nos. 1–4
and No. 5, vol. 1–No. 5,
vol. 9 (February 1962–
June 1965).

BRG has: complete file.

**The Dick: An Occasional
Newsletter of Observation,
Literature & Commentary.**
Vol. 1, no. 1 (February
1967). Edited and largely
written by Sanders although
it does not contain the
Fuck You imprint.

BRG has: sole issue.

Ed Sanders' Catalog. Nos.
1–6 (June/July 1964–
September 1965).

BRG has: no. 3.

Fuck You books include:

Auden, W. H. *The Platonic
Blow*. 1965.

Bergé, Carol. *The Vancouver
Report*. 1964. (BRG)

Burroughs, William S.
*Health Bulletin: APO-33 A
Metabolic Regulator*. 1965.
Fewer than twenty copies of
this publication are extant;
the rest were destroyed.

[Burroughs, William S.]
"Willie Lee." *Roosevelt After
Inauguration*. Cover illustrations by Allen Ginsberg.
1964.

*Despair: Poems to Come Down
By*. Includes contributions
by Ted Berrigan, Paul
Blackburn, John Keys, Al
Fowler, Harry Fainlight, Ed
Sanders, and Szabo. 1964.

Ferlinghetti, Lawrence.
*To Fuck Is to Love Again.
(Kyrie Eleison Kerista), or,
The Situation in the West,
Followed by a Holy Proposal*.
1965. (BRG)

*The Fuck You Quote of the
Week 1* (by Harry Fainlight).
Broadside. September 7,
1964. (BRG)

*The Fuck You Quote of the
Week 2* (by John Ashbery).
Broadside. September 14,
1964. (BRG)

*The Fuck You Quote of the
Week 3* (by Kenneth Koch).
Broadside. September 23,
1964. (BRG)

Continued on page 168

Continued on page 168

Fuck You, a magazine of the arts, no. 5, vol. 4 (1963).

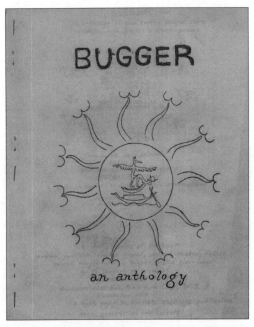

Bugger: An Anthology (New York: Fug-Press, 1964).

Harris, Marguerite. *An Absolute and Glorious New Year 1965*. 1964. (BRG)

Maxims and Aphorisms from the Letters of D. H. Lawrence. Compiled with appended poems by Marguerite Harris. 1964.

Pelieu, Claude. *Automatic Pilot.* Translated by Mary Beach. 1964. Printed by Ed Sanders for City Lights Books. (BRG)

Poems for Marilyn. Includes contributions by Joel Oppenheimer, John Keys, Taylor Mead, and Ed Sanders. 1962. (BRG)

Pound, Ezra. *The Cantos, CX–CXVI.* Cover by Joe Brainard. 1967. (BRG)

Sanders, Ed. *A Description of the Regal Society of Sooey Semen.* 1969.

Sanders, Ed. *Ed Sanders Newsletter.* 1966.

Sanders, Ed. *Fuck God in the Ass: Poems by Ed Sanders.* 1967. (BRG)

Sanders, Ed. *The Toe Queen Poems.* Foreword by Consuela. Cover by Ed Sanders. 1964. (BRG)

Sanders, Ed. *A Valorium Edition of the Entire Extant Works of Thales!: The Famous Milesian Poet, Philosopher, Physicist, Astronomer, Mathematician, Cosmologist, Urstoff-freak, Absent-minded Professor, & Madman;* with an introduction by Aristotle. 1964. (BRG)

Sanders, Ed, ed. *Bugger: An Anthology of Anal Erotic, Pound Cake, Cornhole, Arse-Freak & Dreck Poems.* Includes contributions by Szabo, Allen Ginsberg, Ed Sanders, Ted Berrigan, John Harriman, Ron Padgett, Al Fowler, John Keys, and Harry Fainlight. Cover by Ed Sanders. 1964. (BRG)

Sanders, Ed, Ken Weaver, and Betsy Klein, eds. *The Fugs' Songbook.* 1965. (BRG)

Special thanks to Timothy Murray, from whose unpublished checklist of Fuck You publications this list was compiled.

Locus Solus

John Ashbery, Kenneth
Koch, Harry Matthews,
and James Schuyler

Lans-en-Vercors, France
1961–1962

Locus Solus II (Summer 1961).

Locus Solus. Nos. 1–5
(1961–1962).

BRG has: complete file.

Published in five issues in four volumes, *Locus Solus* could be called the overseas wing of the New York School. Each squat and plain issue looked like the serious literature of the French, a toned-down Gallimard volume perhaps. Included were translations of contemporary French poets such as Marcelin Pleynet alongside the work of, for example, Frank O'Hara, Joseph Ceravolo, or Kenneth Koch (issue 5 even includes a poem by modernist art critic Harold Rosenberg). The magazine was definitely "no nonsense" from the beginning, presenting no manifestoes or editorial statements, just high-quality literature – simply and elegantly presented with care and respect. The editors alternated responsibility, with Schuyler editing numbers 1 and 5, Kenneth Koch developing the "Special Collaborations" issue that was number 2, and John Ashbery editing the double issue, number 3/4, of New Poetry. Harry Matthews was the publisher, the man behind the magazine. Their taste was impeccable.

Art and Literature

John Ashbery

Paris
1964–1967

Art and Literature.
Nos. 1–12 (1964–1967).

BRG has: complete file.

Very high style, intense, and European, following on the heels of *Locus Solus, Art and Literature* was published in Switzerland by Anne Dunn and Rodrigo Moynihan, and edited from Paris by poet John Ashbery. Ashbery produced a remarkable blend of poetry, fiction, and commentary dealing not only with the world of poetry and literature, but with avant-garde art, theater, film, performance, and installation art. In addition, *Art and Literature* ranged geographically and chronologically over a wide variety of literatures. Issue 11 alone, for instance, included Rilke, Kenneth Koch and James Schuyler, Iannis Xenakis (Greece), Witold Gombrowicz (Poland), Cyril Connolly (England), Caspar David Friedrich (Germany), Miroslav Holub (Czechoslovakia), Gunter Kunert (East Germany), and Adrian Stokes (England). The last and twelfth issue of *Art and Literature* has a section dedicated to Frank O'Hara as well as a portfolio of work by Lucian Freud, a group of prose poems by Francis Ponge, a long poem by Barbara Guest, minimalist work by Aram Saroyan and Clark Coolidge, and a portfolio of work by sculptor Ronald Bladen with an essay by Bill Berkson. A remarkably integrated magazine despite its wide range of subjects and sympathies, *Art and Literature* was an elegant showcase for important new work from a variety of sources.

Art   and   Literature
$2.00

An international Review

I

Art and Literature 1
(March 1964).

Living Hand

Paul Auster, Lydia Davis, and Mitchell
Susskind

Paris and New York City
1973–1976

Living Hand. Nos. 1–8
(1973–1976) (two periodi-
cal issues [nos. 1 and 4]
and six monographs).

BRG has: complete file.

Both a little magazine and a small, independent publishing house, *Living Hand,*
which took its name from Keats ("This living
hand, now warm and capable"), was started
in Paris by Paul Auster (*The New York Trilogy,
The Music of Chance, The Art of Hunger, The
Invention of Solitude*), who was then working
as a telephone operator for the Paris Bureau
of *The New York Times* and translating French
poetry. *Living Hand,* which included a great
number of Auster's translations, numbered
eight issues, with numbers 1 and 4 being the
most conventionally magazine-like; the other
numbers were monographs. They included
translations of Paul Celan, Georges Bataille,
Edmond Jabès, and Maurice Blanchot and
other modern European writers, alongside
original work in English by editors Auster
and Davis (who were then married), Allen
Mandelbaum, Sarah Plimpton, Russell Edson,
and Rosmarie Waldrop, among others. *Living Hand* published two volumes of translations by Auster, Jacques Dupin's *Fits and Starts:
Selected Poems* (issue 2) and *The Uninhabited:
Selected Poems of André Du Bouchet* (issue 7),
as well as Auster's own first collection of
poetry, *Unearth* (issue 4). *Living Hand* 3 was
The Thirteenth Woman and Other Stories, a
sparkling collection of short works by Lydia
Davis. *Leaves of Absence,* a collection of poems
by Allen Mandelbaum, an award-winning
translator (of Ungaretti and the *Aeneid,* for
instance), was *Living Hand* 6, and a collection
of work by Sarah Plimpton was *Living Hand*
8. *Living Hand* did not accept unsolicited
submissions and was in the most positive way
the product of an intellectual community
intensely dedicated to avant-garde (in the
sense of on the edge, ahead of its time) writing. In this, and in its concern for the friendship of French and American letters, *Living
Hand* is also and paradoxically part of a cen-
tury-long tradition of ultramodernism.

LIVING HAND · 4

Maurice Blanchot — Death · Halt
Paul Auster — Poems
Simic / Prynne — Sarah Plimpton — 20 pages Reflectors
Anthony Barnett — from Fence Miscanthratai
Russell Edson — 5 (stories) works in Prose
Rosmarie Waldrop — from Nothing Has Changed
Lydia Davis — 2 stories
[Joseph Joubert — From the Notebooks]

— possible, + to be included :
        Prynne (7)
        Simic (10)

Maurice Blanchot
Paul Auster · Sarah Plimpton
Anthony Barnett · Lydia Davis · Rosmarie Waldrop
Russell Edson Joseph Joubert

Blanchot   Blanchot
Auster   Auster
Plimpton   Plimpton
Simic   Barnett
Edson   Davis
Barnett   Waldrop
Davis   Edson
Waldrop   Joubert
Joubert

Back cover:

As it is though, I'll do what little
I can in writing. Only it will be
very little. I'm not capable of
it; and if I were, you would
not go near it at all. For
if you died, you would hardly
dare to live.
            James Agee

Sarah Plimpton — has published work in The Partisan Review, The Paris
Review, Modern Occasions, and Extensions, and
lives in Paris.

Paul Auster, holograph
contents page for *Living
Hand* 4 (1974).

The Paris Review

Poetry editor, Tom Clark

New York City
1964–1974 (nos. 32–56)

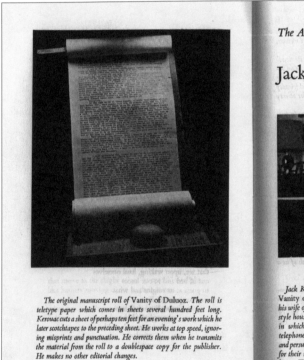

The original manuscript roll of Vanity of Duluoz. The roll is teletype paper which comes in sheets several hundred feet long. Kerouac cuts a sheet of perhaps ten feet for an evening's work which he later scotchtapes to the preceding sheet. He works at top speed, ignoring misprints and punctuation. He corrects them when he transmits the material from the roll to a doublespace copy for the publisher. He makes no other editorial changes.

60

The Art of Fiction XLI

Jack Kerouac

Jack Kerouac is now forty-five years old. His thirteenth novel, Vanity of Duluoz was published earlier this year. He lives with his wife of one year, Stella, and his invalid mother in a brick ranch-style house in a residential district of Lowell, Massachusetts, the city in which he spent all of his childhood. The Kerouacs have no telephone. Ted Berrigan had contacted Kerouac some months earlier and persuaded him to do the interview. When he felt the time had come for their meeting to take place, he simply showed up at the Kerouacs' house. Two friends, poets Aram Saroyan and Duncan McNaughton, accompanied him. Kerouac answered his ring; Berrigan quickly told

61

Ted Berrigan's interview with Jack Kerouac, in *The Paris Review* 43 (Summer 1968).

One of the great literary magazines of the latter half of the twentieth century, *The Paris Review* was founded in 1953 by novelist Peter Matthiessen and Harold Hume. The model for the magazine was Ford Madox Ford's *Transatlantic Review*, especially as it fell under the influence of Ezra Pound, and the idea was to recapture the Paris of the 1930s and the aura of explosive experimentation of that time. Soon after its founding, Matthiessen asked George Plimpton to edit and serve as the public relations arm of the magazine. The first poetry editor was Donald Hall. *The Paris Review* has been remarkably astute in predicting literary success and has indeed published most of the important fiction writers and poets of our time. The *Paris Review* interviews, entitled either *The Art of Fiction* or *The Art of Poetry*, have become known worldwide and have been influential in establishing almost a new literary genre, the author interview. Issue 31 (Winter/Spring 1964), edited by the second poetry editor, X. J. Kennedy, was devoted to an anthology of "Poets of the Sixties" that included, among others, John Hollander, James Dickey, Robert Bly, W. S. Merwin, and James Wright. However, with issue 32 (Summer/Fall 1964), Tom Clark assumed the poetry editorship and began publishing two generations of the New York School in the issues beginning with number 35 (which included Ron Padgett, Aram Saroyan, and an interview with William S. Burroughs). Issue 36 added Barbara Guest, and issue 40 printed three of Ted Berrigan's *Sonnets* and two poems by John Ashbery ("The Bungalows" and "The Chateau Hardware"). Poems in issue 41 were almost all by poets associated with the New York Schools, including Ashbery, Berkson, Coolidge, Gallup, Koch, Lima, Padgett, Schuyler, and Towle. Issue 43 contains the famous interview with Jack Kerouac by Ted Berrigan, witnessed by Aram Saroyan. Clark was poetry editor for ten years and twenty-five issues, until 1974 and issue 56, which contained his own "At Malibu" as well as work by Anne Waldman, Lewis MacAdams, and Alice Notley and a portfolio of "Imaginary Drawings for Book Covers," by George Schneeman.

The Paris Review. Poetry Editor, Tom Clark. Nos. 32–56 (1964–1974).

BRG has: complete file.

Paris Review Editions books, published in association with Doubleday & Company, include:

Baxter, Charles. *Imaginary Paintings and Other Poems.* 1989.

Elmslie, Kenward. *The Orchid Stories.* 1973. (GRD)

Mathews, Harry. *Tlooth.* 1966. (GRD)

Schuyler, James. *Freely Espousing: Poems.* 1969.

Wiebe, Dallas E. *Skyblue the Badass.* 1969.

Zukofsky, Louis. *"A"* 1–12. 1966. (GRD)

Zukofsky, Louis. *"A"* 13–21. 1969. (GRD)

Angel Hair

Anne Waldman and Lewis Warsh

New York City and Bolinas, California
1966–1978

Anne Waldman
and Lewis Warsh.
Photomat portraits,
New York City,
1968.

The Presses and Publications

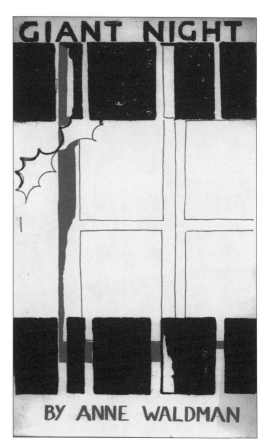

Anne Waldman, *Giant Night* (1968).
Cover by George Schneeman.

"Angel Hair sleeps with a boy in his head" was the line from the Jonathan Cott poem that caught Lewis Warsh's and my fancy, our duetted "ear," and we settled on Angel Hair as the name for our magazine and press. Jon was an old high school friend from New York, where we'd been literary pals exchanging Rilke, Alan Watts, Aldous Huxley, Lady Murasaki, Beckett plays, Berryman's "Homage to Mistress Bradstreet," various "little" magazines (Jon gave me a copy of Ted Berrigan's *"C"* magazine), and our own early and awkward poems. Lewis and I met at a Robert Duncan reading at the 1965 Berkeley Poetry Conference through a friend of Jon's and it was love at first sight. We seemed to be on a similar wavelength – both serious *and* romantic about poetry, studying it *and* the small press "underground" scene outside "the academy." Lewis was already extremely knowledgeable. He knew the work of and had met Jack Spicer, Robin Blaser, other "legends," and was collecting White Rabbit Press books. A voracious reader and writer, he also had several novels under his belt that he'd composed in high school. We founded our press on the spot. By September I had returned to school and Lewis was back on the Lower East Side, settling by Spring 1966 into the apartment at 33 St. Mark's Place and working for the Welfare Department. His salary sponsored our first ventures, in fact. We decided to use printer Ronnie Ballou from Williamstown who printed *Silo* (the Bennington College literary magazine).

His Chapel Press, with the exception of *Silo*, had printed mostly grocery lists until then and his prices were cheap. (I think the first issue was about $150 and the cover was left-over *Silo* paper.) *Angel Hair* had an ultimately modest run of six issues, although the press continued through marriage, separation, and divorce in myriad – both simple and elegant – ways: mimeo, offset, in addition to the occasional letterpress-printed broadsides and books.

— *Anne Waldman*
  Boulder, Colorado, September 15, 1997

Alice Notley, *Incidentals in the Day World* (1973). Cover by Philip Guston.

The Presses and Publications

*A*ngel Hair helped define the community of poets on the Lower East Side in the late 60s (as *"C"* magazine, *Kulchur, Fuck You, a magazine of the arts, Yugen,* and *Mother* had done in the early part of the decade). Jonathan Cott introduced Anne Waldman and me to one another at the Berkeley Poetry Conference in Summer 1965, and part of our impetus for starting the magazine was to publish his work along with our own, and the few other poets we knew, like Gerard Malanga and Chuck Stein. Anne was editing *Silo* at Bennington College, so it was convenient – once we gathered material for the first issue – to use the same printer and the same Fabriano paper stock for the cover (a different color for every issue). When Anne graduated in June 1966 she moved into my apartment, a large floorthrough at 33 St. Mark's Place in Manhattan (now a body piercing shop) and within a year we began publishing books (Lee Harwood's *The Man with Blue Eyes* and Gerard Malanga's *3 Poems for Benedetta Barzini* were the first titles) as well as continuing the magazine. We lived together in that apartment for three years,

and the table of contents of *Angel Hair* reflects not only our evolving tastes as poets but the constant stream of visitors who passed through our door: Ted Berrigan was a nightly guest, and we invariably hosted a party every Wednesday night after the readings at The Poetry Project. Our plan as editors was to focus on poets of the New York School and also to include West Coast writers like Robert Duncan, Joanne Kyger, Ebbe Borregaard, and Jim Koller whom we'd met on our travels. The magazine stopped after six issues when Anne and I separated, but we both continued publishing books under the Angel Hair imprint until 1978.

— *Lewis Warsh*
Brooklyn, New York, September 1997

Angel Hair. Nos. 1–6 (Spring 1966–Spring 1969). Cover by George Schneeman (6).

BRG has: complete file. BRG also has: *Angel Hair Catalogs* No. 2 (May 1969), 8 (Spring 1973), 9 (Spring 1975). Covers by Joe Brainard (9), Emilio Schneeman (8), George Schneeman (2).

Angel Hair books include:

Berkson, Bill. *Recent Visitors.* Cover and drawings by George Schneeman. 1973. (BRG)

Berkson, Bill. *Shining Leaves.* Cover by Alex Katz. 1969. (BRG)

Berrigan, Ted. *Many Happy Returns.* Broadside. 1967.

Berrigan, Ted. *Nothing for You.* 1977. (BRG)

Brainard, Joe. *I Remember.* 1970. (BRG)

Brainard, Joe. *More I Remember.* 1972. (BRG)

Brainard, Joe. *More I Remember More.* 1973. (BRG)

Brodey, James. *Identikit.* Cover photograph by Bob Cato. 1967. (BRG)

Brownstein, Michael. *3 American Tantrums.* Cover by Donna Dennis. 1970.

Bye, Reed. *Some Magic at the Dump.* 1978.

Carroll, Jim. *4 Ups and 1 Down.* Cover by Donna Dennis. 1970. (BRG)

Carter, Charlotte. *Sheltered Life.* Cover by Raphael Soyer. 1975. (GRD, SC)

Clark, Tom. *Neil Young.* 1970. (BRG: signed by the author)

Clark, Tom. *Sonnet.* Broadside. 1968. (BRG)

Clark, Tom, and Ron Padgett. *Bun.* Cover by Jim Dine. 1968. (BRG)

Coolidge, Clark. *Ing.* Cover by Philip Guston. 1968. (BRG)

Corbett, William. *Columbus Square Journal.* Cover by Philip Guston. 1976. (BRG)

Cott, Jonathan. *Elective Affinities.* 1970.

Creeley, Robert. *In London.* 1970. Printed by The Grabhorn-Hoyem Press. (BRG)

Continued on page 180

Anne Waldman comments: "Our first little pamphlet had been English poet Lee Harwood's *The Man with Blue Eyes*. Artist and writer Joe Brainard (one of my all-time heroes!) had generously agreed to design a cover for the little book (Lee's first) and offered us several possibilities. After we decided on the one with simple, unmistakable Brainard lettering I went ahead and had it printed on blue paper without further consultation. And the whole project went to press. Several weeks later I proudly handed Joe a copy and he seemed both surprised and amused. 'Blue? I'd meant it to be white. But that's okay.' "

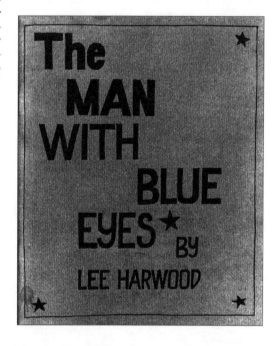

Lee Harwood, *The Man with Blue Eyes* (1966). Cover by Joe Brainard.

Denby, Edwin. *Snoring in New York.* Cover by Rudy Burckhardt. 1974. (BRG)

Elmslie, Kenward. *Girl Machine.* 1971. (BRG)

Fagin, Larry. *Parade of the Caterpillars.* Cover by George Schneeman. 1968. (BRG)

Fagin, Larry. *Twelve Poems.* Cover by George Schneeman. 1972. (BRG)

Fagin, Larry, and George Schneeman. *Landscape.* 1972. (BRG)

Gilfillan, Merrill. *Truck.* Cover by Joe Brainard. 1970. (BRG)

Giorno, John. *Birds.* 1971.

Greenwald, Ted. *Makes Sense.* Cover by George Schneeman. 1975.

Harwood, Lee. *The Man with Blue Eyes.* 1966. Cover by Joe Brainard. (BRG)

Kyger, Joanne. *Joanne.* Photograph of the author by Bill Berkson. 1970. (BRG)

Malanga, Gerard. *3 Poems for Benedetta Barzini.* Photograph of the author by Stephen Shore. 1967. (BRG)

Mayer, Bernadette. *The Basketball Article.* 1975.

Mayer, Bernadette. *Eruditio Ex Memoria.* Cover by the author. 1977. (BRG)

Mayer, Bernadette. *The Golden Book of Words.* Cover by Joe Brainard. 1978. (BRG)

Mayer, Bernadette. *Moving.* Covers by Ed Bowes. Drawings by Rosemary Mayer. 1971. (BRG)

Notley, Alice. *Incidentals in the Day World.* Cover by Philip Guston. 1973. (BRG)

O'Hara, Frank. *Oranges.* Cover by George Schneeman. 1969. (BRG)

Rosenberg, David. *Blues of the Sky.* Interpreted from the Ancient Hebrew Book of Psalms. Cover by George Schneeman. 1974.

Rosenberg, David. *Some Psalms.* Cover by Hannah Wilke. 1973. (BRG)

Rosenthal, Bob. *Cleaning Up New York.* Cover by Rochelle Kraut. 1976. (BRG)

Schiff, Harris. *I Should Run for Cover But I'm Right Here.* Covers by Rudy Burckhardt. 1978.

Schiff, Harris. *Secret Clouds.* Cover by Joe Brainard. 1970.

The Presses and Publications

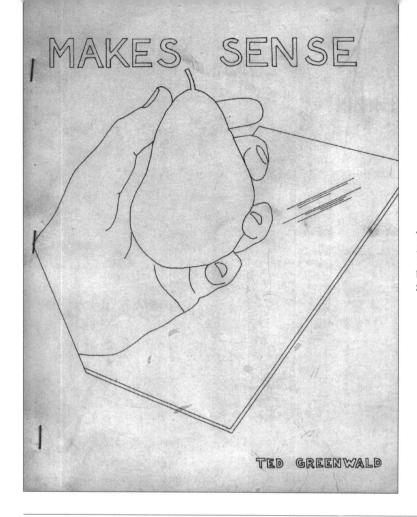

Ted Greenwald,
Makes Sense
(1975). Cover
by George
Schneeman.

Schjeldahl, Peter. *Dreams.* Cover by James Rosenquist. 1973. (BRG)

Schuyler, James. *Verge.* Broadside. 1971. Printed by Andrew Hoyem. (BRG)

Stanton, Johnny. *Slip of the Tongue.* Cover and drawings by George Schneeman. 1969. (BRG)

Stein, Charles. *The Virgo Poem.* 1967. (BRG)

Thomas, Lorenzo. *Dracula: A Long Poem.* Cover by Britton Wilkie. 1973. (GRD, SC)

Thomas, Lorenzo. *Fit Music.* Cover by Cecilio Thomas. 1972. (SC)

Torregian, Sotère. *The Golden Palomino Bites the Clock.* Cover by George Schneeman. 1967. (BRG)

Veitch, Tom. *Eat This: A Story.* Cover by Greg Irons. 1974. (GRD)

Vermont, Charlie. *Two Women.* Cover photograph by Harry Gross. 1971. (BRG)

Waldman, Anne. *Giant Night.* Cover by George Schneeman. 1968. (BRG)

Waldman, Anne. *Icy Rose.* Broadside. 1971. Printed by the Cranium Press.

Waldman, Anne. *O My Life!* Cover by George Schneeman. 1969. (BRG)

Waldman, Anne. *Up Through the Years.* Cover by Joe Brainard. 1969.

Warsh, Lewis. *The Maharajah's Son.* 1977. (BRG)

Warsh, Lewis. *Moving Through Air.* Covers by Donna Dennis. 1968. (BRG)

Warsh, Lewis, and Tom Clark. *Chicago.* 1970. Printed by The Grabhorn-Hoyem Press. (BRG)

Weiner, Hannah. *Clairvoyant Journal 1974.* Cover photograph of the author by Tom Ahern. 1978. (GRD)

Wieners, John. *Asylum Poems.* Cover by George Schneeman. 1969. (BRG)

Wieners, John. *Hotels.* Cover by Gordon Baldwin. 1974. (BRG)

Wilkie, Britton. *Limits of Space and Time.* 1971. (GRD)

Big Sky

Bill Berkson

Bolinas, California
1971–1978

Big Sky 4 (1972).
Cover by Philip Guston.

Big Sky began in 1971 during a perceptible lull in adventurous poetry publishing. The previous year I had moved to Bolinas, California, from New York where my parting shot had been a single-issue compendium of art and literature called *Best & Company*. When I arrived, the literary community in Bolinas numbered fewer than a dozen people, mainly poets like Joanne Kyger who had been associated with the Spicer and Duncan circles in San Francisco, plus a couple of prior interlopers from New York, Tom Clark and Lewis Warsh. By 1971, our neighbors included David and Tina Meltzer, Lewis and Phoebe MacAdams, Robert Creeley and Bobbie Louise Hawkins, and, briefly, Philip Whalen. Joe Brainard's *Bolinas Journal* was the first Big Sky book, soon followed by *The Cargo Cult* by John Thorpe. The name was suggested by Tom Veitch who lived around the lagoon, in Stinson Beach, and who reminded me of the line from a Kinks song, "Big Sky looks down on all the people." For the magazine, my original concept was a comic-book format, which was impractical for small print runs, so I held to something

like comic-book size and worked with friends who had enough offset-printing skills to crank out the pages on an old multilith on overnight binges in assorted redwood sheds. My original editorial stance was to accept whatever arrived from those invited to contribute. After two chaotic issues, I put this policy to rest, devoting the next number solely to Clark Coolidge. With *Big Sky* 4 – bearing its great wrap-around Philip Guston cover and especially powerful contributions by Creeley, Ron Padgett, and Bernadette Mayer – I hit my stride as an editor. Six years later, having published twelve issues of the magazine and more than twenty books, I decided I'd done the job.

— Bill Berkson
San Francisco, California, September 1997

Big Sky. Nos. 1–11/12 (1971–1978). Covers by Gordon Baldwin (10), Norman Bluhm (6), Celia Coolidge (3), Red Grooms (9), Philip Guston (4), Greg Irons (1), Alex Katz (2).

BRG has: nos. 1–4.

Big Sky books include:

Anderson, David. *The Spade in the Sensorium.* Cover by Philip Guston. 1974. (BRG)

Berkson, Bill. *Enigma Variations.* Cover and drawings by Philip Guston. 1975. (APP)

Berkson, Bill. *Terrace Fence.* 1971. (BRG)

Berkson, Bill, and Larry Fagin. *Two Serious Poems & One Other.* 1971. (BRG)

Berkson, Bill, and Joe LeSueur. *Homage to Frank O'Hara.* 3rd revised edition. 1988. (GRD)

Brainard, Joe. *Bolinas Journal.* 1971. (GRD)

Brodey, Jim. *Blues of the Egyptian Kings.* Cover by Greg Irons. 1975.

Carey, Steve. *Gentle Subsidy.* 1975. (GRD)

Coolidge, Clark. *Moroccan Variations.* Broadside. 1971. Printed at the Cranium Press.

Coolidge, Clark. *Polaroid.* 1975. Published with Adventures in Poetry. (BRG)

Fagin, Larry. *Seven Poems.* 1976. (BRG)

Gallup, Dick. *Above the Tree Line.* 1976. (GRD)

Greenwald, Ted. *The Life.* Cover drawing by the author. 1974. (BRG)

Gustafson, Jim. *Tales of Virtue and Transformation.* Cover by Greg Irons. 1974.

Kyger, Joanne. *All This Every Day.* Cover photograph of the author by Frances Pelizzi. 1975. (BRG)

MacAdams, Lewis. *I Have Been Tested and Found Not Insane.* 1974.

Mayer, Bernadette. *Studying Hunger.* Cover portrait of the author by Ed Bowes. 1975. Published with Adventures in Poetry.

Notley, Alice. *Phoebe Light.* Cover by Alex Katz. 1973.

Padgett, Ron. *Crazy Compositions.* Cover by George Schneeman. 1974.

Thorpe, John. *The Cargo Cult.* 1972. (GRD)

Veitch, Tom. *Death Collage and Other Poems.* Cover by the author. 1976. (BRG)

Waldman, Anne. *Spin Off.* 1972.

Watten, Barrett. *Opera Works.* 1975. (GRD)

The Poetry Project

St. Mark's Church-in-the-Bowery

New York City
1966–

The Poetry Project, located in the landmark St. Mark's Church-in-the-Bowery
in New York City's East Village, has for more
than thirty years been this country's premier
venue for new and experimental poetries.
Since 1966, the Project has offered readings,
performances, writing workshops, lectures,
symposia, publications, publishing facilities,
audiotape and document archives, and most
recently a site on the World Wide Web. Readers, performers, and teachers at The Poetry
Project have included Allen Ginsberg, John
Ashbery, Alice Walker, William S. Burroughs,
Sam Shepard, Adrienne Rich, Robert Creeley,
Diane di Prima, Kenneth Koch, Audre Lord,
John Cage, Yoko Ono, Imamu Amiri Baraka
(LeRoi Jones), Nicanor Parra, Jim Carroll,
and Patti Smith. Among the Project's former
directors are Joel Oppenheimer, Anne Waldman, Ron Padgett, Bernadette Mayer, and

Eileen Myles. The Poetry Project has always
been staffed completely by poets. Programs
and publications are geared to challenge,
inform, and inspire working writers, while
remaining accessible to the general public.
It has been said that The Poetry Project has
presented more poetry readings than any
other organization in history; and though
live programming has been a fundamental
emphasis, publishing has also been a high
priority. In the period from 1966 to the early
1980s, a steady stream of magazines and
books emanated from the Project's mimeograph machine. The Poetry Project started
publishing its literary magazine, *The World*,
in 1967 and began issuing *The Poetry Project
Newsletter* in 1972. Also appearing at regular
intervals were various workshop-produced
magazines. Other publishers availed themselves of the Project's publishing facilities

(i.e., typewriters, mimeograph, tables, and staplers). Among the presses that produced books at St. Mark's were Angel Hair, Adventures in Poetry, "C" Press, Telephone Books, Frontward Books, Jim Brodey Books, Crony Books, Dead Duke Books, Misty Terrace, Andrea Doria Books, and Remember I Did This For You. The list of magazines published at The Poetry Project included *Telephone*, *Adventures in Poetry*, *Un Poco Loco*, *Mag City*, the *4, 3, 2 Review*, *The Harris Review*, *Reindeer*, the *12th Street Rag*, *Caveman*, *Unnatural Acts*, *Little Light*, and *Tangerine*, as well as many one-shot reviews and anthologies. *Gandhabba* magazine and the *11th St. Ruse* were mimeographed at The Poetry Project as late as 1987 and 1995, respectively. By 1987, Poetry Project publications were produced using desktop computers and commercial printers. *The World* is now (October 1997) in its fifty-third issue and has been anthologized three times by major publishing houses. As of October 1997, 166 issues of *The Poetry Project Newsletter* have appeared. In the recent period, short-run publications have included *Project Papers*, edited by Ed Friedman; *Cuz*, edited by Richard Hell; and *Milk*, edited by Gillian McCain.

— *Ed Friedman*
   New York City, October 1997

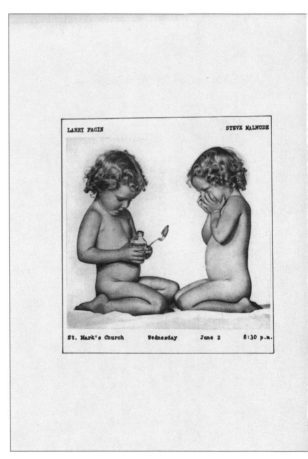

Collage for flyer for a poetry reading, The Poetry Project, St. Mark's Church, for Larry Fagin and Steve Malmude, 1971. Work on paper by Ron Padgett.

The World

Edited by Joel Sloman, Anne Waldman,
and others

New York City
1967–

The World 1 (January 1967).
Cover by Dan Clark.

In the Spring of 1966, I couldn't wait to graduate from Bennington, and get back "home" (which meant Macdougal Street and subsequently St. Mark's Place) and the "literary life." I had edited *Silo* magazine at school, and Lewis Warsh and I had founded *Angel Hair* magazine and books at the Berkeley Poetry Conference in the Summer of 1965. The Fall of 1966 was a critical time for me with Frank O'Hara's tragic death, but I was also hired as an assistant to the newly christened Poetry Project, a place where "only" poets could get jobs. Troubadour translator and New York poet Paul Blackburn had hosted open readings in the parish hall at St. Mark's the previous year, after moving the scene from the Metro coffee house. Joel Oppenheimer, another poet, was named Director. He had worked as a printer and wrote columns for the *Village Voice* in characteristic lower case. Younger poet Joel Sloman, who'd been a protégé of Denise Levertov, came on as primary assistant. We were being funded by Lyndon Johnson's Office of Economic Opportunity through a sociologist from the New School who had raised funding specifically to "benefit alienated youth on the Lower East Side." He would interview the staff, the participants, do a "study." So, a pilot project. We were "all" guinea pigs. We took the command seriously. When we started *The World*, there had been a lull in the little magazine blitz, di Prima and LeRoi

Jones's *Floating Bear* was subsiding, Ed Sanders's *Fuck You, a magazine of the arts* and *"C"* magazine, edited by Ted Berrigan, weren't coming out regularly. *Carpe diem!* A not-so-efficient brainstorm as it turned out, Joel Sloman and I sent out stencils to our desired contributors in mailing tubes that were to be returned with hot-from-the-muse in-progress works. They came back mangled, or improperly typed. Banged out in creative fervor. Holes for "o's" from those with expressive macho typewriters. No, that sheet has to go under the blue part shiny side up, you dummies! Exasperation, but soon it started to look good *in the tradition,* as we in the Mimeo Revolution say. Long hours late at night in the office minding the machines. Then we'd have a collation party the next day with the heavy-duty stapler. The over-inked pages had a certain charm. A page of an Edwin Denby play we printed, still readable but mottled, turned into a gorgeous work. George Schneeman often added color and visual flair to the magazine, and one of his works hangs over the peripatetic desk still. The other covers were fabulous! Artists Joe Brainard, Philip Guston, Yvonne Jacquette, Larry Rivers, Alex Katz, and others joined the mix. Joel's issue number one included work by Jack Anderson, Ted Berrigan, Jim Brodey, Michael Brownstein, Ruth Krauss, Gerard Malanga, Joel Oppenheimer, John Perreault, Carol Rubenstein, **continued**

The World 22
(April 1971). Cover
by John Giorno.
Guest editor:
Tom Clark.

continued Rene Ricard, Peter Schjeldahl, Anne Waldman, Lewis Warsh, Gary Youree, and others. I took over from Joel Sloman after the first issues, which had a number edited by Sam Abrams. I think I was "in Chief" by the end of 1967 and was then named Director of the Project in 1968 and continued the magazine through the next decade, which included some fine guest editorships: Tom Clark, Lewis Warsh (the Prose Issue), Ron Padgett (the Translation Issue), to name a few. Bernadette Mayer was a stalwart co-worker in 1974. The magazine was always too big, messy, uneven, democratic, inclusive, raw, and even boring at times. Hundreds of writers appeared in its 8 1/2 x 11 pages. The impulse was always toward the *immediate* community, so it covers most of the so-called New York School plus what comes after, with a bow toward Black Mountain, the Beats, San Francisco Renaissance, and the New York Scene (not "school"), as well as many independent folk and younger writers from workshops. It was arty, political, experimental, classy, corny, unaligned. In 1976 or so after many issues, when I headed out West with Allen Ginsberg to start up the Jack Kerouac School of Disembodied Poetics at the Naropa Institute in Boulder, Colorado, the first thing I did was purchase a mimeo machine at a used office equipment store in Denver for $38 so I'd feel more at home.

— *Anne Waldman, "Running Off* The World*"

The World. To date: Nos. 1– (January 1967–). *The World* is still in operation. Covers by Bill Beckman (7), Jack Boyce (5), Joe Brainard (9, 14, 25), Tom Clark (11), Fielding Dawson (6), Donna Dennis (4, 13), Bruce Erbacher (18), Larry Fagin (10), Cliff Fyman, and others (41), John Giorno (22), Mimi Gross (26), Philip Guston (29), Louise Hamlin (36), Jean Holabird (33), Yvonne Jacquette (21), Alex Katz (28), Rochelle Kraut (35), Linda Lawton (31), Rosemary Mayer (45), Rory McEwen (27), Pat Padgett (24), Larry Rivers (30), George Schneeman (3, 8, 19), Rick Veitch (15), Tom Veitch (20), Britton Wilkie (23), Trevor Winkfield (32).

BRG has: nos. 1–11, 13–16, 18–39, 41, 45.

Flyer for The Poetry
Project workshops
and readings,
Fall/Winter 1972.

```
                         THE POETRY PROJECT
                    St. Marks Church In-the-Bowery
                        10th Street & 2nd Avenue
                             NYC 10003

WORKSHOP SCHEDULE

Monday                    Prose              Seymour Krim
Tuesday                   Poetry             Joel Oppenheimer
Wednesday                 Playwriting        Murray Mednick
Thursday (afternoon 2PM)  Poetry             Joel Oppenheimer
Thursday                  Poetry             Sam Abrams
Friday                    Poetry             Ted Berrigan


All workshops are at 8:30 PM (except Thursday afternoon) in the
Old Courthouse, 2nd Avenue & 2nd Street.  FREE to all, but
especially directed to the young writer (17-25 years).  For
further information call 982-8825 between 2-5 PM Mon. thru Fri.


READING SCHEDULE

Wednesday       November 22  - Benefit for FOR NOW magazine
Wednesday       November 29 - George Kimball, Harry Lewis
Wednesday       December 6  - John Ashbery
Wednesday       December 13 - Catherine Murray, Mary Ferrari
Wednesday       December 20 - Robert Creeley
Wednesday       December 27 - To be announced
Wednesday       January 3   - John Wieners
Wednesday       January 10 - Kenneth Koch
Wednesday       January 17 - Andrei Codrescu, Charles Goldman
Wednesday       January 24 - Lewis MacAdams
Wednesday       January 31 - Robert Kelly

All readings are at 8:30 PM at the parish hall in the CHURCH.
CONSULT THE VILLAGE VOICE or EVO FOR CHANGES, ADDITIONS ETC.


THE WORLD

is the poetry magazine of the Poetry Project.  It comes out
once a month.  Send manuscripts (with self-addressed envelope)
to Anne Waldman, Editor at the address above or submit through
the workshops.

WELCOME to the Poetry Project.
```

The Poetry Project Newsletter

*Ron Padgett, Ted Greenwald, Bill
Mackay, Frances LeFevre, Vicki
Hudspith, Ed Friedman, and others*

*New York City
1972–*

**The Poetry Project
Newsletter.** To date: Nos. 1–
(December 1972–). *The
Poetry Project Newsletter*
is still in operation.

BRG has: nos. 1–62.

Begun in 1972, *The Poetry Project Newsletter* was mimeographed on the Gestetner machine in the Project's office; its corner-stapled pages listed new publications and upcoming events of interest to the Project's community. Most of these had to do with poetry, but there were also announcements of plays, performances, and art exhibits, as well as an occasional plea for a cheap apartment to rent or kittens in need of a home. Early issues made almost no mention of Poetry Project events, since at that time, the Project's mailing list of 250 or so received weekly flyers publicizing the programs at St. Mark's. Over the years, the newsletter expanded to include poems, articles, columns, reviews, comics, ads, and calendars of Project events, becoming – and, sadly, remaining – one of the few publications that regularly list and review poetry books from small- and medium-sized presses. During the 1980s, typed stencils and mimeography gave way to typesetting and offset printing. Then, as personal computers became affordable, typesetting and paste-up gave way to desktop publishing. Today, each thirty-two-page issue is mailed to a list of over 3,500 and is distributed nationally for sale at newsstands and bookstores; subscriptions are available to institutions and individuals. Although it continues to draw upon the Project for its sense of locale, the publication also addresses the interests of a national (and somewhat international) community of readers who share an interest in the more communicative and adventurous aspects of contemporary poetry.

— *Ed Friedman*
New York City, October 1997

ZZZZZ (1977).
Cover by Alex Katz.

Z Press

Kenward Elmslie

Calais, Vermont

1973–

Z Press produced the eponymous one-shot magazines *Z, ZZ, ZZZ, ZZZZ, ZZZZZ*, and *ZZZZZZ* in the 1970s, perhaps following in the footsteps of the Once series edited in England in the early 1960s by Tom Clark (*Once, Twice, Thrice, Ice, Frice*, etc.). *Z*, for which Trevor Winkfield drew the logo and cover, also included other work by him, including prose poems. It also had poems by Ted Berrigan, Michael Brownstein, Pat Nolan, Keith Abbott, and Charles North, and by Brad Gooch, who was to become a successful novelist and the biographer of Frank O'Hara. The third issue, printed by the Poets Press, included work by John Ashbery, Paul Violi, Trevor Winkfield, Douglas Crase, Ann Lauterbach, Tim Dlugos, John Wieners, Kenward Elmslie, Lorenzo Thomas, and Joanne Kyger. The cover and logo were by Donna Dennis, and the issue included "Hotels," a portfolio of eight of her images, printed on glossy paper. The cover for *ZZZZ* was a drawing by Joe Brainard of Beetle Bailey, in homage and bagging Z's, and with the sixth issue the last Z could be found hidden on the moose's nose, drawn by Alex Katz.

This issue included some of the usual suspects (Kenneth Koch, Ted Berrigan, Alice Notley, and Frank O'Hara) but added some experimentalists such as Barrett Watten, Bob Perelman, and Paul Hoover. Z Press continues to publish books, broadsides, records, and cassettes from time to time (including work by Joe Brainard and Kenward Elmslie) and keeps most of its publications in print and well distributed, being in this way a little unusual or lucky.

Z. Nos. 1–6 (1973–1977): Z (1973), ZZ (1974), ZZZ (1974), ZZZZ (1974), ZZZZZ (1976), ZZZZZZ (1977). Covers by Joe Brainard (ZZZZ), Donna Dennis (ZZZ), Alex Katz (ZZZZZ), Ron Padgett (ZZ), Karl Torok (ZZZZZ), Trevor Winkfield (Z).

BRG has: complete file.

Z Press books and other publications include:

Ashbery, John, and James Schuyler. *A Nest of Ninnies.* 1975. (BRG)

Brainard, Joe. *29 Mini-Essays.* 1978.

Brainard, Joe, Anne Waldman, and Michael Brownstein. *Almost Heaven.* Poster. 1973.

Brownstein, Michael. *Strange Days Ahead.* Cover photograph by August Sander. 1975. (GRD)

Bye, Reed. *Border Theme.* 1981. (BRG)

Denby, Edwin. *Miltie Is a Hackie.* 1973. (BRG)

Elmslie, Kenward, and Donna Dennis. *26 Bars: A Collaboration.* 1987.

Finlay, Ian Hamilton. *Heroic Emblems.* 1978.

Matthews, Harry. *Selected Declarations of Dependence.* Illustrated by Alex Katz. 1977.

Padgett, Ron. *The Tulsa Kid.* 1979. (BRG)

Winkfield, Trevor. *Nativity.* Drawings by Karl Torok. 1974. (BRG)

For a complete listing of Z Press publications, the reader is referred to: William C. Bamberger, *Kenward Elmslie: A Bibliographical Profile* (Flint, Mich.: Bamberger Books, 1993).

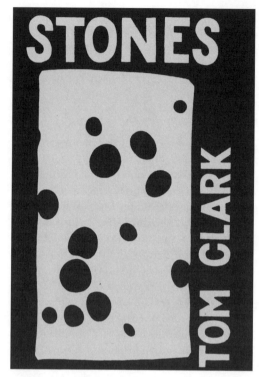

Tom Clark, *Stones* (1969). Cover by Joe Brainard.

Into the Mainstream with Harper & Row

1969–1970

The five books of New American Poetry published by Harper & Row were:

Clark, Tom. *Air.* Cover design by Joe Brainard. 1970. (BRG, GRD)

Clark, Tom. *Stones.* Cover by Joe Brainard. 1969. (BRG, GRD)

Coolidge, Clark. *Space.* Cover by Jasper Johns. 1970. (BRG, GRD)

Gallup, Dick. *Where I Hang My Hat.* Cover by George Schneeman. 1970. (GRD)

MacAdams, Lewis. *The Poetry Room.* Cover photographs by Phoebe MacAdams. 1970. (GRD)

Although Indiana-based Bobbs-Merrill published two lively anthologies of New York School poetry (*The World Anthology* in 1969 and *Another World* in 1971, both edited by Anne Waldman) and a few books of poetry including Waldman's own *Baby Breakdown* (1970) and *Life Notes* (1973), the most glorious publishing moment for some of the young second-generation New York School poets may have been the publication of five books of poetry by the giant, unmistakably mainstream, New York–based publisher Harper & Row. As poet Larry Fagin explains, the apotheosis of the mainstreaming of the New American Poetry, or at least a stream of it, occurred under editor Fran McCullough: "McCullough was an editor at Harper & Row in the late '60s. Through the poet Donald Hall, she became friendly with Tom Clark, editing his book, *Stones.* She was staunchly supportive of the younger New York School writers and admired Ron Padgett's book *Great Balls of Fire*. Soon, she invited Tom to submit a second book, *Air,* and solicited books from Padgett (*Others*), Dick Gallup (*Where I Hang My Hat*), Clark Coolidge (*Space*) and Lewis MacAdams (*The Poetry Room*). Padgett withdrew his manuscript – a collection of collaborations with other poets – and the remaining four titles appeared simultaneously in 1970."

Clark Coolidge,
Space (1970). Cover
by Jasper Johns.

Adventures in Poetry 2
(July 1968).
Front cover by
Joe Brainard.

Adventures
in Poetry

Larry Fagin

New York City
1968–1976

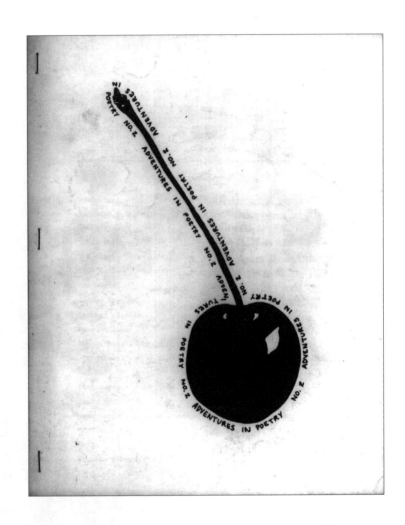

he title derives from a children's textbook, *Adventures in Reading*. I was trying for a kind of funky elegance like *o to 9*, a little fancier than *"C"* or *Lines*. A typical issue was 300–350 copies, consuming thirty reams of 24# mimeograph paper, run through the Gestetner machine of The Poetry Project at St. Mark's Church. Most numbers were as thick as possible – as many as fifty double-sided pages. I purchased a state-of-the-art Novus ½" stapler from Germany that cut through an issue like it was butter, a very satisfying sensation. After the final editing, typing, proofing, correcting, and mimeographing, a bunch of us would set up long tables in the Parish Hall, often after a reading, and collate and staple late into the night. Working at the Project and attending hundreds of readings over the years was a big advantage. If I heard something I especially liked at a reading, I would rush to the podium and claim the manuscript for *Adventures*. I was rarely refused. Editing was a good way to make friends (and, hopefully, not many enemies). I loved what Joe Ceravolo was writing then, as well as poems by Ron Padgett, Ted Berrigan, Dick Gallup, Tony Towle, et al. – the second-generation New York School crowd. But older poets contributed, too, and work from the West Coast, Chicago, and London was solicited. *Adventures* avoided the grab bag mode of publishing one or two pieces each from many contributors. Often, several poets were featured with up to a dozen poems each. One number was entirely devoted to three writers. There was an all-prose issue. Number 10 was the "anonymous" issue – no authors were credited; not even the name of the magazine appeared; the covers were pornographic comic strips. I couldn't pay the authors or cover artists, though once I commissioned Dick Gallup, who was in a slump, at $5 per poem, and he came up with his wonderful "Charged Particles" and several other beauties. Few legitimate publishers were taking on the kind of writing I like, so in 1970 Adventures published its first pamphlet, Tom Veitch's *My Father's Golden Eye*. Books by John Ashbery, John Godfrey, Clark Coolidge, and John Giorno soon followed. Writers who were completely **continued**

Adventures in Poetry. Nos. 1–12 (March 1968–Summer 1975). Covers by Anonymous (10), Joe Brainard (2), Rudy Burckhardt (2), Jim Dine (6), Rory McEwen (11), Ron Padgett (1), Aram Saroyan (7), George Schneeman (5).

BRG has: nos. 1, 2, 5–8, 10–12.

Adventures in Poetry, Catalogs. Edited by Larry Fagin. Nos. 1–2 (1973–1975). Covers by Bill Brodecky (1) and Alice Neel (2).

BRG has: complete file.

Adventures in Poetry books include:

Anonymous [Clark Coolidge and Larry Fagin]. *Tonto Lavoris*. 1973. (BRG)

Ashbery, John. *The New Spirit*. 1970. (BRG)

Bartlett, Jennifer. *Cleopatra I–IV*. 1971. (BRG)

Baxter, Glen. *Drawings*. 1974. (BRG)

Baxter, Glen. *The Khaki*. 1973. (BRG)

Berkson, Bill, and Frank O'Hara. *Hymns of St. Bridget*. Cover by Larry Rivers. 1974. (BRG)

Berrigan, Ted. *The Drunken Boat*. A translation of Rimbaud. Drawings by Joe Brainard. 1974. (BRG)

Biggs, Thazarbell. *We Are Integrated and Wonderfully Made*. 1976. (BRG)

Brown, Rebecca. *For the 82nd Airborne*. 1976. (BRG)

Brownstein, Michael, and Ron Padgett. *Kiss My Ass!/Suffering Succotash*. 1971. (BRG)

Carey, Henry. *Chrononhotonthologos: The Most Tragical Tragedy, That Ever Was Tragediz'd by Any Company of Tragedians*. Presented by Ron Padgett and Johnny Stanton. 1971.

Continued on page 196

continued off the radar screen – Steve
Malmude, Richard Snow, Richard Elliott,
Jamie MacInnis, Curtis Faville, Rebecca
Brown – and painters Joseph White and
Jennifer Bartlett made their debuts with
Adventures pamphlets. One unsolicited
manuscript was accepted: *We Are Integrated
and Wonderfully Made*, poems describing the
major body organs, written in lilting dog-
gerel by Mrs. Thazarbell Biggs, a registered
nurse. There were a number of abandoned
Adventures projects – an anthology of children's poems, translations of French poets,
and pamphlets by Dale Herd, Ed Marshall,
Alfred Starr Hamilton, John Wieners, and
others. The magazine lasted through 1975.
Money was becoming scarce, and at the end
of 1976, after about thirty-seven books, I gave
it a rest.

— *Larry Fagin*
  New York City, September 1997

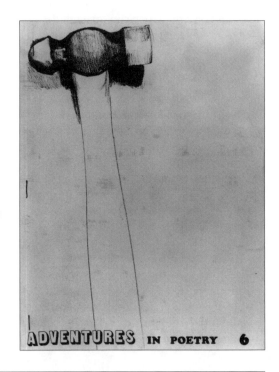

Adventures in Poetry 6
(1970). Cover by
Jim Dine.

Carroll, Jim, and Lewis
MacAdams. [Two Poems].
Illustration by George
Schneeman. 1973. (BRG)

Cendrars, Blaise. *Kodak.*
Translated by Ron Padgett.
1976. (BRG)

Coolidge, Clark. *Polaroid.*
1975. Published with Big
Sky. (BRG)

Coolidge, Clark. *The So
(Poems of 1966–67).* Cover
by Brice Marden. 1971.
(BRG)

Coolidge, Clark. *Suite V.*
1973. (BRG)

Crabtree, Lee. *An Unfinished
Memoir.* Edited by Peter
Schjeldahl. Cover photo-
graph by Linda Schjeldahl.
1974. (BRG)

Dawson, Fielding. *The Girl
with the Pale Cerulean Eyes/
The Man with the Grey Hair.*
Cover by the author. 1974.
(BRG)

Denby, Edwin. *Snoring in
New York.* Cover photograph
by Rudy Burckhardt. 1974.
Published in association
with Angel Hair. (BRG)

Elliott, Richard. *A Song and
a Diary for A.* Cover by
Edward Gorey. 1973. (BRG)

Elmslie, Kenward. *City
Junket.* Cover by Alex Katz.
1972. (BRG)

Faville, Curtis. *Ready.*
Cover by Hugh Kepets.
1975. (BRG)

Ferrari, Mary. *The Flying
Glove.* Cover and drawings
by Susan Hall. 1973.

Giorno, John. *Cum.* Cover
by Les Levine. 1971. (BRG)

Godfrey, John. *The Music of
the Curbs.* Cover drawing by
Michael Goldberg. 1976.
(BRG)

Godfrey, John. *26 Poems.*
Cover by Robert Indiana.
1971. (BRG)

Greenwald, Ted. *Making a
Living.* Cover by Gordon
Matta-Clark. 1973.

Larbaud, Valery.
*RLDASEDLRAD LES
DLCMHYPBDF.* Trans-
lated by Ron Padgett.
Covers by Lindsay
Stamm Shapiro. 1973.

The Presses and Publications

John Ashbery, *The New Spirit* (1970). Cover photograph of the author by unknown photographer.

MacInnis, Jamie. *Hand Shadows*. Covers by Bruce Erbacher. 1974. (BRG)

Malmude, Steve. *Catting*. Cover by John Wesley. 1972.

Mann, Edward L. *Central Avenue*. Cover by George Schneeman. 1971. (BRG)

Mayer, Bernadette. *Studying Hunger*. 1975. Published in association with Big Sky.

North, Charles. *Elizabethan and Nova Scotian Music*. Cover and drawings by Jane Freilicher. 1974. (GRD)

Obenzinger, Hilton. *Bright Lights! Big City!* 1974. (BRG)

O'Hara, Frank. *Belgrade, November 19, 1963*. 1973. (BRG)

Owen, Maureen. *Country Rush*. Cover and drawings by Yvonne Jacquette. 1973. (BRG)

Padgett, Ron, and Larry Fagin, eds. *Book of Methods (For Getting Children Interested in Writing)*. 1971. (BRG)

Padgett, Wayne. *Three Kings*. 1972. (BRG)

Schuyler, James. *A Sun Cab*. Cover and drawings by Fairfield Porter. 1972. (BRG)

Snow, Richard. *The Funny Place*. Cover by Red Grooms. 1973.

Spicer, Jack. *Admonitions*. [1973]. (BRG)

Towle, Tony. *Lines for the New Year (Poems 1963–65)*. Cover by Allan D'Arcangelo. 1975.

Veitch, Tom. *My Father's Golden Eye*. 1970. (BRG)

Waldman, Anne. *West Indies Poems*. Cover and drawings by Joe Brainard. 1972. (BRG)

Warsh, Lewis. *Today*. Covers by Alan Saret. 1974. (BRG)

White, Joseph. *Palace of the Oriental*. Cover drawing by the poet. 1973. (BRG)

United Artists

Lewis Warsh and Bernadette Mayer

Lenox, Massachusetts, and New York City

1977–

Ted Berrigan, *The Sonnets*
(1982). Front cover by
Louise Hamlin.

Bernadette Mayer and I co-founded *United Artists* magazine in 1977. We were living in relative isolation in Lenox, Massachusetts, and editing a magazine put us in touch with poets and friends we had left behind in New York. We managed to buy an inexpensive mimeo machine in Pittsfield and we produced the magazine in the living room of our large apartment on the main street of Lenox. The beauty of mimeographing is that we could control every aspect of production ourselves, that I could stay up all night and produce a new issue by morning if I wanted. The first issue reflects our geographical shift and contains work by ourselves and our immediate neighbors, Clark Coolidge and Paul Metcalf. Our idea was, whenever possible, to publish large amounts of a few poets' work in each issue, as opposed to one or two poems by a lot of people. Among the regular contributors to subsequent issues were Ted Berrigan, Alice Notley, Diane Ward, and Bill Berkson. *United Artists* was probably the last of the great mimeo magazines since by the mid-80s everyone had computers and all the magazines became perfect-bound with glossy covers so the bookstores would distribute them. We published eighteen issues, from 1977 to 1983, and during this time we returned to New York City and began publishing United Artists Books, which I continue editing into the present.

— *Lewis Warsh*
Brooklyn, New York, September 1997

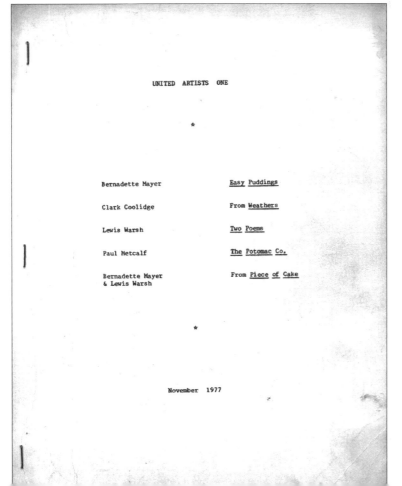

United Artists 1
(November 1977).

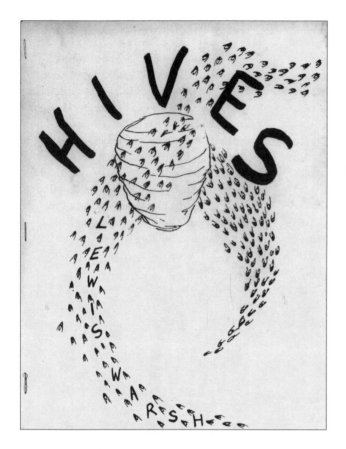

Lewis Warsh, *Hives* (1979). Front cover by Rosemary Mayer.

United Artists. Nos. 1–18 (November 1977–December 1983). Covers by Louise Hamlin (16), Yvonne Jacquette (17), Rosemary Mayer (18).

BRG has: complete file.

United Artists books include:

Berrigan, Ted. *The Sonnets.* Covers by Louise Hamlin. Frontispiece portrait by Joe Brainard. 1982. (BRG)

Berrigan, Ted, and Harris Schiff. *Yo-Yo's with Money.* Front cover by Rosina Kuhn. Photographs by Rochelle Kraut. 1979. (BRG)

Brodey, Jim. *Judyism.* Cover by Martha Diamond. 1980.

Carey, Steve. *The California Papers.* Cover by Peter Kanter. 1981.

Collum, Jack. *The Fox.* Covers by Annie Hayes and William Kough. 1981. (GRD)

Coolidge, Clark. *Own Face.* 1978. (BRG)

Lenhart, Gary. *One at a Time.* Cover by Louise Hamlin. 1983. (GRD)

Notley, Alice. *Songs for the Unborn Second Baby.* Cover by George Schneeman. 1979. (BRG)

Schiff, Harris. *In the Heart of the Empire.* Cover by George Schneeman. 1979. (BRG)

Vermont, Charlie. *Selected Poems.* Cover by Alice Notley. 1980. (BRG)

Warsh, Lewis. *Hives.* Front and back covers by Rosemary Mayer. 1979. (BRG)

The completed video was included in the exhibition *A Secret Location on the Lower East Side: Adventures in Writing, 1960–1980,* presented in the Berg Exhibition Room, The New York Public Library, January 24–July 25, 1998. Stills from it appear below and on the following pages.

Portraits and Home Movies, 1968–1969, by Larry Fagin and Julie Harrison

During the Fall of 1968 and through the next Spring, I fooled around with a cheap super-8 movie camera, making three-minute portraits of poet friends. I completed seven of these, planned others, and hoped to add music. I also shot some rolls of "our gang" goofing off at a beautiful pink house on Long Island, which belonged to Bill Berkson's mother. Another roll shows the ongoing poker game at Dick Gallup's apartment. This ritual was eventually moved to George Schneeman's and had a fifteen-year run. Hannah Weiner took the wedding footage. Joan Inglis and I were married by Michael Allen, the pastor of St. Mark's Church-in-the-Bowery. Both the ceremony and the reception were held in the Schneemans' large apartment on St. Mark's

Place. Lewis Warsh was my best man and Anne Waldman was the bridesmaid. Attendees were a who's who of the East Village poetry and art scene. In spite of (or because of) social upheaval and the war in Vietnam, it was a time of giddy, even joyful, group activity: collaborative writing, little magazines and pamphlets, weekly poetry readings, endless parties, rock concerts, dope smoking, wild sex, and political protests. You can look it up. Twenty-eight years later, these little reels of film turned up in a box in my closet. There were some exposure problems (I never really knew what I was doing), but much of the footage was presentable. Julie Harrison cleaned it up and transferred it to videotape, then we set about editing and laying in some music for the portraits. Ron Padgett did the commentary for the group scenes in his inimitable, down-home manner.

— *Larry Fagin*
New York City, 1997

Lewis Warsh, from his New York Diary 1967:

The alarm rings: it's 2:00 P.M. I get up, dress & go downstairs to buy the *Post*. It's Halloween. Call the typewriter repair shop

& learn that it will cost $25 to have my typewriter repaired. Read a few chapters from *A Confederate General from Big Sur*.

Anne returns. I go out, take some packages to the post office on 14th Street. Then I go to the library around the corner.

I get a new library card but there are no books I want to take out. Take more packages to the P.O. on 4th Avenue. Return

home; it's almost dark out. Anne comes home. Peter comes by. We talk about Peter Viereck who is going to read at

The Presses and Publications

St. Mark's. Anne cooks dinner. Peter leaves. I re-write part of an old poem on Anne's typewriter. At about 9:00 I go to the

church to the reading which started at 8:30. Meet Shelly at door to the church. She's going to a big Halloween party at the

Village Theater. Reading has not yet started. There aren't many people there: Anne & Ted & Larry & Peter. After the first

set I leave. It's Halloween. Kids are running through the street asking people for money. In front of Gem Spa I meet Katie

& Debbie & their kids. There are three cops on the corner. We all go upstairs. I give the kids all the Halloween candy. . . .

Center

Carol Bergé

*Woodstock, New York, and
Santa Fe, New Mexico
1970–1984*

Center. Nos. 1–13
(1970–1984), and
Supplement: Special
Issue, vol. 1 (1983).

BRG has: complete file.

Center contained a wide range of fiction and other prose, including considerable avant-garde dance and art criticism. Bergé's editorial philosophy was influenced by John Cage's theories developed in his class on new music at the New School, by Jackson Mac Low's performance pieces at the Judson Memorial Church, and by her work with the Fluxus Group and others. As she noted in an autobiographical memoir for Gale's *Contemporary Authors:* "Kenneth King's, Phoebe Neville's, Yvonne Rainer's, Simone Forti's 'new dance' would cause me to see ordinary walking as dance. Yvonne's 'The Mind Is a Muscle,' Carolee [Schneemann's] 'The Queen's Dog,' a funny piece by Phoebe Neville parodying The Hippie Walk on a tightrope, all at Judson. Al Hansen made me think about news and newspapers when he ground them in a blender. Opera would never be the same again after being in Dick Higgins's 'Opera' and Central Park looked different after having seen it on stilts with Ray Johnson. 'Poetry in Motion' changed from a phrase to a meaningful infusion after being in Jackson Mac Low's theater pieces…. The revelation: it is all music, all a poem being lived, all dance. A gift, back to the givers, full circle … moving at the edges where poetry, music, dance, sculpture and painting overlapped and melded and caused our ordinary lives to be suffused into art."

Center 1 (1970). Cover
photograph of Georgia
O'Keeffe in Abiquiu,
New Mexico, by
Michael Vaccarro.

My career as a writer burgeoned as one of the LIGHT YEARS poets who met at the Deux Mégots Coffeeshop in the East Village in the 1960s. We read our work aloud weekly and were published in early magazines of the "Mimeo Revolution," as well as in traditional media. By 1970, I knew that half of us had moved into prose, with a plethora of eager experimentation in modes hitherto unexplored, and I sensed there was a place for a magazine to represent this new writing. The first issue of *Center* set the tone: I invited friends to send me "non-form prose from known writers, exciting work unacceptable in the usual media. . . ." Susan Sherman produced number 1 on a mimeo machine: thirty-four pages; the response was so enthusiastic that numbers 2 and 3 went to fifty-two and sixty-two pages, which established the median size of issues. I printed an issue when I'd received "enough" interesting manuscripts. If a piece excited me, I felt it would interest, excite, and challenge my peers to try new ways to create, to innovate. *Center* became a forum for writers whose avant-garde ideas have become, over the ensuing years, part of the tradition in literature. Of the 150 writers published in *Center*, about sixty have produced books since 1970 containing material which was first seen in its pages. Writers wanted to be published in it. The print run was always tiny, from 200 to 450 copies, yet the circulation was triple that, because copies circulated hand-to-hand, mind-to-mind, in a flurry of excitement. Editing and publishing *Center*, from 1970 to 1984, was a joy: the energy produced by the writing coming to my desk in Woodstock (1970–1974) and five subsequent loci was an intensely stimulating ingredient in my life. I met many incredibly talented people through their writings, many of whom became close friends. Generous grants to publish plus pay the authors came from the NEA through the Coordinating Council of Little Magazines starting with number 2, and I went to offset and saddle-stitch or perfect-binding through number 13 (the "Final Issue"). In the 1980s there were two Center Chapbooks of new prose, and in the early 1990s Center Press published two books of innovative fiction by other writers, and co-published with Tribal Press my own collected fiction, *Zebras, or, Contour Lines* – these are all *Center* magazine offshoots. It has been a steady stream for twenty-seven years of applied devotion to adding to the literature, with lovely perks alongside.

— *Carol Bergé*

o to 9

Bernadette Mayer and
Vito Hannibal Acconci

New York City
1967–1969

of things just pass things   pure up cize   pass think it here/on(to
this, that is, to the s/In the first days of the year 1911, a badly d
ressed young man/teeth and fists, he smashed eternity to smithereens.
Then/women were remembered in the icy fog./Lute/He died like the sun/
studio last year while eating lemons./There, then, they did it ov/iii
ii/iiiii/I am putting on the topsoil i/In Wiltshire there dwelt a Far
mar of indifferent wealth,/him for a garment or two, and so tooke him
into seruice:/eously: wel apparelled he was, and well monied, & might
/heard that hee had married a wife in Wilshire, not farre/the comming
of hir trecherous husband, who returned within a/him with lookes ful
of death, made him this answer: I villaine,/cast them in his face, &
said, Now lustful whoremaister, go/22/23/first and then fold and even
/1, 2, 3, 4, 5,/face them, they are cheek by/steps, shops noses, ear
a, eyes/A surface of/an apple/As there were four where anyone seldom/
s it, and he is it. And ther/   /   /ad made it. Whether he had
m/The field of Carnac is a large, open space where eleven/buried. Th
e fact of the duel required that the stones be/representation of the
python, because, according to Pausanias,/been. "Let us look for the
reason, a thing no one has thought/l'Ecole Polytechnique, an engineer
, a M. de la Sauvagere./as ever were Pelloutier, Deric, Latour d'Auve
rgne, Penhoet/them), if anyone should, after all these opinions, ask
me mine,/sharp, clear tones swelled louder as they came nearer and/ra
ising her arm as if to hide under it, she turned her head/by little t
he soil assumed its usual level and everyone went/road, and the sun,
which made our shoulders smart beneath/dinner/dinner/nds folded befor
e you -- I t/The engine/Carter's body/A treasure/Dahlstrom said/Polic
e found/———/——/et to mention that -- during/'Twas in the month of
December, and in the year 1883,/and was first seen by the crew of a G
ourdon fishing boat,/Beautiful Railway Bridge of the Silvery Tay!/Upw
ards of two miles and more,/Beautiful Railway Bridge of the Silv'ry T
ay!/It must have been an awful sight,/at me stealing away from my/tic
k/tick/t, noticeable, unmistakable((/all   all/ide the left half of
the hum/Six Works by/to/is/listeners/just/gardens,/and eo-/plug in yo
ur hands, as well/There is a changling that can't/s means you. I mea
n that. I/Why don't you tell every one about it, he said to her/His
attention was disturbed by the sudden lodging of a beebee/Beeflesh. U
p in the interesting hive his wife and baby bees/u point away. Come
to the po/of things just pass things   pure up cize   pass think it
here/on(to this, that is, to the s/In the first days of the year 1911
, a badly dressed young man/teeth and fists, he smashed eternity to s
mithereens. Then/women were remembered in the icy fog./Lute/He died
like the sun/studio last year while eating lemons./There, then, they
did it ov/iiiii/iiiii/I am putting on the topsoil i/In Wiltshire ther
e dwelt a Farmar of indifferent wealth,/him for a garment or two, and
so tooke him into seruice:/eously: wel apparelled he was, and well mo
nied, & might/heard that hee had married a wife in Wilshire, not farr
e/the comming of hir trecherous husband, who returned within a/him wi
th lookes ful of death, made him this answer: I villaine,/cast them i
n his face, & said, Now lustful whoremaister, go/22/23/first and then
fold and even/1,2,3,4,5,/face them, they are cheek by/steps, shops
noses, ears, eyes/A surface of/an apple/As there were four where anyo
ne seldom/s it, and he is it. And ther/   /   /ad made it. Whet
her he had m/The field of Carnac is a large, open space where eleven/
buried. The fact of the duel required that the stones be/representat
ion of the python, because, according to Pausanias,/been. "Let us lo
ok for the reason, a thing no one has thought/l'Ecole Polytechnique,a
n engineer, a M. de la Sauvagere./as ever were Pelloutier, Deric, Lat
our d'Auvergne, Penhoet/them), if anyone should, after all these opin
ions, ask me mine,/sharp, clear tones swelled louder as they came nea
rer and/raising her arm as if to hide under it, she turned her head/by
little the soil assumed its usual level and everyone went/road, and t

o to 9 3 (January 1968).

"What is a body artist? Someone who is his own test tube," quips painter David Salle about performance artist, filmmaker, and writer Vito Hannibal Acconci, probably the prime example of an artist who experiments on himself and his own life, using his body and its movements as his materia artistica. Born in New York City in 1940, Acconci returned to the Lower East Side in 1964 to teach at Brooklyn College and the School of Visual Arts after graduating from Holy Cross College and the Iowa Writers' Workshop. Acconci was first a writer, and with his sister-in-law Bernadette Mayer edited one of the most experimental of all the early mimeo magazines. *o to 9* included works by a phalanx of literary experimentalists, including the minimalist works of Aram Saroyan and Clark Coolidge, along with the graphic works of artists Sol LeWitt, Michael Heizer, and Robert Smithson, and performance-oriented work by Jackson Mac Low, Steve Paxton, and Acconci himself. Art historian Kate Linker places Acconci's earliest language-oriented work as a poet, including *o to 9*, in the perspective of his later accomplishments: "Zeroing in on or 'targeting' language, the works attempt to materialize language, to give words body and weight – substance but not depth. Throughout the pieces, language points to itself, reflexively describing its motion over the page along with its capacities for accumulation, juxtaposition, and interplay. These early poems comprise a series of ruthlessly logical operations on poetic space. Although the literalism of the language indicates an assault on the 'expressive' author or self, the poems reinforce the modernist prescription to acknowledge the limits of the medium. They renounce language's referential function, its ability to evoke a world off the page; instead their aim, Acconci has written, was to 'Use language to cover a space rather than uncover a meaning.' " In the tradition of little magazines of the 1960s, *o to 9* published a supplement and several books in addition to the magazine.

0 to 9. Nos. 1–6 (April 1967–July 1969), and Supplement to No. 6, entitled *Street Works* (1969).

BRG has: complete file.

0 to 9 books include:

Acconci, Vito Hannibal. *Four Book.* 1968. (BRG)

Mayer, Bernadette. *Story.* 1968. (BRG)

Mayer, Rosemary. *Book: 41 Fabric Swatches.* 1969. (BRG)

Piper, Adrian. Untitled booklet, whose first line is "one block was randomly selected from a map of New York City." 1968. (BRG)

Saroyan, Aram. *Coffee Coffee.* 1967. (BRG)

Aram Saroyan,
Coffee Coffee (1967).

In "A Lecture at the Naropa Institute, 1989,"
Poetics Journal *(1990), Bernadette Mayer discusses the conception and structure of* Story:

"This is the first book I ever published. I published it myself. It's called *Story*. It has no page numbers. It's about thirty pages. The way it came into being was I wrote a story that was about falling down, tripping and falling down. It was nicely written, experimentally so, but it seemed dull. So I tried to figure out what to do with it; and being a twenty-year-old person at the time, I went overboard and made a structure that is like a diamond shape where I accumulated other texts. I was very interested in American Indian myths at that time so I included a Kwakiutl myth about hats and about smoking; their description of a hoop and arrow game; and then an Italian folk tale about fourteen men who went to hell; another Italian tale about a man who sold cloth to a statue; then from Coos myth texts, a story of the five world makers, and the man who became an owl. Then I accumulated some lists from the dictionary of other words for beginning, middle and end. There's a recipe for true sponge cake, there's a 19th-century letter about etiquette, a couple of quotes from Edgar Allan Poe, and an article by the biologist Louis Agassiz about coral reefs. Each of these things I thought was relevant to the diamond shaped nature or accumulation of the story....

"As I was saying to Clark Coolidge, there is some aspect of this work that I can't remember (as to how I did it). I took the longest work which was the story I'd written about falling, and I made that begin at the beginning and end at the end. Everything was going on in the exact middle of the work, and at the beginning and end only one thing was going on and it was gradually accumulating and decreasing.

"To make things worse, I decided to interrupt the text at random moments with all the words I could think of that would mean story.... There are fifty-one ... anecdote, profile, life-story, scenario, love-story, lie, report, western, article, bedside reading, novel, thumbnail sketch, talk, description, real-life story, piece, light reading, confessions, dime novel, narrative poem, myth, thriller.

"It was interrupted at random. The confluences were amazing. All of a sudden it would say detective story, and the section that was randomly chosen to be a detective story really became one. Or could become one in the reader's mind. Probably more so than in my mind."

But even this, though it passes through great ones of that, does not undergo such ones of that other as one of those that rises from something of sixty-four of these to the thing of it.

He emerges, blind, on a beach and sleeps.

Laboratory utensils: funnels, beakers, flasks, desiccators, canisters, bottles and test tube holders.

When they threw it, they made it roll along, and people would shoot at it.

Frogs, flowers in the shapes of globes, a kangaroo.

Certainly there will be a person.

How people and things fall: from the tree, in battle, from her shoulders, to the sea, ill, on a Monday, to the widow, in the second syllable, on her lips, from her lips, into two classes, and among, away, back, back on, behind, down on, flat, for, foul of, from grace, in, inwith, off, on, out, short, through, to and under.

The former remains within the thing of one of them.

He shuts himself inside a hollow tree to escape a hail storm.

Household utensils: dustpans, fly swatter, colander, garbage pail, wastebasket, ice bucket, juicer, child's hot plate.

Origin.

Once in a while one of them would hit it when he shot at it.

Novel

There was a child whose name was Fourteen.

May be in a tree or up it, or on their way up it, or

Bernadette Mayer, from *Story* (1968).

Lines

Aram Saroyan

New York City
1964–1967

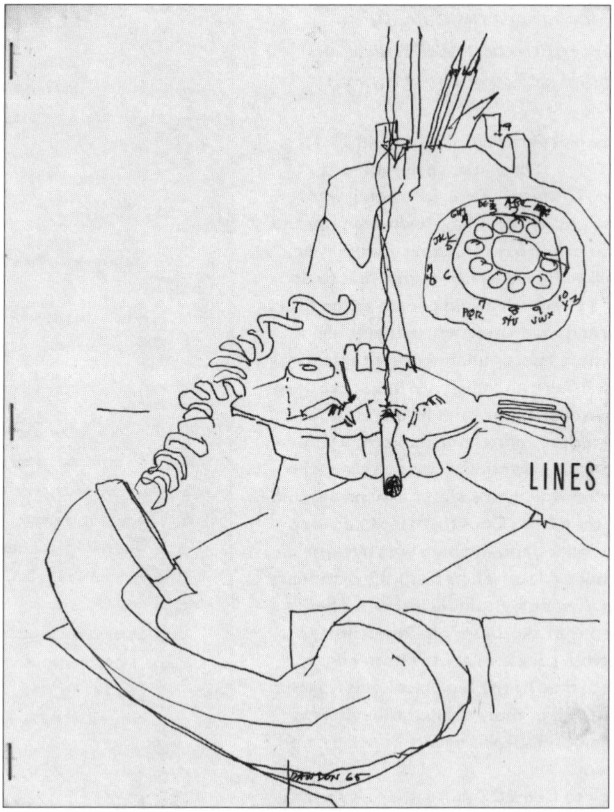

Lines 5 (May 1965). Cover by Fielding Dawson.

Lines. Nos. 1–6 (September 1964–November 1965). Covers by Fielding Dawson (5), Richard Kolmar (4), Aram Saroyan (1–3, 6).

BRG has: complete file.

Lines books include:

Berrigan, Ted, with Ron Padgett. *Noh.* 1965. (Lines Broadsheet, No. 1.)

Coolidge, Clark. [*Clark Coolidge*]. 1967. (BRG)

Coolidge, Clark. *Flag Flutter and U.S. Electric.* Cover design by the author. 1966. (BRG)

Greenwald, Ted. *Lapstrake.* Cover by Joe Brainard. 1965. (BRG)

Kolmar, Richard. *Games.* Cover by Larry Zox. 1966. (BRG)

Perreault, John. *Camouflage.* 1966. (BRG)

Saroyan, Aram. [*Aram Saroyan*]. 1967. (BRG)

Saroyan, Aram. [*Works*]. 1966. (BRG)

Stein, Gertrude. [*Poems*]. 1967.

Aram Saroyan, the son of one of America's most beloved novelists, grew up on New York's West End Avenue and attended Trinity School, a private prep school in the same neighborhood. He attended the University of Chicago for a while and had his first poem published in the *Nation*. Returning to New York, he worked at Bookmasters bookstore near Times Square and at Virginia Admiral's Academy Typing Service (she was a poet and the mother of actor-to-be Robert De Niro). After traveling cross-country to show his poems to Robert Creeley, then in Placitas, New Mexico, Saroyan was finally ready, at age twenty-one, to start his own little magazine, *Lines*, in 1964. In *Friends in the World* (Coffee House Books, 1992), he recalled: "I was eager to make contact with my literary contemporaries, and the little magazine was a nice entree into the milieu. Young poets need a place to publish, and the magazine gave me an excuse to make contact with anyone whose work I liked." As it turned out, he published the work of at least four of the most talented male poets of his generation: Ted Berrigan with his aggressively mimeo *"C"* magazine; Ron Padgett with his delicately weird and offset *White Dove Review*; Tom Clark, poetry editor of the prominently non-mimco *Paris Review*; and Clark Coolidge, whose first book, *Flag Flutter and U.S. Electric*, was published by *Lines* in 1966. Saroyan joined Berrigan when he visited Jack Kerouac in Lowell, Massachusetts, for his legendary *Paris Review* interview. The look of mimeo was perfect for Saroyan and for *Lines*, which published the community of poets whom he admired, in their more "abstract" or minimalist moments. The strikingly simple covers and the carefully composed pages make *Lines* among the most elegant of all the 1960s mimeograph magazines. Saroyan published six issues of the magazine and several books (including Ted Greenwald's *Lapstrake* and John Perreault's *Camouflage*), before leaving New York, and the 60s, to begin a different life: "When I started to write again in Bolinas, California, it wasn't minimal poetry anymore, but a long poem about my life, marriage, and fatherhood. Strawberry Saroyan had been born at the hospital in Stoneham, Massachusetts on October 20, 1970."

Aram Saroyan, Bolinas, California, 1972. Photograph by Larry Fagin.

Telegraph Books

Victor Bockris, Aram Saroyan, and Andrew Wylie

New York City
1971–1973

Patti Smith, *Seventh Heaven* (1972). Photograph by Judy Linn.

Telegraph Books include:

Bockris, Victor. *In America.* Cover photograph of the author by Aram Saroyan. 1972. (GRD)

Clark, Tom, Ron Padgett, and Ted Berrigan. *Back in Boston Again.* Introduction by Aram Saroyan. Cover photograph by Rudy Burckhardt. 1972. (GRD)

Malanga, Gerard. *Poetry on Film.* Cover photograph by the author. 1972. (BRG)

Polk, Brigid. *Scars.* Cover by the author. 1972. (GRD)

Saroyan, Aram. *Poems.* Cover photograph by Gailyn Saroyan. 1972. (BRG)

Saroyan, Aram. *The Rest.* Cover photograph by the author. 1971. (GRD)

Smith, Patti. *Seventh Heaven.* Photograph by Judy Linn. 1972. (GRD)

Weatherly, Tom. *Thumbprint.* Cover photograph by Elsa Dorfman. 1971. (SC)

Wylie, Andrew. *Gold.* Cover photograph by Gerard Malanga. 1972. (GRD)

Wylie, Andrew. *Tenderloin.* Cover photograph by Aram Saroyan. 1971. (GRD)

Born in Harvard Square, Telegraph Books were edited from Cambridge, Massachusetts, printed and perfect-bound in Philadelphia, and published in New York (essentially from Andrew Wylie's bookstore on Jones Street in Greenwich Village). They were, and still are, instantly recognizable. Aram Saroyan and Wylie first discussed the series after they had both read at a benefit for a socialist bookstore in Cambridge, and Saroyan describes the purpose behind their project in *Friends in the World* (Coffee House Press, 1992): "We wanted to do something specifically for our own generation along the lines of what Ferlinghetti had done for the Beat Generation with his City Lights Books. We spent a lot of time talking about the poets we would publish and also decided that, like City Lights's Pocket Poets series, the books should have a standardized size and format. . . . Victor [Bockris] had a working partnership with a printer outside Philadelphia and handled the nuts-and-bolts work of seeing that the books looked the way we wanted them to: mass paperback dimensions with a photograph, usually of the author, on the cover. When the first copy of my collection, *The Rest*, arrived, Gailyn and I were both amazed at the care and professionalism of the product. It was a real new book we held in our hands. After titles by Andrew and me, Victor went on to produce books by Tom Weatherly, Gerard Malanga, a memoir by Ron Padgett, Tom Clark and Ted Berrigan, and *Seventh Heaven* by Patti Smith, her first poetry collection. She had been recommended to Andrew by Malanga, and Andrew, who had a quick eye for new talent, had been immediately won over both by her work and her tough-girl street style with its undercurrent of sweetness."

Tom Weatherly, *Thumbprint* (1971). Photograph by Elsa Dorfman.

Contact 6 (January
1973): Tom Pickard
issue. Cover photo-
graph of Tom Pickard
by Bockris-Wylie.

Contact

Jeff Goldberg

Philadelphia

1972–1973

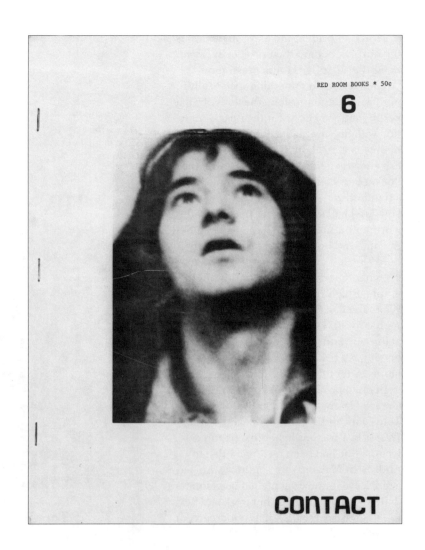

RED ROOM BOOKS ★ 50¢

6

CONTACT

The Presses and Publications

Published over the course of only two months in the winter of 1972–1973, *Contact* consisted of seven issues and was the creation of poet-lyricist-musician Jeff Goldberg, egged on by a combine known as Bockris-Wylie (Andrew Wylie and Victor Bockris, recently and formerly of Telegraph Books). The attitudes and poses of the cover stars gave the magazine a tinge of rock glory or Rimbaudian flair, most evident in the first three issues, which focus on the work of Goldberg ("A Week in Philadelphia" in all three) and his friends Ken Bluford and Marty Watt, Philadelphians all. These issues of the magazine are graced with the New York savoir faire of a great number of collaborations between Bockris and Wylie (culminating in a long review article on Wylie by Ken Bluford in issue 3). With number 4, the Larry Fagin issue, the magazine changes course, devoting most of its nearly thirty pages to one poet, a formula it continued using to great effect. The Fagin issue includes tributes by friends in prose and poetry, and a sampling of Fagin's own poetry. The cover of the issue is, of course, a photograph of Fagin with a typewriter. The next and final three issues follow the same format (as does Opal Nations's London-based *Strange Faeces*, which came out at this time, and with a Larry Fagin issue too). *Contact* ends with issues devoted, respectively, to Anne Waldman, British poet Tom Pickard, and John Wieners. This last issue (number 7) includes an excellent survey of Wieners's work by the late Burroughsian scholar Eric Mottram that was also published in *Poetry Information* (employing another important strategy developed by entrepreneurial little magazine publishers of the 1970s: reprinting).

Contact. Nos. 1–7 (1972–1973).

BRG has: complete file.

Little Caesar

Dennis Cooper

Los Angeles
1976–1980

Little Caesar. Nos. 1–11
(1976–1980).

GRD has: complete file.

Little Caesar books include:

Britton, Donald. *Italy.*
Cover by Trevor Winkfield.
1981. (MSS)

Cooper, Dennis. *Tiger Beat.*
1978. (GRD)

Cooper, Dennis, ed.,
assisted by Tim Dlugos.
*Coming Attractions: An
Anthology of American
Poets in Their Twenties.*
1980. (MSS)

Dlugos, Tim. *Entre Nous:
New Poems.* 1982. (GRD,
MSS)

Dlugos, Tim. *Je suis ein
Americano.* Cover photo-
graph by Richard Elovich.
1979.

Gerstler, Amy. *Yonder.*
Cover photographs by
Judith Spiegel. 1982. (BRG)

Koertge, Ron. *Sex Object.*
1979.

Lally, Michael. *Hollywood
Magic.* 1982. (GRD, MSS)

MacAdams, Lewis. *Africa
and the Marriage of Walt
Whitman and Marilyn
Monroe.* 1982. (GRD)

Malanga, Gerard. *100 Years
Have Passed: Prose Poems.*
1978. (GRD)

Schjeldahl, Peter. *The Brute.*
Cover and drawings by
Susan Rothenberg. 1981.
(GRD)

Skelly, Jack. *Monsters.* Cover
designed by Stephen Spera
from a photograph by
Sheree Levin. 1982. (GRD)

Coming Attractions: An Anthology of American Poets in Their Twenties, edited by Dennis Cooper, assisted by Tim Dlugos (1980).

Despite its visual resemblance to the teen idol magazine *Tiger Beat* (the covers tell the story, featuring images of Adolphe Menjou, John F. Kennedy, Jr. at age sixteen, Arthur Rimbaud, Warhol star Eric Emerson, poet John Wieners, and completely naked rock star Iggy Pop), *Little Caesar* was a very serious attempt to widen the subjects of and audiences for poetry: "We want a literary magazine that's read by Poetry fans, the Rock culture, the Hari Krishnas, the Dodgers. We think it can be done, and that's what we're aiming at. . . . We have this dream where writers are mobbed everywhere they go, like rock stars and actors. People like Patti Smith (poet/rock star) are subtly forcing their growing audiences to become literate, introducing them to Rimbaud, Breton, Burroughs and others. Poetry sales are higher than they've been in fifteen years. In Paris ten year old boys clutching well worn copies of Apollinaire's ALCOOLS put their hands over their mouths in amazement before paintings by Renoir and Monet." Running along pretty much like a "punk poetry 'zine" for its first three issues, *Little Caesar* then shifted gears a bit, devoting issue 4 to Rimbaud, 5 to poet, filmmaker, and photographer Gerard Malanga, and 6 to John Wieners. With issue 8 it was back to a neo-punk look and sported a "new wave rock theme," including an interview with Johnny Rotten and an article by Jeff Goldberg, himself the editor of the rock music–influenced *Contact*. Goldberg wrote on the Ramones and the "Origins of the New Wave: Forest Hills." The Saroyan/Wylie/Bockris Telegraph Books series provided both a visual and literary model, but *Little Caesar* was strikingly of its time, perfectly Californian, new wave, and queer without providing a manifesto for anything, being in your face about most things and up front about few. In addition to the anthology *Coming Attractions*, books published by Little Caesar Press included Tim Dlugos's *Je suis ein Americano*, Ronald Koertge's *Sex Object*, a newly translated version of Rimbaud's *Voyage en Abyssinie et au Harrar*, Gerard Malanga's *100 Years Have Passed*, and editor Cooper's collection of poems *Tiger Beat*. Cooper went on to organize the fantastically successful Beyond Baroque Readings in Venice, California, and is a novelist of some power, grace, and controversy.

Frontward Books

Bob Rosenthal and Rochelle Kraut

New York City
1976–1979

Susie Timmons, *Hog Wild* (1979). Cover by Susie Timmons.

"Susie Timmons goes nutso genius and what appears looks like a poem and it's definitely okey-doke. 'We are the Spanish Harps/ Vwing Vwing Vwing.' 'Keep on going old sappy head.' More than okey-doke. As good as going to see superman or eating breakfast."

— Ed Friedman, review of *Hog Wild* in
  L=A=N=G=U=A=G=E 11 (January 1980)

A part of the third wave of New York
School poetry, Frontward Books began
life in 1976 with the publication of a collaborative performance novel, *Bicentennial Suicide,*
by Nuyorican Poets Cafe stalwart Bob Holman
and Bob Rosenthal. In all, the press published
nine mimeographed books, noteworthy for
their often hand-colored covers with drawings by Rochelle Kraut. Rosenthal, later to
become Allen Ginsberg's assistant, reminisces
in "Mimeography: Friends Forever": "In some
ways, mimeo publishing poetry books was an
outgrowth of the War in Korea, where corpo-
ral Ted Berrigan had run the mimeo machine
in his unit, later producing his own magazine
"C" using the new skill of mimeography. I was
in Chicago just starting to write poetry and
Ted was teaching at Northwestern University,
where I sat in somewhat shyly on his classes
but didn't really get to know him until he was
told that I had a car. He told me he needed
someone to drive him and the stencils for his
wife's (Alice Notley's *Chicago*) mimeo magazine over to a little church. I obliged and
he taught me to use the mimeo. I can't forget him taking off his pants and running the
machine wearing his skivvies, a Pall Mall hanging off his lips. So my friends and I started our
own mimeo mag (the *Milk Quarterly*) and later
Rochelle Kraut and I published a series of
mimeo books under the imprint of Frontward
Books, which eventually banded together to
combine our bookrate mailings, calling themselves Packet Poets. I eventually taught dozens
of people how to use the mimeo machine
and spent light-years walking around in collating circles reading the works of poets from
all across the country. . . . Everyone felt that
these books were merely holding space on
the shelves until the major publishers picked
them up and brought out 'real' editions. But
the publishing boom of the time was soon
over, and these books were really for real."

Alice Notley, *A Diamond Necklace* (1977). Hand-colored
cover by Rochelle Kraut.

Frontward Books include:

Berrigan, Ted. *A Feeling for
Leaving.* Hand-colored
cover by Rochelle Kraut.
1975. (BRG)

Friedman, Ed. *The Black Star
Pilgrimage/The Escape Story.*
Front and back covers by Ed
Bowes. 1976. (BRG)

Hackman, Neil. *Small Poems
to God.* Cover by Rudy
Burckhardt. 1979. (BRG)

Holman, Bob, and Bob
Rosenthal. *Bicentennial
Suicide.* 1976. (BRG)

Kraut, Rochelle. *Circus
Babys.* 1975. (BRG)

Notley, Alice. *A Diamond
Necklace.* Hand-colored
cover by Rochelle Kraut.
1977. (BRG)

Rosenthal, Bob. *Lies About
the Flesh.* Cover by Rochelle
Kraut. 1977. (BRG)

Timmons, Susie. *Hog Wild.*
Cover and drawings by the
author. 1979. (BRG)

Toth, Steve. *Rota Rooter.*
1976. (BRG)

Siamese Banana

Johnny Stanton

New York City

1972–1978

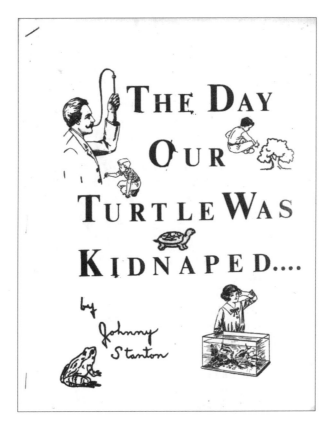

Johnny Stanton, *The Day Our Turtle Was Kidnaped.* . . . (1978).

Siamese Banana books include:

Anderson, David. *Under Western Eyes.* 1970. (BRG)

Auster, Paul, trans. *A Little Anthology of Surrealist Poems.* Cover by George Schneeman. 1972. (BRG, GRD)

Brainard, Joe. *The Banana Book.* Cover and drawings by the author. 1972. (BRG)

Brainard, Joe. *The Friendly Way.* Cover and drawings by the author. 1972. (BRG)

Brainard, Joe. *Some Drawings of Some Notes to Myself.* 1971.

Brainard, Joe, ed. *The Cigarette Book.* Cover by the editor. 1972. (BRG)

Brainard, Joe, and Anne Waldman. *Self Portrait.* 1972. (BRG)

Brown, Rebecca. *Mouse Works.* Cover and illustrations by Martha Diamond. 1971. (BRG)

Cohen, Keith. *Madness in Literature.* 1970. (BRG)

Obenzinger, Hilton. *Thunder Road.* 1970. (BRG)

Stanton, Johnny. *The Day Our Turtle Was Kidnaped.* . . . 1978. (BRG)

Veitch, Tom. *Death College.* Cover by the author. 1970. (BRG)

Weingarten, Don. *Lord Scum's Hotel.* Cover and illustrations by the author. 1971.

First it was a NEWSPAPER,
Then it was a PRESS,
Then it was a GANG.

I worked at a neighborhood youth center and one day our fearless director barked at me, "Jumping butterballs, you're supposed to be a writer, why don't you start a center newspaper."

"You betcha," I meowed.

This idea for a newspaper collected a bunch of oddball kids: Fat John, Ginzo, Pokey, Caggie, Lilley, et al.

The painter Joe Brainard had suggested the newspaper's name in another context: The SIAMESE BANANA from Vol. XXVII of Ripley's Believe It or Not.

The paper's motto became: If the Facts Don't Fit, Change Them. After that it was easy to start up an artsy-literary press. The philosophy was simple: Writers and Artists, you have nothing to lose, so unite in the SB Press. The technology was easy: electronic stencils.

Meanwhile, back in the 'hood, wiseguy newspaper kids got infected by literary bugs. But these kids were from the TV dope fiend generation. They wanted to form a gang.

"How about a name?"

"Exterminator Angels?"

"No way!"

"Military Gangsters from the Super Id?"

"Fuck off, Mr. Stanton."

"Please, you guys, just call me Stanton."

"Okay Stanton, how about the SBG?"

"Right on! The SBG. I'm a member."

We tore up and down every house we performed in. Kicked ass and then some. Ahead of our time and underneath it.

— *Johnny Stanton*
  New York City, November 1997

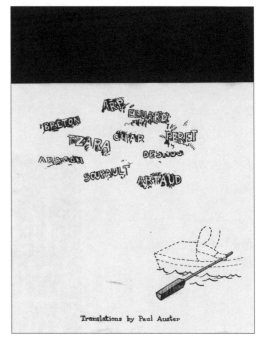

Paul Auster, trans., *A Little Anthology of Surrealist Poems* (1972). Cover by George Schneeman.

Dodgems

Eileen Myles
New York City
1977

Dodgems. Nos. 1–2 (1977).

BRG and GRD have:
complete files.

Dodgems 1 (1977).

I've never liked mimeo. Sure, it's fast and it's cheap but it doesn't look like a book. If you can do it yourself, why bother? Why not just xerox your favorite new poems from time to time and hand 'em to your friends? Or better still, why not stylishly fold your latest into your back pocket and show it to the several people who matter? How many people's taste do you trust? I mean, who actually understands poetry? I publish my poems in mimeo magazines. I like to see them breathe beyond my own typewriter though I'm much happier when they're typeset. . . . Somebody once described mimeo publication as "punk publishing" and that made it work for me for awhile. But not really. When someone asks me if I've got a book I say Yeah . . . but it's just mimeo. That usually means you can't get it. It's not available or else Sure, but I don't like it anymore. Was the 60s the Golden Age of Mimeo? That makes me think it's a dated idea. Mimeo. But I think it's too late for all

that. The best poems should be well-packaged, I'm not even thinking about big-house books (oh, sure), it's not even like comparing cable to prime-time teevee, it's like comparing – there's no comparison, view-master to movies – no comparison. I just mean mimeo vs. a book-book. A nice shiny book-book. Doesn't money make money? Won't people take your poems more seriously in a great typeface with a far-out cover, expensive, in color. Wouldn't this here ratty publication be more "influential" (influential on what – Genius critic Denis Donoghue says poetry now occupies a "marginal" place. Like the funniest lines in *Mad* magazine?) if it was typeset? Wouldn't I be more excited about writing for it? You go to the New York Small Press Bookfair and see endless publications, books & magazines in full glossy grandeur, nice commercial high-production values. You say Wow, don't these books look pretty! Pick one up & sniff the nice new cover – but don't look inside – *pure dreck.* . . . But I like these shiny books: they look commercial, real, they look American. If only the stupid publishers and the brilliant poets could get together. Mimeo skirts all that so the publisher is the poet's best friend or even the poet and that's that. Your family won't believe it's a book but so what. They also are unable to read your poems. So I have only set my hand once to mimeo publishing but it was an act of revenge in my heart – we did an anthology of poems ourselves in response to another slicker inferior one. Mimeo was effective in this case – fast & cheap. It wasn't like killing someone, it was like throwing a beer in their face.

A FRESH YOUNG VOICE FROM THE PLAINS

Eileen Myles, *A Fresh Young Voice from the Plains* (New York: Power Mad Press, 1981). Cover photograph of the author by Irene Young.

— *Eileen Myles*
in The Poetry Project Newsletter
(March 1982)

[None of the issues of Dodgems *were produced through mimeography.]*

*Vehicle
Editions*

*Annabel Lee
[née Levitt]*

*New York City
1976–*

Ted Berrigan, *Train Ride*
[1978]. Cover by Joe
Brainard.

I started Vehicle Editions as an enthusiastic cottage industry, working out of a railroad flat in Little Italy, printing by letterpress at Center for Book Arts a couple of blocks away, binding in the kitchen, storing the books under the bed, making limited editions by hand. I had already worked in publishing uptown as well as in a union offset printing shop as an A.B. Dick 360 operator and as a computer and hot lead typesetter. Authors, artists, craftspeople, apprentices, and the publisher worked in close collaboration to ensure that the format of each book reflected its contents. As one reviewer wrote, "Each book is custom designed to fit its contents." *Score*, a score of the dance piece *Lazy Madge* with writings by choreographer Douglas Dunn, was the first "commercially" produced Vehicle Edition. Published in 1977 in an edition of about 500 copies, it served both the dance and the literary communities as a document of multidisciplinary collaborative work. Ted Berrigan's *Train Ride* was produced with materials tested for at least 250 years. The edition is 1,500 copies printed letterpress – the typeface is monotype Gill Sans,

the same used throughout the British railway system. Artist Joe Brainard not only designed the cover but also contributed to the overall design and editorial decisions. *Smithsonian Depositions & Subject to a Film* by Clark Coolidge was produced on a Xerox machine using a high grade of bond paper in an almost square format to achieve a unique book object containing most unusual essays on subjects that might otherwise seem mundane: the making of the movie *Jaws* and the work of sculptor Robert Smithson. Instead, these are a couple of Coolidge's most intriguing works.

— Annabel Lee
Ancram, New York, September 1997

Vehicle Editions books include:

Allen, Roberta. *The Traveling Woman*. Cover and drawings by the author. 1986.

Beltrametti, Franco. *Airmail Postcards*. 1979. (BRG)

Berrigan, Ted. *Train Ride (February 18th, 1971) for Joe*. Cover by Joe Brainard. [1978]. (BRG, GRD)

Coolidge, Clark. *Smithsonian Depositions and Subject to a Film*. 1980. (BRG)

Dunn, Douglas, and Annabel Levitt. *Score*. 1977. (BRG)

Guest, Barbara. *Quilts*. 1980.

Knowles, Christopher. *Typings, 1974–1977*. 1979. (GRD)

Lally, Michael. *Just Let Me Do It: Love Poems, 1967–1977*. 1978. (GRD)

Levitt, Annabel. *Calisthenics of the Heart*. 1976.

Levitt, Annabel. *Continental 34s*. 1977. (GRD)

Levitt, Annabel. *The Erie-Lackawanna Railroad Train Poem*. Broadside. 1979.

Notley, Alice. *When I Was Alive*. Cover by Alex Katz. 1980.

Pettet, Simon. *Conversations with Rudy Burckhardt About Everything*. 1987. (APP)

Phillips, Jayne Anne. *Counting*. 1978. (GRD)

Phillips, Jayne Anne. *Fast Lanes*. Drawings by Yvonne Jacquette. 1984. (GRD, RBK)

Ratcliff, Carter. *Give Me Tomorrow*. Portraits by Alex Katz. 1983. (GRD)

Schuchat, Simon. *Light & Shadow*. 1977.

Schuchat, Simon. *Wushan Gorge*. Broadside. 1979?

Shimun, Surma D'Baitmar. *Assyrian Church Customs and the Murder of Mar Shimun*. 1983.

Winter, Leon de. *The Day Before Yesterday: Six Stories*. Translated from the Dutch by Scott Rollins. 1985.

Telephone 2 (n.d.).
Cover by Sonia Fox.

Telephone

Maureen Owen

New York City
1969–1984

Telephone. Nos. 1–18
(1969–1983). Covers by
Joe Brainard (3), Donna
Dennis (6), Sonia Fox (2),
Joe Giordano (11), John
Giorno (7), Hugh Kepets
(12, 14), Dave Morice (16),
Paula North (6, 9), Lauren
Owen (4), Charles Plymell
(8), Emilio Schneeman (5),
George Schneeman (1),
Britton Wilkie (10).

BRG has: nos. 1–12, 14, 16.

Telephone Books include:

Bennett, Will. *Zero.* Cover
by George Schneeman.
1984. (GRD)

Berrigan, Sandy. *Summer
Sleeper.* 1981.

Brodey, Jim. *Last Licks.*
1973.

Brown, Rebecca.
The Barbarian Queen. 1981.

Brown, Rebecca.
The Bicycle Trip. 1974. (BRG)

I came to the Lower East Side by way of San Francisco, Japan, and Bronson, Missouri. I was with Lauren Owen at the time, and when we got to New York, we stayed at the apartment of his friends from Tulsa, Ron and Patty Padgett. Ron and another pal, Johnny Stanton, told me about The Poetry Project at St. Mark's. I immediately took myself over there and began going to readings and meeting other poets. Anne Waldman was bringing out *The World*, and it was very exciting. I started thinking about doing books and putting a magazine of my own together. I went over to St. Mark's and asked Anne if I could use the Gestetner to launch my new press. She and Larry Fagin instructed me in the use of stencils, which was not as easy as it sounded, a tricky business at best. I added illustrations. My light table was a window. I would hold the stencil up against the window and trace the drawing I wanted to use. Tom Veitch, whom I barely knew, volunteered to run the Gestetner for me and show me how to actually mimeograph. I'll never forget that first page coming off the big roller. Like a miracle, the dark stencil had yielded up a page bright white with words embossed in shiny black ink.

Mimeo is the greatest way to do a publication. It's immediate, street wise, hands on, open to change to the last second before the machine starts to hum, and the ink sits up on the page like art. It's sensual and sexy, raw and real. Alone in the big empty church of St. Mark's late into the night with only the sound of the mimeograph "kachucking" and the pages swishing down. Although I went on to mimeo on my own, on long late nights in that big church, Tom Veitch will always be a saint to me. After we ran off the pages we stacked them to dry, and some days later I gathered every friend I'd made and their friends and we collated. One of the beautiful things about mimeo is the sense of community. People collated and stapled and took copies to hand around. In that beginning time, I did two Telephone Books: Rebecca Wright's *Elusive Continent* and David Rosenberg's *Frontal Nudity* and a first issue of the magazine, *Telephone*. I was hooked.

— *Maureen Owen*
    Guilford, Connecticut, September 1997

Brown, Rebecca. *3-way Split*. 1978.

Cataldo, Susan. *Brooklyn Queens Day*. 1982.

Friedman, Ed. *The Telephone Book*. 1979. (APP)

Hamill, Janet. *The Temple*. 1980.

Hartman, Yuki. *Hot Footsteps*. 1976.

Howe, Fanny. *The Amerindian Coastline Poem*. Cover and centerfold drawing by Hugh Kepets. 1975. (BRG)

Howe, Fanny. *Fanny Howe's Alsace-Lorraine*. Cover and drawings by Colleen McCallion. 1982. (BRG)

Howe, Susan. *Hinge Picture*. 1974. (BRG)

Howe, Susan. *Secret History of the Dividing Line*. 1978. (BRG)

Nolan, Pat. *Drastic Measures*. 1981.

Norton, Joshua. *Pool*. Cover by Charles Plymell. 1974.

Plymell, Charles. *Over the Stage of Kansas*. Cover by the author. 1973. (BRG)

Pommy-Vega, Janine. *Morning Passage*. Cover drawing by Martin Carey. 1976.

Rosenberg, David. *Frontal Nudity*. Cover by George Schneeman. 1972. (BRG)

Torregian, Sotère. *Amtrak Trek*. Cover drawing and calligraphy by the author. 1979.

Weigel, Tom. *Audrey Hepburn's Symphonic Salad and the Coming of Autumn*. Covers by Monica Weigel. 1980. (BRG)

Weigel, Tom. *Twenty four Haiku After the Japanese*. 1982.

Wilkie, Britton. *The Celestial Splendor Shining Forth from Geometric Thought, & On the Motion of the Apparently Fixed Stars*. 1977.

Wright, Rebecca. *Ciao Manhattan*. 1977.

Wright, Rebecca. *Elusive Continent*. Cover and drawings by Denise Green. 1972.

Clothesline/
Jim Brodey Books

Jim Brodey

New York City
1965, 1970,
1977–1980

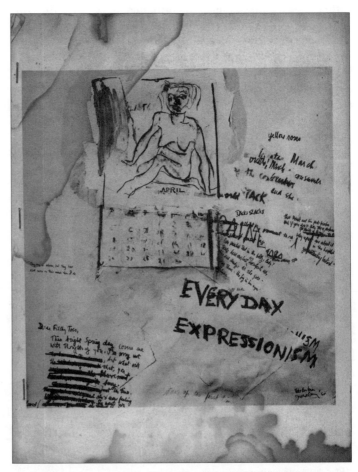

Clothesline, vol. 1, no. 1 (September 1965). Cover by Michael Goldberg and
Bill Berkson.

Clothesline was edited by young poet Jim Brodey, whose charm and wit were winning enough to secure the likes of Frank O'Hara (his teacher at the New School), Kenneth Koch, Tony Towle, John Giorno, John Perreault, Kathleen Fraser, Michael Goldberg, and Bill Berkson for the magazine, which lasted for only two (very distant from each other) issues (1965 and 1970). Brodey returned the graciousness of his own elders when he was barely an elder himself, and became an important force for poetry in the 1970s, as suggested by poet John Godfrey in his preface to Brodey's collected poems, *Heart of the Breath, Poems 1979–1992*: "On several occasions he directed workshops at The Poetry Project, and his hour-long visits to fellow poets could, on a good day, be workshops in themselves. North America contains reams of collaborations aired-out during such visits. Brodey could be extremely sensitive to and appreciative of the poems of others, and his encouragement led many younger poets to publish and often edit their own magazines. He could be an intense and inspiring friend." Jim Brodey Books was personal and very small, publishing only four books, including Brodey's own *Piranha Yoga* (published to coincide with a reading Brodey gave with Allen Ginsberg on December 8, 1977) and Eileen Myles's *The Irony of the Leash*. Jim Brodey Books was occasional in the best sense of the word, belonging as it did to the core of the poet/publisher's life (". . . there is one poem we all write out of our entire existence alive. There is also the poem in the air we breathe, its vapors and juices renew us always."). There were always, after all, newer and more exciting things to be done.

Eileen Myles, *The Irony of the Leash* (1978). Cover by Steve Levine.

Clothesline. Vol. 1, no. 1–vol. 2, no. 2 (September 1965–1970).

BRG has: complete file.

Jim Brodey Books/ Clothesline Editions books include:

Brodey, Jim. *Fleeing Madly South.* Cover by Bill Beckman. 1967.

Brodey, Jim. *Piranha Yoga.* Introduction by John Godfrey. Photographs by James Hamilton. 1977. (BRG)

Myles, Eileen. *The Irony of the Leash.* Cover by Steve Levine. 1978. (BRG)

Savage, Tom. *Personalities.* Cover by Alice Notley. 1978.

Remember I Did
This For You/
A Power Mad Book

Steve Levine and Barbara Barg

New York City
1978–1979

**Remember I Did This For
You/A Power Mad Book
books include:**

Lenhart, Gary. *Drunkard's
Dream.* Cover by Rae
Berolzheimer. 1978. (BRG)

Masters, Gregory. *In the Air.*
Cover by Rae Berolzheimer.
1978. (BRG)

Scholnick, Michael. *Perfume.*
Cover by Rae Berolzheimer.
1978. (BRG)

Wright, Jeff. *Charges.* Cover
by Jim Moser. 1979. (BRG)

Remember I Did This For You press was
conceived for reasons I am unable to
fully recall. But seriously, its aim was essentially like that of most other mimeograph
poetry presses: to publish the then younger
poets whose work was worthy and unavail-
able in book form, to further establish those
writers' (and the publisher's) reputations
in the community of poets, and to reach
out to whatever audience for their work
might exist. The name of the press was a
tongue-in-cheek one; it was meant to reflect
the somewhat self-serving nature of such
publishing. Three of the Remember I Did
This For You books were brought out simultaneously, with seemingly identical covers.
This was an attempt to create interest in the
books and present them as parts of an ongoing series, to distinguish them from the
mass of similar productions, and to establish
a visual identity for the press. Unfortunately,
unlike the more notable mimeo presses of
the time, Remember I Did This For You was
short-lived and had only four terrific publications to its name.

— *Steve Levine*
Brooklyn, New York, October 1997

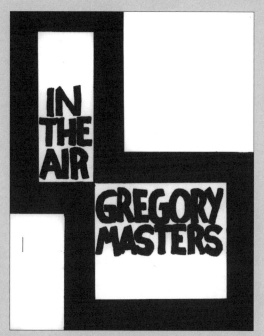

Gregory Masters, *In the Air* (1978). Cover by Rae Berolzheimer.

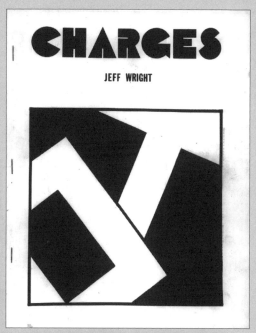

Jeff Wright, *Charges* (1979). Cover by Rae Berolzheimer.

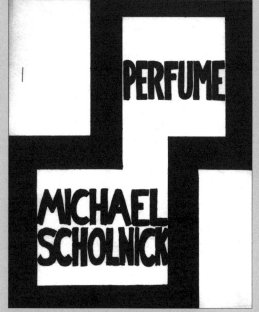

Michael Scholnick, *Perfume* (1978). Cover by Rae Berolzheimer.

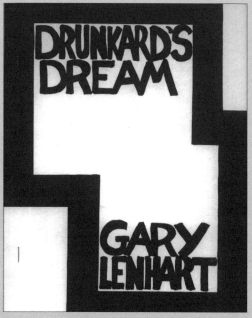

Gary Lenhart, *Drunkard's Dream* (1978). Cover by Rae Berolzheimer.

Remember I Did This For You/A Power Mad Book

Mag City

Gary Lenhart,
Gregory Masters,
and Michael
Scholnick

New York City
1977–1983

Mag City. Nos. 1–14 (1977–
1983). Covers by David
Borchard (10), Rudy Burck-
hardt (14), Louise Hamlin
(9), Yvonne Jacquette (6),
Alex Katz (14, back cover),
Barry Kornbluh (2, 13),
Rochelle Kraut (11),
George Schneeman (12),
Lee Sherry (3).

BRG has: nos. 2, 3, 6, 9–14.
MSS has: publisher's papers.

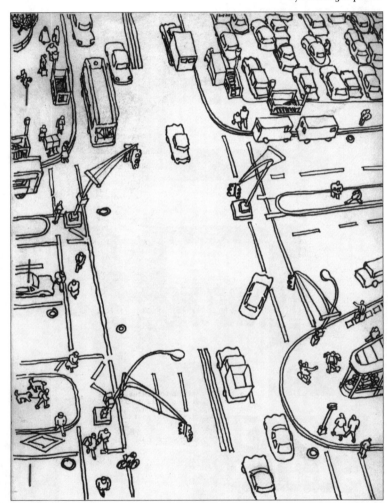

Mag City 6 (1979). Cover
by Yvonne Jacquette.

The Presses and Publications

Mag City was a party in print. It was started to give a form to a literary scene that existed in the East Village, disenchanted with mainstream values. In the mid-70s this neighborhood provided for a confluence of young artists, poets, musicians. The workshops led by Ted Berrigan and Alice Notley at The Poetry Project at St. Mark's Church were where the third generation of New York School poets began to develop. Everyone attended the Monday and Wednesday night readings at the Project and would then convene in various bars afterward – Les Mykta, Grassroots, Orchidia, El Centro. Most of the poets worked part-time jobs or worked a few months and took off a few months. We wanted to be ready for the poem. We lived for poetry and were grateful to have discovered there were others like us out there whose priorities were complementary. Michael Scholnick, Gary Lenhart, and I lived in a tenement on East 12th Street. Other poets had preceded us there. We had no heat or hot water for two very cold winters. We didn't know to be outraged. We assumed that was part of our training for being poets. The three of us were together a lot and we went to The Poetry Project and the Nuyorican Poets Cafe in its early days on East Sixth Street. Michael had had Miguel Algarin as a teacher at Rutgers so we were welcomed there and encouraged to get up and read our poems. The tradition of small press publishing emboldened us to publish our poems ourselves. But by the time we got *Mag City* going in 1977, offset printing was cheap enough and then the Xerox copier became available. Michael came up with the name and we asked our comrades for their poems. From the beginning our idea was to publish hefty chunks of work, as no other magazines were doing that. At a typical meeting, we'd read each poem aloud and come to a consensus. There were never any arguments. If one of us believed strongly enough

in a work, the others usually trusted enough to defer. We usually drew from the locals and then sent off letters to others whose work we admired. Sometimes we received material from as far away as China, where our friend Simon Schuchat was sojourning. We were honored to also publish Allen Ginsberg, Edwin Denby, Rudy Burckhardt, Ted Berrigan, Alice Notley, Ed Sanders, James Schuyler, Ron Padgett, and Bonnie Bremser in our pages. Publishing precedents were Lewis Warsh and Anne Waldman's Angel Hair Press, Ted Berrigan's "C" Press, Ed Sanders's *Fuck You, a magazine of the arts*, Larry Fagin's *Adventures in Poetry*, and Lewis Warsh and Bernadette Mayer's *United Artists* magazine and books. Among our friends, Simon Schuchat's *4, 3, 2 Review*, Eileen Myles's *Dodgems* and the one-shot *Ladies Museum*, Elinor Nauen, Maggie Dubris, and Rachel Walling's *KOFF* magazine, Jeff Wright's Hard Press poetry postcard series, Tom Savage's *Gandhabba*, Tom Weigel's *Tangerine* magazine and anthologies, served up similar delights. The work printed in the fourteen issues of *Mag City* is too diverse to classify. It's mostly confessional and personal. The work is decidedly unacademic, meaning the poems' emphasis is content, not form, leaving rough edges, all the more for impact. If the work wasn't always politically engaged, it offered reactions and responses to the malaise in this company. We were weathering a decade of Republican leadership that was contemptuous of free expression, individual peculiarities, social justice, and fun. The poems were often chatty and attempted to be accessible and entertaining by discoursing in common speech. They celebrated the common, the daily, and immediate.

— *Greg Masters*
New York City, November 1995

L=A=N=G=U=A=G=E

Charles Bernstein and Bruce Andrews

New York City
1978–1981

Charles Bernstein, Susan Bee, and their daughter, Emma, 1985. Photograph by Chris Felver.

The early to mid-1970s marked a rising ferment of experimental activity in the poetry world: the most extreme texts of the previous decade tumbling out, the coming (or returning) into print of earlier radical modernist works shaking up the apparent canon, the development of new preoccupations and modes of working that could not be contained within the mainstream or even within the available (and established) alternatives, and cross-pollinations with other art forms confronting similar problems and opportunities – all against a backdrop of political and social unsettling, at home and abroad. Face-to-face communities of aesthetically radicalized poets sprang up in the San Francisco Bay area, New York, and Washington, where new reading series, presses, and magazines set the stage for intense discussions of new poetic possibilities as well as critical and historical thinking about poetry by the poets themselves (rather than by scholars or critics). Animated discussion of poetics went on in letters, in conversation, and in public talks, but there was no print forum for these ongoing exchanges. And so, in 1977, in consultation with Ron Silliman in California, we sketched out plans for a New York–based, self-produced magazine of information and commentary, *L=A=N=G=U=A=G=E*. The first issue appeared in February 1978 and went out to our initial subscribers – about 200 by the end of the first year – and was also distributed through a few bookstores. The first three volumes were typed on legal-size sheets on an IBM Selectric typewriter, sprayed to prevent smearing, and then pasted into our format by our designer, Susan Bee. The initial run was offset printed, although we often produced additional copies by photocopying. We stopped publishing the magazine in 1981, with our fourth volume, a perfect-bound book co-published with the Toronto magazine *Open Letter*. In 1984, Southern Illinois University Press published an anthology, *The L=A=N=G=U=A=G=E Book*, including about half of what we had published; this anthology was reissued by the press in 1997.

— *Bruce Andrews and Charles Bernstein*
New York City, September 1997

L=A=N=G=U=A=G=E. 1978–1981. Vols. 1–3 consist of thirteen issues (9 and 10 were a double issue), three supplements, and one table of contents for vols. 1–4. Vol. 4 was published as an issue of the Canadian journal *Open Letter* (Fifth Series, no. 1, Winter 1982). *Open Letter* is edited by Frank Davey; the *L=A=N=G=U=A=G=E* issue was edited by Charles Bernstein and Bruce Andrews.

GRD has: complete file.

Also issued was: *Legend*, collaborations by Bruce Andrews, Charles Bernstein, Ray DiPalma, Steve McCaffery, and Ron Silliman. 1980. Co-published with the Segue Foundation. (GRD)

L=A=N=G=U=A=G=E 4
(August 1978).

LOUIS ZUKOFSKY

 The first (& for a long time the only) to read Pound & Williams with what we wld recognize as modern eye & ear. Ear tuned tautly toward a double function: intrinsic, language as he found it (i.e., parole); extrinsic, musical composition, determining wholeness, aesthetic consistency, perfect rest. But for whom language began with sight (thus *Bottom* -- love : reason :: eye : mind -- in wch love contains all the significations Benjamin, so like LZ, gave the term aura). In his writing, language (L) synthesizes polar impulses rising dialectically from an equally problematic material base:

```
music ──────────────── speech
              \    /
               \  /
          L     \/
               /\
              /  \
perception ──────────── the visible
```

Not the tongue his parents spoke, it always carries some trace of Other (hence *Catullus*), tending toward objectification. Each line &/or stanza a study in balance, silence (peace) proposed as maximum stress in all directions, thus active. This never-to-be resolvd equilibrium of the spoken within the written within the spoken, etc., is for him the motivating center of craft (the final 28 lines of *"A" 23*, last words, escort the reader thru the alphabet, letters are presences).
 "A living calendar...: music, thought, drama, story, poem" (23). A characteristic distinction: the title is *"A"*, not *A*. Its open-ended interconnectedness in *1-6* marks the debt to *The Cantos*, but from 7 (w/ wch he chose to represent himself in the Objectivist issue of *Poetry*, 2/31) forward, a new conceptualization as to the function of part-to-whole relations in the formation of a longpoem starts to emerge: each moment is a totalization, complete to itself, capable of entering into larger structures as a relational fact. This integrity of units is radically unlike *Maximus* or *Passages*, tho it includes (requires!) the capacity to incorporate a piece in open form (*"A" 13* his *Paterson*) -- this empowers Zukofsky, & he alone, to complete such a work.

"In editing *L=A=N=G=U=A=G=E*, we said we were 'emphasizing a spectrum of writing that places attention primarily on language and ways of making meaning, that takes for granted neither vocabulary, grammar, shape, syntax, program, or subject matter.' And that refusal to take things for granted can in turn pose a direct challenge to social norms about vocabulary, grammar, process, shape, syntax, program & subject-matter.... Faced with rules or patterns of constraint – the negative face of ideology – writing can respond with a drastic openness. Here, an open horizon gets defined, dynamically, by failures of immediate sense – surrenders, even – which are failures in the working of this *negative power*. To look for – & make – problems, to open up new relationships by crazed collision – laying bare the device...."

— Bruce Andrews, "Poetry as Explanation, Poetry as Praxis" in
 The Politics of Poetic Form, edited by Charles Bernstein (New York:
 Roof, 1993)

Joglars 3 (1966).
Cover by John Furnival.

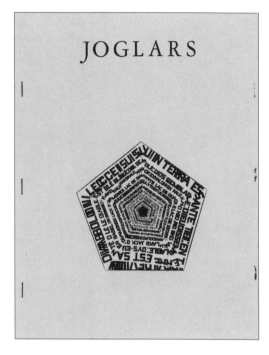

Joglars

Clark Coolidge and George
[Michael] Palmer

Cambridge, Massachusetts,
and Providence, Rhode Island
1964–1966

The first push toward *Joglars* came in the Summer of 1963 at Vancouver in Warren Tallman's kitchen. Charles Olson was telling a bunch of young poets how we ought to start a magazine to publish poets' correspondence, specifically that between Charles and Bob Creeley. So Fred Wah, Michael Palmer, and I began discussing a possible three-way editorship. But when we all got home the plan broke in two, Fred starting *Sum* in New Mexico and Michael and I *Joglars* from Cambridge (MP) and Providence (CC). We did the first two issues together and then I did the third one myself when Michael went to Europe. The title came from Michael, and his interest in the Troubadours. Like most starting poets I think we wanted primarily to find and show more of the work we were fascinated with (it was such a rich period, compared to now) plus get in touch with the poets who were writing it. Issue 3 shows my increasing interest in the younger New York School poets, and a brief brush with the Concrete movement. And now it strikes me as odd that we didn't publish Olson in the magazine. Or Creeley. A life of its own.

— Clark Coolidge
    The Berkshires, Massachusetts, September 23, 1997

Joglars. Nos. 1–3
(1964–1966).

BRG has: complete file.

This

Barrett Watten and
Robert Grenier; later
Barrett Watten

Iowa City and San
Francisco
1971–1982

"One could see, without reading any of the words in the issue, that *This* 1 issued a double appeal to fresh beginnings and revered ancestors. The cover displays drawings by Grenier's very young daughter Amy done at the stage when signification was just beginning to emerge from marks on paper (i.e., when big circles first mean heads and two smaller circles with centered dots mean eyes). Balancing this originary gesture, inside were photos of the masters: one of Charles Olson, who had died the previous year, and one shot from street level of the very old Pound.... The issue's simultaneous claim to originariness, a tradition, and a productive future follows the basic patterns of Pound's, Zukofsky's and Olson's manifestos."

— Bob Perelman, *The Marginalization of Poetry: Language Writing and
Literary History* (Princeton, N.J.: Princeton University Press, 1996)

In his landmark critical history, *The Marginalization of Poetry: Language Writing and Literary History*, Bob Perelman stressed the importance of the creation of literary venues (magazines and small presses) for the nurturing of new writing, singling out *This* for particular attention, as "the first self-conscious journal of what would become known as language writing. The name and character of the movement were uninvented at the time, nor were many of the future participants in touch yet, but the magazine was clearly motivated by a sense of literary progress." In his discussion, Perelman places *This* and language writing in the context of literary history, providing for it a distinguished genealogy: "At the time there were many writers, involved in different social formations and providing various formal models, from which language writing would arise. A short list would include figures associated with Black Mountain, the New York School, the San Francisco Renaissance: Charles Olson, Frank O'Hara, and Jack Spicer, each of whom had recently died but whose work was still appearing; Robert Creeley, Robert Duncan, Larry Eigner; the aleatory work of Jackson Mac Low and John Cage; John Ashbery, Ted Berrigan, Alice Notley, Clark Coolidge, Bernadette Mayer, and Ron Padgett; Tom Raworth, David Bromige, and Michael Palmer. The Objectivists were still active and were in fact a much stronger presence than they had been in prior decades: George Oppen had just won the Pulitzer Prize and Louis Zukofsky was in the process of finishing "*A*."... Compared to the range of formal possibilities and social groupings and postures this partial list includes, the work and literary information in *This* 1 was quite limited. But [the magazine was] important in its positing of literary space. It established, at least in embryonic form, a way of connecting private reading and writing desires with some sense of public consequence and thus with a future. All the above writers could conceivably be used, not simply read."

This. Nos. 1–12
(1971–1982).

BRG has: complete file.

This Press books include:

Andrews, Bruce.
Sonnets (Momento Mori).
1980. (GRD)

Coolidge, Clark.
The Maintains. 1974.

Coolidge, Clark.
Quartz Hearts. 1978.

Eigner, Larry. *Country,
Harbor, Quiet, Act, Around:
Selected Prose*. Introduction
by Douglas Woolf. Edited
by Barrett Watten. 1978.
(BRG, GRD)

Greenwald, Ted. *You Bet!*
1978. (GRD)

Grenier, Robert. *Series:
Poems 1967–1971*. Cover by
Francie Shaw. 1978. (BRG)

Harryman, Carla. *Under the
Bridge*. 1980. (GRD)

Perelman, Bob. *Primer*.
1981.

Silliman, Ron. *Ketjak*.
1978. (GRD)

Watten, Barrett. *Decay*.
1977. (GRD)

Watten, Barrett. *1–10*.
1980. (GRD)

From
Robert Grenier,
30 from Sentences
(1978).

Sentences

Robert Grenier

*Berkeley, California,
and Cambridge,
Massachusetts
1978*

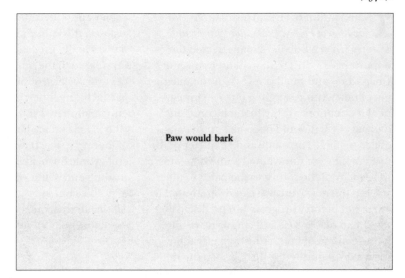

Paw would bark

**Sentences appeared in the
following forms:**

Grenier, Robert. *Sentences.*
1 portfolio, approx. 500
sheets. Cambridge, Mass.:
Whale Cloth Press, 1978.
(BRG)

Grenier, Robert. *Sentences
Toward Birds.* Kensington,
Calif.: L Publications, 1978.
(BRG)

Grenier, Robert. *30 from
Sentences.* 16 sheets. Cam-
bridge, Mass.: Whale Cloth
Press, 1978. (BRG)

Robert Grenier's exemplary project of the late 1970s culminated in the 1978 publication of 500 cards in a blue Chinese cloth box with ivory clasps. In many ways, *Sentences* serves as the prototype or even the apex of language writing. Barrett Watten talks about Grenier's work in the fifth issue of *L=A=N=G=U=A=G=E* (October 1978): "The work is unavoidably an object. A production number – five hundred index cards, boxed, one poem per card. Intended to be read in any order (ideally all at once), it denies book format, in which binding would give only one of all possible readings page-by-page. Any sequence is a chance ordering, any poem could come next. The words rise off the page as the mind would like – well-lit, pure, detached – 'in eternity.' The heavy white paper (field) sets off the IBM Selectric type (thing) as utter contrast in order to dismantle the apparatus of conveyance and release the word and its effect. Yet the work is physically awkward, a mechanical problem, and calls attention to itself as visual format. . . . *Sentences* is a distillation of six years' close attention to 'everything going on all the time.' Out of voices heard, bird calls, shape of landscape, bolt from the blue, Kerouac's 'void bowl slant,' some perceptible shift makes a denotative signal, as bird pistols brain with peculiar stop to all sound. One kind of perception in the taxonomy of this work then shows parallels of language to the world outside. . . . Voice invested with power to make real (symbolism) is finally undermined. Any person's voice noted shows desire bending to an unyielding other. Cued by dissonance under scrutiny of arbitrary white, the sum total of the cards exposes the point in the mind where structure collapses into words. Not the work objectified (as a 'point of rest'), but language brought to light through the failure of object (a 'point of unrest'). . . . Is that enough? There are no sentences in *Sentences*, like a glass ball nearly impossible to find. The work refuses closure (capital letter, period meaning a 'completed thought') in being completely self-contained. It might be the only constitution possible for the republic in which one would want to live."

From
Robert Grenier,
30 from Sentences
(1978).

THE BUS DRIVER

and the black stream

Tottel's

Ron Silliman

Oakland and San Francisco
1970–1981

From *Tottel's* 13
(1973).

Named after the first anthology of English poetry, *Tottel's Miscellany* of 1557, Ron Silliman's mimeo *Tottel's* published mostly controversial and always innovative work. In each of eighteen issues devoted to the work of a single poet (among them, Robert Grenier, David Gitin, Thomas Meyer, Clark Coolidge, Ray DiPalma, David Melnick, Bruce Andrews, and Larry Eigner), all associated with language writing (if only as models), Silliman printed the most radically disjunctive work he could find. One of the original San Francisco language poets, he seemed driven by his own catholic and authentic background to organize (he has been a prison and tenants rights organizer, editor of the *Socialist Review*, a lobbyist, and teacher). Silliman's biographical statement in Michael Lally's anthology *None of the Above: New Poets of the U.S.A.* (1976) can serve as a good introduction to *Tottel's:* "I started out as a conventional writer of lyrical poems, but, as the forms I'd inherited, common to any writer circa '65/'66, had no more reason or meaning for their existence than conformity & habit, I became quickly frustrated & bored. I wanted something more than a half-art. The pseudo-formalist approach of the post-Projective writers, with which I experimented for a time, offered no real solution. At best, the equation of the page to 'scored speech' was a rough metaphor & it excluded more of the world than it could bring in. . . . Thus when Coolidge & then Grenier extended the definition of language beyond discourse, it seemed that a reinvestigation of the whole act of writing was not only possible, but necessary. Any other tendency now is mere decoration." Silliman has published an influential collection of essays, *The New Sentence* (1987), and edited a defining anthology of language writing, *In the American Tree* (1986). Two of his own volumes, *Ketjak* (1978) and *Tjanting* (1981), are widely respected for their radical experimentation and lively rebelliousness. He has taken as his literary mothers Gertrude Stein and Laura Riding, which helps explain his conflation of politics and poetics: "poetics must be concerned with the process by which writing is organized politically into literature" and "there can be no such thing as a formal problem in poetry which is not a social one as well."

Tottel's. Nos. 1–18 (1970–1981).

BRG has: nos. 4–15, 17.

The first gathering of individuals who were to become known as "language poets" was edited by Ron Silliman under the title "The Dwelling Place: 9 Poets." Published in *Alcheringa*, it included work by Bruce Andrews, Barbara Baracks, Clark Coolidge, Lee De Jasu, Ray DiPalma, Robert Grenier, David Melnick, Silliman himself, and Barrett Watten. Silliman's three pages of excellent and informative notes, entitled "Surprised by Sign (Notes on Nine)," characterize his selection as "a fix in time of writing which bears a family resemblance." He also clearly describes the poets' common concerns: "What connects these writers beyond my impression of a connection is what I take to be a community of concern for language as the center of whatever activity poems might be and for poetry itself as the perfection of new forms as additions to nature. Which raises questions, problems, answers, solutions, recalls old modes (half forgotten modernists such as Arensberg, say, or the work of certain Russian Futurists) and reflects concerns that have not previously been so extensively explored in the context of American poetry (e.g., for the work of such as Lacan or Barthes). Some have come to this more or less isolately, while others have found use in the work of their peers." His essay includes capsule biographies, sometimes provided by the writers themselves as in the case of Bruce Andrews, first alphabetically: "Bruce Andrews. Books: *Edge, A Cappella, Corona.* '(A) stress on these characteristics and using them as organizing principles when syntax is attenuated: sound, texture, weight, discreteness, silence, targets, rhythms, presence, physicality.' Professor of Political Science, Fordham University."

From *Alcheringa*,
New Series, vol. 1,
no. 2 (1975).

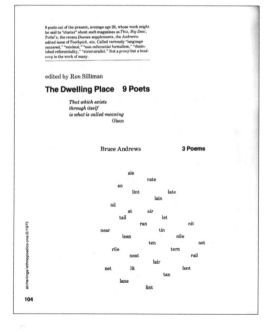

Vort 2 (vol. 1, no. 2)
(Winter 1972).

Vort

Barry Alpert

Silver Spring, Maryland
1972–1976

For all but one of its nine issues, *Vort* followed the same pattern in its plain, large-format issues, creating a little critical universe for each of two authors. The sole divergence from the pattern was the fifth issue, which was devoted wholly to Robert Kelly and his work. Perhaps more an encyclopedia in parts than a magazine or journal, the issues included a photograph of each author, a small collection of each author's work, three or four critical studies, homages, commentaries, and long and detailed interviews with each author by editor Alpert. Throughout its existence, *Vort* covered the following writers: Ed Dorn and Tom Raworth, Anselm Hollo and Ted Berrigan, David Bromige and Ken Irby, Fielding Dawson and Jonathan Williams, Robert Kelly, Gilbert Sorrentino and Donald Phelps, David Antin and Jerome Rothenberg, Jackson Mac Low and Armand Schwerner, and, in the last issue, Guy Davenport and Ronald Johnson. Planned but never completed were issues on the work of John Ashbery, John Cage, Jack Hirschman, David Meltzer, and Something Else Press alumni. *Vort* is an unfortunately unfinished encyclopedia of the New American Poetry, but is still very useful for the information it contains and still important "for those to whom criticism is a fine art."

Vort. Vols. 1, nos. 1–3; vol. 2, nos. 1–3; vol. 3, nos. 1–3 (1972–1976).

BRG has: complete file.
GRD has: complete file.

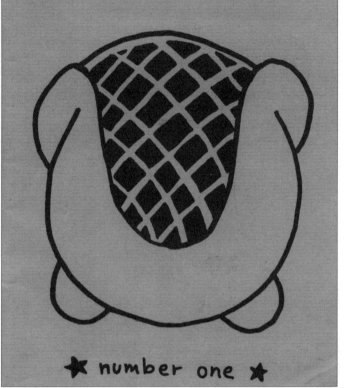

Hills

Bob Perelman and
Michael Waltuch; later
Bob Perelman

*Iowa City; Cambridge,
Massachusetts; San
Francisco; and
Berkeley, California
1973–1983*

Hills 1 (March 1973).
Front cover by
Francie Shaw.

Edited by Bob Perelman, and following him all over the country, *Hills* was the sweetest of all language-centered journals, with covers often resembling cows. The first issue, from Iowa City, was co-edited with Michael Waltuch and included the work of Iowa poet Darrell Gray, as well as some experimental and exotic work by Kit Robinson and Josephine Clare. Included also are some of the earliest translations (by Anselm Hollo, Eliot Anderson, and editor Perelman) of the Slovenian poet Tomaz Salamun. All the work in this first issue is clustered toward the top of the page, leaving white space below. *Hills* 2 is typed on a more elegant typewriter (perhaps by Bob Grenier) and some of his *Sentences* appear within, for instance: "SWEET/expect accept object." *Hills* 4 was typeset by Barrett Watten, and includes work by Ron Silliman, Carla Harryman, Bruce Andrews, and Fanny Howe as well as Iowan and *Poetry Comics* editor Dave Morice. With issue 5, Perelman and the magazine moved to San Francisco, and the cover is appropriately reproduced from a photo by Jon Winet of Center Ice, The Cow Palace. The very famous and important double issue 5/6 prints a number of the "Talks" then given in different San Francisco venues (including the San Francisco Art Institute, 80 Langton Street, and various lofts and apartments). According to Perelman, the talk series began in 1977 and numbered nearly forty over the next five or so years: "A 'talk' is a broad designation – was the situation educational, creational, dramatic? Was information to be presented or were values to be embodied: was the focus on the speaker or the community or the speaker and audience? The answers varied. All speakers were presented with a common problem: to say something in public. In various cases this meant talking spontaneously, referring to notes and texts, reading written out essays, or abandoning written essays in midstream." Talkers included Bill Berkson, Barrett Watten on "Russian Formalism and the Present," Steve Benson with "Views of Communist China," Bob Perelman on "The First Person," Michael Davidson on "The Prose of Fact," and Ron Silliman on "The New Sentence." *Hills* 8 includes a play by Carla Harryman entitled *The Third Man*. Its cast included Steve Benson and Kit Robinson.

Hills. Nos. 1–9 (1973–Spring 1983). Covers by Francie Shaw (1, 2).

BRG has: nos. 1–2.
GRD has: nos. 4–9.

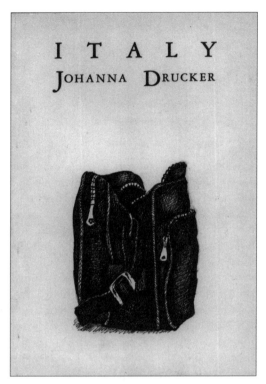

Johanna Drucker, *Italy* (1980). Cover by the author.

The Figures

Geoffrey Young and Laura Chester; later Geoffrey Young

Berkeley, California, and Great Barrington, Massachusetts 1975–

The Figures books include:

Auster, Paul. *Wall Writing.* 1976. (BRG)

Benedetti, David. *Nictitating Membrane.* Prints by Allen Schiller. 1976. (BRG)

Benson, Steve. *As Is.* 1978. (BRG)

Benson, Steve. *Blue Book.* Cover image by Ross Bleckner. 1988. Published in association with Roof. (GRD)

Bernheimer, Allen. *Cafe Isotope.* 1980. (GRD)

Chester, Laura. *My Pleasure.* Cover reproduction of a painting by Guy Williams. 1980. (GRD)

Clark, Tom. *Baseball.* Cover and other illustrations by the author. 1976. (GRD)

Davidson, Michael. *The Prose of Fact.* Cover reproduction of a painting by Richard Diebenkorn. 1981. (GRD)

Davis, Lydia. *Story and Other Stories.* Cover photograph by Lizbeth Marano. 1983. (GRD)

Dewdney, Christopher. *Spring Trances in the Control Emerald Night.* 1978. (GRD)

Drucker, Johanna. *Italy.* Cover and drawings by the author. 1980. (GRD)

Einzig, Barbara. *Disappearing Work: A Recounting.* Cover by Mercy Goodwin. 1979. (GRD)

Fraser, Kathleen. *Each Next: Narratives.* 1980. (GRD)

Gold, Artie, and Geoff Young. *Mixed Doubles: Fifteen Poems.* 1975.

Hejinian, Lyn. *Writing Is an Aid to Memory.* 1978. (GRD)

Perelman, Bob. *7 Works.* Cover by Francie Shaw. 1978.

Raworth, Tom. *Ace.* Illustrations by Barry Hall. 1977.

Rice, Stan. *Some Lamb.* 1975. (GRD)

Robinson, Kit. *Down and Back.* 1978. (BRG)

Rodefer, Stephen. *The Bell Clerk's Tears Keep Flowing.* 1978. (GRD)

Silliman, Ron. *Tjanting.* Introduction by Barrett Watten. 1981. (GRD)

Young, Geoff. *Subject to Fits.* Cover by Mel Bochner. 1980. (BRG)

Geoff Young and Laura Chester began The Figures in 1975 in Berkeley, claiming the name of the press from Charles Olson's *Maximus Poems.* Young and Chester had earlier edited one *Stooge* magazine, which had provided them with the experience in publishing they needed to begin their small press. It has since grown to be one of the three or four most important publishers of experimental writing in the country, with over fifty titles currently in print. Its first publication, *Mixed Doubles: Fifteen Poems* by Artie Gold and Geoff Young, was an elegant limited edition. But the press really hit its stride three years later, in 1978, with a host of titles by younger language-centered writers in simpler but carefully produced "trade" editions with good covers. Among the important books The Figures published in 1978 were Steve Benson's *As Is,* Kit Robinson's *Down and Back,* Rae Armantrout's *Extremities,* Christopher Dewdney's *Spring Trances in the Control Emerald Night,* and Bob Perelman's *7 Works.* Although never again equaling in one year this *annus mirabilis* of language writing, the press has gone on to achieve a solid list including, among other important works, Lydia Davis's *Story and Other Stories*; Clark Coolidge's *The Crystal Text*; Johanna Drucker's *Italy*; Steve Benson's *Blue Book*; Lyn Hejinian's *Oxota, a Short Russian Novel;* and festschrifts for James Schuyler in 1991 and Bernadette Mayer in 1995; as well as *Ted: A Personal Memoir of Ted Berrigan* by Ron Padgett (1993).

Steve Benson,
Blue Book (1988).
Cover image by
Ross Bleckner.

BLUE BOOK
STEVE BENSON

Roof

*James Sherry and Tom Savage;
later James Sherry*

*New York City
1976–*

ROOF: an anthology of poetry from the Naropa I nstitute, Bou lder, Colorad o, summer of 1976. $2.00

*Roof: An Anthology of
Poetry from the Naropa
Institute, Boulder, Colorado
(Summer 1976). Cover
by Lee Sherry.*

Roof. Nos. 1–10
(1976–1979).

GRD has: complete file.

Roof books include:

Andrews, Bruce. *Wobbling.*
1981. Co-published with the
Segue Foundation. (GRD)

Bernstein, Charles.
Controlling Interests. 1980.
Co-published with the
Segue Foundation. (GRD)

Davies, Alan. *Active 24
Hours.* 1982. Co-published
with the Segue Foundation.
(GRD)

Day, Jean. *A Young Recruit.*
1988.

Gottlieb, Michael. *Ninety-six
Tears.* 1981. Co-published
with the Segue Foundation.
(GRD)

Grenier, Robert. *A Day at
the Beach.* 1984. Co-pub-
lished with the Segue
Foundation.

McCaffery, Steve. *North of
Intention: Critical Writings,
1973–1986.* 1986. (GRD)

Seaton, Peter. *The Son
Master.* 1982. (GRD)

Sherry, James.
Part Songs. 1978.

Silliman, Ron. *The Age of
Huts.* Cover drawing by
Lee Sherry. 1986. (GRD)

Silliman, Ron. *The New
Sentence.* 1987. (GRD)

Weiner, Hannah.
Little Books – Indians. 1980.
Co-published with the
Segue Foundation. (GRD)

Roof was to hold all the different writing tendencies under it. The first issue included many of America's best-known writers of the time: Ashbery, Creeley, Duncan, and Ginsberg to name a few. It also contained many new writers who were at Naropa for that session. The well-known writers were supportive of what I was doing so long as it furthered the aims of their writing, but they were not supportive of alternative tendencies in writing that cut across the grain of the established conflict in American letters. (At the time, the conflict was between the day-to-day personism of the New York School/Beat group against the "Academic" modernism. Looking back on it today, we see the conflict as the two sides of the Objectivist tendency, but then it was a serious cultural conflict between liberal academics and the counterculture.) I did not feel that the established writers were interested in the same issues as the younger writers, so for the second issue of *Roof* I put out the word that I was publishing new writing by new writers. I met and published Bruce Andrews, Charles Bernstein, and Ron Silliman, and others of what was to become language poetry. Soon after I published the third issue of *Roof*, Andrews and Bernstein started *L=A=N=G=U=A=G=E*, a magazine devoted to critical writing by poets. The energy of the moment swung decisively in the direction of a more complex and political prosody as opposed to simplified prosody with political

or personal content. The tendency included a group of about ten poets in New York, twenty in the Bay area, five in D.C., and a few others scattered about the country and in Canada who began to read each other in a different way than we read any other poetry. In the beginning of language writing, there were public "Talks" and private meetings to discuss what poetry might be, and publications like *Roof*, *L=A=N=G=U=A=G=E*, *This*, *Hills*, and *Sun & Moon* to publish and promote it. People began to derisively call it a school and attack both its methods and its politics, but it was clear that most, not all, of the talented younger writers were interested in these issues. I began to publish longer sections of people's work at the same time that the poets were writing longer pieces, and grouping poets by geography. In 1978, I began to publish books, with my own *Part Songs*. Since then, Roof has published about one hundred books including several by Ron Silliman, Bruce Andrews, Hannah Weiner, Kit Robinson, Bob Perelman, Jackson Mac Low, Nicole Brossard, and Diane Ward. Roof is also known for critical books such as Bernstein's edited *The Politics of Poetic Form: Poetry and Public Policy*, Alan Davies's *Signage*, Steve McCaffery's *North of Intention*, and Ron Silliman's *The New Sentence*.

— *James Sherry*
New York City, November 1997

Là-Bas, experimental poetry and poetics

Douglas Messerli

College Park, Maryland

1976–1979

Là-Bas. Nos. 1–13
(1976–1979).

GRD has: nos. 1–12.

The thirteen mimeographed issues of the newsletter *Là-Bas* were published with great style and verve (as well as care and continuity). Editor Messerli described its mission in the first issue: "*Là-Bas* is sent free to poets who in their poetry have shown an interest in a poetry which (as Harold Norse in a letter to *Là-Bas* recently described) is not 'poured into moulds,' and whose poetry has reflected a valuing of the poetic process over artifact. Certainly *Là-Bas* is not entirely a new idea; the great mimeo magazines such as *0–9*, "*C,*" *The Floating Bear*, the Once series, *Open Space* and *The World* have all in the past supported similar principles. But there is always a need for such publications to remind us that poetry is a force as much as a form. And, currently – while there are many 'little' magazines publishing exciting poetry – there are very few publications intrinsically involved with the necessary interchange between the individual poet and the poetry community at large. Moreover, *Là-Bas* is something new, one hopes, not merely a new version of an old idea. *Là-Bas* prints not only new poetry, but revisions and reactions (response to poetry, theory, news of interest to poets – whatever). And, most importantly, because it is a poet's publication, not a publisher's, *Là-Bas* seeks new ideas and suggestions. . . . Like the poetry it publishes, *Là-Bas* will not be poured into moulds."

The Presses and Publications

Là-Bas 3 (1976).

SHADE

CHARLES BERNSTEIN

Sun & Moon

Douglas Messerli

College Park, Maryland,
and Los Angeles
1976–

Sun & Moon: A Quarterly of Literature and Art. Nos. 1–18 (1976–1986).

BRG has: nos. 2–5.
GRD has: nos. 1–12.

Sun & Moon Press books include:

Ahern, Tom. *Hecatombs of Lake.* 1984. (Sun & Moon Contemporary Literature Series, No. 21.) (GRD)

Antin, David. *Who's Listening Out There?* 1979. (Sun & Moon Contemporary Literature Series, No. 4.) (GRD)

Bernstein, Charles. *Content's Dream: Essays 1975–1984.* 1986. (GRD)

Bernstein, Charles. *Shade.* Cover by Susan Bee Laufer. 1978. (Sun & Moon Contemporary Literature Series, No. 1.) (BRG, GRD)

Brownstein, Michael. *Oracle Night: A Love Poem.* Cover drawing by the author. 1982. (Sun & Moon Contemporary Literature Series, No. 13.) (BRG)

Cory, Jean Jacques. *Particulars.* 1980. (Sun & Moon Contemporary Literature Series, No. 8.)

Darragh, Tina. *On the Corner to Off the Corner.* 1981. (Sun & Moon Contemporary Literature Series, No. 10.)

DiPalma, Ray. *Cuiva Sails.* 1978. (Sun & Moon Contemporary Literature Series, No. 2.) (GRD)

Frank, Peter. *The Travelogues (1971–1977).* 1982. (Sun & Moon Contemporary Literature Series, No. 12.) (GRD)

Greenwald, Ted. *Word of Mouth: A Poem.* 1986. (GRD)

Hejinian, Lyn. *The Cold of Poetry.* 1994. (GRD)

Herbert, F. John. *The Collected Poems of Sir Winston Churchill.* 1981. (Sun & Moon Contemporary Literature Series, No. 9.) (GRD)

Charles Bernstein, *Shade* (1978).
Cover by Susan Bee Laufer.

S*un & Moon* magazine ran from 1976 to 1986, publishing eighteen issues, and Sun & Moon Press began in College Park, Maryland, in 1978 with the publication of poet Charles Bernstein's *Shade* with a cover by Susan Bee Laufer. The press and magazine soon moved to Los Angeles. It is almost impossible to overestimate the importance of Sun & Moon to the community of experimentally minded writers in the United States, West or East Coast. A vibrant and flourishing publishing concern, continuing in the footsteps of New Directions, Sun & Moon has effectively established a new avant-garde tradition for the end of the twentieth century and the beginning of the twenty-first. The press and the magazine mix cultures past and present.

The books are beautifully and carefully produced and printed in runs of 1,000 to 2,000 copies, which, according to proprietor Messerli, keeps the unit costs down. Among the many avant-garde and experimental writers Sun & Moon has published are Henry James, André Breton, Gertrude Stein, Djuna Barnes, Jackson Mac Low, Barrett Watten, Lyn Hejinian, and Charles Bernstein in the Classics series, Lewis Warsh, Johnny Stanton, Curtis White, and Paul Auster in the New American Fiction series, and Rae Armantrout, Clark Coolidge, and Dennis Phillips in the New American Poetry series.

Inman, P. *Platin.* 1979. (Sun & Moon Contemporary Literature Series, No. 5.) (GRD)

Mac Low, Jackson. *From Pearl Harbor to FDR's Birthday: 7 December 1981–30 January 1982: Poems.* 1982. (Sun & Moon Contemporary Literature Series, No. 14.)

Messerli, Douglas. *Dinner on the Lawn.* 1979; rev. edition 1982. (Sun & Moon Contemporary Literature Series, No. 7.)

Messerli, Douglas, ed. *Contemporary American Fiction.* 1983. (Sun & Moon Contemporary Literature Series, No. 18.)

Sherry, James. *In Case.* 1981. (Sun & Moon Contemporary Literature Series, No. 11.) (GRD)

Stehman, John. *Space Dictation.* 1978. (Sun & Moon Contemporary Literature Series, No. 3.) (GRD)

Vance, Ronald. *I Went to Italy and Ate Chocolate.* 1979. (Sun & Moon Contemporary Literature Series, No. 6.) (BRG)

Warsh, Lewis. *A Free Man.* 1991.

Warsh, Lewis. *Methods of Birth Control.* 1983. (Sun & Moon Contemporary Literature Series, No. 16.) (GRD)

Weinstein, Jeff. *Life in San Diego.* Cover and art work by Ira Joel Haber. 1983. (Sun and Moon Contemporary Literature Series, No. 17.) (GRD)

Wine, James. *Longwalks.* 1982. (Sun & Moon Contemporary Literature Series, No. 14.)

For further information on Sun & Moon Press, including the complete catalog of its publications, the reader is referred to the Sun & Moon website at: http://www.sunmoon.com

Tuumba Press

Lyn Hejinian

Willits and Berkeley, California
1976–1984

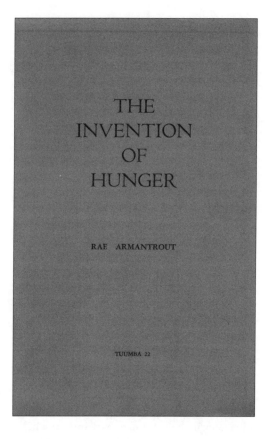

Rae Armantrout,
The Invention of
Hunger (1979).

Tuumba issued fifty booklets, a poster, and a broadside. They are:

Andrews, Bruce. *Praxis.*
1978. (Tuumba 18.) (BRG)

Armantrout, Rae. *The*
Invention of Hunger. 1979.
(Tuumba 22.) (GRD)

Baracks, Barbara. *No Sleep.*
1977. (Tuumba 11.) (GRD)

Benson, Steve. *The Busses.*
1981. (Tuumba 32.) (GRD)

Bernheimer, Alan. *State*
Lounge. 1981. (Tuumba 33.)
(GRD)

Bernstein, Charles. *Senses*
of Responsibility. 1979.
(Tuumba 20.) (BRG)

Bromige, David. *P-E-A-C-E.*
1981. (Tuumba 34.) (GRD)

Coolidge, Clark. *Research.*
1982. (Tuumba 40.)

Day, Jean. *Linear C.* 1983.
(Tuumba 43.)

DiPalma, Ray. *Observatory*
Gardens. 1979. (Tuumba 24.)
(GRD)

Dreyer, Lynne. *Step Work.*
1983. (Tuumba 44.) (GRD)

Eigner, Larry. *Flat and*
Round. 1980. (Tuumba 25.)
(GRD)

Eisenberg, Barry. *Bones' Fire.*
1977. (Tuumba 7.) (GRD)

Eshleman, Clayton. *The*
Gospel of Celine Arnauld.
1977. (Tuumba 12.) (GRD)

Faville, Curtis. *Wittgenstein's*
Door. 1980. (Tuumba 29.)
(GRD)

Fraser, Kathleen. *Magritte*
Series. 1977. (Tuumba 6.)
(GRD)

Greenwald, Ted. *Smile.*
1981. (Tuumba 31.) (BRG)

Grenier, Robert. *Cambridge*
M'ass. Poster. 1979.

Grenier, Robert. *Oakland.*
1980. (Tuumba 27.) (BRG)

Hall, Doug. *Beyond the Edge.*
1977. (Tuumba 8.)

Harryman, Carla. *Percentage.*
1979. (Tuumba 23.) (GRD)

Harryman, Carla. *Property.*
1982. (Tuumba 39.) (GRD)

Hejinian, Lyn. *Gesualdo.*
1978. (Tuumba 15.) (GRD)

Hejinian, Lyn. *The Guard.*
1984. (Tuumba 50.) (GRD)

Hejinian, Lyn. *A Thought Is*
the Bride of What Thinking.
1976. (Tuumba 1.) (GRD)

Higgins, Dick. *Cat Alley:*
A Long Short Novel. 1976.
(Tuumba 5.)

Continued on page 258

The Presses and Publications

Logo of Tuumba Press,
designed by Lyn Hejinian.

I founded Tuumba Press in 1976. It was a solo venture in that I had no partner(s) or assistant(s) but it was not a private nor solitary one; I had come to realize that poetry exists not in isolation (alone on its lonely page) but in transit, as experience, in the social worlds of people. For poetry to exist, it has to be given meaning, and for meaning to develop there must be communities of people thinking about it. Publishing books as I did was a way of contributing to such a community – even a way of helping to invent it. Invention is essential to every aspect of a life of writing. In order to learn how to print, I invented a job for myself in the shop of a local printer. The shop was in Willits, California – a small rural town with an economy based on cattle ranching and logging; the owner of the shop (the printer, Jim Case) was adamant that "printing ain't for girls," but he took me on three afternoons a week as the shop's cleaning lady. A year later I moved to Berkeley, and purchased an old Chandler-Price press from a newspaper ad. I knew how to run the press but not much about typesetting; friends (particularly Johanna Drucker and Kathy Walkup) taught me a few essentials and a number of tricks. The first eleven chapbooks (printed in Willits in 1976–1977) had a slightly larger trim size than those I did myself (in a back room of the house in Berkeley) – I was using leftover paper in

Willits, but in Berkeley I bought paper from a local warehouse and used the trim size that was the most economical (creating the least amount of scrap). The list of authors of the first books makes it clear that for the first year and a half I was looking to various modes of "experimental," "innovative," or "avant-garde" writing for information; the subsequent chapbooks represent a commitment to a particular community – the group of writers who came to be associated with "Language Writing." The chapbook format appealed to me for obvious practical reasons – a shorter book meant less work (and expense) than a longer one. But there were two other advantages to the chapbook. First, most of the books I published were commissioned – I invited poets to give me a manuscript by a certain date (usually six months to a year away) – and I didn't want to make the invitation a burden. And second, I wanted the Tuumba books to come to people in the mode of "news" – in this sense, rather than "chapbook" perhaps one should say "pamphlet." It is for this reason, by the way, that I didn't handsew the books; they are all stapled – a transgression in the world of fine printing but highly practical in the world of pamphleteering.

— *Lyn Hejinian*
Berkeley, California, September 1997

TUUMBA 28

DOCTOR WILLIAMS' HEIRESSES

Alice Notley

Alice Notley,
Doctor Williams'
Heiresses (1980).

Howe, Fanny. *For Erato:*
The Meaning of Life. 1984.
(Tuumba 48.) (GRD)

Howe, Susan. *Thorn, Thistle,*
Apron Leaf. Broadside. 1976.

Howe, Susan. *The Western*
Borders. 1976. (Tuumba 2.)
(GRD)

Inman, P. *Ocker.* 1982.
(Tuumba 37.) (GRD)

Irby, Kenneth. *Archipelago.*
1976. (Tuumba 4.) (GRD)

Kahn, Paul. *January.* 1978.
(Tuumba 13.) (GRD)

Kostelanetz, Richard.
Foreshortenings, and Other
Stories. 1978. (Tuumba 14.)
(GRD)

Lipp, Jeremy. *Sections from*
Defiled by Water. 1976.
(Tuumba 3.) (GRD)

Mandel, Tom. *EncY.* 1978.
(Tuumba 16.) (BRG)

Mason, John. *Fade to Prompt.*
1981. (Tuumba 35.)

Melnick, David.
Men in Aida: Book One. 1983.
(Tuumba 47.) (GRD)

Notley, Alice. *Doctor*
Williams' Heiresses. 1980.
(Tuumba 28.) (GRD)

Palmer, Michael. *Alogon.*
1980. (Tuumba 30.) (GRD)

Perelman, Bob. *a.k.a.* 1979.
(Tuumba 19.) (GRD)

Perelman, Bob. *To the*
Reader. 1984. (Tuumba 49.)
(GRD)

Price, Larry. *Proof.* 1982.
(Tuumba 42.) (GRD)

Robinson, Kit. *Riddle Road.*
1982. (Tuumba 41.) (GRD)

Robinson, Kit. *Tribute to*
Nervous. 1980. (Tuumba
26.) (GRD)

Rodefer, Stephen. *Plane*
Debris. 1981. (Tuumba 36.)

Seaton, Peter. *Crisis*
Intervention. 1983. (Tuumba
45.) (GRD)

Silliman, Ronald. *ABC.*
1983. (Tuumba 46.) (GRD)

Silliman, Ronald. *Sitting Up,*
Standing, Taking Steps. 1978.
(Tuumba 17.) (GRD)

Watten, Barrett. *Complete*
Thought. 1982. (Tuumba
38.) (GRD)

Watten, Barrett. *Plasma*
Paralleles "X". 1979.
(Tuumba 21.) (GRD)

Wilk, David. *For You/For*
Sure. 1977. (Tuumba 9.)
(GRD)

Woodall, John. *Recipe:*
Collected Thoughts for
Considering the Void. 1977.
(Tuumba 10.) (GRD)

Poet Charles Bernstein on the economics of small press literary publishing, using Sun & Moon Press as an example:

"The printing bill runs from $2600 to $4000 as you go from 1000 to 2000 copies. [Douglas] Messerli estimates the cost of editing a 100-page poetry book at $300: this covers all the work between the press receiving a manuscript and sending it to a designer (including any copyediting and proofreading that may be necessary as well as preparation of front and back matter and cover copy). Typesetting is already a rarity for presses like Sun & Moon, with authors expected to provide computer disks wherever possible. Formatting these disks (converting them into type following specifications of the book designer) can cost anywhere from $300 to $1000, one of those variable labor costs of small press operations. The book designer will charge about $500. The cover will cost an additional $100 for photographic reproduction or permission fees or both. Publicity costs must also be accounted for, even if, as at Sun & Moon, no advertising is involved. Messerli estimates publicity costs at $1500, which covers the cost of something like 100 free copies distributed to reviewers, postage and packing, mailings and catalog pages, etc. The total cash outlay here, then, for 2000 copies, is around $6,800. (For the sake of this discussion, overhead costs – rent, salaries, office equipment, phone bills, etc. – are not included; such costs typically are estimated at about 30 percent more than the cost of production.)

"If all goes well, Sun & Moon will sell out of its print run in two years. Let's say Sun & Moon prints 2000 copies of the book and charges $10 retail; let's also say all the books were sold. That makes a gross of $20,000. Subtract from this a 50 percent wholesale discount (that is, most bookstores will pay $5 for the book) and that leaves $10,000. Subtract from this the 24 percent that Sun & Moon's distributor takes (and remember that most small presses are too small to secure a distributor with a professional sales force). That leaves $7600. Now last, but not to be totally forgotten, especially since I am a Sun & Moon author, the poet's royalty; typically no advance would be paid and the author would receive 10 percent of this last figure or $760. That leaves $6840 return to the publisher on a cash cost of about $7000. As James Sherry noted years ago in L=A=N=G=U=A=G=E: a piece of paper with nothing on it has a definite economic value. If you print a poem on it, this value is lost. Here we have a vivid example of what Georges Bataille has called general economy, an economy of loss rather than accumulation. Poetry is a negative – or let's just say poetic – economy."

Charles Bernstein, from "Provisional Institutions: Alternative Presses and Poetic Innovation," *Arizona Quarterly*, vol. 51, no. 1 (Spring 1995) and Qwerty Arts (http://www.qwertyarts.com/books/bernstein.html).

Some Other Presses and Publications:

The checklists which precede and follow are decidedly preliminary. As David Meltzer rightly noted after compiling his "SF Poetry Chronology" in *The San Francisco Poets* (New York: Ballantine, 1971), p. 309: "I could see a dedicated bibliographer coming out of his cave after a decade's work with a book as fat as a phonebook – and still not having gotten it all down. The life of poetry is that way. It moves fast and quick and usually it moves on."

A key to the abbreviations used for divisions of The New York Public Library appears on page 55.

A Preliminary Checklist

Abracadabra. Luxembourg. Edited by Marcello Angioni. Nos. 1–3 (1977–1978).

BRG has: complete file.

Accent Editions.
New York City. Tom Weigel[?].

Weigel, Tom. *Little Heart.* 1981.

Weigel, Tom. *Sonnets.* Cover by Rochelle Kraut. 1980. (BRG)

Acker, Kathy.

Acker, Kathy. *The Adult Life of Toulouse Lautrec.* 6 vols. San Francisco and New York: Self-published and TVRT, 1975–1976. (BRG, RBK)

Acker, Kathy. *I Dreamt I Was a Nymphomaniac!: IMAGIN-ING.* 6 Parts. San Francisco: Self-published and Empty Elevator Shaft Poetry Press and musicmusic corpora-tion, 1974. (BRG)

Ahnoi. North Bergen, New Jersey. Edited by Joel S. Lewis. Nos. 1–3 (1979–1980).

BRG has: complete file. GRD has: no. 1.

Alternative Press. Detroit and Grindstone City, Michigan. Edited by Ann and Ken Mikolowski. Nos. 1–16 (1971–1989).

Alternative Press. Detroit and Grindstone City, Michigan. Ann and Ken Mikolowski.

Berrigan, Ted. *Landscape with Figures.* Broadside. 1978.

Clark, Tom. *Back in Tulsa.* Broadside. 1971. (RBK)

Creeley, Robert. *For Betsy and Tom.* Broadside. 1970.

Eshleman, Clayton. *One of the Oldest Dreams.* Broadside. 1971. (RBK)

Ginsberg, Allen. *Milarepa Taste.* Broadside. 1971. (RBK)

Knight, Etheridge. *For Black Poets Who Think of Suicide.* Broadside. 1970.

Mikolowski, Ann. *Port Hope Beacon*. Broadside. [1975?].

Mikolowski, Michael. *Three Hundred Six*. Broadside. 1978.

Padgett, Ron, with Glen Baxter. *The Modified Educator Stared at His Shoe*. Broadside. 1978.

Snyder, Gary. *Clear Cut*. Broadside. 1974.

Warsh, Lewis, and Tom Clark. *Ode to Negativity*. Broadside. 1970.

Am Here Books/Immediate Editions. Santa Barbara, California. Richard Aaron.

Clark, Tom. *The Rodent Who Came to Dinner*. 1981. (BRG)

Di Prima, Diane. *The Mysteries of Vision: Some Notes on H.D.* 1988. (GRD)

Notley, Alice. *Tell Me Again*. 1982.

Sanders, Edward. *The Cutting Prow*. 1981. (GRD)

American Theatre for Poets. New York City. Diane di Prima.

The American Theatre for Poets Inc. Presents February 14, 1965, William Burroughs: Valentine's Day Reading at the East End Theatre. Pamphlet. 1965.

The American Theatre for Poets Inc. Presents the New York Poets Theatre. The Travelers Watch a Sunrise by Wallace Stevens, Murder Cake by Diane di Prima, Love's Labor by Frank O'Hara. Pamphlet. 1958.

The American Theatre for Poets Inc. The New York Poets Theatre in 1965. The Plays Include: Unpacking the Black Trunk by Kenward Elmslie and James Schuyler, Shopping and Waiting by James Schuyler, The Sideshow by Arthur Williams, and The Wednesday Club by Kenward Elmslie and James Schuyler. Pamphlet. 1964. (BRG)

Di Prima, Diane. *Like*. 1960.

Guest, Barbara. *Port: A Murder in One Act*. 1964.

Koch, Kenneth. *Guinevere, or the Death of the Kangaroo*. 1961.

O'Hara, Frank. *Awake in Spain*. 1960. (BRG)

Schuyler, James. *Shopping and Waiting: A Dramatic Pause*. 1953. (BRG)

Amphora. San Francisco and Berkeley, California. Edited by Thomas Head. Nos. 1–8 (1970–1972). Cover by Charles Amirkhanian (6).

BRG has: no. 6, guest-edited by David Gitin.

Andrea Doria Books. New York City. Tom Weigel.

Goldstein, Lenny. *Both Sides of the Goat*. Cover by Monica Weigel. 1981. (BRG)

Hughes, Helena. *Kiss My Lips*. Cover by Rochelle Kraut. 1979. (BRG)

Scholnick, Michael, and Tom Weigel. *A Hot Little Number*. Cover by Rochelle Kraut. 1979. (BRG)

Weigel, Tom. *Panic Hardware*. Cover by Doug Morrissey. 1979. (BRG)

Weigel, Tom, ed. *The Full Deck Anthology: Poetry 1959–1981*. 1981. (BRG)

See also **Tangerine.**

Annex. Ann Arbor, Michigan. Edited by Brita Bergland and Tod Kabza. Nos. 1–3 (1975–1977): No. 1: *Biscuit* (1975); No. 2: *Flora Danica* (1976); No. 3: *Terraplane* (1977).

GRD has: complete file.

The Ant's Forefoot. Toronto, Canada. Edited by David Rosenberg. Nos. 1–11 (Fall 1967–September 1973).

GRD has: nos. 1–3, 6–9, 11.

Arif Press. Berkeley, California. Wesley B. Tanner.

Berkson, Bill. *Ants*. 1974. (BRG)

Codrescu, Andrei. *& Grammar & Money*. 1973. (RBK)

Ferlinghetti, Lawrence. *Love Is No Stone on the Moon: Automatic Poem*. 1971. (GRD)

Hawkins, Bobbie Louise. *15 Poems*. 1974. (RBK)

Kyger, Joanne. *Desecheo Notebook*. Designed by Wesley Tanner. 1971. (RBK)

Kyger, Joanne. *Trip Out and Fall Back*. Cover and drawings by Gordon Baldwin. 1974. (BRG)

McClure, Joanna. *Extended Love Poem*. 1978. (RBK)

Spicer, Jack. *The Red Wheelbarrow*. 1971.

Tanner, Wesley. *Hymn to the Sun*. 1972. (RBK)

Waldman, Anne. *Sun the Blond Out*. 1975. (BRG, RBK)

The Ark. San Francisco. Edited by Philip Lamantia and Sanders Russell. No. 1 (Spring 1947). Covers by Ronald Bladen.

BRG has: sole issue.

Ark II/Moby I. San Francisco. Edited by Michael McClure and James Harmon. No. 1 (1956–1957).

BRG has: sole issue.

Ark III. San Francisco. Edited by James Harmon. No. 1 (Winter 1957).

BRG has: sole issue.

Ark Press. Berkeley, California. Thomas Parkinson.

Duncan, Robert, and Jack Spicer. *An Ode and Arcadia*. 1974. (BRG, RBK)

Parkinson, Thomas. *Homage to Jack Spicer, and Other Poems: Poems 1965–1969*. 1970. (BRG)

Parkinson, Thomas. *Men, Women, Vines*. 1959.

Artists' Workshop Press. Detroit, Michigan. John Sinclair.

Semark, Jim. *Book of Humors*. 1965. (Artists' Workshop Books, No. 1.)

Sinclair, John. *This Is Our Music.* Introduction by Charles Moore. 1965. (Artists' Workshop Books, No. 3.)

Tysh, George. *Sit Up Straight.* 1965. (Artists' Workshop Books, No. 2.)

Wieners, John. *Hart Crane, Harry Crosby, I See You Going Over the Edge.* 1966. (Broadside No. 2.) (BRG)

Younkins, Jerry. *Write About My Buddies: They're Dead: Commemorating the Death of Stephen Wilson.* 1965. (Artists' Workshop Books, No. 7.)

See also **Change**; **Whe're**; **Work.**

Assembling. New York City. Compiled by Richard Kostelanetz and others. Nos. 1–10 (1970–1980).

BRG has: no. 8. GRD has: no. 9.

Asylum's Press. New York City. Charles Bernstein and Susan Bee [Laufer].

Bernstein, Charles. *Parsing.* 1976. (BRG)

DiPalma, Raymond. *Marquee: A Score.* 1977. (BRG)

Greenwald, Ted. *Use No Hooks.* Cover by Pat Steir. 1980. (BRG)

Laufer, Susan Bee. *Photogram.* 1978.

Seaton, Peter. *Agreement.* 1978.

Joanne Kyger, *Desecheo Notebook* (Berkeley, Calif.: Arif Press, 1971). Designed by Wesley Tanner.

Athanor. New York City. Edited by Douglas Calhoun. Contributing editor, George Butterick. Vol. 1, nos. 1–6 (Winter/Spring 1971– Spring 1975).

BRG has: complete file.

Attaboy! Boulder, Colorado. Edited by Linda Bohe and Phoebe MacAdams. Vols. 1–2 (1976–1977).

BRG has: complete file.

Audit/Poetry and Audit/Fiction. Buffalo, New York. Edited by Michael Anania and Charles Doria. Vol. 1, no. 1–vol. 12 (February 1960–1981).

BRG has: vol. 4, no. 1 (Frank O'Hara issue); vol. 4, no. 3 (Robert Duncan issue).

Avalanche. Berkeley, California. Edited by Richard Krech. Nos. 1–3 (1966–1967).

BRG has: no. 3 (special Rock and Roll issue).

Awede Press. Windsor, Vermont. Brita Bergland.

Andrews, Bruce. *Jeopardy.* 1980. (GRD)

Royet-Journoud, Claude. *The Maternal Drape; or The Restitution.* Translated by Charles Bernstein. 1985. (GRD)

Sherry, James. *Converses.* 1982. (GRD)

Waldrop, Keith. *Intervals.* 1981. (GRD)

Waldrop, Rosmarie. *Nothing Has Changed.* 1981. (GRD)

Weiner, Hannah. *Sixteen.* 1983. (GRD)

Bacedifogu. San Francisco. Edited by Larry Fagin. No. 1 (1962).

BRG has: sole issue.

Baloney Street. Ventura, California. Edited by Michael-Sean Lazarchuk. Nos. 1–7 (?–1973).

BRG has: nos. 1, 6, 7.

Bed. Vancouver, British Columbia, Canada. Edited by George Stanley and Scott Watson; Scott Watson and Stan Persky. Vols. 1–4 (1975–1976).

Dick Higgins, *What Are Legends* (Berkeley, Calif.: Bern Porter, 1960).

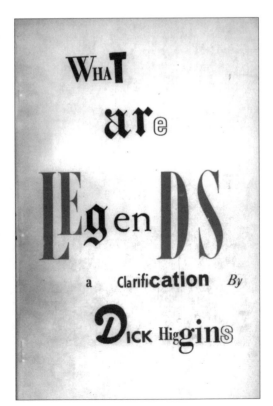

Berkeley Miscellany. Berkeley, California. Edited by Robert Duncan. Nos. 1–2 (1948–1949).

BRG has: complete file.

Berkeley Poetry Conference. Berkeley, California, 1965.

Checklists of separate publications of poets at the First Berkeley Poetry Conference, 1965. Berkeley, Calif.: Cody's Books, 1965. Compiled for Cody's by the editors of Oyez. (BRG)

University of California, Berkeley. Letters and Science Extension. *Bibliography. Olson's Poetry and Mythology Seminars.* Mimeographed sheet, 1965. (BRG)

Bern Porter. Berkeley, California. Bern Porter.

Duncan, Robert. *Heavenly City, Earthly City.* Drawings by Mary Fabilli. 1947. (BRG)

Higgins, Dick. *What Are Legends.* 1960. (BRG)

Lamantia, Philip. *Erotic Poems.* 1946. (BRG, RBK)

Patchen, Kenneth. *Panels for the Walls of Heaven.* 1946. (RBK)

Rexroth, Kenneth. *A Bestiary for My Daughters, Mary & Katherine.* 1955.

Schevill, James. *Selected Poems, 1945–1959.* 1960. (GRD)

Best and Company. New York City. Edited by Bill Berkson. One-shot (1969).

BRG has: sole issue.

Bezoar. Gloucester, Massachusetts. Edited by Fred Buck, Thorpe Feidt, Paul Kahn, and others. Vol. 1, no. 1–vol. 21, no. 4 (April 1975–November? 1981).

BRG has: vol. 3, no. 1; vol. 4, no. 1; vol. 4, numero 3; vol. 5, number whatever; vol. 6, no. 1 (*Special Buffalo/ Yellowstone National Park Eternal Embarrassment Bezoar*); vol. 7, no. 2 (*3 Poems 3 Poets*); vol. 9, no. 2; vol. 10, no. 2; vol. 11, no. 2; vol. 12, nos. 1, 3, 5; vol. 13, nos. 2, 3; vol. 14, nos. 2, 4; vol. 15, no. 1; Issue 59? (Winter 1979); vol. 17, no. 2; vol. 19, nos. 2 (*Birds and Paradise Bezoar*), 4; vol. 20, no. 1 (*The Secret Graces of Our Enemies Bezoar*); vol. 21, no. 2 (*Heads and Tales Bezoar*).

Big Table. Chicago. Edited by Irving Rosenthal (no. 1) and Paul Carroll (nos. 2–5). Nos. 1–5 (Spring 1959–1960).

BRG has: complete file.

Bingo. New York City. Edited by Susie Timmons. No. 1 (1980). Folded sheet.

BRG has: sole issue.

Black Mountain College. Black Mountain, North Carolina.

Cage, John. *Haiku.* 1952.

Dawson, Fielding. *6 Stories of the Love of Life.* 1949.

Olson, Charles. *Letter for Melville, 1951.* 1951. (RBK)

Olson, Charles. *This.* Designs by Nicola Cernovich. 1952. (RBK)

Olson, Charles. *To ALL Those Who Care For Black Mountain College and What It Stood For, and Now More Than Ever Stands For, in American Education.* 1954.

Blewointment. Vancouver, British Columbia, Canada. Bill Bissett and Martina Clinton. Vol. 1 (1963–1973?), plus five unnumbered special issues: *The Combind Blewointment Open Picture Book nd th news* (1972); *And* by Gerry Gilbert (April 1971); special issue dedicated to the Len Forest–Jack Long film *In Search of Inno-cence*, Blewointmentpress poverty isshew (March 1972); "untitled issue with initial work by Michael Coutts from 67 July."

Blewointment Press. Vancouver, British Columbia, Canada. Bill Bissett.

Bissett, Bill. *Blew Trewz.* 1971. (GRD)

Bissett, Bill. *Th Fifth Sun.* Cover designs by the author. 1975. (BRG)

Bissett, Bill. *(Th) Gossamer Bed Pan.* 1974. (GRD)

Bissett, Bill. *Th High Green Hill.* 1972. (GRD)

Bissett, Bill. *Image Being.* 1975. (GRD)

Bissett, Bill. *Ready for Framing.* 1982. (APP)

Bissett, Bill. *Soul Arrow.* 1980. (BRG, GRD)

Bissett, Bill. *Sunday Work?* 1969.

Bissett, Bill. *Venus.* Photographs by Bertrand Lachance. 1975. (GRD)

Bissett, Bill. *Wht Poetiks.* 1967.

Bissett, Bill. *The Wind Up Tongue.* 1976. (BRG)

Clinton, Martina. *Yonder Glow.* 1971.

Farrell, Lance. *Inside Loves Out: Pome and 6 Drawings.* 1967.

Lachance, Bertrand. *Street Flesh.* 1972. (GRD)

Lachance, Bertrand. *Tes Rivières T'attendent; Song for th Peopul of Kanada.* Drawings by Bill Bissett. 1971. (GRD)

levy, d.a. *Zen, Concrete: Translations & a New Interpretation of Buddhist Doctrines.* 1968. (BRG)

Nichol, bp. *The Captain Poetry Poems.* 1970.

West, Ken. *Wire.* 1970.

Blue Beat. New York City. Edited by George Montgomery and Erik Kiviat. No. 1 (March 1964).

BRG has: sole issue.

Blue Pig. Paris, France, and Northampton, Massachu-setts. Nos. 1–23 (1969–1975). No. 10 is *No Eating* by Ted Greenwald (1970?), no. 11 is *Cheapness Means Forgiveness* by George Tysh (1970), no. 12 is *Brain Damage* by Larry Fagin (1970), no. 13 is *Workday* by Jack Collum, no. 15 is *Histoires Naturelles* by Robert Hebert (1971), no. 17 is *Pleasant Butter* by Tom Raworth (1972), no. 19 is *The New Money* by Ted Greenwald (1973), no. 22 is the Philip Lopate issue (n.d.), and no. 23 is *Cloister* by Ted Greenwald (1975).

BRG has: nos. 3, 7, 8, 10, 12, 16, 22. GRD has: nos. 1–4, 7–16, 18–19.

Blue Suede Shoes. Berkeley, California. Edited by Keith Abbott. Nos. 1–20 (1970–1973).

GRD has: nos. 2, 4–20.

Blue Suede Shoes. Monterey, Berkeley, and Davis, California. Keith Abbott.

Abbott, Keith. *The Closet: A Verse Drama in One Act.* 1972.

Abbott, Keith. *Joie de Vivre.* 1972.

Abbott, Keith. *Keith Abbott's Being Alone with a Girl.* Drawings by Opal L. Nations. 1975.

Abbott, Keith. *A Midsummer Nights Dream.* Broadside. 1973.

Carey, Steve. *Fleur-de-lis.* 1969. (BRG)

Clark, Tom. *Captain America.* Broadside. 1971.

Lazarchuk, Michael-Sean. *Face.* 1974.

Nolan, Pat. *Bob Hope in a Buick.* 1971.

Sowl, Michael. *Can "Ice Knockey" Teams Provide Chocolate Winter?* 1974.

Blue Wind Press. Iowa City, Iowa, and Berkeley, California. George Mattingly.

Abbott, Keith. *Erase Words: Poems, 1971–1975.* 1977. (GRD)

Abbott, Keith. *Gush.* 1975. (GRD)

Abbott, Keith. *Rhino Ritz: An American Mystery.* 1979. (GRD)

Berrigan, Ted. *So Going Around Cities: New and Selected Poems, 1958–1979.* Dust jacket by Donna Dennis. Illustrations by George Schneeman. 1980. (BRG)

Burroughs, William S. *The Book of Breeething.* 1980.

Burroughs, William S. *Port of Saints.* 1980. (BRG, GRD)

Gilfillan, Merrill. *Light Years: Selected Early Poems, 1969–1972.* 1972. (GRD)

Gilfillan, Merrill. *To Creature.* 1975.

Gitin, David. *This Once: New and Selected Poems, 1965–1978.* 1979. (GRD)

Gray, Darrell. *Something Swims Out.* Front cover by George Mattingly. [1972?]. Issued as *Search for Tomorrow,* Special Number A. (BRG)

Hollo, Anselm. *Finite Continued.* Photographs by David Abrams. 1980. (GRD)

Lally, Michael. *Rocky Dies Yellow: 1967–1972.* 1975. (GRD)

Mattingly, George. *Breathing Space.* 1975. (GRD)

Mattingly, George. *Darling Bender.* Poems by W. S. Merwin and others, with George Mattingly. 1971. (BRG)

Thomas, Lorenzo. *Chances Are Few.* 1979. (GRD, SC)

See also **Search for Tomorrow.**

Bobbs-Merrill. Indianapolis, Indiana, and New York City.

Brownstein, Michael. *Brainstorms.* Drawings by Donna Dennis. 1971. (BRG)

Oppenheimer, Joel. *In Time: Poems, 1962–1968.* 1969. (GRD)

Waldman, Anne. *Baby Breakdown.* 1970. (BRG)

Waldman, Anne. *Life Notes.* Cover by Joe Brainard. 1973. (BRG)

Boink! Berkeley, California. Edited by Dean Faulwell. No. 1 (Spring 1973).

GRD has: sole issue.

Boke Press. New York City. Joe Brainard.

Berrigan, Ted. *Living with Chris.* Illustrations and cover by Joe Brainard. 1965. (BRG)

Elmslie, Kenward, and Joe Brainard. *The Baby Book.* 1965. (BRG)

Elmslie, Kenward, and Joe Brainard. *The 1967 Game Calendar.* 1967.

Elmslie, Kenward, and Joe Brainard. *Shiny Ride.* 1972. (GRD)

Padgett, Ron, and Joe Brainard. *100,000 Fleeing Hilda.* Cover and drawings by Joe Brainard. 1967.

Waldman, Anne. *On the Wing.* Cover by Joe Brainard. 1968. Published dos-à-dos with Lewis Warsh, *Hijacking.* (BRG)

Warsh, Lewis. *Hijacking.* Cover by Joe Brainard. 1968. Published dos-à-dos with Anne Waldman, *On the Wing.* (BRG)

Bombay Gin. Jack Kerouac School of Disembodied Poetics, Naropa Institute, Boulder, Colorado. Various editors. Nos. 1–7 (Summer 1976–Summer/Fall 1979); *Bombay Gin* continues into the 1990s. Covers by Robert Duncan (6), Dick Gallup (3), Cary Meschl (5), Alice Notley (7).

BRG has: nos. 1, 3–7.
GRD has: nos. 1–7.

Bones. New York City. Edited by Katherine Greef and Terence Anderson. Nos. 1–3 (Fall 1967–Spring 1971).

BRG has: nos. 1–2.

Boston Eagle. Boston, Massachusetts. Edited by William Corbett, Lee Harwood, and Lewis Warsh. Nos. 1–3 (1973–1974).

BRG has: complete file.

Brilliant Corners. Chicago. Edited by Art Lange. Nos. 1–10 (1975–1979).

BRG has: complete file.

Broadside Press. Detroit, Michigan. Dudley Randall.

Baker, Houston. *A Many Colored Coat of Dreams: The Poetry of Countee Cullen.* 1974. (GRD, SC)

Brooks, Gwendolyn. *Beckonings.* 1975. (GRD, SC)

Brooks, Gwendolyn. *Report from Part One.* 1972. (GRD, SC)

Brooks, Gwendolyn, and others. *A Capsule Course in Black Poetry Writing.* 1975. (GRD, SC)

Clifton, Lucille. *All of Us Are All of Us.* Broadside. 1974. (RBK)

Danner, Margaret, and Dudley Randall. *Poem/Counterpoem.* 1966. (SC)

Dixon, Melvin. *Climbing Montmartre.* Broadside. 1974. (RBK)

Giovanni, Nikki. *Black Judgement.* 1968. (GRD, SC)

Rosmarie and Keith
Waldrop, *Light Travels*
(Providence, R.I.:
Burning Deck, 1992).
Designed by Keith
Waldrop.

Harper, Michael. *To an Old Man Twiddling Thumbs.* Broadside. 1975. (RBK)

Knight, Etheridge. *Belly Song and Other Poems.* 1973. (GRD, SC)

Knight, Etheridge. *Poems from Prison.* 1968. (GRD, SC)

Madhubuti, Haki. *Directionscore: Selected and New Poems.* 1971. (GRD, SC)

Major, Clarence. *The Cotton Club: New Poems.* 1972. (GRD, SC)

Randall, Dudley. *Ballad of Birmingham (On the Bombing of a Church in Birmingham).* Broadside. 1965. (RBK)

Randall, Dudley. *Cities Burning.* 1968. (GRD, SC)

Walker, Margaret. *October Journey.* 1973. (GRD, SC)

Buffalo Stamps. Chevy Chase, Maryland, and Chicago. Edited by Simon Schuchat, Mat Stover, and Alec Bernstein. Vol. 1, nos. 1–7 (1971–1973). Cover by Gregory Corso (3/4).

BRG has: vol. 1, nos. 2, 3/4, 6 (*The Last Buffalo*).

Burning Deck. Ann Arbor, Michigan, and Durham, Connecticut. Edited by James Camp, D. C. Hope, Bernard Waldrop. Nos. 1–4 (1962–1965).

Burning Deck. Providence, Rhode Island. Keith and Rosmarie Waldrop.

Andrews, Bruce. *Corona.* 1973. (BRG, RBK)

Ashley, Mary. *Truck: A Dance.* 1972. (RBK)

Crozier, Andrew. *The Veil Poem.* 1974. (RBK)

DiPalma, Raymond. *Max: A Sequel.* 1974. (RBK)

Mac Low, Jackson. *Four Trains . . . 4–5 December 1964.* 1974. (RBK)

Owens, Rochelle. *Poems from Joe's Garage.* 1973. (RBK)

Silliman, Ron. *Nox.* 1974. (RBK)

Strand, Mark. *The Sargeantville Notebook.* 1973. (RBK)

Taggart, John. *Pyramid Canon.* 1973. (RBK)

Tysh, George. *Shop [and] Posh.* 1973. (RBK)

Waldrop, Keith. *My Nodebook for December.* 1971. (BRG, RBK)

Waldrop, Keith and Rosmarie. *Words Worth Less.* 1973. (RBK)

Waldrop, Keith and Rosmarie. *Until Volume One.* 1973. (RBK)

Waldrop, Rosmarie. *Camp Printing.* 1970? (BRG, GRD)

Waldrop, Rosmarie and Keith. *Light Travels.* Designed by Keith Waldrop. 1992.

Camels Coming. Albuquerque, New Mexico, and Reno, Nevada. Edited by Richard Morris. Nos. 1–8/9 (1965–1968).

Cape Goliard. London. Tom Raworth and Barry Hall.

Berrigan, Ted. *In the Early Morning Rain.* Cover and drawings by George

Ray Bremser, *Blowing Mouth* (Cherry Valley, N.Y.: Cherry Valley Editions, 1978). Front cover photograph by Jonas Kover.

Schneeman. 1970. (BRG)

Blackburn, Paul. *Bryant Park.* Broadside. 1968.

Burroughs, William S. *The Last Words of Dutch Schultz.* 1970.

Creeley, Robert. *A Sight.* 1967.

Ginsberg, Allen. *T. V. Baby Poems.* 1967.

Hollo, Anselm. *Works, 1959–1969.* 1970.

Kelly, Robert. *Kali Yuga.* 1970.

Krolow, Karl. *Invisible Hands: Poems.* 1969.

Mitchell, Adrian. *Out Loud.* 1968.

Olson, Charles. *Letters for Origin, 1950–1956.* 1970. (GRD)

Olson, Charles. *The Maximus Poems.* 1960.

Padgett, Ron, and Jim Dine. *The Adventures of Mr. and Mrs. Jim and Ron.* Cover by Jim Dine. 1970. (BRG)

Prynne, J. H. *Kitchen Poems.* 1968. (BRG)

Raworth, Tom. *Moving.* Illustrations by Joe Brainard. 1971. (GRD)

Tarn, Nathaniel. *Where Babylon Ends.* 1968.

Tarn, Nathaniel, ed. *Con Cuba: An Anthology of Cuban Poetry of the Last Sixty Years.* 1969.

Wieners, John. *Nerves.* 1970. (BRG)

Caveman. New York City. Edited by Simon Schuchat. Unnumbered; number of issues unknown (1977–1981).

BRG has: issues dated June 13, 1977; January 13, 1978; May 27, 1981; December 7, 1981.

Change. Detroit, Michigan. Published by Artists' Workshop. Edited by John and Leni Sinclair and Charles Moore. Nos. 1–2 (Fall/Winter 1965–Spring/Summer 1966).

BRG has: complete file.

Cherry Valley Editions. Cherry Valley, New York. Mary Beach, Charles Plymell, and others.

Bremser, Ray. *Blowing Mouth.* Front cover photograph by Jonas Kover. 1978. (BRG)

Norton, Joshua. *The Blue and the Gray: Poems.* 1975. (GRD)

Owen, Maureen. *The No-Travels Journal.* Cover and drawings by Hugh Kepets. 1975. (BRG)

Raphael, Dan. *Energumen.* 1976.

Chicago. Chicago. Edited by Alice Notley. Vol. 1, no.1–vol. 6 (double issue) (February 1972–March 1973). Covers by George Schneeman (vol. 1, no. 1; vol. 5, no. 1). 6 issues.

BRG has: complete file.

Chicago. European Edition. Wivenhoe, Essex, England. Edited by Alice Notley. Nos. 1–3 (1973–1974). Covers by George Schneeman.

BRG has: complete file.

Cicada. New York City.
Edited by Carter Ratcliff.
One-shot (1970).

BRG has: sole issue.

Circle. Berkeley, California.
George Leite. Nos. 1–10
(1944–1948).

Clown War. Brooklyn,
New York. Edited by Bob
Heman and Stephen
Fairhurst (co-editor of
some issues). Nos. 1–31?
(February 1972–1989?).

BRG has: nos. 8, 11, 14, 23,
24, 31. GRD has: nos. 1–4,
6–9, 11–17, 19–26.

Coach House Press.
Toronto, Canada. Stan
Bevington and others.

Atwood, Margaret. *Murder
in the Dark.* 1983. (GRD)

Bowering, George. *Curious.*
1974.

Bowering, George, and
Robert Hogg. *Robert
Duncan: An Interview by
George Bowering and Robert
Hogg, April 19, 1969.* 1971.
(A Beaver Kosmos Folio.)

Coleman, Victor. *America.*
1972. (GRD)

Davey, Frank. *Arcana.* 1973.
(RBK)

Davey, Frank, and Fred
Wah, eds. *The SwiftCurrent
Anthology.* 1986. (GRD)

Dawson, Fielding. *On
Duberman's Black Mountain
and B. H. Friedman's
Biography of Jackson Pollock.*
1973. (BRG)

Gilbert, Gerry. *From Next
Spring.* 1977. (GRD)

Steve McCaffery,
Carnival (Toronto:
Coach House Press,
1973).

Some Other Presses and Publications: A Preliminary Checklist

Kiyooka, Roy. *The Fontainebleau Dream Machine: 18 Frames from a Book of Rhetoric.* 1977. (GRD)

Kiyooka, Roy. *Nevertheless These Eyes.* 1967.

Kiyooka, Roy. *StoneD Gloves.* Photographs by the author. 1971?

McCaffery, Steve. *Carnival.* 1973. (BRG)

Nichol, bp. *The Martyrology,* Books 1 & 2. 2nd ed. 1977.

Nichol, bp. *The Martyrology,* Books 3 & 4. 1976.

Nichol, bp. *The Martyrology,* Book V, Chain 8. 1979.

Padgett, Ron, and Tom Veitch. *Antlers in the Treetops.* 1973. (BRG)

UU, David. *Chopped Liver.* 1981. (GRD)

Wah, Fred. *Among.* 1972. (GRD)

Warsh, Lewis. *Part of My History.* 1972. (BRG)

Collection. Hove, Sussex, England. Edited by Peter Riley. Nos. 1–7? (March 1968–1970?). 5 issues. No. 4/5 with *Tzarad* 3/4.

GRD has: nos. 1–5.

Columbia University Press for the Frank O'Hara Foundation. New York City.

Brownstein, Michael. *Highway to the Sky.* 1969. (GRD)

Ceravolo, Joseph. *Spring in This World of Poor Mutts.* 1968. (GRD)

Elmslie, Kenward. *Motor Disturbance.* 1971. (GRD)

Koethe, John. *Domes.* 1973. (GRD)

Combustion. Toronto, Canada. Edited by Raymond Souster. Nos. 1–15 (January 1957–1966). *Island* 6 (1966) issued as *Combustion* 15.

BRG has: no. 2.

Communications Co. New York City.

Di Prima, Diane. *Revolutionary Letters.* 1968.

Contact. Toronto, Canada. Edited by Raymond Souster. Nos. 1–10 (1952–1954).

Coyote's Journal. Eugene, Oregon, and San Francisco. Edited by James Koller, Edward Van Aelstyn, and William Wroth. Nos. 1–10 (1964–1974), plus a special issue (1982).

BRG has: no. 1.

Coyote's Journal. Eugene, Oregon, and San Francisco. James Koller, Edward Van Aelstyn, and William Wroth.

Kyger, Joanne. *The Fool in April: A Poem in Two Parts.* 1966.

Whalen, Philip. *Every Day: Poems.* 1965. (GRD)

Whalen, Philip. *Higrade: Doodles, Poems.* 1966. (GRD)

Whalen, Philip. *You Didn't Even Try.* 1967. (GRD)

Woolf, Douglas. *Signs of a Migrant Worrier.* 1965.

Cranium Press. San Francisco. Clifford Burke.

Abbott, Keith. *Putty.* 1971. (RBK)

Blazek, Douglas. *Two Poems.* Broadside. 1970.

Burke, Clifford. *Griffin Creek: Poems.* 1972. (RBK)

Carey, Steve. *Smith Going Backward.* 1968.

Carey, Steve. *Two Poems.* 1966.

Coyote's Journal 2 (1965). Art by Ralph Turner.

Duerden, Richard. *The Left Hand & the Glory of Her.* 1967. (GRD)

Duncan, Robert. *Bring It Up from the Dark.* Broadside. 1970.

Ginsberg, Allen. *Who Be Kind To.* Broadside. 1967. (RBK)

Körte, Mary Norbert. *A Breviary in Time of War.* 1970.

McClure, Michael. *The Mammals.* 1972. (BRG)

Nolan, Pat. *Blues.* Broadside. 1973.

Nolan, Pat. *The Chinese Quartet: Poems.* 1973.

Perkoff, Stuart. *Song for Max Finstein.* Broadside. 1973.

Pickard, Tom. *The Skull Masks.* Broadside. 1971.

Sky, Gino. *Sweet Ass'd Angels, Pilgrims and Boogie Woogies.* Cover woodcut by Genevra Sloan. Illustrations by Dana Sloan. 1973.

Welch, Lew. *Redwood Haiku and Other Poems.* 1972. (BRG, RBK)

Wild, Peter. *Sonnets.* 1967.

Credences. Kent, Ohio, and Buffalo, New York. Edited by Robert Bertholf. Nos. 1–8/9 (1975–1980); new series, vol. 1, no. 1–vol. 3, no. 2 (1981–1985). 14 issues in 12.

BRG has: complete file.

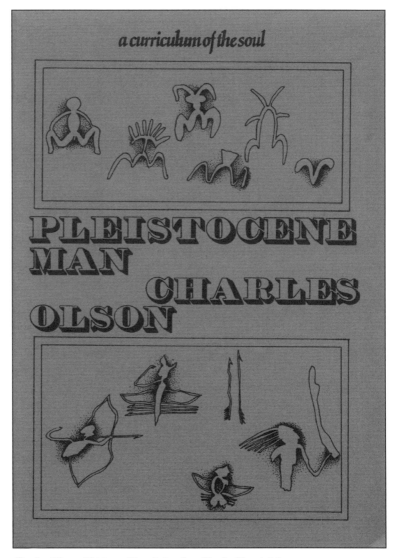

Charles Olson, *Pleistocene Man: Letters from Charles Olson to John Clarke During October 1965* (Canton, N.Y.: A Curriculum of the Soul, 1968). Front cover by Guy Berard.

Some Other Presses and Publications: A Preliminary Checklist

Cronopios. Madison, Wisconsin. Edited by James Stephens and David Hilton. Nos. 1–7 (November 1966–May 1970).

BRG has: no. 7. GRD has: complete file.

Crony Books/Dead Duke Books. New York City. Greg Masters.

Lenhart, Gary. *Bulb in Socket.* Cover by Louise Hamlin. 1980. (BRG)

Masters, Greg. *My Women and Men Part 2.* 1980. (BRG)

Myles, Eileen, and Anne Waldman. *Polar Ode.* Cover by Steve Levine. 1979. (BRG)

Scholnick, Michael. *Beyond Venus.* 1980. (BRG)

A Curriculum of the Soul. Institute of Further Studies, Canton, New York. Plan by Charles Olson; general editor, John Clarke.

Lansing, Gerrit. *Analytic Psychology, or The Soluble Forest Is Swimming Across.* 1983. (A Curriculum of the Soul, No. 23.) (BRG)

MacAdams, Lewis. *Dance as Individual Body-Power.* 1972. (A Curriculum of the Soul, No. 16.) (GRD)

McNaughton, Duncan. *Dream.* 1973. (A Curriculum of the Soul, No. 2.) (GRD)

Olson, Charles. *Pleistocene Man: Letters from Charles Olson to John Clarke During October 1965.* Front cover by Guy Berard. 1968.

Sanders, Ed. *Egyptian Hieroglyphs.* Cover by Guy Berard. 1973. (A Curriculum of the Soul, No. 17.) (GRD)

Wah, Fred. *Earth.* 1974. (A Curriculum of the Soul, No. 6.) (GRD)

d.a.levy. *See* **levy, d.a.**

Dave Haselwood Books. San Francisco. Dave Haselwood.

Ferlinghetti, Lawrence. *After the Cries of the Birds.* 1967. (BRG)

McClure, Michael. *Dream Table. 30 Cards.* 1965.

McClure, Michael. *Unto Caesar.* 1965.

Wieners, John. *Chinoiserie.* 1965.

Wieners, John. *The Hotel Wentley Poems: Original Versions.* 2nd revised edition. 1965. (BRG, MSS)

Dental Floss. West Branch, Iowa. Edited by Allan Kornblum. Vol. 1, nos. 1–5 (1975–1984).

BRG has: nos. 1–3. GRD has: complete file.

Diana's Bimonthly. Providence, Rhode Island. Edited by Tom Ahern. Vols. 1–3; vol. 4, nos. 1–6; vol. 5, nos. 1–3; vols. 7–10 (1972–1983).

BRG has: complete file.

The Difficulties. Kent, Ohio. Edited by Tom Beckett. Vol. 1, no. 1–vol. 3, no. 2 (1980–1989).

GRD has: vol. 1, no. 2–vol. 3, no. 2.

DiMaggio, Joe, Press. *See* **Joe DiMaggio Press.**

Doones. Bowling Green, Ohio. Edited by Ray DiPalma. Vol. 1, nos. 1–4 (1969–1971).

BRG has: complete file.

Doones Press. Bowling Green, Ohio. Ray DiPalma.

Benveniste, Asa. *Listen.* 1975.

DiPalma, Ray, and Stephen Shrader. *Macaroons.* 1969.

Gilfillan, Merrill. *9:15.* 1970.

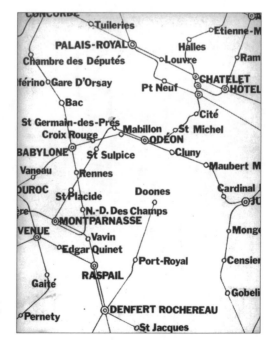

Doones, vol. 1, no. 4 (1971). Cover by Stephen Shrader.

Gray, Darrell. *The Beauties of Travel.* Cover by John Whelan. 1971. (BRG)

Greenwald, Ted. *Miami.* 1975.

Hollo, Anselm. *Spring Cleaning Greens,* from *Notebooks, 1966–1973.* Cover by Elisabeth Brandfass. 1973. (BRG)

Lally, Michael. *What Withers.* 1970.

Painted Horses. Edited by Ray DiPalma. Cover by Steven Schrader. One-shot. 1970. (BRG)

Raworth, Tom. *Tracking.* Cover by Fielding Dawson. 1972. (BRG)

Shelter. Edited by Ray DiPalma. Cover by John Whelan. One-shot. 1972. (BRG)

Shirt. Edited by Ray DiPalma. Cover by Elisabeth Brandfass. One-shot. 1973. (BRG)

Silliman, Ron. *Mohawk.* 1973. (BRG)

Slater, Robert. *Blues & Apologies.* 1970.

Dot Books. New York City. R. Meyers [Richard Hell].

Stern, Theresa [Richard Meyers/Richard Hell and Tom Miller/Tom Verlaine]. *Wanna Go Out?* Cover by Richard Meyers. 1973.

Wylie, Andrew. *Yellow Flowers.* Cover by Andrew Wylie. 1972.

Drainage. Cambridge, Massachusetts. Edited by Neil Barrett. Nos. 1–2 (1967). Cover photographs by Nick Welsh.

BRG has: complete file.

E 1 (1976).

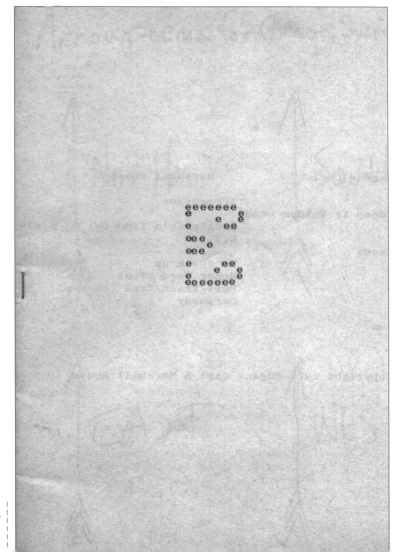

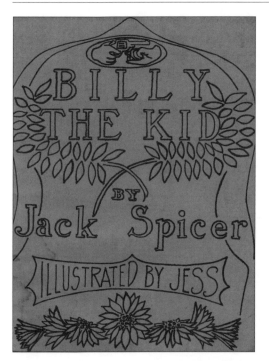

Jack Spicer, *Billy the Kid* (Stinson Beach, Calif.: Enkidu Surrogate, 1959). Front cover by Jess (Collins).

Dream Sheet. New York City. Edited by Diane Wakoski. No. 1–? (1965–?).

Dust. Paradise, California. Edited by Len Fulton. Vols. 1–5 (nos. 1–17) (Spring 1964–Fall 1971).

GRD has: vol. 1, no. 2–vol. 5.

E. Den Haag and Utrecht, Holland, and Rockville, Maryland. Edited by Eugene Carl and Marshall Reese. [Vol. 1] No. 1–vol. 2, no. 2 (1976).

E pod. Baltimore, Maryland. Edited by Kirby Malone and Marshall Reese. Nos. 1–6 (Spring 1978–1980).

Ear. New York City. Edited by Ted Greenwald and Lorenzo Toumes [Thomas]. No. 1 (1964).

BRG has: sole issue.

Elephant. New York City. Edited by John Perreault. Nos. 1–3 (Summer 1965–1966).

BRG has: complete file.

The End [& variations of]. Oakland and Monte Rio, California. Edited by Pat Nolan and others. Nos. 1–9 (1972–1975).

BRG has: nos. 2 (*The Living End*), 7 (*The End in Itself*), 8 (*The End Over End*).

Enkidu Surrogate. Stinson Beach, California. Robert Duncan and Jess (Collins).

Duncan, Robert. *Faust Foutu: An Entertainment in Four Acts*. Cover and drawings by the author. 1959. (BRG)

Spicer, Jack. *Billy the Kid*. Illustrated by Jess (Collins). 1959. (BRG)

Experimental Review. Woodstock, New York. Edited by Robert Duncan and Sanders Russell. Nos. 1–3 (August 1940–September 1941).

BRG has: no. 2 (1940).

Fathar. Buffalo, New York, and Bolinas, California. Edited by Duncan McNaughton. Nos. 1–7 (June 1970–March 1975).

BRG has: One (no. 1, June 1970), 2 (no. 2, December 1970), Sixty-six (no. 6, September 1974), Zayin (no. 7, March 1975).

Features. San Francisco. Published by Pants Press. Edited by Bill Presson; later Scott Cohen. Nos. 1–3 (1970–1972).

BRG has: no. 3.

Also published:

Clark, Tom. *Car Wash*. 1971. (BRG)

The Fifties. Pine Island, Minnesota. Edited by Robert Bly. Nos. 1–3 (1958–1959). Continues as *The Sixties*.

BRG has: complete file.

Fire Exit. Boston, Massachusetts. Vol. 1, no. 1 (1968) edited by Fanny Howe, Ruth Whitman, and William Corbett, joined by Ben E. Watkins as Associate Editor for vol. 1, no. 2 (1968). No. 3 (n.d.) edited by William Corbett. Front cover photograph by Rob Brown and back cover drawing by Gerald Goble. No. 4 (1974) edited by William Corbett. Front cover by Robert Nunnelley. Also four unnumbered issues, all dated April, no year given, all edited by William Corbett. Covers by Philip Guston, Ray Kass, Robert Nunnelley, David Von Schlegell.

BRG has: complete file.

Also published:

Palmer, Michael. From *Without Music*. Dated 1 May 1975. A Fire Exit Broadside.

First Issue. New York City. Edited by Bill Wertheim. Nos. 1–9? (1968–1975?).

BRG has: nos. 1, 2, 4. GRD has: complete file.

Flash of Pasadena. Pasadena, California. Edited by David Laidig. No. 1 (March 28, 1971).

Folder. New York City. Edited by Daisy Aldan. Nos. 1–4 (Winter 1953–1956).

BRG has: nos. 1, 2, 4, all incomplete.

Folklore Center. New York City.

The Folklore Center Presents Fielding Dawson & Robert Newman, Sunday, December 1, 1966. 3 pp. (BRG)

Fire Exit (April, no year given). Front cover by Philip Guston.

Some Other Presses and Publications: A Preliminary Checklist

Reading, Dick Gallup [and] Johnny Stanton at the Folklore Center, 221 Sixth Avenue, Sunday, October 24th, 8:30 p.m. Poster. [1965]. (BRG)

Waldman, Anne, and Lewis Warsh. Two-page announcement for a poetry reading at The Folklore Center, Sunday, November 27, 1966. (BRG)

Foot. Berkeley, California. Edited by Richard Duerden. Nos. 1–8 (1962–1980?). Covers by Diane Sophia (6), Philip Whalen (2).

BRG has: nos. 2, 6.

4, 3, 2 Review. New York City. Edited by Simon Schuchat. Nos. 1–7 (1976–1978). Covers by Rochelle Kraut.

BRG has: complete file.

Free Lance Press. *See* **levy, d.a.**

Friction. The Annals of the Jack Kerouac School of Disembodied Poetics. Boulder, Colorado. Edited by Randy Roark. Nos. 1–7 (Fall 1982–Summer 1984).

BRG has: nos. 2/3 (*Documents from the Kerouac Conference*), 5/6 (*Obscure Destinies*, edited by Allen Ginsberg), 7 (Clark Coolidge issue).

GRD has: nos. 1, 4–7.

From a Window. Tucson, Arizona. Edited by Paul Malanga and Bobby Byrd. Nos. 1–6 (April 1965–November 1966).

BRG has: no. 1.

Frontier Press. West Newbury, Massachusetts. Harvey Brown.

Dorn, Edward. *The Cycle*. Drawings by the author. 1971. (BRG)

Dorn, Edward. *The Rites of Passage*. 1965. (GRD)

Dorn, Edward. *Songs Set Two, a Short Count*. Designed by Graham Mackintosh. 1970. (BRG)

Duncan, Robert. *Hekatombe*. Broadside. 1996.

H.D. (Hilda Doolittle). *Hermetic Definitions*. 1971.

Kelly, Robert. *Cities*. 1971. (BRG)

Kelly, Robert. *In Time*. 1971.

Long, Haniel. *If He Can Make Her So*. 1968.

McClure, Michael. *The Surge*. 1969.

Prynne, J. H. *Into the Day*. 1972.

Sanders, Ed. *Peace Eye*. 1965. (BRG)

See also **Niagara Frontier Review.**

Fubbalo. Buffalo, New York. Edited by Edward Budowski. Vol. 1, nos. 1–2 (Summer 1964–Summer 1965).

BRG has: complete file.

Fulcrum Press. London. Stuart Montgomery.

Dorn, Edward. *Geography*. 1965. (GRD)

Dorn, Edward. *Idaho Out*. Cover drawing by the author. 1965. (BRG)

Dorn, Edward. *The North Atlantic Turbine*. 1967. (BRG)

Finlay, Ian Hamilton. *Canal Game*. 1967. (APP)

Pickard, Tom. *High on the Walls*. 1967. (GRD)

Rothenberg, Jerome. *Between: Poems 1960/63*. 1967. (GRD)

Snyder, Gary. *The Back Country*. 1967. (BRG)

Snyder, Gary. *A Range of Poems*. 1966. (BRG)

Full Court Press. New York City. Anne Waldman, Ron Padgett, and Joan Simon.

Burroughs, William S. *Letters to Allen Ginsberg, 1953–1957*. 1982. (BRG)

Denby, Edwin. *Collected Poems*. 1975.

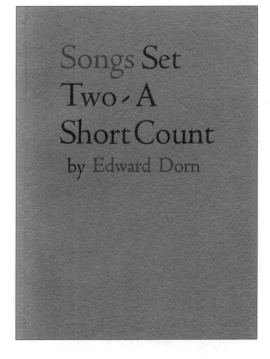

Edward Dorn, *Songs Set Two, a Short Count* (West Newbury, Mass.: Frontier Press, 1970). Designed by Graham Mackintosh.

Fagin, Larry. *I'll Be Seeing You: Selected Poems, 1962–1976.* 1978. (BRG)

Godfrey, John. *Dabble: Poems 1966–1980.* 1982. (GRD)

O'Hara, Frank. *Selected Plays.* 1978. (BRG)

Gandhabba. New York City. Edited by Tom Savage. Vol. 1, nos. 1–5 (January 1984–1987).

BRG has: no. 5. GRD has: nos. 1–4.

Ganglia. Orangeville, Ontario, Canada. Published by Ganglia. Nos. 1–7; Series 2, nos. 1–2 (1965–1967; October 1969–1971).

Ganglia. Toronto, Canada. David Aylward and bp Nichol.

Nichol, bp. *Scraptures: Second Sequence.* 1965. (BRG)

Nichol, bp. *A Vision of the U. T. Stacks.* 1966.

Nichol, bp. *The Year of the Frog: A Study of the Frog from Scraptures: Ninth Sequence.* 1967.

See also **grOnk.**

Genesis : Grasp. New York City. Edited by Richard Meyers [Richard Hell] and David Giannini. Vol. 1, no. 1–vol. 2, no. 1/2 (1968–1971). 6 issues.

BRG has: nos. 3, 4.

Also published:

Giannini, David. *Opens: A Folder of 6 Broadsides.* Cover by the author. 1971.

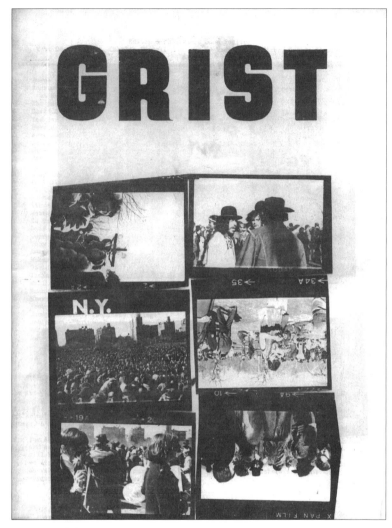

Grist 12 (1967?).

Some Other Presses and Publications: A Preliminary Checklist

The Harris Review 2
(1971). Front cover by
Gerard Malanga.

Hartman, Yuki. *One of Me.*
1970. Supplement to vol. 1,
no. 4. (BRG)

Meyers, Richard. *Fun: A
Folder of Four Poems.* Cover
by the author. 1970.

Schuchat, Simon. *Svelte.*
Introduction by Lewis
MacAdams. 1971.
Supplement to vol. 2, no.
1/2. (BRG)

Stomach, Ernie. *uh.* 1971.
Supplement to vol. 2, no.
1/2.

The Genre of Silence.
New York City. Edited
by Joel Oppenheimer,
Joel Sloman, and Anne
Waldman. One-shot (June
1967). Cover photograph
by Joe Dankowski.

BRG has: sole issue.

**The Grabhorn-Hoyem
Press.** San Francisco.
Robert Grabhorn and
Andrew Hoyem.

Ginsberg, Allen. *Howl, for
Carl Solomon.* 1971.

Ginsberg, Allen. *The
Moments Return: A Poem.*
Three drawings by Robert
LaVigne. 1970.

Johnson, Ronald. *Songs of
the Earth.* 1970.

Rosenberg, Jim. *Notes for the
Foundation of a Theory of
Meter: An Essay by Jim
Rosenberg Toward an
Understanding of Projective
Verse and Beyond.* 1970.
(RBK)

Grape Press. Stinson Beach, California. Tom Veitch.

Brownstein, Michael. *30 Pictures.* Cover from a 1956 photograph by Winston Robot. Back cover photograph of the author by Anne Waldman. 1972. (BRG)

Codrescu, Andrei. *The History of the Growth of Heaven.* 1971. (GRD)

Codrescu, Andrei. *Secret Training.* 1973. (GRD)

Veitch, Tom. *Cooked Zeros.* 1970. (BRG)

Grey Fox Press. Bolinas, California. Donald Allen.

Dorn, Edward. *Selected Poems.* 1978.

Kerouac, Jack. *Heaven & Other Poems.* 1977. (BRG)

O'Hara, Frank. *Early Writing.* 1977. (BRG)

O'Hara, Frank. *Poems Retrieved.* 1977. (BRG)

O'Hara, Frank. *Standing Still and Walking in New York.* 1975. (BRG)

Spicer, Jack. *One Night Stand and Other Poems.* 1980. (GRD)

Welch, Lew. *How I Work as a Poet & Other Essays.* 1973. (BRG)

Welch, Lew. *Ring of Bone: Collected Poems, 1950–1971.* 1973. (BRG)

Whalen, Philip. *Decompressions: Selected Poems.* 1978. (GRD)

Whalen, Philip. *Enough Said: Fluctuat Nec Mergitur: Poems 1974–1979.* 1980. (GRD)

Whalen, Philip. *Scenes of Life at the Capital.* 1971. (GRD)

Grist. Lawrence, Kansas. Edited by John Fowler. Nos. 1–14 (December 1964–December 1967).

GRD has: nos. 1–12, 14.

grOnk. Toronto, Canada. Published by Ganglia Press. Edited by D. W. Harris, bp Nichol, and others. Series 1, no. 1–series 8, no. 8 (January 1967–1971), including:

Ball, Nelson. *Force Movements: 1966–1969.* 1969. (grOnk Series 3, No. 4.)

Birney, Earle. *Pnomes Jukollages & Other Stunzas.* 1969. (grOnk Series 4, No. 3.)

McCaffery, Steve. *Maps: A Different Landscape.* 1972. (grOnk Series 6, No. 8.)

McCaffery, Steve. *A Section from Carnival.* 1969. (grOnk Series 5, No. 2.)

McCaffery, Steve. *Transitions to the Beast: Post Semiotic Poems.* 1970. (grOnk Series 6, No. 2/3.)

Nichol, bp. *Ganglia Press Index.* 1972. (grOnk Series 8, No. 7.)

UU, David. *Motion/Pictures.* 1969. (grOnk Series 4, No. 1.)

Wagner, D. R. *Sprouds and Vigables.* 1969. (grOnk Series 3, No. 7.)

Gum. Iowa City. Edited by Dave Morice. Nos. One/half–9 (March 1970–January 1973).

BRG has: no. 7 (1972).

Hacker, Marilyn.

Hacker, Marilyn. *The Terrible Children.* New York, 1967. (BRG)

Hanging Loose. Brooklyn, New York. Edited by Dick Lourie, Emmett Jarrett, and Ron Schreiber. Nos. 1–71 (1966–1997) to date.

BRG has: no. 1. GRD has: complete file to date.

Hanging Loose. Brooklyn, New York. Dick Lourie, Emmett Jarrett, and Ron Schreiber.

Adam, Helen. *Ghosts and Grinning Shadow: Two Witch Stories.* Collage by the author. 1979. (GRD)

Akin, Katy. *Impassioned Cows by Moonlight: Poems.* 1974.

Kashner, Sam. *Driving at Night.* 1976. (GRD)

Lally, Michael. *Attitude: Uncollected Poems of the Seventies.* 1982.

Lourie, Dick. *Anima.* Illustrations by Harley Elliott. 1976. (GRD)

Ratner, Rochelle. *Combing the Waves.* 1979. (GRD)

Schreiber, Ron. *Living Space.* 1973. (GRD)

Torgersen, Eric. *Ethiopia.* 1976.

The Happy Press. Iowa City, Iowa. Dave Morice.

Morice, Dave, ed. *The Cutist Anthology.* 1979. (BRG)

See also **Poetry Comics.**

The Hard Press. New York City. Jeff Wright.

The Hard Press published nearly 100 poetry postcards including:

Acker, Kathy. *Homage to Baudelaire.* 1980.

Baraka, Amiri. *Important Sonnet.* 1980.

Berrigan, Ted. *Postcard from the Sky.* 1980.

Carey, Steve. *A Birthday Poem for Alice Notley.* 1980.

Dubelye, Didi Susan. *From Translations of Dali.* 1977.

Greenwald, Ted. *Thinking.* 1978.

Lazarchuk, Michael-Sean. *Zip Gun.* 1980.

Lesniak, Rose. *Merry Christmas.* 1979.

Notley, Alice. *Sea.* 1977.

Weiner, Hannah. *From the International Code of Signals.* 1978.

Hardware Is Now Software. New York City. Edited by Diane Wakoski and Harry Lewis. No. 1 (1965?).

BRG has: sole issue.

The Harris Review. New York City. Edited by Harris Schiff. 2 unnumbered issues (1971: Poultry Season, Baseball Season). Cover by Gerard Malanga (2).

BRG has: complete file.

Haselwood, Dave, Books. *See* **Dave Haselwood Books.**

The Hasty Papers. Binghamton, New York. Edited by Alfred Leslie. One-shot (1960).

Paul Blackburn,
*Three Dreams and
an Old Poem*
(Buffalo, N.Y.:
Intrepid Books,
1970).

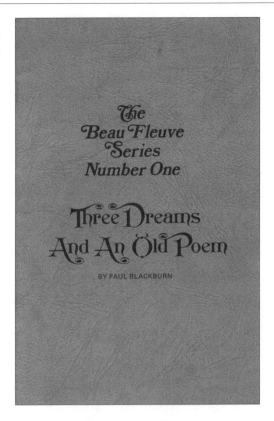

The
Beau Fleuve
Series
Number One

Three Dreams
And An Old Poem

BY PAUL BLACKBURN

In the Light. Chicago.
Edited by Jim Hanson. Nos.
1–7 (1975–1980).

BRG has: no. 5/6. GRD has:
no. 1.

Input. Valley Stream, New
York. Edited by Peter
Salmansohn and F. Roth.
Nos. 1–5 (December
1963–Spring 1965).

GRD has: complete file.

Insect Trust Gazette.
Philadelphia, Pennsylvania.
Edited by Robert Besara,
Leonard Belasco, Jed Irwin,
and William Levy. Nos. 1–3
(1964–1968).

BRG has: complete file.

Instant Editions. New York
City. Peggy de Coursey.

Berrigan, Edmund.
Dinosaur. Cover by the
author. 1982. (BRG)

Interim Books. New York
City. Jay Socin.

Beck, Julian. *Songs of the
Revolution.* 1963. (GRD)

Blossom, Roberts.
Excusology of the Ocean.
1964. (GRD)

Congdon, Kirby. *Iron Ark: A
Bestiary.* 1962. (BRG)

Dawson, Fielding. *An Essay
on New American Fiction.*
Cover by the author. 1963.
(BRG)

Hernton, Calvin. *The
Coming of Chronos to the
House of Nightsong.* 1964.
(SC)

Payne, John Burnett. *At the
Corner of Third Avenue and
14th Street.* 1970. (BRG)

Hearse. Eureka, California.
Edited by E. V. Griffith. Nos.
1–17 (1957–1972).

Hit Singles. New York City.
Edited by Vincent Katz and
Paul Schneeman. No. 1
(1977). Cover by Thomas
Burckhardt.

BRG has: sole issue.

Holt, Rinehart and Winston.
Chicago.

Padgett, Ron. *Great Balls of
Fire.* Dust jacket by Joe
Brainard. 1969. (GRD)

Horus. San Francisco.
Edited by Larry Fagin [Stan
Persky]. Nos. 1–3 (1962).

BRG has: nos. 1, 3.

HOW(ever). San Francisco.
Edited by Kathleen Fraser
and others. Vol. 1, no. 1–vol.
6, no. 4 (December 1983–
January 1992).

GRD has: complete file.

A Hundred Posters.
Dorchester, Massachusetts.
Edited by Alan Davies. Nos.
1–38 (January 1976–
February 1979).

BRG has: nos. 16, 21, 27.

The Illiterati. Waldport and
Wyeth, Oregon; later
Pasadena, California.
Published by Untide Press.
Edited by Kemper
Nomland, and others. Nos.
1–6 (Spring 1943–1955).

BRG has: nos. 4(1945), 6
(1955).

Imago. Calgary, Alberta,
Canada; later Vancouver,
British Columbia, Canada.
Edited by George Bowering.
Nos. 1–20 (1964–1974).

GRD has: complete file.

IO IO IO IO IO IO I

DOCTRINE OF SIGNATURES

Io Magazine $3

5

Io 5 (Summer 1968). Front cover picture
taken from a natural history by Buffon.

Intransit. Eugene, Oregon.
Published by Toad Press.
Edited by Bill Thomas, with
various guest editors.
Unnumbered (1965–
1969).

BRG has: *Intransit: The
Andy Warhol–Gerard
Malanga Monster Issue*
(1968). GRD has: *Intransit:
The Philip Whalen Issue*
(1967).

Intrepid. Buffalo, New York.
Edited by Allen De Loach.
Nos. 1–39/41 (1964–
1980).

GRD has: nos. 2–39/41.

Intrepid Books. Buffalo,
New York. Allen De Loach.

Blackburn, Paul. *Three
Dreams and an Old Poem.*
1970. (Beau Fleuve Series,
No. 1.)

Bremser, Ray. *Black Is Black
Blues.* 1971. (Beau Fleuve
Series, No. 4.)

Cirocco, William. *Narcissus.*
1971. (Beau Fleuve Series,
No. 7.)

Coleman, Victor. *Some
Plays: On Words.* 1971.
(Beau Fleuve Series, No. 6.)

De Loach, Allen. *From
Maine.* 1970. (Beau Fleuve
Series, No. 3.)

Di Prima, Diane. *Brass
Furnaces Going Out: Song,
After an Abortion.* 1976.
(BRG)

Kerman, Judith. *Confessions.*
1974. (Beau Fleuve Series,
No. 8.)

Mottram, Eric. *William
Burroughs: The Algebra of
Need.* 1971. (Beau Fleuve
Series, No. 2.) (BRG)

Juillard 9 (1972). Front
cover by Trevor Winkfield.

Orlovsky, Peter. *Dear Allen:
Ship Will Land Jan 23, 58.*
1971. (Beau Fleuve Series,
No. 5.) (BRG)

Io. Berkeley, California,
and elsewhere. Edited by
Richard Grossinger and
Lindy Hough. Published
by North Atlantic Books.
Nos. 1–36 (ca. 1965–1986).

GRD has: complete file.

See also **North Atlantic
Books.**

Island. Toronto, Canada.
Edited by Fred Wah. Nos.
1–7/8 (September
1964–1966). *Island* 4
(1965) is Fred Wah's
Lardeau; Island 6 (1966)
issued as *Combustion* 15.

Island Press. Toronto,
Canada. Fred Wah.

Rodefer, Stephen. *The
Knife.* 1965.

Wah, Fred. *Lardeau.* 1965.
(*Island* 4.)

Jawbone. Washington, D.C.
Doug Lang.

Brodey, Jim. *Unless.* 1977.

Lang, Doug. *Hot Shot.* Cover
by the author. 1977.

Ward, Diane. *Trop-I-Dom.*
Cover by Tad Wanveer.
1977. (BRG)

Winch, Terence. *The
Attachment Sonnets.* Cover by
Diane Ward. 1978. (BRG)

Jihad Press. New York City.

Jones, LeRoi (Imamu Amiri
Baraka). *Black Art.* 1966.
(BRG)

Jimmy & Lucy's House of K.
Berkeley, California. Edited
by Andrew Schelling and
Benjamin Friedlander. Nos.
1–9 (May 1984–1989).

BRG has: nos. 5–6, 8–9.
GRD has: nos. 1–7.

Also published:

Friedlander, Benjamin.
*Built Up Clark Coolidge
Glosses.* Cover by the author.
1984. 5 pages.

Joe DiMaggio Press.
Bexleyheath, Kentucky.
John Robinson.

Baxter, Glen. *Stories.*
Drawings by the author.
1973. (BRG)

Lax, Robert. *Selections.*
1978.

MacSweeney, Barry. *Dance
Steps.* 1972.

Marley, Brian. *The Second
Before You Hit the Sidewalk:
Poems.* 1972.

McCarthy, Ulli. *Horsetalk.*
1972.

Vas Dias, Robert. *Making
Faces.* 1975.

Journal of Black Poetry.
San Francisco. Edited by Joe
Goncalve. Vol. 1, nos. 1–17
(Fall/Winter 1966–Summer
1973).

GRD has: nos. 1–8. SC has:
complete file.

Juillard. London. Edited by
Trevor Winkfield. Nos. 1–9
(Spring 1968–1972). Covers
by Glen Baxter (8), Joe
Brainard (6), Jasper Johns
(1), Trevor Winkfield (7, 9).

BRG has: nos. 1, 6–9.

Just Friends. New York City. Edited by Tom Disch. Nos. 1–3 (1969–1970).

BRG has: no. 2.

Kayak. San Francisco. Edited by George Hitchcock. Nos. 1–64 (Autumn 1964–May 1984).

BRG has: nos. 1, 8, 10, 13. GRD has: complete file.

Kayak Books. Santa Cruz and San Francisco. George Hitchcock.

Alegria, Fernando. *Instructions for Undressing the Human Race.* English version by Matthew Zion and Lennart Bruce. Illustrations by Matta. [1968?] (GRD)

Alegria, Fernando. *Ten Pastoral Psalms.* English versions by Bernardo Garcia and Matthew Zion. Drawings by Suzanne Vanlandingham. 1967.

Bruce, Lennart. *Letter of Credit.* 1973. (RBK)

Carver, Raymond. *Winter Insomnia.* Prints by Robert McChesney. 1970. (GRD)

Fraser, Kathleen. *Change of Address & Other Poems.* 1966.

Hammer, Louis. *Bone Planet.* 1967. (GRD)

McCord, Howard. *Fables & Transfigurations.* 1967.

Simic, Charles. *Somewhere Among Us a Stone Is Taking Notes.* Prints by George Hitchcock. 1969. (BRG)

Simic, Charles. *What the Grass Says.* 1967. (BRG)

KOFF. New York City. Edited by Rachel Walling, Elinor Nauen, and Maggie Dubris. Nos. 1–3 (1977–1978).

BRG has: no. 3.

KOFF Magazine Press. New York City. Edited by Rachel Walling, Elinor Nauen, and Maggie Dubris.

Mancini, Maria. *Surprise Surprise Surprise That's Not My Finger (The Collected Poems and Selected Correspondence & Reminiscences of Maria Mancini).* Edited by Maggie Dubris and Elinor Nauen. Reproductions of photographs by John Schlesinger. 1985. (BRG)

L. Berkeley and Kensington, California. Edited by Curtis Faville. Vol. 1, no. 1–vol. 2, no. 1/2 [nos. 1–2/3, 4/5] (1972–1974). 3 issues.

BRG has: complete file.

L Publications. Kensington, California. Curtis Faville.

Berkson, Bill. *Blue Is the Hero: Poems 1960–1975.* 1976. (GRD)

Faville, Curtis. *Stanzas for an Evening Out: Poems 1968–1977.* 1977. (GRD)

Greenwald, Ted. *Common Sense.* 1978. (GRD)

The Ladies Museum. New York City. Published by Rag On Press. Edited by Eileen Myles, Susie Timmons, and Rochelle Kraut. No. 1 (1977).

BRG has: sole issue.

Kayak 25 (1971).

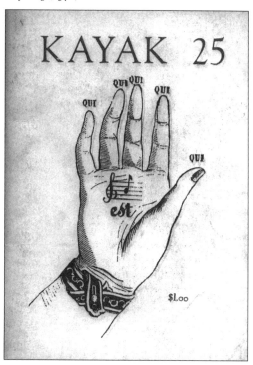

Some Other Presses and Publications: A Preliminary Checklist

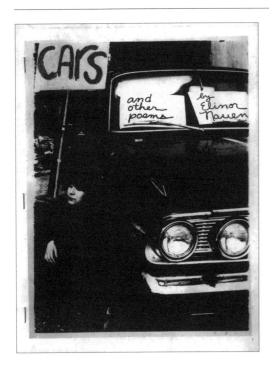

Elinor Nauen,
*Cars and Other
Poems* (New York:
Misty Terrace
Press, 1980).

Life Magazine. New York
City. Edited by Tom Veitch
from a workshop at the St.
Mark's Poetry Project. No. 1
(1970).

BRG has: sole issue.

**Life of Crime, Newsletter of
the Black Bart Poetry
Society.** Oakland,
California. Edited by Steve
LaVoie and Pat Nolan. Vol.
1, no. 1–vol. 2, no. 6
(1982–1983). 12 issues.

BRG has: vol. 1, no. 1; volume louder, number: dou-
ble (1983).

Little Light. New York City.
Edited by Susan Cataldo.
Nos. 1–3 (1980). Covers by
Susie Cataldo (2), Tina
Swanson (3).

BRG has: complete file.

Leon Press. New York City.

Fagin, Larry. *Eternal Quest.*
1968. (BRG)

Leon. *More Pictures of Leon.*
1970. (BRG)

Leon. *Pictures of Leon.* 1968.
(BRG)

Leon. *The Portable Leon.*
N.d. (BRG)

**levy, d.a. (books written or
published by d.a.levy under
his several imprints).**
Cleveland, Ohio, and elsewhere.

*465: An Anthology of
Cleveland Poets.* Cleveland: 7
Flowers Press, 1966. (BRG)

levy, d.a. *The Beginning of
Sunny Dawn: A Short Story.*
Cleveland: Ghostflower
Press, 1968. (GRD)

levy, d.a. *Cleveland
Undercovers.* Cleveland: 7
Flowers Press, 1966. (BRG)

levy, d.a. *The North American
Book of the Dead.* Cleveland:
Free Lance Press, 1965.
(GRD)

levy, d.a. *Poem for Beverly.*
Cover by the author.
Cleveland: Cold Mountain,
1968. (BRG)

levy, d.a. *Poem for Julie.*
Cleveland: Grass Coin,
1967. (BRG)

levy, d.a. *Prose: On Poetry in
the Wholesale Education &
Culture System.* Milwaukee,
Wisc.: Gunrunner Press,
1968. (BRG)

levy, d.a. *Songs for Dead
Children.* San Francisco:
Black Rabbit Press, 1969.
(BRG)

levy, d.a. *Suburban
Monastery Death Poem.*
Cleveland: Zero Edition,
1968. (BRG)

Randall, Margaret. *Poems of
the Glass.* Cleveland:
Renegade Press, 1964.
(GRD)

Salamon, Russell.
Parent[hetical po]pies: Poems.
Cover and prints by d.a.levy.
Cleveland: Renegade Press,
1964. (GRD)

Sanders, Ed. *King Lord/
Queen Freak.* Cleveland:
Renegade Press, 1964.

A Tribute to Jim Lowell.
Cleveland: Ghost Press,
1967. (GRD)

See also **Blewointment Press;
Marrahwannah Newsletter;
Marrahwannah Quarterly;
Silver Cesspool; Swamp
Erie Pipe Dream; The Willie.**

Madrona. Seattle,
Washington. Edited by
Charles Webb. Vol. 1–vol. 6,
nos. 1–19 (Summer 1971–
Spring 1984; publication
suspended 1980–1983).

BRG has: volume double
issue 11/12 (December
1975, Cid Corman issue).
GRD has: vol. 1, no. 1–vol.
5, no. 17/18.

Magazine. New York City.
Edited by Lewis Ellingham.
Nos. 1–6 (1964–1966).

BRG has: nos. 3, 4.

Marrahwannah Newsletter.
Cleveland, Ohio. Published
by Renegade Press. Edited
by d.a.levy. Nos. 1–2 (1966).

See also **levy, d.a.**

Marrahwannah Quarterly.
Cleveland, Ohio. Published
by Renegade Press. Edited
by d.a.levy. Vol. 1, no. 1–vol.
4, no. 2 (1964–1968).

GRD has: complete file,
except for vol. 3, no. 1; vol.
4, no. 1.

See also **levy, d.a.**

**Matchbook, a Journal
of 1-Word Poetry.** Iowa
City, Iowa. Edited by Joyce
Holland (a.k.a. Dave
Morice). Nos. A–M (1973).

BRG has: nos. A–D, F, J, M.

Membrane Press. Kenosha,
Milwaukee, and Shorewood,
Wisconsin. Karl Young.

Bergé, Carol. *The Unex-
pected: Poems Based in the
Elements.* 1976.

Einzig, Barbara. *Color.* 1976.
(BRG)

Einzig, Barbara. *Robinson
Crusoe: A New Fiction.* 1983.

Enslin, Theodore. *Opus O.*
1979.

Filliou, Robert. *Six Fillious:
being B. P. Nichol's translation of Robert Filliou's 14
chansons et 1 charade into
English (+ Filliou's original
text) + Steve McCaffery's
translation of George Brecht's
translation of Robert Filliou's
14 chansons et 1 charade
into English into English
(+ Brecht's translation into
English, 14 songs and 1
riddle) + Dick Higgins' translation of Dieter Roth's translation of Robert Filliou's 14
chansons et 1 charade into
German into English (+ Roth's
translation into German, 14
chansons und 1 Ratsel [sic]).*
1978. (BRG, GRD)

The Four Horsemen.
*The Prose Tattoo: Selected
Performance Scores.* By
Rafael Barreto-Rivera,
Paul Dutton, Steve
McCaffery, and bp Nichol.
Cover drawings by the
authors. 1983. (BRG)

Kostelanetz, Richard.
Constructs Two: Stories.
1978. (APP)

Mac Low, Jackson. *54th
Light Poem for Ian Tyson.*
1978.

Nathanson, Tenney. *The
Book of Death.* 1975. (GRD)

Nichol, bp. *Translating
Translating Apollinaire: A
Preliminary Report from a
Book of Research.* Intro-
duction by the author.
Research notes by Hart
Broudy, Dick Higgins, Steve
McCaffery, Richard Truhlar,
and Karl Young. 1979.
(GRD)

Olson, Toby. *Aesthetics.*
1978.

Olson, Toby. *Home.* 1976.
(BRG)

Olson, Toby. *Vectors.* 1972.

Rosenblum, Martin J. *Home.*
1971. (GRD)

Rothenberg, Jerome.
Abulafia's Circles. 1979.

Rothenberg, Jerome. *The
Notebooks.* 1976. (JWS)

Taggart, John. *Dodeka.*
Introduction by Robert
Duncan. 1979. (GRD)

Tarn, Nathaniel. *The
Microcosm.* 1977.

Wiegner, Kathleen.
Encounters. 1972.

Young, Karl. *Ecosystems.*
Broadside. 1976.

Young, Karl. *First Book of
Omens from Middle American
Dialogues.* 1976. (GRD)

Young, Karl. *From Prints.*
Broadside. 1976.

See also **Stations.**

Miam. San Francisco.
Edited by Tom Mandel.
Nos. 1–6 (1977–October
1978).

The Milk Quarterly.
Chicago. Published by the
Yellow Press. Edited by
Peter Kostakis, Darlene
Pearlstein, Bob Rosenthal,
and others. Nos. 1–11/12
(1972–1978). Covers by Jay
Lynch (8), Brian Ogelsby
(2), Peter Panek (6).

BRG has: nos. 2 (edited by
Peter Kostakis), 3 (edited
by Richard Friedman), 5
(edited by Bob Rosenthal),
6 (edited by Peter Kostakis),
8 (edited by Darlene
Pearlstein).

Mother 5 (Summer
1965). Front cover by
Joe Brainard.

MULCH 4

Mulch 4 [vol. 2, no. 2]
(Winter 1973–1974).
Front cover drawing by
Basil King.

Misty Terrace Press. New York City. Michael Scholnick.

Fyman, Cliff. *Stormy Heaven.* 1981. (BRG)

Hughes, Helena, and James Schuyler. *Collabs.* 1980. (BRG)

Nauen, Elinor. *Cars and Other Poems.* 1980. (BRG)

Scholnick, Michael, and Tom Weigel. *Nations and Peace.* Cover photograph by Rudy Burckhardt. 1980. (BRG)

Montana Gothic. Missoula, Montana. Edited by Peter Koch. Nos. 1–6 (1974–1977).

BRG has: no. 5, with cover illustration by Bill Yenne. GRD and RBK have: complete files.

Montemora. New York City. Edited by Eliot Weinberger. Nos. 1–8 (1975–1981).

BRG has: nos. 6–8. GRD has: complete file.

Montemora also published supplements or monographs, including the following:

Blau DuPlessis, Rachel. *Wells.* 1980. (GRD)

Howe, Susan. *The Pythagorean Silence.* 1982. (BRG)

Kirschen, Mark. *Pier's End.* 1980. (GRD)

Oppen, Mary. *Poems & Transpositions.* 1980. (GRD)

Sobin, Gustaf. *Wind Chrysalid's Rattle.* 1980. (GRD)

Mother, a Journal of New Literature. Northfield, Minnesota; Galesburg, Illinois; New York City; and Buffalo, New York. Edited by David Moberg, Jeff Giles, Peter Schjeldahl, Lewis MacAdams, and others. Nos. 1–10 (April 1964–May 1969) [nos. 9 and 10 issued as sound recordings]. Covers by Joe Brainard (3, 5), Mike Goldberg (7), George Schneeman and Joe Brainard (8), Michael Steiner (4).

BRG has: nos. 3–5, 7, 8.

Mother Press. New York City. Peter Schjeldahl, Lewis MacAdams, and others.

Gallup, Dick. *The Bingo.* Introduction by Ron Padgett. Cover by Joe Brainard. 1966.

Giorno, John. *Poems by John Giorno.* Cover by Robert Rauschenberg. 1967.

Zukofsky, Louis. *After I's.* 1964. Published with Boxwood Press of Pittsburgh, Pennsylvania. (BRG)

Mudra. San Francisco. Bob and Eileen Callahan.

Meltzer, David. *The Eyes, the Blood.* 1973. Printed at the Cranium Press. (RBK)

Mulberry. New Haven, Connecticut. Edited by David Pollens, David Wasser, Norman Stein, and Patrick McEntee. Nos. 1–3 (1972–1973).

BRG has: complete file.

Mulch. New York City; Amherst and Northampton, Massachusetts. Edited by David Glotzer, Basil King, and Harry Lewis. Vol. 1, no. 1–vol. 4, no. 1 (April 1971–Spring/Summer 1976). 7 issues.

Multiples. Missoula, Montana. Edited by W. R. Borneman and Paul S. Piper. Nos. 1–7 (1981?–Fall 1986). Nos. 1–5 entitled: *Zetesis* 1, *Popular Poetix* 2, *African Golfer* 3, *Wrld wr* 4, *1733 South 5 West* 5.

BRG has: no. 3. GRD has: nos. 4–7.

My Own Mag. Hertfordshire, England. Edited by Jeff Nutall. Nos. 1–17 (1964–September 1966).

BRG has: nos. 5–12, 14–16.

Nagy, Tibor de. *See* Tibor de Nagy.

Neon. Brooklyn, New York. Edited by Gilbert Sorrentino. Nos. 1–4, and two supplements (1956–1960).

New Star Books. Vancouver, British Columbia, Canada. Rolf Maurer.

Bissett, Bill. *Living with th Vishyun.* 1974. (GRD)

Bowering, George. *Autobiology.* 1972. (GRD)

Persky, Stan. *Slaves.* 1974.

Randall, Margaret. *Spirit of the People.* 1975. (GRD)

Stanley, George. *You: Poems, 1957–1967.* Paintings by Paul Alexander. 1974. (GRD)

New York Times. New York City. Edited by Allen Appel and Paul Violi. Nos. 1–3 (1970–1971). Covers by Nick Loving (3), Phyllis Rosenzweig (1), Bill Zavatsky (2).

BRG has: complete file.

Niagara Frontier Review. Buffalo, New York. Published by Frontier Press. Edited by Harvey Brown. Unnumbered (Summer 1964–Spring 1966).

The Niagara Magazine. Brooklyn, New York. Edited by Neil Baldwin. Nos. 1–12/13 (Summer 1974–Fall 1980). 13 issues in 12.

GRD has: complete file.

Nomad. London. Edited by Donald Factor and Anthony Linick. Nos. 1–10/11 (Winter 1959–Autumn 1962). 11 issues in 10.

BRG has: no. 7.

North Atlantic Books. Berkeley and Richmond, California, and Plainfield, Vermont. Richard Grossinger and Lindy Hough.

Di Prima, Diane. *Selected Poems, 1956–1976.* 1977. (BRG, RBK)

Enslin, Theodore. *Ranger.* 1978. (GRD)

Gerrit Lansing, *The Heavenly Tree Grows Downward* (Berkeley, Calif.: North Atlantic Books, 1977). Front cover photograph by Charles Stein.

Enslin, Theodore. *Synthesis 1–24.* 1975. (GRD)

Grossinger, Richard. *The Long Body of the Dream.* 1974. (GRD)

Grossinger, Richard. *The Windy Passage from Nostalgia.* 1974.

Kelly, Robert. *The Alchemist to Mercury.* Edited by Jed Rasula. 1981. (GRD)

Lansing, Gerrit. *The Heavenly Tree Grows Downward.* Front cover photograph by Charles Stein. 1977.

Palmer, Michael, ed. *Code of Signals.* 1983. (GRD)

See also **Io.**

The Nurse's Hip Flask. Boston, Massachusetts.

BRG has: vol. 1, no. 5 (December 10, 1981). Folded broadside.

O Press. Oakland, California. Leslie Scalapino.

Grenier, Robert. *What I Believe: Transpiration, Transpiring: Minnesota.* 1981? (GRD)

O Press. Washington, D.C., and New York City. Michael Lally.

Andrews, Bruce. *Vowels.* 1976. (BRG)

Drum, David. *Facade: A Bunch of Poems.* 1976.

Winch, Terence. *Irish Musicians.* 1974. (BRG)

Oannes Press. Berkeley, California.

Adam, Helen. *San Francisco's Burning.* Illustrated by Jess (Collins). 1963.

Objects. Evanston, Illinois. Edited by Steve Hamilton. No. 1 (1975).

BRG has: sole issue.

Oculist Witnesses. Dorchester, Massachusetts. Edited by Alan Davies. Nos. 1–3 (Summer 1975–1976). Cover by George Schneeman (1).

BRG has: nos. 1, 3.

See also **Other Publications.**

Oink! Chicago. Edited by Paul Hoover and Jim Leonard. Nos. 1–19 (1971–1985).

BRG has: nos. 5,8. GRD has: nos. 2–19.

Oink Books. Chicago. Richard Friedman.

Faulwell, Dean. *A Giraffe Vomits in the Treetops.* 1972.

Faulwell, Dean. *The January Sonnets.* 1973.

Hoover, Paul. *Hairpin Turns.* 1972.

Hoover, Paul. *The Monocle Thugs.* 1977.

Leonard, Jim. *The Frequency of Inexperience.* 1972.

Only Prose. New York City. Edited by John Perreault and Jeff Weinstein. No. 1 (July 1971).

BRG has: sole issue.

Ole. Bensonville, Illinois, and San Francisco. Published by Mimos Press. Edited by Doug Blazek. Nos. 1–8 (1963–1967).

Also published:

Blazek, Doug, ed. *The Ole Anthology.* Glendale, Calif.: Poetry X/Change, 1967. (BRG, GRD)

The Once Series [each issue was subtitled "a One Shot Magazine," with a different title]. Brightlingsea, England. Edited by Tom Clark. 1966–1968. 11 issues, including *Once, Twice, Thrice, Thrice and ¹/₂, Frice, Vice, Spice, Slice, Ice,* and *Nice.*

BRG has: *Thrice, Frice, Vice, Slice, Ice,* and *Nice.*

Once Books. Brightlingsea, England. Tom Clark.

Clark, Tom. *Airplanes.* Introduction by Aram Saroyan. 1966. (BRG)

Padgett, Ron. *Tone Arm.* Cover by Tom Clark. 1967. (BRG)

Veitch, Tom. *Toad Poems.* Cover by Tom Clark. 1966. (BRG)

One. London. Edited by David Chaloner. Nos. 1–3 (Summer 1971–Spring 1976).

BRG has: complete file.

Open Letter. Toronto and Vancouver, British Columbia, Canada. Edited by Frank Davey. Vols. 1–10 (1966–1998) to date.

BRG has: nos. 1–3, 5, 7. GRD has: complete file to date.

Open Skull. San Francisco. Edited by Douglas Blazek. No. 1 (1967).

BRG has: sole issue.

Open Skull Press. San Francisco. Douglas Blazek.

Blazek, Douglas. *Zany Typhoons.* 1970. (GRD)

Bukowski, Charles. *All the Assholes in the World and Mine.* 1966. (BRG)

Deutsch, Joel. *Space Heaters.* 1969. (BRG)

Kryss, T. L. *Nuclear Roses & Quiet Rooms.* 1969.

levy, d.a. *The Beginning of Sunny Dawn and Red Lady.* Cover by Doug Blazek. 1969. (BRG)

Lifshin, Lyn. *Why Is the House Dissolving?* 1968.

Miller, Brown. *Fertilized Brains: Prayers & Profanities.* 1968. (BRG)

Miller, Brown, ed. *Lung Socket.* Front cover by Doug Blazek. 1968. (BRG)

Moore, Robert Nelson. *I Was There.* 1968.

Open Window. New York City. Edited by Paul Schneeman and Vincent Katz. Nos. 1–2 (Spring 1976–Fall 1976).

BRG has: complete file.

Brown Miller, ed., *Lung Socket* (San Francisco: Open Skull, 1968). Front cover by Doug Blazek.

Or, oar, ore. Boulder, Colorado. Edited by David Sandberg. Nos. 1–2 (1966). No. 1 (April 1966) entitled *Or, oar, ore,* no. 2 (December 1966) entitled *O'er.*

BRG has: complete file.

Oriental Blue Streak. Placitas, New Mexico. Edited by Larry Goodell and Joe Bottone. 1968.

BRG has: sole issue.

Other Publications. Buffalo, New York; and Dorchester, Lancaster, and Boston, Massachusetts. Alan Davies.

Davies, Alan. *Split Thighs.* 1975.

Gottlieb, Michael. *Local Color: Eidetic Deniers.* 1978. (*Oculist Witnesses,* No. 4.) (GRD)

Saroyan, Aram. *The Bolinas Book.* 1974. (BRG)

Warsh, Lewis. *Immediate Surrounding.* Cover by George Schneeman. 1974.

Wieners, John. *The Lanterns Along the Wall.* 1972.

Some Other Presses and Publications: A Preliminary Checklist

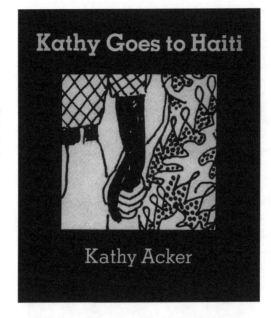

Kathy Acker, *Kathy Goes to Haiti* (Toronto: Rumour, 1978). Drawings by Robert Kushner.

Out of Sight. San Francisco. Edited by Gino Clays. Vol. 1, nos. 1–2 (1966).

BRG has: vol. 1, no. 2.

Out of This World, a one-shot magazine. New York City. Edited by John Perreault. No. 1 (Summer 1973). Cover by Ira Joe Haber.

BRG has: sole issue.

Out There. Chicago. Edited by Rose Lesniak. Nos. 1–14 (1973–1979). Covers by Shelly Kraut (1), Alice Notley (4). Nos. 8 and 12 edited by Rose Lesniak and Barbara Barg; no. 12 also guest-edited by Neil Hackman and Kevin Klein.

BRG has: nos. 1, 2, 4, 8, 12. GRD has: nos. 3–14.

The Outsider. New Orleans, Louisiana, and Tucson, Arizona. Edited by Jon Edgar Webb. Nos. 1–4/5 (1961–1969).

BRG has: complete file.

A Pamphlet. Pocatello, Idaho. Edited by Ted Crump.

BRG has: vol. 3, no. 7 (1962).

Panjandrum Press. San Francisco. Dennis Koran and L. J. Harris.

Bruce, Lennart. *Subpoemas.* 1974. (GRD)

Efros, Susan, ed. *This Is Women's Work: An Anthology of Prose and Poetry.* 1974. (GRD)

Gitin, David. *Guitar Against the Wall.* Cover by Wayne Johnson. 1972. (RBK)

Gleason, Madeline. *Here Comes Everybody: New & Selected Poems.* Drawings by Paul Blake. 1975. (GRD)

Leyland, Winston, ed. *Angels of the Lyre: A Gay Poetry Anthology.* 1975. (GRD)

Pants Press. San Francisco. Bill Presson.

Presson, Bill. *Before Next, Before Next.* 1971.

Veitch, Tom, and Clark Coolidge. *To Obtain the Value of the Cake Measure from Zero: A Play in One Act.* Cover by George Schneeman. 1970. (BRG)

See also **Features**.

Paper Air. Blue Bell, Pennsylvania. Edited by Gill Ott. Vol. 1, no. 1–vol. 4, no. 3 (1976–1990).

BRG has: vol. 2, no. 1 (John Taggart issue). GRD has: complete file.

Parenthese. New York City. Edited by John Bernard Myers. Vol. 1, no. 1–vol. 1, no. 6 (1975).

BRG has: nos. 2–4.

Pig Press. London. Richard Caddel.

Corbett, William. *Schedule Rhapsody.* 1980. (BRG)

Un Poco Loco. New York City. Edited by Larry Fagin. 15 unnumbered issues (June 1977–December 1979).

BRG has: complete file.

Pod Books. Baltimore, Maryland. Kirby Malone.

Andrews, Bruce. *Love Songs.* 1982. (GRD)

Bernstein, Charles. *Poetic Justice.* 1979. (GRD)

Cardarelli, Joe, with Anselm Hollo and Kirby Malone. *Phantom Pod.* 1977.

Fisher, Allen. *Hooks: Place 32 Taken Out of Place.* 1975.

Mason, Chris. *Poems of a Doggy.* 1977.

Poetics Journal. Berkeley, California. Edited by Lyn Hejinian and Barrett Watten. Nos. 1–9 (1982–1991).

BRG has: complete file.

Poetry Comics. Iowa City, Iowa. Published by The Happy Press. Edited by Dave Morice. Nos. 1–17 (1979–1982).

BRG has: nos. 1–10, 14–17. GRD has: complete file.

Poetry in Motion. Clinton, New York. Edited by David Lehman and David Rigsbee. Nos. 1–11 (1976–1980).

BRG has: complete file.

Poetry Information. London and Newcastle-upon-Tyne, England. Edited by Peter Hodgkiss. Nos. 1–20/21 (1970–1979/80). 21 issues in 20.

BRG has: no. 15. GRD has: complete file.

Porter, Bern. *See* **Bern Porter.**

Potes & Poets Press. Needham, Massachusetts; and Hartford and Elmwood, Connecticut. Peter Ganick.

Andrews, Bruce. *Excommunicate.* 1982. (BRG)

Bernstein, Charles. *Disfrutes.* 1981.

Coolidge, Clark. *A Geology.* 1981. (BRG)

Davies, Alan. *A An Av Es.* 1981.

Davies, Alan. *Mnemonotechnics.* 1982. (BRG)

Enslin, Theodore. *Meditations on Varied Grounds.* 1982.

Enslin, Theodore. *September's Bonfire.* 1981.

Rahmings, Keith. *Printouts.* 1981.

Weiner, Hannah. *Nijole's House.* 1981.

Quarks. Reno, Nevada. Edited by Richard Morris. No. 1 (1967).

BRG has: sole issue.

Quixote. Madison, Wisconsin. Edited by Morris Edelson. Vol. 1, no. 1–vol. 12, no. 6 (1965–1984?).

Quixote. Madison, Wisconsin. Morris Edelson.

Blazek, Douglas. *Life in a Common Gun [An Informal Book of Communications].* 1968. (APP, GRD)

Reindeer. New York City. Edited by Carter Ratcliff. One-shot (1968).

BRG has: sole issue.

Renaissance. San Francisco. Edited by John Bryan and Michael O'Donoghue. Vol. 1, nos. 1–4 (July 1961–1962).

BRG has: vol. 1, no. 1.

Renegade Press. *See* **d.a.levy.**

Rivoli Review. San Francisco. Edited by Richard Duerden. Nos. 1–2 (1963–1964).

Rocky Ledge. Boulder, Colorado. Edited by Reed Bye and Anne Waldman. Nos. 1–8 (April/May 1979–June/July 1981). Covers by Gordon Baldwin (7), Joe Brain-ard (2), Rudy Burckhardt (6), Donna Dennis (4), Jane Freilicher (8), Alex Katz (5), Joe Lynn (3).

BRG has: complete file.

Rocky Ledge Cottage Editions. Boulder, Colorado. Reed Bye and Anne Waldman.

Bye, Reed. *Erstwhile Charms.* 1980. (BRG)

Waldman, Anne. *First Baby Poems.* 1982. (BRG)

Witkowski, Annie. *Half a Tourist.* 1980. (BRG)

Roi Rogers. New York City. Edited by Bill Zavatsky. No. 1 (n.d.).

BRG has: sole issue.

Roy Rogers. New York City. Edited by Bill Zavatsky. 2 unnumbered issues (1970–1974).

Rumour Publications. Toronto, Canada.

Acker, Kathy. *Kathy Goes to Haiti.* Drawings by Robert Kushner. 1978.

The Runcible Spoon. Sacramento, California. Edited by D. R. Wagner. 2 unnumbered issues (1967); nos. 1–12 (1968–1970).

Runcible Spoon. Sacramento, California. D. R. Wagner.

Blazek, Douglas. *Baptismal Corruption in the Sunflower Patch.* 1969.

Depew, Wally. *Scream Poem.* 1970.

Geer, Dick. *Anna's \ Gram: Distance Is Measured in Perplexity.* 1967.

Kitasono, Katsué. *12 Kitazonos: Some of the Poetry of Kitazono Katsué.* Translated from the Japanese by Sam Grolmes. 1970.

Kryss, T. L. *Look at the Moon Then Wipe the Light from Your Eyes and Tell Me What You See, and Other Obscurities.* 1968. (BRG)

levy, d.a. *Notes: Variations on a Short Poem.* 1970.

levy, d.a. *Tomb Stone as a Lonely Charm.* 1967.

Locklin, Gerald. *The Toad Poems.* 1970. (BRG)

Nichol, bp. *Ballads of the Restless Are: (two versions/common source).* 1968. (GRD)

Nichol, bp. *Beach Head.* 1970. (BRG)

Wagner, D. R. *Plump Poon Poems & Slumped Slit Songs.* 1970.

Salt Lick. Quincy, Illinois. Edited by James Haining. Vol. I–vol. III, no. 1/2 (1969–1980).

BRG has: vol. III, no. 1/2 (1980).

San Francisco Earthquake. San Francisco. Edited by Jacob Herman, Claude Peliau, and Norman Mustill. Nos. 1–5 (Fall 1967–1969).

BRG has: complete file.

Some Other Presses and Publications: A Preliminary Checklist

San Francisco State University [College]. Poetry Center.

San Francisco State College. Poetry Center. *The Poetry Center, San Francisco State College, at Telegraph Hill Neighborhood Association Presents Denise Levertov. Sunday, January 19, 1958.* 3-page flyer. (BRG)

San Francisco State College. Poetry Center. *The Poetry Center, San Francisco State College Presents Charles Olson. Thursday, February 21, 1957.* 3-page flyer. (BRG)

San Francisco State College. Poetry Center. *Poetry Festival. Held at the San Francisco Museum of Art, June 21–24, 1962.* 1962. (BRG)

Sand Dollar. Berkeley, California. Jack and Victoria Shoemaker.

Berkson, Bill. *Saturday Night: Poems 1960–1961.* 1975. (BRG)

Berry, Wendell. *An Eastward Look.* 1974. (RBK)

Bialy, Harvey. *Babalon 156.* 1970. (GRD)

Bialy, Harvey. *The Broken Pot.* 1975. Printed at the Cranium Press.

Bialy, Harvey. *For Timotha.* 1970.

Bialy, Harvey. *Susanna Martin.* Second ed., 1975.

Davidson, Michael. *The Mutabilities and the Foul Papers.* 1976. (GRD)

Davidson, Michael. *Two Views of Pears.* 1973. (BRG)

Greene, Jonathan. *Once a Kingdom Again.* 1978.

Leslie Scalapino, *O* (Berkeley, Calif.: Sand Dollar, 1976). Designed by Wesley Tanner.

Johnson, Ronald. *Radi OS: o I–o IV.* Afterword by Guy Davenport. 1977. (GRD)

McClure, Michael. *The Book of Joanna.* 1973.

Palmer, Michael. *C's Songs.* 1973. (RBK)

Palmer, Michael, and Geoffrey Young, trans. *Relativity of Spring: 13 Poems by Vicente Huidobro.* 1976. (BRG)

Scalapino, Leslie. *O.* Designed by Wesley Tanner. 1976. (BRG, RBK)

Stein, Charles. *Witch-Hazel.* 1975. (BRG)

Saturday Morning. London. Edited by Simon Pettet. Vol. I, nos. 1–4–vol. II, no. 1/2 (New York City issue) (1977–Summer 1978). 5 issues.

BRG has: vol. I, nos. 3, 4; vol. II, no. 1/2.

Schuyler, James.

Schuyler, James. *49 South.* One-shot. Cover by Robert Dash. Southampton, N.Y., n.d. (BRG)

Schuyler, James. *A Picnic Cantata: for four women's voices, two pianos and percussion.* New York, 1954. 4 leaves folded. (BRG)

Seaplane. New York City. Edited by Carter Ratcliff. One-shot (1969).

BRG has: sole issue.

Search for Tomorrow. Iowa City, Iowa. Published by Blue Wind Press. Edited by George Mattingly. Nos. 1–4 (1970–1972), plus Special Number A, Darrell Gray's *Something Swims Out.* Front cover by George Mattingly. 1972?

BRG has: nos. 2 and 3, and Special Number A.

Segue Books. New York City. James Sherry.

Andrews, Bruce. *R & B.* 1981.

Andrews, Bruce, Charles Bernstein, Ray DiPalma, Steve McCaffery, and Ron Silliman. *Legend.* 1980. Co-published with L=A=N=G=U=A=G=E. (BRG)

Bernstein, Charles. *Controlling Interests: Poems.* 1980. (GRD)

Bernstein, Charles, and Susan Bee Laufer. *The Occurrence of Tune.* 1981. (GRD)

Child, Abigail. *From Solids.* 1983. (BRG)

Gottlieb, Michael. *Ninety-six Tears.* 1981. (GRD)

Messerli, Douglas. *Some Distance.* 1982.

Ward, Diane. *Theory of Emotion.* 1979.

See also **Roof** and **Roof Books** on pp. 250–251.

Semi-Colon. New York City. Published by Tibor de Nagy Gallery. Edited by John Bernard Myers. Vol. 1, nos. 1–6; vol. 2, nos. 1–4 (1950–1970?).

BRG has: complete file.

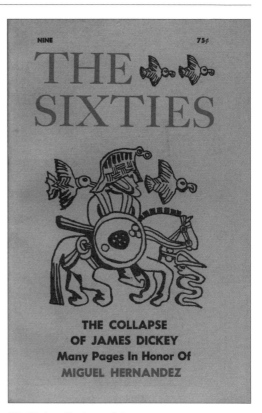

The Sixties 9 (Spring 1967).

Some Other Presses and Publications: A Preliminary Checklist

7 Flowers. *See* levy, d.a.

Shaman Drum. Berkeley, California. Frederic Brunke.

Enslin, Ted. *The Mornings.* 1974. (GRD)

Gifford, Barry. *Persimmons: Poems for Paintings.* 1977. (GRD)

Sanfield, Steve. *Wandering.* 1977. (GRD)

Snyder, Gary. *The Fudo Trilogy: Spel Against Demons, Smokey the Bear Sutra, The California Water Plan.* Illustrated by Michael Corr. 1973. (BRG, RBK)

Staple, Will. *Passes for Human.* 1977. (GRD)

Shameless Hussy. Berkeley, California. Alta.

Alta. *No Visible Means of Support.* 1971.

Griffin, Susan. *Dear Sky.* 1971.

Noda, Barbara. *Strawberries.* 1979.

Shange, Ntozake. *Sassafrass.* 1976.

Shameless Hussy Review. San Lorenzo, California. Edited by Alta. Unnumbered, undated (1974?).

Shell. Waban, Massachusetts. Edited by Jack Kimball. Nos. 1–2/3 (Fall/Winter 1976–Spring/Summer 1977). Cover by Lucas Samaras (2/3).

BRG has: no. 2/3.

Shortstop. Westcliff, Colorado. Edited by Fielding Dawson. No. 1 (July 1964). Broadsheet.

BRG has: sole issue.

Shortstop Press. New York City. Fielding Dawson.

Dawson, Fielding. *Man Steps into Space.* 1965. (BRG)

Dawson, Fielding. *On the Danger of Writers Teaching.* 1976. (GRD)

The Silver Cesspool. Cleveland, Ohio. Published by Renegade Press. Edited by d.a.levy. Nos. 1–3 (1966–1967).

See also levy, d.a.

Sinister Wisdom. Lincoln, Nebraska; Charlotte, North Carolina; and Berkeley, California. Nos. 1–57 (July 1976–Winter/Spring 1996) to date.

GRD has: complete file to date.

The Sixties. Madison, Wisconsin. Edited by Robert Bly. Nos. 1–10 (Fall 1958–1968).

Slit Wrist. New York City. Edited by Paul Brown and Terry Swanson. Nos. 1–3/4 (Spring 1976–Spring 1977). 3 issues.

BRG has: complete file.

Smithereens Press. Bolinas, California. Charley Ross.

Berkson, Bill. *Red Devil.* 1982.

Spencer Holst, *Something to Read to Someone;* Beate Wheeler, *Sixteen Drawings* (Barrytown, N.Y.: Station Hill, 1980). Front cover drawing by Beate Wheeler.

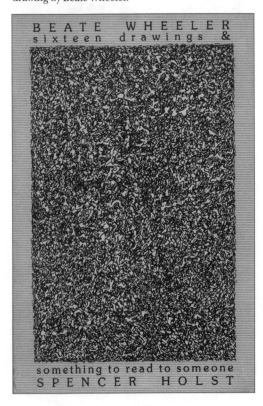

Cardarelli, Joe. *From the Maine Book.* 1983.

Clark, Tom. *Dark as Day.* 1983.

Fagin, Larry. *Nuclear Neighborhood.* Cover by Ken Botto. 1983. (BRG)

Gallup, Dick. *Plumbing the Depths of Folly.* 1983. (BRG)

Lance, Jeanne. *Loose Arrangement.* 1983. (GRD)

McNaughton, Duncan. *Sonny Boy.* 1983.

Shelton, Cindy. *Why Am I Sitting Still?* 1981.

Simmons, Al. *Care Free.* Cover and illustrations by Arthur Okamura. 1984.

Thorpe, John. *Poetry as Air Traffic Control.* 1984.

Snazzy Wah Press.
Bellingham, Washington.
Keith Abbott ?

Abbott, Keith. *Moving Posture.* 1970.

Abbott, Keith. *Short Change.* 1970.

Carey, Mary. *Soft Touch.* 1970. (BRG)

Nolan, Pat. *Rock Me/Roll Me Vast Fatality.* 1970. (BRG)

Some. New York City. Edited by Allen Ziegler, Harry Greenberg, and Larry Zirlin. Nos. 1–10 (Spring 1972–1981).

BRG has: no. 4 (Bill Knott issue). GRD has: nos. 7/8, 10.

Some of Us Press.
Washington, D.C.

Andrews, Bruce. *Edge.* 1973. Printed by Arry Press. (BRG)

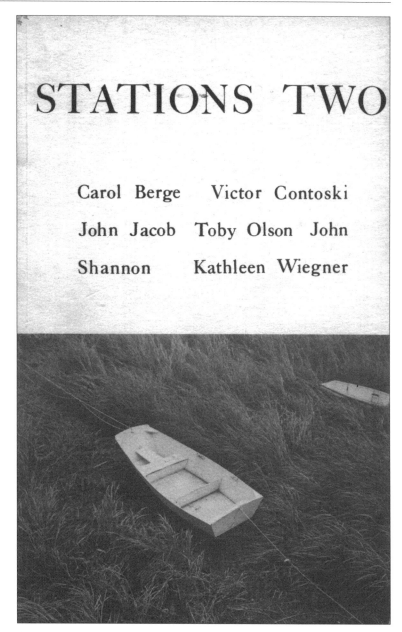

Stations Two (Spring 1973). Front cover photograph by Mark Power.

Some Other Presses and Publications: A Preliminary Checklist

Astronauts of Inner-Space: An International Collection of Avant-garde Activity. 17 Manifestoes, Articles, Letters, 28 Poems & 1 Filmscript (San Francisco: Stolen Paper Review Editions, 1966).

ASTRONAUTS
OF
INNER-SPACE:

AN INTERNATIONAL
COLLECTION
OF AVANT-GARDE
ACTIVITY

17 MANIFESTOES,
ARTICLES, LETTERS,
28 POEMS & 1 FILMSCRIPT

Eshleman, Clayton. *The Lich Gate.* 1980.

Hollo, Anselm. *With Ruth in Mind.* 1979.

Holst, Spencer. *Something to Read to Someone;* Beate Wheeler, *Sixteen Drawings.* Front cover drawing by Beate Wheeler. 1980.

Jaffe, Nora. *Drawings & Relief Sculpture.* 1978.

Kamin, Franz. *Ann Margret Loves You & Other Psychotopological Diversions.* 1980. (GRD)

Kamin, Franz. *Distance Function.* 1977.

Kamin, Franz. *Egz Book of Frogs.* Illustrated by Kathy Bourbonais. 1982.

Kamin, Franz. *Scribble Death.* 1986.

Kelly, Robert. *The Cruise of the Pnyx.* 1979. (BRG)

Mac Low, Jackson. *The Pronouns: A Collection of Forty Dances for the Dancers, 3 February–22 March 1964.* Photographs by Peter Moore. 1979. (GRD)

Quasha, George. *Giving the Lily Back Her Hands.* 1979.

Sanders, Ed. *The Z–D Generation.* 1981.

Dlugos, Tim. *High There.* 1973.

Lally, Lee. *These Days.* 1972. (GRD)

Lally, Michael. *The South Orange Sonnets.* 1972.

Schuchat, Simon. *Blue Skies.* 1973.

Winch, Terry. *Boning Up.* 1972.

Soulbook. Berkeley, California. Edited by Donald Freeman, Bob Hamilton, and others. Vol. 1, no. 1–vol. 13? (1964–1980?). Publication suspended between vol. 3, no. 1 (1970) and vol. 3, no. 2 (1975).

GRD has: nos. 4, 5, 7–9. SC has: nos. 1–3, 9, 10.

Soup. San Francisco. Edited by Steve Abbott. Nos. 1–4 (1980–1985).

BRG has: no. 1. GRD has: nos. 1, 4.

Spanner. London. Edited by Allen Fisher. 26 issues (1974–1986).

Spanner Books. London. Allen Fisher.

Fisher, Allen. *Kessingland Studies.* 1979.

Mottram, Eric. *Elegy 15: Neruda.* 1978.

The Spero. Flint, Michigan. Edited by Douglas and Kathy Casement. Vol. 1, nos. 1–2 (1965–1966).

BRG has: vol. 1, no. 1. GRD has: complete file.

Spit in the Ocean. Pleasant Hill, Oregon. Edited by Ken Kesey. Nos. 1–6 (1974–1981).

BRG has: complete file.

Station Hill Press. Barrytown, New York. George and Susan Quasha.

Auster, Paul. *White Spaces.* 1980. (BRG)

Bernstein, Charles. *Stigma.* 1981.

Eigner, Larry. *Cloud, Invisible Air.* 1978. (BRG)

Enslin, Theodore. *Ranger CXXII & CXXVIII.* 1977.

Stations. Milwaukee, Wisconsin. Published by Membrane Press. Edited by Karl Young. Nos. 1–5 (1972–1978).

Stolen Paper Review. San Francisco. Edited by Jeff Berner. Nos. 1–3 (Spring 1963–Spring 1965).

Stolen Paper Review Editions. San Francisco. Jeff Berner.

Astronauts of Inner-Space: An International Collection of Avant-garde Activity. 17 Manifestoes, Articles, Letters, 28 Poems & 1 Filmscript. 1966. (BRG)

Kandel, Lenore. *Invocation for Maitreya.* 1967.

Kandel, Lenore. *The Love Book.* 1966. (BRG)

Watts, Alan. *Nonsense.* 1967.

Stone Wind. Chicago. Edited by Terry Jacobus. Nos. 1–9 (1972–1975).

BRG has: no. 4.

Stooge. Albuquerque, New Mexico; and San Diego and Berkeley, California. Edited by Geoffrey Young and Laura Chester. Nos. 1–13 (1967–Spring 1975). Covers by John Baldessari (11), William Wegman (9).

BRG has: nos. 7, 9, 11, 13.

Strange Faeces. London. Edited by Opal Nations. Nos. 1–20 (1966–1988).

BRG has: nos. 2, 3 (Ron Padgett issue), 4, 5 (Anne Waldman issue), 6 (Larry Fagin issue), 17, 20.

Street Editions. London.

Notley, Alice. *For Frank O'Hara's Birthday.* Cover by Julia Ball. 1976. (BRG)

Raworth, Tom. *Four Door Guide.* 1979. (BRG)

Suction. Iowa City, Iowa. Edited by Darrell Gray. Nos. 1–2 (May 1969–1971).

BRG has: complete file.

Sugar Mountain. Bolinas, California. Edited by Tom Clark and Lewis Warsh. One-shot (August 1970). Cover photograph of Alice Notley by Jayne Nodland.

BRG has: sole issue.

Sum. Albuquerque, New Mexico; later Buffalo, New York. Edited by Fred Wah. Nos. 1–7 (December 1963–April 1965).

Sun Books. New York City. Bill Zavatsky.

Jacob, Max. *The Dice Cup: Selected Prose Poems.* Edited with an introduction by Michael Brownstein. Translated from the French by John Ashbery and others. 1979. (GRD)

Padgett, Ron. *Toujours l'Amour.* 1976. (GRD)

Padgett, Ron. *Triangles in the Afternoon.* 1979. (GRD)

Schjeldahl, Peter. *Since 1964: New and Selected Poems.* 1978.

Towle, Tony. *Autobiography and Other Poems.* 1977.

Violi, Paul. *Harmaton: A Poem.* Drawings by Paula North. 1977. (GRD)

Violi, Paul. *Splurge!* 1982. (GRD)

Zavatsky, Bill. *Theories of Rain and Other Poems.* 1975. (GRD)

Sunshine. New York City. Edited by Alan Bernheimer. One-shot (May 1971). Cover by Merrill Gilfillan.

BRG has: sole issue.

Swamp Erie Pipe Dream. Cleveland, Ohio. Edited by d.a.levy. Vol. 1, no. 1 (May 1967).

See also **levy, d.a.**

Swollen Magpie Press. Putnam Valley, New York. Paul Violi.

Broadway: A Poets and Painters Anthology. Edited by James Schuyler and Charles North. 1979. (GRD)

Ceravolo, Joe. *Inri.* 1979.

Hartman, Yuki. *Red Rice: Poems.* 1980. (GRD)

Hornick, Lita. *David Antin: Debunker of the Real.* 1979.

North, Charles. *Six Buildings.* 1977.

Towle, Tony. *Works on Paper.* Cover by Larry Rivers. 1978.

Towle, Tony, and James Schuyler. *Gemini: Collaborations.* 1981.

Violi, Paul. *She'll Be Riding Six White Horses: Poems.* 1970.

Violi, Paul. *Some Poems.* 1976. (GRD)

See also **New York Times.**

Talisman. Hoboken, New Jersey. Edited by Edward Foster. No. 1–17 (March 1988–Summer 1997).

Talonbooks. Vancouver, British Columbia, Canada. Founded by David Robinson and others.

Bissett, Bill. *Drifting into War.* 1971. (GRD)

Bissett, Bill. *Pass th Food Release th Spirit Book.* 1973. (GRD)

Bissett, Bill. *Sailor.* 1978. (GRD)

Bissett, Bill. *Selected Poems: Beyond Even Faithful Legends.* Introduction by Len Earley. 1980. (GRD)

Blaser, Robin. *Image Nation 13: The Telephone.* Broadside. 1975.

Blaser, Robin. *Syntax.* 1983. (GRD)

Bowering, George. *Selected Poems: Particular Accidents.* Edited with an introduction by Robin Blaser. 1980. (GRD)

Brown, Jim. *Forgetting.* 1969.

Brown, Jim. *Toward a Chemistry of Reel People.* 1971. (GRD)

Coleman, Victor. *Parking Lots.* Photography by Pamela Harris McLeod. 1972. (GRD)

Dorn, Edward. *The Poet, the People, the Spirit.* Edited by Bob Rose from an initial transcript by Derryll White. 1976. (GRD)

Gilbert, Gerry. *Grounds.* 1976. (GRD)

Marlatt, Daphne. *Selected Writing: Net Work.* Edited with an introduction by Fred Wah. 1980. (GRD)

Marlatt, Daphne. *Steveston.* Photographs by Robert Minden. 1974. (GRD)

Some Other Presses and Publications: A Preliminary Checklist

Jim Carroll, *The
Basketball Diaries*
(Bolinas, Calif.:
Tombouctou, 1978).

McNaughton, Duncan. *A
Passage of Saint Devil.* 1976.
(GRD)

Nichol, bp. *Selected Writing:
As Elected.* Introduction by
Jack David. 1980. (GRD)

Persky, Stan. *Wrestling the
Angel.* 1976. (GRD)

Phillips, David. *Wave.* 1970.

Reaney, James. *Colours in the
Dark.* 1969. (GRD)

Rosenthal, Helene. *Peace Is
an Unknown Continent.*
1968. (GRD)

Rosenthal, Helene. *A Shape
of Fire: Poems.* Photographs
by Mari Berg. 1972. (GRD)

Trower, Peter. *Moving
Through the Mystery.* Visuals
by Jack Wise. 1969. (GRD)

Wah, Fred. *Pictograms from
the Interior of B.C.* 1975.
(BRG)

Wah, Fred. *Selected Poems:
Loki Is Buried at Smoky Creek.*
Edited with an introduction
by George Bowering. 1980.
(GRD)

Tangerine. New York City.
Published by Andrea Doria
Books. Edited by Tom
Weigel. Nos. 1–9 (June
1982–1985).

BRG has: nos. 1, 2, 5.
GRD has: nos. 1–7, 9.

**Text, a magazine of poetry
and essays.** New York City.
Edited by Mark Karlins.
Nos. 1–13 (Winter
1976/77–1981).

BRG has: nos. 1, 2, 6, 8,
9/10, 11.

The. Boulder, Colorado.
Edited by Jack Collom. Nos.
1–14 (1966–1977).

BRG has: nos. 13, 14.
GRD has: nos. 6, 8, 14.

Things. New York City.
Edited by Dick Lourie. Nos.
1–3 (Fall 1964–Spring
1966).

Thirst. New York City.
Edited by Benjamin Sloan
and Vyt Bakaitis. No. 1
(1977).

BRG has: sole issue.

Tibor de Nagy. New York
City. John Bernard Myers.

Ansen, Alan. *The Old
Religion.* 1959. (GRD)

Ashbery, John. *Turandot
and Other Poems.* 1953.
(BRG)

Berkson, Bill. *Saturday
Night: Poems 1960–61.*
1961.

Ceravolo, Joe. *Wild Flowers
Out of Gas.* 1967.

Elmslie, Kenward. *Pavilions.*
1961. (BRG, GRD)

Guest, Barbara. *The
Location of Things.* 1960.
(BRG)

Kallman, Chester. *An Elegy.*
1951. (BRG)

Koch, Kenneth. *Poems.*
1953.

Lima, Frank. *Inventory:
Poems.* 1964. (GRD)

O'Hara, Frank. *A City
Winter and Other Poems.*
1951. (BRG)

O'Hara, Frank. *Love Poems
(tentative title).* 1965. (BRG)

Toothpaste 5 (1971). Front cover photograph by Allan Kornblum.

Some Other Presses and Publications: A Preliminary Checklist

O'Hara, Frank. *Oranges: 12 Pastorals.* 1953.

Schuyler, James. *May 24th or So.* 1966. (BRG)

Towle, Tony. *After Dinner We Take a Drive into the Night.* 1968. (BRG)

See also **Semi-Colon.**

Tish. Vancouver, British Columbia, Canada. Edited by Frank Davey and others. Nos. 1–44 (1961–1971?).

BRG has: no. 38.

Toad Press. Eugene, Oregon. Bill Thomas.

Eigner, Larry. *From the Sustaining Air.* 1967. (BRG)

See also **Intransit.**

Tom Veitch Magazine. San Francisco. Edited by Tom Veitch. Nos. 1–4 (1970–1972).

BRG has: nos. 2, 3. GRD has: complete file.

Tombouctou Press. Bolinas, California. Michael Wolfe.

Carroll, Jim. *The Basketball Diaries.* 1978. (BRG)

Creeley, Bobbie. *Frenchy and Cuban Pete.* 1977.

MacAdams, Lewis. *News from Niman Farm.* 1976. (GRD)

MacInnis, Jamie. *Practicing.* 1980. (BRG)

Saroyan, Gailyn. *Stories and Poems.* 1977.

Scalapino, Leslie. *This Eating and Walking at the Same Time Is Associated All Right.* 1979.

Toothpaste. Iowa City, Iowa. Edited by Allan Kornblum. Nos. 1–7 (1970–1972). Covers by Colin Andre (4), Pat Dooley (3), Allan Kornblum (5), Dave Morice (6).

BRG and GRD have: complete files.

Toothpaste Press. Iowa City, Iowa. Allan Kornblum.

Appel, Allan. *Not So Much Love of Flowers: Poems 1969–1972.* 1975.

Ceravolo, Joseph. *Transmigration Solo.* 1979.

Dorn, Edward. *In Defense of Pure Poetry.* 1978.

Gallup, Dick. *The Whacking of the Fruit Trees: A Poem in 13 Parts.* 1975. (BRG)

Hawkins, Bobbie Louise. *A Sense of Humour: Story.* Drawings by Dave Morice. 1983. (GRD)

Holland, Joyce. *The Tenth J.* 1972. (BRG)

Hollo, Anselm. *Heavy Jars.* 1977.

Kornblum, Allan. *Awkward Song: A Collection of Poems.* 1980.

Lesniak, Rose. *Young Anger.* 1979.

Levine, Steve. *A Blue Tongue: Pamphlet of Poems.* 1976. (RBK)

Levine, Steve. *Pure Notations.* 1981. (GRD)

Mikolowski, Ken. *Little Mysteries: Poems.* 1979.

David Meltzer, *Knots* (Berkeley, Calif.: Tree Books, 1971).

Morice, Dave. *Quicksand Through the Hourglass: Poems and Drawings.* 1979. (GRD)

Morice, Dave. *Snapshots from Europe: A Travelogue.* 1974.

Morice, Dave. *Tilt: A Collection of Poems and Stories.* 1971.

Morice, Dave. *A Visit from St. Alphabet: Poem and Drawings.* 1980. (GRD)

Notley, Alice. *How Spring Comes.* Cover drawing by George Schneeman. 1981. (GRD)

Ratner, Rochelle. *Variations on a Theme in Blue.* 1971.

Salamun, Tomaz. *Snow.* 1973.

Violi, Paul. *Waterworks.* 1972. (RBK)

Waldman, Anne. *Countries: Poems.* 1980.

Toothpick, Lisbon & the Orcas Islands. Seattle, Washington. Edited by Michael Wiater. Vol. 1–vol. 3, no. 1 (1971–1973). 5 issues.

BRG has: complete file.

Towle, Tony.

Towle, Tony. *Poems.* Handset and printed at an A.I.G.A. workshop, Spring 1966. (BRG)

Tree. Santa Barbara, California. Edited by David Meltzer. Nos. 1–6 (1970–1978).

BRG has: no. 5.

Tree Books. Berkeley, California. David Meltzer.

Hirschman, Jack. *Scintilla.* 1971.

Jabès, Edmond. *Elya.* Translated by Rosmarie Waldrop. 1972.

Meltzer, David. *Knots.* 1971.

Truck. Carrboro, North Carolina, and elsewhere. Edited by David Wilk. Nos. 1–21 (1970–1979). 20 issues (no. 19 not issued).

GRD has: nos. 13–16.

Truck Press. St. Paul, Minnesota; Carrboro, North Carolina; and elsewhere. David Wilk.

Bialy, Harvey. *Free-beans for All.* 1973.

Corman, Cid. *William Bronk: An Essay.* 1976. (GRD)

Hough, Lindy. *Outlands & Inlands.* 1978. (GRD)

Hough, Lindy. *The Wake of the Wave.* 1973.

Kahn, Paul. *Heart of the World.* 1975.

Marlatt, Daphne. *Our Lives.* 1975.

Moritz, John. *Cartography.* 1973.

Phillips, Jayne Anne. *Sweethearts.* 1976. (BRG)

Wilk, David. *To the Dreamers.* 1973.

Young, Karl. *To Dream Kalapuya.* 1977. (GRD)

Truck 16 (Summer 1975). Front cover photograph by Jonathan Williams. Front cover design by Bull City Studios, Durham, North Carolina.

UNMUZZLED OX $1

Bukowski   Mac Adams   Snyder
Coolidge   Kostelanetz   Stock
Creeley   Reeve   Wakoski
Crumb   Seidman   Wild
Hine   Shapiro   Et Cetera

Unmuzzled Ox 1 (1971). Cover image by R. Crumb.

Turkey Buzzard Review.
Bolinas, California. Edited
by Dotty LeMieux. Nos. 1–4
(1977–1982). Cover by
Michael Rafferty (2).

BRG has: no. 2.

Turtle Island Foundation.
San Francisco. Bob
Callahan.

Angulo, Jaime de. *Coyote's
Bones: Selected Poetry and
Prose.* Edited by Bob
Callahan. 1974.

Angulo, Jaime de. *The
Lariat: A Novel.* 1974.

Brakhage, Stan. *Film
Biographies.* 1977.

Dorn, Edward. *Recollections
of Gran Apacheria.* 1974.
(BRG)

Olson, Charles. *Spearmint
& Rosemary.* 1975. Printed
by the Five Trees Press.
(RBK)

Ortiz, Simon J. *A Good
Journey.* 1977. (GRD)

Raworth, Tom. *A Serial
Biography.* 1977.

Sanders, Ed. *Fame and Love
in New York.* 1980. (BRG,
GRD)

Sauer, Carl Ortwin. *Northern
Mists.* 1973.

Taggart, John. *Peace on
Earth: Poems.* 1981. (GRD)

12th Street Rag. New York
City. Edited by Joanne
Brahainsky. Nos. 1–2
(1975).

BRG has: no. 2.

Two Charlies Magazine.
Various places. Edited by
Charlie Vermont and
Charlie Walsh. Nos. 1–4
(1973–1976).

BRG has: nos. 2 (1973, from
Alameda, New Mexico, and
Scapoose, Oregon), 4
(October 1976, from
Wichita, Kansas, and
Nashville, Tennessee).

Tzarad. London. Edited by
Lee Harwood. Nos. 1–4
(1965–1969). 3 issues. No.
3/4 with *Collection* 4/5.
Cover by Andy Warhol (2).

BRG and GRD have: com-
plete files.

Unmuzzled Ox. New York
City. Edited by Michael
Andre. Vols. 1–14
(1971–1996) to date.

GRD has: complete file to
date.

Unnatural Acts. New York
City. A collaborative writing
experiment published by
Ed Friedman and
Bernadette Mayer. Nos. 1–5
(1972–1973).

BRG has: no. 5 and two
undated, unnumbered
issues.

The Untide. Waldport,
Oregon. Edited by Kemper
Nomland. Vol. 1, no. 1–vol.
2, no. 12 (1943). 24 issues.

RBK has: vol. 1, nos. 2–12;
vol. 2, nos. 2–4, 8, 12.

Untide Press. Waldport and
Wyeth, Oregon. Kemper
Nomland, William Everson,
and others.

Coffield, Glen. *The Horned Moon*. 1944. (RBK)

Everson, William. *Poems: MCMXLII*. 1945. (BRG)

Everson, William. *The Residual Years: Poems, 1940–1941*. 1944. (RBK)

Everson, William. *The Waldport Poems*. 1944. (BRG)

Everson, William. *War Elegies*. 1944. (RBK)

Patchen, Kenneth. *An Astonished Eye Looks Out of the Air*. 1945. (BRG, RBK)

Sloan, Jacob. *Generation of Journey*. 1945. (BRG)

Walker, John. *Arma Virumque Cano*. 1950. (RBK)

Woodcock, George. *Imagine the South*. 1947. (RBK)

See also **The Illiterati.**

Vanishing Cab. San Francisco. Edited by Jerry Estrin. Nos. 1–6 (1975–1984).

Veitch, Tom, Magazine. *See* **Tom Veitch Magazine.**

Vital Statistics. Eugene, Oregon. Edited by Sandra Braman and Douglas Woolf. Nos. 1–3 (1978–1980).

GRD has: complete file.

Weigel, Tom.

Weigel, Tom. *Corker*. 12 signed and numbered copies, 1985. (BRG)

Weigel, Tom. *Metaphysical Suite*. 1985. (BRG)

Weigel, Tom. *Paradise*

Refused. Introduction by Jackie Curtis. Manuscript Copy No. 2 of 24, n.d. (BRG)

Whe're. Detroit, Michigan. Published by Artists' Workshop. Edited by John Sinclair. No. 1 (Summer 1966).

BRG has: sole issue.

The Willie. San Francisco. Published by Manic Press. Edited by d.a.levy. No. 1 (Summer 1967).

BRG has: sole issue.

Women's Press Collective. Oakland, California. Judy Grahn.

Grahn, Judy. *The Common Woman*. 1979. (GRD)

Grahn, Judy. *Edward the Dyke and Other Poems*. 1971. (GRD)

Grahn, Judy. *A Woman Is Talking to Death*. 1974.

Parker, Pat. *Child of Myself*. 1972. (SC)

Parker, Pat. *Pit Stop: Words*. Photographs by Jackie Howell, Ardena Starks, Paula Wallace, and Robin Wadsworth. Drawings by Wendy Cadden. 1975. (SC)

Work. Detroit, Michigan. Published by Artists' Workshop. Edited by John Sinclair. Nos. 1–5 (Summer 1965–May 1968).

Xexoxial Endarchy (formerly Xerox Sutra Editions). Madison, Wisconsin. Miekal And and Elizabeth Was.

And, Miekal. *The Electric Samsara Lightbook*. 1980.

And, Miekal. *Klee*. 1981.

And, Miekal. *Th he Superna*. 1980.

Essary, Loris. *Anthology Essary*. 1982.

Rosenblum, Martin. *Born Out*. 1982.

Was, Elizabeth. *Classical Plagiarism*. 1982.

Yale Literary Magazine. New Haven, Connecticut. Young American Poets issue (May 1969), edited by Alan Bernheimer and David Watson. (BRG)

Yardbird Reader. Berkeley, California. Published by Yardbird Pub. Cooperative. Vols. 1–5 (1972–1976?).

GRD has: complete file. SC has: no. 5.

Yellow Press. Chicago. Richard Friedman, Peter Kostakis, and Darlene Pearlstein.

Berrigan, Ted. *Red Wagon*. 1976. (BRG)

Carroll, Paul. *New and Selected Poems*. 1978. (GRD)

Chernoff, Maxine. *Utopia TV Store: Prose Poems*. 1979. (GRD)

15 Chicago Poets. Edited by Richard Friedman, Peter Kostakis, and Darlene Pearlstein. 1976. (GRD)

Friedman, Richard. *Physical Culture: Poems*. 1979. (GRD)

Friedman, Richard. *Straight: Poems, 1971–1975*. 1975. (GRD)

Hoover, Paul. *Letter to Einstein Beginning Dear Albert*. 1979. (GRD)

Hoover, Paul. *Somebody Talks a Lot*. 1982. (GRD)

Notley, Alice. *Alice Ordered Me to Be Made*. 1976. (GRD)

Rosenthal, Bob. *Rude Awakenings*. 1982. (GRD)

See also **The Milk Quarterly.**

Zukofsky, Louis.

Zukofsky, Louis. *"A" Libretto*. New York, n.d. 21 pages signed in 1977 by Zukofsky. (BRG)

Some Other Presses and Publications: A Preliminary Checklist

Sources for Further Study

General Sources

Allen, Donald, and Warren Tallman, eds. *Poetics of the New American Poetry.* New York: Grove, 1973.

Anderson, Elliott, and Mary Kinzie, eds. *The Little Magazine in America: A Modern Documentary History.* Yonkers, N.Y.: Pushcart Press, 1978.

Chielans, Edward, ed. *American Literary Magazines, The Twentieth Century.* Westport, Conn.: Greenwood Press, 1992.

Dana, Robert, ed. *Against the Grain: Interviews with Maverick American Publishers.* Iowa City: University of Iowa Press, 1986.

Davidson, Michael. *Ghostlier Demarcations: Modern Poetry and the Material Word.* Berkeley: University of California Press, 1997.

Electronic Poetry Center: http://wings.buffalo.edu/epc/

Faas, Ekbert, ed. *Towards a New American Poetics: Essays and Interviews.* Santa Barbara, Calif.: Black Sparrow Press, 1978.

Glazier, Loss Pequeño. *Small Press: An Annotated Guide.* Westport, Conn.: Greenwood Press, 1992.

Görtschacher, Wolfgang. *Little Magazine Profiles: The Little Magazine in Great Britain, 1939–1993.* Salzburg: University of Salzburg, 1993.

Grenier, Donald, ed. *American Poets Since World War II.* 2 vols. Detroit: Gale Research, 1980.

Henderson, Bill, ed. *The Art of Literary Publishing: Editors on Their Craft.* Wainscott, N.Y.: Pushcart Press, 1980.

Meltzer, David, ed. *The San Francisco Poets.* New York: Ballantine, 1971.

Ossman, David, ed. *The Sullen Art: Interviews with Modern American Poets.* New York: Corinth Books, 1963.

Perloff, Marjorie. *The Dance of the Intellect: Studies in the Poetry of the Pound Tradition.* Cambridge, England, and New York: Cambridge University Press, 1985.

Perloff, Marjorie. *Radical Artifice: Writing Poetry in the Age of Media.* Chicago: University of Chicago Press, 1991.

Perloff, Marjorie, ed. *Poetic License: Essays on Modernist and Postmodernist Lyric.* Evanston, Ill.: Northwestern University Press, 1990.

The Poetry Project website: http://www.poetryproject.com/

Rexroth, Kenneth. *American Poetry in the Twentieth Century.* New York: Herder and Herder, 1971.

Small Press Distribution website: http://www.spdbooks.org/

Soar, Geoffrey, and David Miller. *Interaction & Overlap from the Little Magazine & Small Press Collection at University College London.* London: workfortheeyetodo, 1994.

Sullivan, James D. *On the Walls and in the Streets: American Poetry Broadsides from the 1960's.* Urbana: University of Illinois Press, 1997.

Tallman, Warren. *In the Midst.* Vancouver: Talonbooks, 1992.

Tovey, Eloyde. *A Guide to the New American Poetry: San Francisco Bay Scene, 1918–1960.* Unpublished manuscript, 1984.

Ubuweb visual, concrete, & sound poetry page: http://www.ubu.com/

Vincent, Stephen, and Ellen Zweig. *The Poetry Reading: A Contemporary Compendium on Language and Performance.* San Francisco: Momo's Press, 1981.

Weinberger, Eliot. *Written Reaction: Poetics, Politics, Polemics (1979–1995).* New York: Marsilio Publishers, 1996.

Zurbrugg, Nicholas. "The Multimedia Text," *Art & Design,* vol. 10, no. 11 (November 12, 1995).

Anthologies

Algarín, Miguel, and Miguel Piñero, eds. *Nuyorican Poetry: An Anthology of Puerto Rican Words and Feelings.* Photographs by Gil Mendez. New York: Morrow, 1975.

Allen, Donald, ed. *The New American Poetry, 1945–1960.* New York: Grove, 1960.

Allen, Donald, and George F. Butterick, eds. *The Postmoderns: The New American Poetry Revised.* With a new introduction. New York: Grove, 1982.

Carroll, Paul, ed. *The Poem in Its Skin.* New York: Follett, 1968.

Carroll, Paul, ed. *The Young American Poets.* Introduction by James Dickey. Chicago: Follett, 1968.

DeLoach, Allen, ed. *The East Side Scene: An Anthology of a Time and Place.* Buffalo: State University of New York, 1968; reprint New York: Doubleday/Anchor, 1972.

Hartman, Yuki, and George Slater, eds. *Fresh Paint: An Anthology of Younger Poets.* New York: Ailanthus Press, 1977.

Hoover, Paul, ed. *Post Modern American Poetry: A Norton Anthology.* New York: Norton, 1994.

Lally, Michael, ed. *None of the Above: New Poets of the USA.* Trumansburg, N.Y.: The Crossing Press, 1976.

Messerli, Douglas, ed. *From the Other Side of the Century: A New American Poetry, 1960–1990.* Los Angeles: Sun & Moon Press, 1994. (Sun & Moon Classics; 47.)

Messerli, Douglas, ed. *"Language" Poetries: An Anthology.* New York: New Directions, 1987.

Myers, John Bernard, ed. *The Poets of the New York School.* Philadelphia: Graduate School of Fine Arts, University of Pennsylvania; distributed by Gotham Book Mart and Gallery, New York, 1969.

Padgett, Ron, and David Shapiro, eds. *An Anthology of New York Poets.* Drawings by Joe Brainard. New York: Random House, 1970.

Rothenberg, Jerome, ed. *Revolution of the Word: A New Gathering of American Avant Garde Poetry, 1914–1945.* New York: The Seabury Press, 1974.

Rothenberg, Jerome, ed. *Shaking the Pumpkin: Traditional Poetry of the Indian North Americas.* Rev. ed. Albuquerque: University of New Mexico Press, 1986.

Rothenberg, Jerome, ed. *Technicians of the Sacred: A Range of Poetries from Africa, America, Asia, Europe & Oceania.* 2nd ed., rev. and expanded. Berkeley: University of California Press, 1985.

Rothenberg, Jerome, and Pierre Joris, eds. *Poems for the Millennium: The University of California Book of Modern & Postmodern Poetry.* 2 vols. Berkeley: University of California Press, 1995, 1998.

Solt, Mary Ellen. *Concrete Poetry: A World View.* Bloomington: Indiana University Press, 1970.

Waldman, Anne, ed. *Another World: A Second Anthology of Works from the St. Mark's Poetry Project.* Indianapolis: Bobbs-Merrill, 1971.

Waldman, Anne, ed. *Out of This World: An Anthology of the St. Mark's Poetry Project, 1966–1991.* Foreword by Allen Ginsberg. New York: Crown, 1991.

Waldman, Anne, ed. *The World Anthology: Poems from the St. Mark's Poetry Project.* Indianapolis: Bobbs-Merrill, 1969.

Weinberger, Eliot, ed. *American Poetry Since 1950: Innovators and Outsiders: An Anthology.* New York: Marsilio Publishers, 1993.

McClure, Michael. *Lighting the Corners: On Art, Nature and the Visionary: Essays and Interviews.* Albuquerque: University of New Mexico Press, 1994.

McClure, Michael. *Scratching the Beat Surface.* Photographs by Larry Keenan. San Francisco: North Point Press, 1982.

Poets of the Cities of New York and San Francisco, 1950–1965. New York: E. P. Dutton, 1974. Catalog for a show organized by the Dallas Museum of Fine Arts and Southern Methodist University.

Particular Presses, Magazines, Groups, and Individuals

The Alternative Press

Art Poetry Melodrama: 20 Years of the Alternative Press. Detroit: Detroit Institute of Arts, 1990.

Auerhahn Press

Johnston, Alistair. *A Bibliography of the Auerhahn Press & Its Successor Dave Haselwood Books.* Compiled by a printer. Berkeley, Calif.: Poltroon Press, 1976.

Beat Writing

Bartlett, Lee. *The Beats: Essays in Criticism.* Jefferson, N.C.: McFarland, 1981.

Beat Culture and the New America: 1950–1965. New York: Whitney Museum of American Art/Flammarion, 1995.

Charters, Ann, ed. *The Beats: Literary Bohemians in Postwar America.* 2 vols. Detroit: Gale Research, 1983. (*Dictionary of Literary Biography* Vol. 16.)

William S. Burroughs

Miles, Barry. *William Burroughs: El Hombre Invisible.* London: Virgin, 1992.

Morgan, Ted. *Literary Outlaw: The Life and Times of William S. Burroughs.* New York: Henry Holt, 1988.

Allen Ginsberg

Ginsberg, Allen. *Allen Verbatim: Lectures on Poetry, Politics, Consciousness.* Edited by Gordon Ball. New York: McGraw-Hill, 1974.

Miles, Barry. *Ginsberg: A Biography.* New York: Simon and Schuster, 1989.

Morgan, Bill. *The Works of Allen Ginsberg, 1941–1994: A Descriptive Bibliography.* Foreword by Allen Ginsberg. Westport, Conn.: Greenwood Press, 1995.

Schumacher, Michael. *Dharma Lion: A Biography of Allen Ginsberg.* New York: St. Martin's, 1992.

Jack Kerouac

Charters, Ann. *A Bibliography of Works by Jack Kerouac.* New York: Phoenix Book Shop, 1967.

Charters, Ann. *Kerouac: A Biography.* San Francisco: Straight Arrow Books, 1973.

Clark, Tom. *Jack Kerouac.* San Diego: Harcourt Brace Jovanovich, 1984.

Morgan, Bill. *The Beat Generation in New York: A Walking Tour of Jack Kerouac's City.* San Francisco: City Lights, 1997.

Black Mountain

"Black Mountain and Since: Objectivist Writing in America," *Chicago Review,* vol. 30, no. 3 (Winter 1979).

"The Black Mountain College Issue," *North Carolina Literary Review,* vol. 11, no. 2 (1995).

Dawson, Fielding. *The Black Mountain Book.* New York: Croton Press, Ltd., 1970.

Duberman, Martin. *Black Mountain: An Exploration in Community.* New York: E. P. Dutton, 1972.

Charles Olson

Byrd, Don. *Charles Olson's Maximus.* Urbana: University of Illinois Press, 1980.

Clark, Tom. *Charles Olson: The Allegory of a Poet's Life.* New York: W. W. Norton, 1991.

Maud, Ralph. *Charles Olson's Reading: A Biography.* Carbondale and Edwardsville: Southern Illinois University Press, 1996.

Maud, Ralph. *What Does Not Change: The Significance of Charles Olson's "The Kingfishers."* Madison, N.J.: Fairleigh Dickinson University Press, 1998.

Paul, Sherman. *Olson's Push: Origin, Black Mountain and Recent American Poetry.* Baton Rouge: Louisiana State University Press, 1978.

Black Sparrow Press

Morrow, Bradford, and Seamus Cooney. *A Bibliography of the Black Sparrow Press 1966–1978.* Santa Barbara, Calif.: Black Sparrow, 1981.

Burning Deck

Waldrop, Keith and Rosmarie. *A Century in Two Decades: A Burning Deck Anthology 1961–1981.* Providence, R.I.: Burning Deck, 1982.

Caterpillar

Eshleman, Clayton, ed. *A Caterpillar Anthology.* New York: Doubleday/Anchor, 1971.

City Lights

Cook, Ralph T. *City Lights Books: A Descriptive Bibliography.* Metuchen, N.J.: Scarecrow Press, 1992.

Coach House Press

Tweny/20. Toronto: Coach House Press, 1985. The twenty-year catalog of the press.

Corinth Books

Wilentz, Ted, and Bill Zavatsky. "Behind the Writer, Ahead of the Reader: A Short History of Corinth Books," pp. 595–613 in Anderson and Kinzie, *The Little Magazine in America* (1978).

Ethnopoetics and Deep Image Poetry

Rothenberg, Jerome. *Pre-Faces and Other Writings.* New York: New Directions, 1981.

Rothenberg, Jerome, and Diane Rothenberg, eds. *Symposium of the Whole: A Range of Discourse Toward an Ethnopoetics.* Berkeley: University of California Press, 1983.

The Floating Bear

Di Prima, Diane, and LeRoi Jones. *The Floating Bear: A Newsletter.* La Jolla, Calif.: Laurence McGilvery, 1973. Reprinted with an introduction and notes adapted from interviews with Diane di Prima.

Gotham Book Mart

"Special Gotham Book Mart Issue," *Journal of Modern Literature*, vol. 4, no. 4 (April 1975).

Grove Press

O'Brien, John, ed. "Grove Press Number," *The Review of Contemporary Fiction*, vol. 10, no. 3 (Fall 1990).

Jargon Society

Bell, Millicent. *The Jargon Idea.* Providence, R.I.: Brown University, 1963. Reprinted from *Books at Brown* 19 (May 1963).

Edelstein, J. M. *A Jargon Society Checklist 1951–1979.* Published in conjunction with an exhibition of Jargon publications at Books & Co., New York City, March 15–April 14, 1979.

Kulchur and Kulchur Foundation

Hornick, Lita. *The Green Fuse.* New York: Giorno Publishing Systems, 1989.

Hornick, Lita. "Kulchur, a Memoir," pp. 281–297 in Anderson and Kinzie, *The Little Magazine in America* (1978).

Hornick, Lita. *Night Flight.* Photography by Gerard Malanga. New York: Kulchur, 1982.

Language Writing

[Andrews, Bruce.] *Bruce Andrews Contemporary Poetics as Critical Theory II.* Issued as *Aerial* 9. Washington, D.C.: Edge Books, 1998.

Andrews, Bruce. *Paradise & Method, Poetics & Praxis.* Evanston, Ill.: Northwestern University Press, 1996.

Andrews, Bruce, and Charles Bernstein, eds. *The L=A=N=G=U=A=G=E Book.* Carbondale: Southern Illinois University Press, 1984.

Bernstein, Charles. *Content's Dream: Essays 1975–1984.* Los Angeles: Sun & Moon, 1986.

Bernstein, Charles. *A Poetics.* Cambridge, Mass.: Harvard University Press, 1992.

Bernstein, Charles, ed. "Language Sampler," *The Paris Review*, no. 86 (Winter 1982).

Bernstein, Charles, ed. *The Politics of Poetic Form.* New York: Roof, 1990.

Lazer, Hank. *Opposing Poetries*. 2 vols. Evanston, Ill.: Northwestern University Press, 1996. (Vol. 1: Issues and Institutions; vol. 2: Readings.)

Messerli, Douglas, ed. *"Language" Poetries: An Anthology*. New York: New Directions, 1987.

Perelman, Bob. *The Marginalization of Poetry: Language Writing and Literary History*. Princeton, N.J.: Princeton University Press, 1996.

Perelman, Bob, ed. *Writing/Talks*. Carbondale: Southern Illinois University Press, 1985.

Silliman, Ron. *In the American Tree*. Orono, Maine: National Poetry Foundation, 1986.

Silliman, Ron, ed. "Language Writing," *Ironwood* 20 [vol. 10, no. 2] (Fall 1982).

Silliman, Ron, ed. *The New Sentence*. New York: Roof, 1987.

Ward, Geoff. *Language Poetry and the American Avant-Garde*. London: British Association for American Studies, 1993.

[Watten, Barrett.] *Barrett Watten Contemporary Poetics as Critical Theory*. Issued as *Aerial* 8. Washington, D.C.: Edge Books, 1995.

Watten, Barrett. *Total Syntax*. Carbondale: Southern Illinois University Press, 1985.

levy, d.a.

Crane, Michael. *American Renegades: Kenneth Patchen, d.a.levy, D. R. Wagner*. Boulder, Colo.: CU Art Galleries, 1992.

Golden, Mike, ed. *The Buddhist Third Class Junkmail Oracle*. New York: Seven Windows, forthcoming.

levy, d.a. *Zen Concrete & etc*. Edited by Ingrid Swanberg. Madison, Wisc.: Ghost Pony Press, 1991.

Ukanhavyrfuckincitibak; d.a.levy: A Tribute to the Man; An Anthology of His Poetry. Edited by r.j.s. [Robert J. Sigmund]. Cleveland: Ghost Press, 1968.

Naropa Institute/Jack Kerouac School of Disembodied Poetics

Waldman, Anne, and Andrew Schelling. *Disembodied Poetics: Annals of the Jack Kerouac School*. Albuquerque: University of New Mexico Press, 1994.

Waldman, Anne, and Marilyn Webb, eds. *Talking Poetics from Naropa Institute: Annals of the Jack Kerouac School of Disembodied Poetics*. 2 vols. Boulder, Colo.: Shambhala, 1978, 1979.

The New York School

Gooch, Brad. *City Poet: The Life and Times of Frank O'Hara*. New York: Knopf, 1993.

Gruen, John. *The Party's Over Now*. New York: Viking Press, 1972.

Lehman, David. *The Last Avant-Garde: The Making of the New York School of Poets*. New York: Doubleday, 1998.

Perloff, Marjorie. *Frank O'Hara: Poet Among Painters*. New York: George Braziller, 1977.

Ward, Geoff. *Statutes of Liberty: The New York School of Poets*. New York: St. Martin's, 1993.

Sources for Further Study

The New York School: Second Generation

Clark, Tom. *Late Returns: A Memoir of Ted Berrigan.* Bolinas, Calif.: Tombouctou Books, 1985.

Fischer, Aaron. *Ted Berrigan: An Annotated Checklist.* New York: Granary Books, 1998.

Lewis, Joel, ed. *Ted Berrigan: On the Level Everyday: Selected Talks on Poetry and the Art of Living.* Jersey City, N.J.: Talisman House, 1997.

Padgett, Ron. *Ted: A Personal Memoir of Ted Berrigan.* Great Barrington, Mass.: The Figures, 1993.

Waldman, Anne, ed. *Nice to See You: Homage to Ted Berrigan.* Minneapolis: Coffee House Press, 1991.

Wolf, Reva. *Andy Warhol, Poetry, and Gossip in the 1960s.* Chicago: University of Chicago Press, 1997.

Origin

Corman, Cid, ed. *The Gist of Origin 1951–1971: An Anthology.* New York: Grossman, 1975.

The Paris Review and Locus Solus

Sawyer-Lauçanno, Christopher. *The Continual Pilgrimage: American Writers in Paris, 1944–1960.* San Francisco: City Lights, 1992.

San Francisco Renaissance

Davidson, Michael. *The San Francisco Renaissance: Poetics and Community at Mid-century.* New York: Cambridge University Press, 1989.

French, Warren. *The San Francisco Poetry Renaissance, 1955–1960.* Boston: Twayne, 1991.

Kherdian, David. *Six San Francisco Poets.* Fresno, Calif.: The Giligia Press, 1969.

Robert Duncan

Bertholf, Robert J. *Robert Duncan: A Descriptive Bibliography.* Santa Rosa, Calif.: Black Sparrow, 1986.

Fass, Ekbert. *Young Robert Duncan: Portrait of the Poet as Homosexual in Society.* Santa Barbara, Calif.: Black Sparrow, 1983.

Kenneth Rexroth

Hamalian, Linda. *A Life of Kenneth Rexroth.* New York: Norton, 1991.

Jack Spicer

Blaser, Robin. "The Practice of Outside," in *The Collected Books of Jack Spicer.* Edited with a commentary by Robin Blaser. Los Angeles: Black Sparrow, 1975.

Ellingham, Lewis, and Kevin Killian. *Poet Be Like God: Jack Spicer and the San Francisco Renaissance.* Middletown, Conn.: Wesleyan University Press, 1998.

Spicer, Jack. *The House That Jack Built: The Collected Lectures of Jack Spicer.* Edited with an afterword by Peter Gizzi. Hanover, N.H.: University Press of New England, 1998.

Semina and Wallace Berman

Hertz, Uri. "Wallace Berman issue," *Third Rail* 9 (1988).

Solnit, Rebecca. *Secret Exhibition: Six California Artists of the Cold War Era.* San Francisco: City Lights, 1990.

Wallace Berman: Support the Revolution. Amsterdam: Institute for Contemporary Art, 1992.

Wallace Berman Retrospective, October 24– November 26, 1978. Los Angeles: Fellows of Contemporary Art, 1978. Catalog for a show at the Otis Art Institute Gallery.

Gary Snyder

McNeil, Katherine. *Gary Snyder: A Bibliography.* New York: Phoenix Book Shop, 1983.

Something Else Press

Frank, Peter. *Something Else Press: An Annotated Bibliography.* [New Paltz, N.Y.]: Documentext/McPherson & Company, 1983.

New Lazarus Review, vol. 2, no. 1 (1979), no. 3/4 (1980). Includes Dick Higgins's two-part essay "The Something Else Press – notes for a history to be written some day –".

Spanner 9 (January 1977): issue focusing on Dick Higgins and the Something Else Press.

Sun & Moon Press

Sun & Moon website: http://www.sunmoon.com

White Rabbit Press

Johnston, Alastair. *A Bibliography of the White Rabbit Press.* Berkeley, Calif.: Poltroon Press, 1985.

Yugen, Totem Press

Baraka, Amiri. *The Autobiography of LeRoi Jones.* New York: Freundlich Books, 1984.

Z Press

Bamberger, William C. *Kenward Elmslie: A Bibliographical Profile.* Flint, Mich.: Bamberger Books, 1993.

Acknowledgments

The authors could not have managed this book without the benefit of the advice, knowledge, and memories of a whole community of artists and writers. For their counsel, support, and intelligent writing, we are most grateful. Larry Fagin, Lewis Warsh, and Anne Waldman were a constant source of information, support, and, most of all, spirit. We benefited greatly on many levels from conversations, contributions, and ongoing input from Bruce Andrews, Carol Bergé, Bill Berkson, Charles Bernstein, Clark Coolidge, Steve Dickison, Aaron Fischer, Ed Friedman, Julie Harrison, Lyn Hejinian, Fran Herndon, Kevin Killian, Joanne Kyger, Gerrit Lansing, Annabel Lee, Steve Levine, Jackson Mac Low, Michael Mann, Greg Masters, Bill Morgan, Timothy Murray, Eileen Myles, Maureen Owen, Ron Padgett, Ron Patterson, Bob Rosenthal, Jerome Rothenberg, Ed Sanders, Aram Saroyan, George Schneeman, Carolee Schneemann, James Sherry, Ron Silliman, George Stanley, Johnny Stanton, and Gary Sullivan.

In addition, we would like to acknowledge and salute our in-house team: Barbara Bergeron for keeping us on time and for her keen and perspicacious eye, as well as her eloquent pen; Karen Van Westering for support and direction; and Marc Blaustein for attentively shaping our sprawling compilations. Xan Mazzella and Emily Y. Ho were ferocious terriers in the search for obscure bibliographic citations and real-time coordinates of persons both known and unknown.

The New York Public Library's Henry W. and Albert A. Berg Collection of English and American Literature is fortunate to have received considerable support for publications based upon materials in the collection. This book would not have been possible without the Judge and Mrs. Samuel D. Levy Fund and the very gracious generosity of our friend, Mr. Leonard Milberg.

- - - - - - -

Steven Clay dedicates this book to his wife, Julie Harrison, and their daughters, Ruby and Naomi.

About the Berg Collection

The New York Public Library's Henry W. and Albert A. Berg Collection of English and American Literature is one of America's most celebrated collections of literary first editions, rare books, autograph letters, and manuscripts. The founding collection was assembled and presented to the Library, with an endowment, by Dr. Albert A. Berg (1872–1950), a famous New York surgeon and trustee of the Library, in memory of his brother, Dr. Henry W. Berg (1858–1938). Both men found relaxation from their medical careers in collecting the works and memorabilia of English and American men and women of letters.

The collection's more than 35,000 printed items and 115,000 manuscripts cover the entire range of two national literatures with particular emphasis on the nineteenth and twentieth centuries. The earliest manuscript in the Berg Collection is a contemporary transcription of John Donne's poems dating from 1619, and the two earliest books are chronicles printed by William Caxton in 1480. Among the division's holdings one can find rarities considered museum pieces by the book world, including manuscripts of T. S. Eliot's early poems and the original typescript of *The Waste Land*; the holograph diaries of Virginia Woolf; two copies of the extremely rare first edition of Edgar Allan Poe's *Tamerlane*; the Bristol edition of William Wordsworth and Samuel Taylor Coleridge's *Lyrical Ballads*; and Robert Browning's *Pauline*. The literary archive of Fanny Burney, including *Evelina*, *Cecilia*, and *Camilla* in manuscript and her diary and letters as prepared for the press, forms a unique source for the study of the Burneys and their wide circle. First editions of the works of Dr. Johnson, Sterne, Smollett, Sheridan, Burns, Blake, together with Defoe, Swift, Addison and

Steele, Richardson, and Fielding, are well represented.

The collection of works by the principal authors of the nineteenth century includes many first editions, manuscripts, and letters. The Berg Collection houses important holdings of the American writers Washington Irving, Nathaniel and Sophia Hawthorne, Ralph Waldo Emerson, Henry David Thoreau, Mark Twain (Samuel Clemens), and Walt Whitman and the British writers Emily Brontë, Lewis Carroll (Charles Dodgson), Rudyard Kipling, and Elizabeth Barrett Browning. Items in the collection include many of Charles Dickens's public reading copies of his work; William Makepeace Thackeray's letters, manuscripts, sketchbooks, and drawings; "Alice's copy" of the first edition of *Alice's Adventures in Wonderland*; John Keats's last letter to Fanny Brawne; and Mark Twain's manuscripts of *A Connecticut Yankee in King Arthur's Court* and *Following the Equator*. The present century is represented by strong holdings in Arnold Bennett, Joseph Conrad, T. S. Eliot, George Gissing, Thomas Hardy, James Joyce, John Masefield, Eugene O'Neill, George Bernard Shaw, Virginia Woolf, W. H. Auden, and Jack Kerouac. Material dealing with the Irish Literary Renaissance is another important feature of the collection. Notable items include the papers of Lady Gregory, the moving spirit of the Dublin Abbey Theatre and guardian of W. B. Yeats's poetic talent, and the surviving literary archives of Sean O'Casey, many of whose papers were destroyed by fire. The Georgian Poetry movement and the Bloomsbury group are also well documented.

As a research collection, the Berg Collection's primary focus is the acquisition of works of modern and contemporary writers. Manuscript poems by Robert Lowell are next to manuscripts and letters by James Russell Lowell. A massive collection of Gertrude Stein's printed works is followed by those of John Steinbeck. The early history of the Provincetown Playhouse is reflected in the archive of two writers closely connected with its founding: George Cram Cook and Susan Glaspell. In recent years the division has added to its collection the archives of Vladimir Nabokov, W. H. Auden, Robert Graves, Jean Garrigue, Muriel Rukeyser, May Sarton, Philip Levine, Kenneth Koch, Lewis Warsh, and Paul Auster, as well as the papers of James Sibley Watson, co-owner of *The Dial*, the major journal of literary modernism in the 1920s; the papers of Frances Steloff and the Gotham Book Mart, the major American bookstore specializing in modern literature; and the Ann and Samuel Charters Collection of Beat literature.

Index

Page numbers in **boldface** refer to main entries for presses and publications. Page numbers in *italics* refer to illustrations.

Young, La Monte, 32; and *An Anthology of Chance Operations*, 32, *140*, 140–141; and *Beatitude East*, 32

Yugen, 28, **73**, *73*; and Diane di Prima, 89; and LeRoi Jones, 75, 91, 108, 159

Illustration Sources and Permissions

Sources

Illustrations are from materials in The New York Public Library's Henry W. and Albert A. Berg Collection of English and American Literature (primarily from the Robert A. Wilson Collection, the Ann and Samuel Charters Collection, the Lewis Warsh Papers, and the Kenneth Koch Papers) except as noted below:

FROM THE NEW YORK PUBLIC LIBRARY:
General Research Division: pp. 52, 126, 162 (*Fits of Dawn*), 256, 277, 281, 283, 294, 295

Manuscripts and Archives Division: p. 216

Miriam and Ira D. Wallach Division of Art, Prints and Photographs: p. 5

OTHER SOURCES:
Collection of Steven Clay: pp. 21, 273

Courtesy of Elsa Dorfman: pp. 39, 166

Courtesy of Larry Fagin: pp. 201–203

Courtesy of Aaron Fischer: p. 84

Courtesy of George Schneeman: p. 165

Permissions

For permission to reproduce images on the following pages, we thank:

New Directions Publishing Corporation: pp. 94, 96

Andy Warhol Foundation for the Visual Arts/ ARS, New York: p. 118 (cover © 1998 Andy Warhol Foundation for the Visual Arts/ARS, New York)